Peter Brook
A Theatrical Casebook

'So far as Brook's English-speaking audience is concerned, his career consists of a brilliantly lit road from *Love's Labour's Lost* to *A Midsummer Night's Dream* followed by 17 lost years . . . Hence the justification for this book . . . Brook's productions are as transient as any other theatrical event. But they have spawned a formidable archive of eye-witness reports and analytical commentaries, some of which (as David Williams's selection reveals) are of manifest brilliance.'

Irving Wardle, *Foreword*

This Casebook provides the first comprehensive documentation in English of Peter Brook's wide-ranging work in the theatre. Brook's major English productions of the 1960s – *King Lear*, *The Marat/Sade*, *Oedipus*, *The Tempest*, *A Midsummer Night's Dream* – are reconstructed through rehearsal logs, interviews, and reviews. His experimental 'Theatre of Cruelty' season – which lead on to controversial productions of *The Screens* and *US* – is placed in context through the eye-witness testimony of his collaborators. There are rare accounts of Brook's journeys with his Paris-based Centre for International Theatre Research: to Persepolis for the realisation of the *Orghast* project, and to Africa and America with *The Conference of the Birds*. Brook's renowned Paris productions – *Timon of Athens*, *The Ik*, *Ubu*, *The Cherry Orchard*, *Carmen*, *The Mahabharata* – are all explored in detail via rehearsal journals, textual extracts, and critical commentary. Both insiders and outsiders have their say: independent critics examine the political and artistic implications of the work while Brook's colleagues at the C.I.R.T. bear witness to his uncompromising search for vital theatre.

Since graduating from the University of Kent, where he wrote a thesis about Brook's work with the cooperation of the C.I.C.T., David Williams has worked as an actor, journalist, editor and lecturer. He is currently convener of Drama at the Australian National University. *Contemporary Directors' Theatre* (Macmillan), co-written with Dr David Bradby, is to be published in 1988.

The cover photograph shows a rehearsal of *The Tragedy of Carmen* at the Bouffes du Nord, Paris in 1981. From left to right: Zehava Gal (Carmen), Howard Hensel (Don José), Peter Brook. (Photo: Marc Enguerand).

Peter Brook
A Theatrical Casebook

compiled by
DAVID WILLIAMS

A Methuen Paperback

'Come and see
real flowers
of this painful world'
Basho

A Methuen Dramabook

First published as a paperback original in 1988
in Great Britain by Methuen London Ltd,
11 New Fetter Lane, London EC4P 4EE
and in the United States of America
by Methuen Inc, 29 West 35th Street, New York, NY 10001

Selection, Chronology, Commentary and Translations
copyright © 1988 by David Williams
For details of the copyright in individual articles,
see Acknowledgements

Photoset by Rowland Phototypesetting Ltd,
Bury St Edmunds, Suffolk
Printed in Great Britain by Richard Clay Ltd,
Bungay, Suffolk

British Library Cataloguing in Publication Data

Peter Brook: a theatrical casebook.
1. Brook, Peter, *1925–* – Criticism
and interpretation
I. Williams, David, *1957–*
792'.0232'0924   PN2598.B69

ISBN 0-413-15700-8

'Why theatre at all? What for? Is it an anachronism, a super-annuated oddity, surviving like an old monument or a quaint custom? Why do we applaud, and what? Has the stage a real place in our lives? What function can it have? What could it serve? What could it explore? What are its special properties?'
(*The Empty Space*)

'For me there is only the travelling on paths that have heart, on any path that may have heart. There I travel, and the only worthwhile challenge is to traverse its full length. And there I travel looking, looking, breathlessly'
(*The Teachings of Don Juan*, Carlos Castaneda)

'Come. Don't let anything stop you.
Whatever stops you becomes an idol'
(The Hoopoe in *Conference of the Birds*)

'I know of one acid test in theatre. It is literally an acid test. When a performance is over, what remains?'
(*The Empty Space*)

Contents

List of Illustrations

Acknowledgements

Every effort has been made to contact the copyright holders of all the extracts appearing in this book, and the editor is grateful to the following for granting permission:

Farid Ud-Din Attar: Routledge and Kegan Paul Ltd from *The Conference of the Birds*.

Georges Banu: Georges Banu from *Alternatives Théâtrales*.

Maurice Bénichou: Hatier/Maurice Bénichou from *La Cerisaie*.

Kenneth Bernard: Kenneth Bernard/Joel Schechter from *Theatre*.

Peter Brook and Jean-Claude Carrière: The Dramatic Publishing Company, Connecticut from *The Conference of the Birds*.

Denis Cannan and Colin Higgins: The Dramatic Publishing Company, Connecticut from *The Ik*.

Jean-Claude Carrière: C.I.C.T./Jean-Claude Carrière from *La Tragédie de Carmen*.

Marius Constant: C.I.C.T./Marius Constant from *La Tragédie de Carmen*.

John Heilpern: Faber and Faber Ltd from *Conference of the Birds: The Story of Peter Brook In Africa*.

Ted Hughes: Faber and Faber Ltd/Ted Hughes from *Oedipus*.

Albert Hunt and Michael Kustow: Albert Hunt and Michael Kustow from *US*.

John Kane: John Kane from *The Sunday Times*.

Martine Millon: Centre National de la Recherche Scientifique from *Les Voies de la Création Théâtrale*.

J. B. Priestley: Blackie and Son Ltd from *Anton Chekhov*.

David Selbourne: Methuen London from *The Making of a Midsummer Night's Dream*.

Eric Shorter: The British Theatre Association from *Drama*.

Anthony Smith: Methuen London/Anthony Smith from *Orghast At Persepolis*.

John C. Trewin: J. C. Trewin from *Peter Brook: A Biography*.

Colin Turnbull: Jonathan Cape Ltd/Simon and Schuster Inc from *The Mountain People*.

Jean-Pierre Vincent: Jean-Pierre Vincent/C.I.C.T. from *Timon d'Athènes*.

David Williams: Cambridge University Press/David Williams from *New Theatre Quarterly*.

xii

Foreword

The word 'journey' has been worked to death as a metaphor for everything that happens in the theatre, but there is no avoiding it in discussing the career of Peter Brook. Even before he cut loose from the institutional stage, he was known to his colleagues as 'the pathfinder'. As Britain's first star director to emerge without serving any kind of apprenticeship, he hacked out a route for others to follow. As Peter Hall says, 'He paved the way for all of us; he made us feel that if he could do it, we could try too.' His 1950 production of *Ring Round the Moon* set the tone for postwar theatre as decisively as the New Look did for clothes design. His 1964 Theatre of Cruelty season for the RSC launched the age of Artaud on the British stage. In between, he was in perpetual transit between the West End, films, classical production, and the opera house: a Pied Piper pursued by an audience who knew that he would take them somewhere they had never been before. Then, in 1970, he withdrew from the magic triangle of London, Broadway, and Right Bank Paris, and the real journey began.

He was 45 at the time, and professionally he had nothing more to prove: which is a danger point in any career – particularly that of theatre directors, who are notoriously prone to reach the summit and then vanish into some kind of monastic retreat. The news that Brook was quitting Vanity Fair to set up a little research group (to be called C.I.R.T.) with no production deadlines evoked a whole network of escapist assocations, from Copeau's Burgundian *cuverie* to Tyrone Guthrie's Co. Monaghan jam factory.

The associations were false, as I had the luck to discover in the autumn of 1970 when, the day after reviewing the Stratford opening of Brook's *A Midsummer Night's Dream*, I took off for the Shiraz Festival – safely out of reach, so I thought – only to be awoken by a phone-call from Brook who was staying in the same hotel. He proposed a bit of sight-seeing. And it was in his company that I first saw Persepolis and the stupendous rock tombs of Naqsh-i-Rustam; and from him that I learned something of the *ta'zieh* and the other old Persian dramatic forms that had fired his imagination.

This was Brook on the trail of a fresh project, soaking up every impression that came his way from the devious byways of Iranian etiquette to handy phrases in Farsi from his cab driver. He was not a man in any danger of creative paralysis.

The following year I revisited Shiraz for the two parts of *Orghast*, and saw a different side of him. This time he had a show to put on. Rehearsing into the small hours of the morning with naphtha flares lighting up the Zoroastrian fire temple, his whiplash voice cut across the desert as if directing a technical run-through at Drury Lane. At the royal opening of *Orghast II*, the company arrived at Naqsh-i-Rustam to find that the site had been closed by security men (all roads for miles around being cordoned off whenever the Pahlavis were on the move). After a moment of cold fury, Brook spirited the troupe away to a nearby tea-house and kept them there, deaf to frantic pleas from Iranian officials, until the mess had been sorted out. Then, in his own time, he made his return to the waiting spectators and the performance took place. The Shahbuna was heard to complain that the royal party were being treated as common people while the actors were behaving like kings: which is no bad description of how Brook handled the episode.

Those were two journeys I was able to share: both enriching. I had never seen such a country, nor the preparation and performance of such theatrical work. I was keen to tell the story when I got home, but when I did I found it had dwindled into a traveller's tale. Either it prompted the awed reverence befitting some distant wonder, or the derisive snigger betokening the latest fashion in the Emperor's New Clothes. No reports of the time succeeded in lodging the actual event in public memory. Even less did they succeed with Brook's subsequent journey to Africa. *Orghast* may have been an exercise in auto-destructive art with a life-span no longer than a firework; but at least some tapes survive, and a text. The African improvisations have no existence outside the memory of those who saw and performed them.

So far as Brook's English-speaking audience is concerned, his career consists of a brilliantly lit road from *Love's Labour's Lost* to *A Midsummer Night's Dream* followed by 17 lost years, fitfully illuminated by travellers' tales and occasional touring shows some of which, like *The Ik*, looked pretty odd when viewed out of context. Whatever anybody's personal judgement on the separate products of the C.I.R.T. troupe, they constitute a body of work as important as any in the history of stage directing. Other directors have assumed creative supremacy, displaced the playwright, reformed the arts of acting and stage design, devised new relationships with the spectator, and turned the theatre into an instrument of their dreams. But no one before Brook has gone to the length of rejecting theatrical capitals to seek his primary audience elsewhere, and setting out to transform theatrical expression – the most nationalistic of the arts – into an international language. Whatever the chances of achieving this aim, the immediate point is that it has become the life's work of an artist who has repeatedly been right in the past; that it has thrown up a succession of landmark productions; and that the line of research connects with one of the deepest aspirations of the human race. It is possible that the exploit will end in an impasse, and renewed acquiescence in Babel. But no one is entitled to dismiss it without doing something to explore the route.

Hence the justification for this book. It cannot, and does not seek to recapture the experience of the spectator. Brook's productions are as transient as any other theatrical event. But they have spawned a formidable archive of eye-witness reports and analytical commentaries, some of which (as David Williams's selection reveals) are of manifest brilliance.

Brook has been lucky in his commentators. I am thinking not so much of professional reviewers as of colleagues and observers who have got close to him, noted his work methods and preliminary exercises as well as the 'Grand Exercise' of public performance, and then recorded their impressions in as many words as it takes. The usual penalty for joining the entourage of a great director is that you turn into a courtier and your brain is taken away. But there are no tame house scribes to be found among Brook's circle, from Charles Marowitz's mercilessly sceptical journals through to the full-length studies by A. C. H. Smith, John Heilpern, and David Selbourne, and the essays of Albert Hunt and Kenneth Bernard. The value of this material is that it comes from intelligent writers with something to say: not from selfless acolytes relaying the master's pronouncements. The framework Mr Williams has devised for them confirms his own place in their independent-minded company.

The framework is crucial. Good as the eye-witness material may be, it has evaporated like the performances it records: lost in little magazine and old newspaper cuttings; or buried away in books addressed to different kinds of reader. Selbourne's *The Making of A Midsummer Night's Dream* is strictly for students of rehearsal technique; Heilpern's *Conference of the Birds*, a brilliantly funny travel book that anybody could read with pleasure. No single commentator has ever done full justice to Brook. Collective testimony, however, is another matter. To echo

Brook, it is a question of finding a form that encompasses all the contradictions. Bring the scattered evidence together, as in a palaeological reconstruction, and it takes on a shape greater than its separate parts, and from which a story can be read.

The story this book tells has the quality of a primal legend. It is about a man with an urgent message to deliver who finds himself wandering about in a labyrinth. If he were a saint or a poet, he would be the sole guardian of the message, and would go through dark nights in fear of forgetting it. Being a theatre director, our hero is in rather a different case. He travels in company, and his labyrinth is furnished with seductive side-shows. Although obsessed with faith and meaning, he does not carry them in himself. They are nobody's property, and can only be discovered, released, and lost again in the course of an endlessly renewed search. His task is to keep up the search, and resist the tempting delusion of ever arriving at a destination.

I am trying to avoid religious imagery. From one aspect this is the story of a spiritual quest. But as soon as you begin describing it like that, it starts sounding ridiculous. Brook, a pilgrim? What spiritual exercises lead to his productions of *The Little Hut*, *Irma la Douce*, and *The Perils of Scobie Prilt*? Still more absurd, of course, would be to view him as a commercial entertainer, cunningly applying the techniques of Shaftesbury Avenue to the sacred texts of India and Persia.

The hopelessness of trying to pin him into either category is illustrated by the experience of a radio producer who had invited Brook to take part in a discussion on his film, *Meetings With Remarkable Men*. During the warm-up, Brook placed his finger-tips earnestly together and delivered his well-known opening gambit – 'What we were trying to do was something extremely complicated, and at the same time utterly simple . . .' Before he had time to get into his stride, though, his eye fell on a copy of *Variety* and, instantly forgetting about the life of spiritual adventure, he snatched it up to see what kind of business the film was doing in New York. The guru was abruptly elbowed aside by the showman.

This is not a story against Brook. Showmanship, as he says in this book, is honourable. And he is right. Believing they have developed beyond it is the nemesis of directors. No matter how rarefied the project or how prolonged the rehearsals, there must be a show in the end. And in Brook's case, it is the instinct of the showman, with his sensual vigour and intolerance of boredom, that have anchored his work in the real world.

Besides the guru and the showman, there is another duality to be reckoned with: anonymity and personality. How is it that a director who seems never to have given a line-reading in his life, and who devotes inexhaustible ingenuity to coaxing his actors into creating the performance, has nevertheless unveiled a sequence of productions that are stamped through to the centre with his own signature? The quick answer to that is Selection: the main power of any director – selection of material, actor, and of what actors offer in rehearsal. 'What is achieved determines what is to follow', Brook says. That sounds objective; but when it comes to deciding what has been achieved, it is Brook who calls the shots.

A more satisfactory answer is to be found by returning to the labyrinthine story of this book. The most obvious discovery is that Brook's productions follow an organic pattern, each giving birth to the next in a way that is more common among playwrights than among their interpreters. Seemingly unrelated works – like *The Ik* and *Ubu* – develop amplified resonance through being brought together within a larger unit: and, although Brook has long since given up writing plays (and is inclined to mistrust all but a few playwrights), he has repeatedly been able to imagine the kind of work needed by a particular time, and bring it into existence through research, collaborative exercise, and theatrical magic. The results pass his own test, as work exceeding the powers of any single artist; but equally confirm him as their prime creator.

Less obviously, signs of submerged biography stir through the material like the 'secret plays' that Brook detects in Shakespeare. Taking *King Lear* as the starting point (with its notorious deletion of the one act of disinterested sympathy in the entire play), the prospect is one of unrelieved desolation, extending through the Weiss productions to *US*. These are expressions of anthropological despair, re-examining the nature of man in the light of Auschwitz and Vietnam by a process of immersion in the 'destructive element'.

Desolation, admittedly, is a prevailing characteristic not only of Brook's mid-career, but of the whole history of 'director's theatre', which was originally founded on the abandoned shell of the Christian church. Like Copeau and Reinhardt, Brook was very much in the Sisyphean business of constructing secular rituals to replenish the spiritual vacuum: beginning fruitfully with Artaud, and going on to appropriate the innovations of the Living Theatre, Grotowski, and Joseph Chaikin's Open Theatre. The result sometimes appeared distinctly synthetic, and justified Marowitz's complaint that Brook was becoming a purveyor of *avant-garde* novelties to middle-class customers. It is also worth noting that the blackest of these works were produced while he was still a prisoner of the 'glamour circuit': before he kicked the careerist ladder aside and went his own way.

The turning point came at the end of this period. First, with the robustly phallic conclusion to *Oedipus* (for once, a contrived directorial effect, which caused a great row with the management): and, conclusively, with the communal spectacle of *A Midsummer Night's Dream*, in which Theseus/Oberon's parting line – 'Meet we all at break of day' – applied to everybody in the house: court, immortals, mechanicals, and audience alike.

Since then, the spectacle of human degradation has receded from Brook's stage. It is not that his view of the human animal has changed: nowhere does it come over more bleakly than in *The Ik*, which draws directly on anthropology to deny that the social impulse plays any essential part in the survival of the species. But a comparison of the Turnbull narrative and the acting text shows Brook making the point without charnel house horrors. It goes without saying that humanity's greatest enemy is Sartre's 'hairless, flesh-eating creature, man himself'. There is nothing to be gained by repeating it. The Theatre of Cruelty no longer offers a fitting platform for the atrocities of mankind.

Instead, Brook has turned to fables of healing and reconciliation: products of ancient cultures that have had their own sight of Armageddon and survived without losing their capacity for fun, sex, and human companionship. National classics renewed every day in the mouths of village story-tellers, these are the richest sources he has tapped since Shakespeare. And, as with Shakespeare, he approaches them as storehouses of universal power for which it is his business to find the key. It is not a question of an over-sophisticated European prostrating himself before a primitive altar. Simplicity is the goal. As the poet Vyasa puts it in *The Mahabharata*: 'One should always listen to stories. It's enjoyable, and sometimes it makes things better.' But he only earns the right to say that after the Hindu epic has been fractured and reassembled through a spectrum of international sensibilities; so that it takes on the colours of the *commedia* and Kabuki, and even the exotic blare of the nagaswaram comes from a Danish trumpeter who had to practise for three months before he could get a note out of the instrument.

The work, as all who saw it will agree, has meaning. So, as this book reveals, does the process by which it was prepared. In both, you see a heroic structure being cantilevered out into the void. The message I take away from this is that whatever disgrace humanity has brought upon itself in this century, it can perhaps reconstruct itself like a theatrical performance.

IRVING WARDLE

Preface

When Peter Brook first invited me to write some short pieces about his International Centre for Theatre Research in Paris, I knew it would be very difficult to be objective about work that has coloured so much of my professional and personal life, work that has impassioned me for more than a decade. 'Ah, but true objectivity comes from passion,' came the reply. Maybe so with Chekhov, I thought, flattered but unconvinced.

I am now able to state quite bluntly that in my case passion merely breeds passion. I emerge from the process of compiling this book more deeply moved and engaged than from other similar projects, having reread the mountain of literature that has built up in the wake of Brook's work, and reassessed my own responses to what I have seen in Les Bouffes du Nord, his theatre, and elsewhere. And the simple truth is that I have never been as consistently stimulated, excited and provoked anywhere else: I am an avid fan – and I make no apologies for that. Here is a theatre of energy, movement and life, as enraging as it is engaging, in its disrespect for the imposed canons of convention: a theatre that confronts reality, while refusing all pat dogmas, morals, solutions: a theatre that demands the spectator's imaginative complicity in the most direct and alluring way, for it is the spectator's creativity that is celebrated here too.

My concerns here have been to trace Peter Brook's development as a director from his first major rupture with mainstream theatre in the early Sixties to the epic story-telling ventures of his International Centre today. I have tried to find that material which best conveys what was involved: both for the participants during the working process (never just a means to an end for Brook) and for audiences. As it stands, this record of more than twenty years' work must remain a fragment: all that is still visible of experiences far more substantial: a taste of things past and to come. I have constantly been reminded of the story of the blind men describing an elephant, never coming near to the totality – and simplicity – of the beast itself.

Another image has underpinned the work on this book. There is a dance in Bharat Natyam which recounts an episode from the life of

Krishna. Fearing her child has put something in his mouth, his mother demands that he open it and show her. After an initial refusal, he opens up and she peers in, only to be amazed and even terrified by what she sees: for all of the worlds co-exist in her baby's mouth – sacred and profane, divine and demonic, the metaphysical and the everyday. When Krishna closes his mouth again, this vision of an absolute reality fades, and his mother is unable to recall what she has seen; life returns to normal. And yet she is profoundly transformed.

A brief word about the organisation of this book. My original intention was to focus on Brook's work after he left London to found the C.I.R.T. in Paris. But further research revealed that the impulses which activated his later journeys could be traced to his 1962 RSC production of *King Lear*, which is where this book begins. The articles come from a wide variety of sources: I have placed my initials after my own commentary, which links up each item. Brook founded the Centre for International Theatre Research (C.I.R.T.) in Paris in 1970; it subsequently became known as the Centre for International Theatre Creation (C.I.C.T.). Both acronyms appear throughout the book.

My thanks go to the following, who have been invaluable to me in this work over the last few years: at the Centre in Paris, Peter Brook and the wonderful Nina Soufy, Maurice Bénichou, Malik Bowens, Jean-Claude Carrière, Alain Maratrat, Maurice McLelland, Vittorio Mezzogiorno, Yoshi Oida, Toshi Tsuchitori, Lou Zeldis. And heartfelt thanks to Bruce Myers; Ludwik Flaszen at the Polish Teatr Laboratorium; Joseph Chaikin, Simon Trussler, Albert Hunt, Daniel Charlot, Habib Tanvir; Georges Banu, the foremost scholar of Brook's work in Europe today; Dr David Bradby, a teacher and friend throughout this period, and a constant source of strength and encouragement: and, finally, Nick Hern and Marcy Kahan at Methuen. Although this book must to some degree be dedicated to all of the above, it is really for Rachel Williams.

D.W.

Chronology of Peter Brook's Work

1925 March 21: birth of Peter Brook, London.

1942 *Doctor Faustus* by Christopher Marlowe, Torch Theatre, London (with an amateur cast): Brook still a student at Oxford.

1944 *A Sentimental Journey* film from the novel by Laurence Sterne.

1945 *The Infernal Machine* by Jean Cocteau, Chanticleer Theatre Club, London.
The Barretts of Wimpole Street by Rudolf Besier, 'Q' Theatre, London.
Pygmalion by Bernard Shaw, for an ENSA tour of England and Germany.
Man and Superman by Bernard Shaw, Birmingham Repertory Theatre (with Paul Scofield as John Tanner).
King John by William Shakespeare, Birmingham Repertory Theatre (with Paul Scofield as Philip the Bastard).
The Lady from the Sea by Henrik Ibsen, Birmingham Repertory Theatre (with Paul Scofield as Doctor Wangel).

1946 *Love's Labour's Lost* by William Shakespeare, Shakespeare Memorial Theatre, Stratford-upon-Avon (with Paul Scofield as Don Adriano de Armado, David King-Wood as Berowne).
The Brothers Karamazov adapted by Alec Guinness from the novel by Dostoyevsky, Lyric Theatre, Hammersmith (with Alec Guiness as Mitya).
Vicious Circle (*Huis Clos*) by Jean-Paul Sartre, Arts Theatre, London (with Alec Guinness as Garcin, Beatrix Lehmann as Inès, Betty Ann Davies as Estelle).

1947 *Romeo and Juliet* by William Shakespeare, Shakespeare Memorial Theatre, Stratford (with Laurence Payne as Romeo, Daphne Slater as Juliet).
Men without Shadows and *The Respectable Prostitute* (double bill) by Jean-Paul Sartre, adapted by Kitty Black, Lyric Theatre, Hammersmith (with Mary Morris as Lucie in *Men without*

Shadows: Betty Ann Davies as Lizzie in *The Respectable Prostitute*). Brook writes dance criticism for the *Observer*.

1948 *Boris Godunov* by Mussorgsky, Royal Opera House, Covent Garden.
La Bohème by Puccini, Royal Opera House, Covent Garden.

1949 *Dark of the Moon* by Howard Richardson and William Berney, Lyric Theatre, Hammersmith; later transferred to Ambassador's Theatre, London (with William Sylvester as John, Sheila Burrell as Barbara Allen).
The Marriage of Figaro by Mozart, Royal Opera House, Covent Garden.
The Olympians by Bliss, Royal Opera House, Covent Garden.
Salomé by Richard Strauss, Royal Opera House, Covent Garden: designed by Salvador Dali (with Ljuba Welitsch as Salome).

1950 *Ring round the Moon* by Jean Anouilh, adapted by Christopher Fry, Globe Theatre, London (with Paul Scofield as Hugo and Frederic, Claire Bloom as Isabelle, Margaret Rutherford as Mme Desmortes).
Measure for Measure by William Shakespeare, Shakespeare Memorial Theatre, Stratford (with John Gielgud as Angelo, Barbara Jefford as Isabella): tour to West Germany.
The Little Hut by André Roussin, adapted by Nancy Mitford, Lyric Theatre, Hammersmith (with Robert Morley as Philip, Joan Tetzel as Susan, David Tomlinson as Henry).

1951 *La Mort d'un Commis Voyageur* (*Death of a Salesman*) by Arthur Miller, Belgian National Theatre, Brussels.
A Penny for a Song by John Whiting, Haymarket Theatre, London (with Alan Webb, Denys Blakelock, Virginia McKenna, Ronald Squire).
The Winter's Tale by William Shakespeare, Phoenix Theatre, London (with John Gielgud as Leontes, Diana Wynyard and Flora Robson).
Marriage to Natasha Parry.
Colombe by Jean Anouilh, adapted by Denis Cannan, New Theatre, London (with Yvonne Arnaud as Mme Alexandra, Joyce Redman as Colombe).

1952 *The Beggar's Opera* (film) adapted from John Gay (with Laurence Olivier as Macheath).

1953 *Venice Preserv'd* by Thomas Otway, Lyric Theatre, Hammersmith
(with John Gielgud as Jaffier, Paul Scofield as Pierre, Eileen
Herlie as Belvidera).
The Little Hut, Coronet Theatre, New York (with Anne Vernon
as Susan).
Box For One, television play by Peter Brook.
Faust by Charles Gounod, Metropolitan Opera, New York (with
Jussi Bjoerling, Victoria de los Angeles, Nicola Rossi-Lemeri).
King Lear (television film, New York) with Orson Welles.

1954 *The Dark is Light Enough* by Christopher Fry, Aldwych Theatre,
London (with Edith Evans as Countess Rosmarin Ostenburg).
Both Ends Meet by Arthur Macrae, Apollo Theatre, London (with
Brenda Bruce as Margaret, Arthur Macrae as Tom, Alan Webb
and Miles Malleson).
House of Flowers by Truman Capote, music by Harold Arlen,
Alvin Theatre, New York (with Pearl Bailey).

1955 *The Lark* by Jean Anouilh, translated by Christopher Fry, Lyric
Theatre, Hammersmith (with Dorothy Tutin as Joan, Richard
Johnson as the Earl of Warwick, Donald Pleasence as the
Dauphin).
Titus Andronicus by William Shakespeare, Shakespeare Memorial
Theatre, Stratford-upon-Avon: transferred to London in 1956
(with Laurence Olivier as Titus, Anthony Quayle as Aaron,
Vivien Leigh as Lavinia).
Hamlet by William Shakespeare, Phoenix Theatre, London (with
Paul Scofield as Hamlet, Diana Wynyard as Gertrude, Alec
Clunes as Claudius, Mary Ure as Ophelia): on tour to Moscow –
twelve performances at the Moscow Arts Theatre.
The Birthday Present and *Report From Moscow*, television films by
Peter Brook.

1956 *The Power and the Glory* adapted from Graham Greene's novel by
Denis Cannan and Pierre Bost, Phoenix Theatre, London (with
Paul Scofield as the Priest, Harry H. Corbett as the Lieutenant
of Police).
The Family Reunion by T. S. Eliot, Phoenix Theatre, London
(with Paul Scofield as Harry, Sybil Thorndike as Amy, Gwen
Ffrangçon-Davies as Agatha).
A View from the Bridge by Arthur Miller, Comedy Theatre,
London (with Anthony Quayle as Eddie, Mary Ure as
Catherine).

La Chatte sur un toit brûlant (*Cat On a Hot Tin Roof*) by
Tennessee Williams, translated André Obey, Théâtre Antoine,
Paris (with Jeanne Moreau as Maggie).

1957 *The Tempest* by William Shakespeare, Shakespeare Memorial
Theatre, Stratford, and later at Theatre Royal, Drury Lane,
London (with John Gielgud as Prospero).
Heaven and Earth by Peter Brook and Denis Cannan (television
film).
Eugene Onegin by Tchaikovsky, Metropolitan Opera, New York,
designed by Ralf Gérard, conducted by Dimitri Mitropoulos
(with Georges London as Eugene).
Titus Andronicus at the Théâtre des Nations, Paris: European
tour to Venice, Belgrade, Warsaw, Vienna, Zagreb.

1958 *Vue du pont* (*A View from the Bridge*) by Arthur Miller, translated
by Marcel Aymé, Théâtre Antoine, Paris (with Raf Vallone as
Eddie, Lila Kedrova as Beatrice).
The Visit by Friedrich Dürrenmatt, adapted by Maurice Valency,
Lynn Fontanne Theatre, New York (with Lynn Fontanne and
Alfred Lunt).
Irma la Douce by Alexandre Breffort, Lyric Theatre, London
(with Keith Michell as Nestor-le-Fripe, Elizabeth Seal as Irma),
English version by Julian More, David Heneker and Monty
Norman, music by Marguerite Monnot.

1959 *The Fighting Cock* translated from Jean Anouilh's *l'Hurluberlu* by
Lucienne Hill, ANTA Theatre, New York (with Rex Harrison as
the General, Natasha Parry as Sophie).

1960 *Le Balcon* by Jean Genet, Théâtre de Gymnase, Paris (with Marie
Bell, Loleh Bellon, Roger Blin, Charles Denner).
Moderato Cantabile (film) from Marguerite Duras's novel (with
Jeanne Moreau and Jean-Paul Belmondo).

1961 Summer: 3 months' filming William Golding's *Lord of the Flies*
on the island of Vieques, Puerto Rico, photography by Gerry
Feil, Tom Hollyman. Edited in Paris by Brook and Feil.

19 *King Lear* by William Shakespeare, Royal Shakespeare
Theatre, Stratford (with Paul Scofield as Lear, Diana Rigg
as Cordelia, Irene Worth as Goneril, Patience Collier as
Regan, Alec McCowen as the Fool, Tom Fleming as Kent, Brian
Murray as Edgar, Ian Richardson as Edmund, Alan Webb as

Gloucester). Transfer to the Aldwych Theatre, London, in December.

1963 *The Physicists* by Friedrich Dürrenmatt, translated by James Kirkup, Aldwych Theatre, London (with Irene Worth as Mathilde von Zahnd, Alan Webb as Ernesti, Michael Hordern as Beutler, Cyril Cusack as Möbius).
The Tempest by William Shakespeare, Royal Shakespeare Theatre, Stratford-upon-Avon: directed in collaboration with Clifford Williams (with Tom Fleming as Prospero).
The Perils of Scobie Prilt a musical by Julian More and Monty Norman: for one week only at New Theatre, Oxford (with Michael Sarne and Nyree Dawn Porter).
La Danse de Sergent Musgrave translated from John Arden's *Serjeant Musgrave's Dance*, Théâtre de l'Athénée, Paris (with Laurent Terzieff as Musgrave).
Le Vicaire (*The Representative*) by Rolf Hochhuth, Théâtre de l'Athénée, Paris: co-directed with François Darbon (with Jean Topart as the Doctor).
May: *Lord of the Flies* shown at the Cannes Film Festival; in August, released in New York.
May: *King Lear* at Théâtre des Nations, Paris.

1964 January/February: four-week Theatre of Cruelty season (LAMDA Theatre, London).
Spring: tour of *King Lear* in E. Europe/USA. May, in New York (State Theatre).
June: *The Screens* by Jean Genet (Donmar Rehearsal Rooms, Covent Garden).
July: release of *Lord of the Flies* (BLC/British Lion) in London, followed by general release.
August 20: *The Persecution and Assassination of Marat as Performed by the Inmates of the Asylum of Charenton under the Direction of the Marquis de Sade (The Marat/Sade)* by Peter Weiss (RSC Aldwych); cast including Patrick Magee (Sade), Ian Richardson (Marat), Glenda Jackson (Corday), Clifford Rose (M. Coulmier), Bob Lloyd (Jacques Roux), Susan Williamson (Simone Everard); design, Sally Jacobs; music, Richard Peaslee.

1965 New Year's Honours List, Brook awarded CBE.
February 1: first of Brook's university lectures on *The Theatre Today*, later published in revised form as *The Empty Space*.

October 19: *The Investigation* by Peter Weiss (RSC public reading at the Aldwych); prepared by Brook, David Jones; translation by Alexander Gross.
Publication in English of *Shakespeare our Contemporary* by Jan Kott, with Brook's introduction.

1966 January/March: *Marat/Sade* in New York (Martin Beck Theatre); awarded 3 Tonies, 4 Drama Critic Awards.
February: *Marat/Sade* recorded on disc, New York.
May: *Marat/Sade* filmed at Pinewood Studios, London (17 days' shooting) with American tour cast (United Artists).
August 1–10: Grotowski and Cieslak in London with the RSC.
October 13: *US* (RSC, Aldwych); cast including Glenda Jackson, Mark Jones, Bob Lloyd, Pauline Munro, Clifford Rose, Barry Stanton, Mike Williams, Leon Lissek, Morgan Sheppard, Mike Pratt, Hugh Sullivan, Patrick O'Connell; design, Sally Jacobs; music, Richard Peaslee; written material, Denis Cannan, Adrian Mitchell; documentary advisers, Michael Stott, Michael Kustow; Brook's associate directors, Geoffrey Reeves, Albert Hunt.

1967 March: *Marat/Sade* film premièred at Odeon, Haymarket, London.
Summer: *Tell me Lies* filmed in London in 4 weeks.

1968 February: *Tell me Lies* released New York (13th), London (17th, at Gala Royal, Edgware Road).
March 19: *Oedipus* by Seneca (National Theatre at the Old Vic); adaptation by Ted Hughes from translation by David Anthony Turner; cast including John Gielgud (Oedipus), Irene Worth (Jocasta), Colin Blakely (Creon), Ronald Pickup (Messenger), Frank Wylie (Tiresias); design, Jean Monod; music, Richard Peaslee; co-director, Geoffrey Reeves.
May: Brook in Paris (Mobilier National, Gobelins) working in private with international Théâtre des Nations group including Joe Chaikin, Victor Garcia, Claude Roy; forced to leave for London, in June.
July 18: Shakespeare's *The Tempest* (Round House, Chalk Farm, London); international group including Yoshi Oida, Bob Lloyd, Natasha Parry, Sylvain Corthay, Philippe Avron, Pierre Jorris, Bernadette Ouffroy.
September: publication of *The Empty Space*.

1969 January/April: filming *King Lear* in Jutland, Denmark; followed by seven months editing in Paris.

1970 August 27: Shakespeare's *A Midsummer Night's Dream* (RSC, Stratford); cast including Alan Howard (Theseus/Oberon), Sarah Kestelman (Hippolyta/Titania), John Kane (Philostrate/Puck), Ben Kingsley (Demetrius), Frances de la Tour (Helena), Christopher Gable (Lysander), Mary Rutherford (Hermia), Philip Locke (Egeus/Quince), Barry Stanton (Snug), David Waller (Bottom); design, Sally Jacobs; music, Richard Peaslee. December: two performances of *Dream* at Roundhouse. Creation of C.I.R.T., Paris; directors, Brook and Micheline Rozan.
November 1: work starts in la Salle Perret of the Mobilier National.

1971 January: *Dream* in New York (Billy Rose Theatre) as part of fourteen-week USA/Canada tour. March: two-week residence of *Dream* at the Brooklyn Academy of Music, New York. Brook wins Tony award for best direction.
June 10: transfer of *Dream* to Aldwych, London.
August 28: *Orghast* (Persepolis, Iran, as part of the 5th Shiraz International Festival of Arts); company including Malik Bowens (Mali), Michèle Collison (USA), Claude Confortès (France), Sylvain Corthay (France), Daniel Kamwa (Cameroon), Andreas Katsulas (USA), Bob Lloyd (Britain), Paloma Matta (Spain), Joäo Mota (Portugal), Pauline Munro (Britain), Bruce Myers (Britain), Yoshi Oida (Japan), Natasha Parry (Britain), Irene Worth (Britain), Lou Zeldis (USA) plus 10 Persian actors and 5 musicians; writer, Ted Hughes; designers, Eugene Lee, Franne Lee, Jean Monod; composer, Richard Peaslee; Brook's co-directors, Arby Ovanessian (Iran), Geoffrey Reeves (Britain), Andrei Serban (Rumania).
Release of *King Lear* film (Athena Laterna Films) at Prince Charles, London, in July; cast including Paul Scofield (Lear), Irene Worth (Goneril), Patrick Magee (Cornwall), Cyril Cusack (Albany), Tom Fleming (Kent), Alan Webb (Gloucester), Ian Hogg (Edmund), Bob Lloyd (Edgar), Jack MacGowran (Fool), Barry Stanton (Oswald), Anne-Lise Gabold (Cordelia), Susan Engel (Regan); produced by Michael Birkett.

1972 April 25: C.I.R.T. public demonstrations of exercises (Théâtre Récamier, Paris).

Limited public performances/improvisations of Handke's
Kaspar.
European tour of RSC *Dream*.

1973   December (1972) / February (1973): Journey to Africa:
Conference of the Birds (Algeria, Niger, Nigeria, Dahomey, Mali);
Malik Bowens (Mali), Sylvain Corthay (France), Michele
Collison (USA), Andreas Katsulas (Greek-American), Bruce
Myers (Britain), Yoshi Oida (Japan), Natasha Parry (Britain),
Lou Zeldis (USA), Ayansola (Nigeria), Miriam Goldschmidt
(West Germany), François Marthouret (France), Helen Mirren
(Britain), plus Daniel Charlot, John Heilpern, Daniel
Odimbossoukou; composer, Elizabeth Swados (USA); stage
managers, Mary Evans, Bob Applegarth. July 1/October 12:
Journey to America (California with El Teatro Campesino,
Colorado, Minnesota, New York and the Brooklyn Academy of
Music); Malik Bowens, Michèle Collison, Richard Cohen
(musician), Sylvain Corthay, Miriam Goldschmidt, Sally Jacobs,
Andreas Katsulas, François Marthouret, Helen Mirren, Bruce
Myers, Yoshi Oida, Natasha Parry, John Schimmel (musician),
Andrew Schloss (musician), Nina Soufy (assist. manager),
Elizabeth Swados (composer), Lou Zeldis; stage managers, Mary
Evans, Bob Applegarth.
World tour of RSC *Dream*; including USA, Japan.

1974   October 15: Shakespeare's *Timon d'Athènes* (C.I.C.T., Bouffes
du Nord, Boul'd de la Chapelle, Paris 10; part of Paris Festival
d'Automne); French version by Jean-Claude Carrière; cast
including François Marthouret (Timon), Malik Bowens
(Apemantus), Bruce Myers (Alcibiades); Brook's co-director,
Jean-Pierre Vincent.

1975   January 12: *Les Iks* (C.I.C.T., Bouffes du Nord; part of Festival
d'Automne); cast including Andreas Katsulas (Colin Turnbull),
Malik Bowens, Michele Collison, Miriam Goldschmidt, Bruce
Myers, Yoshi Oida (the Ik); associate director, Yutaka Wada.
May: free improvised versions of Attar's *The Conference of the Birds*
performed to restricted audiences, Bouffes du Nord.
April/June: *Timon/Les Iks* alternating in repertory at the Bouffes
du Nord 24–26 April: International Colloquy on theatre
(Théâtre Récamier, Paris): theme – collective creation; including
Jean-Louis Barrault, Peter Brook, Armand Gatti, Tadeusz
Kantor, Ariane Mnouchkine, Jean-Claude van Itallie, Shuji

Terayama, Peter Weiss.
June/July: Brook in Poland (Wroclaw, Warsaw) for Université
des Explorations du Théâtre des Nations; involved in lectures,
discussions, workshops etc. with Eugenio Barba, Joe Chaikin,
Victor Garcia, Andre Gregory, Jerzy Grotowski, Luca Ronconi.
15–18 July: international colloquy on theatre/culture at
UNESCO, Paris; including Brook and Grotowski, along with 30
artists from 25 countries.

1976 January 15: *The Ik*, six-week season at the Round House, London.
May: *The Ik* at Caracas Festival of Latin American Theatre,
Venezuela; S. American tour.
October/November: six-week tour of *The Ik* around USA
universities; followed by E. European tour.

1977 May/August: shooting *Meetings with Remarkable Men*
(Afghanistan and Pinewood Studios, London); edited by Brook
in Paris during *Ubu* rehearsal period.
November 23: Jarry's *Ubu aux Bouffes* (C.I.C.T., Bouffes du
Nord); cast including Andreas Katsulas (Père Ubu), Michèle
Collison/Miriam Goldschmidt (Mère Ubu), Malik Bowens, Urs
Bihler (West Germany), Mireille Maalouf (Lebanon), Alain
Maratrat (France), François Marthouret, Yoshi Oida,
Jean-Claude Perrin (Switzerland); percussion by Toshi
Tsuchitori (Japan).
1977/8: European and Latin American tour of *Ubu* (over 150
performances worldwide).

1978 May: *Ubu* at Young Vic, London. July: *Ubu* as French
representative at Théâtre des Nations, Caracas.
October 4: Shakespeare's *Antony and Cleopatra* (RSC, Stratford);
cast including Alan Howard (Mark Antony), Glenda Jackson
(Cleopatra), Jonathan Pryce (Octavius Caesar), Patrick Stewart
(Enobarbus), David Suchet (Pompey), Marjory Bland (Octavia),
Richard Griffiths (clown); design, Sally Jacobs; music, Richard
Peaslee.
October 27: Shakespeare's *Mesure pour Mesure* (C.I.C.T.,
Bouffes du Nord); French version by Jean-Claude Carrière; cast
including François Marthouret (Duc), Bruce Myers (Angelo),
Clémentine Amouroux (Isabelle), Andreas Katsulas (Pompé);
three-month run.

1979 Short European tour of *Mesure pour Mesure*.
   July 15: Attar's *Conference of the Birds* (C.I.C.T., Cloître des
   Carmes, Avignon; part of 33rd Festival d'Avignon); cast
   including Maurice Bénichou (France), Urs Bihler, Malik
   Bowens, Michèle George (France), Miriam Goldschmidt,
   Andreas Katsulas, Arnault Lecarpentier (France), Mireille
   Maalouf, Alain Maratrat, Bruce Myers, Yoshi Oida, Natasha
   Parry, Jean-Claude Perrin, Tapa Sudana (Bali). Musicians –
   Blaise Catala, Linda Daniel, Alain Kremski, Amy Rubin, Toshi
   Tsuchitori; design, Sally Jacobs; ancient Balinese masks, private
   collection of Jacques Fassola; contemporary Balinese masks
   created by Ida Bagus Anom, Wayan Tangguh.
   Performed with a version of Birago Diop's *L'Os* (adapted by Malik
   Bowens and Jean-Claude Carrière); cast including Malik
   Bowens (Mor Lam), Yoshi Oida (Moussa), Mireille Maalouf
   (Awa), Andreas Katsulas (Mame Magatte). Short European tour
   before return to Bouffes du Nord, Paris, for two-month run
   beginning October 6.
   September 13: London première of Brook's film of G. I.
   Gurdjieff's *Meetings with Remarkable Men* (Libra Films, New
   York); cast including Dragan Maksimovic (Gurdjieff), Terence
   Stamp (Prince Lubovedsky), Warren Mitchell (Gurdjieff's
   father), Athol Fugard (Skridlov), Natasha Parry (Vivitskaia),
   Bruce Myers (Yelov), Donald Sumpter (Pogossian), Mikica
   Dimitrijevic (young Gurdjieff), Colin Blakely, Tom Fleming,
   Ian Hogg; music, Thomas de Hartmann, Laurence Rosenthal
   and Alain Kremski (sound track released on disc – Disque Vare
   Sarabande (1979) STV 81129); photography, Gilbert Taylor. (To
   present day, *Meetings* shown twice a week at St Ambroise cinema,
   Paris XIe).

1980 March/April: *The Ik, Ubu, L'Os, Conférence* performed at
   Adelaide Festival, Australia; filmed as *Stages* (Macau Light
   Films).
   May/June: *The Ik, Ubu, L'Os, Conférence* performed at La Mama
   Annexe, New York.
   October/December: *L'Os, Conférence* revived at Bouffes du
   Nord.

1981 March 18: Chekhov's *La Cerisaie* (C.I.C.T., Bouffes du Nord);
   cast including Natasha Parry (Lioubov Ranevskaia), Claude
   Everard (Epikhodov), Nathalie Nell (Varia), Michel Piccoli

(Gaev), Maurice Bénichou (Yacha), Niels Arestrup (Lopakhine),
Joseph Blatchley (Trofimov), Michèle Simonnet (Charlotta),
Anne Consigny (Ania); music, Marius Constant; design, Cloé
Obolensky; associate director, Maurice Bénichou.
November 23: *La Tragédie de Carmen* (C.I.C.T./Théâtre
National de l'Opéra de Paris co-production, Bouffes du Nord);
cast including Hélène Delavault/Zehava Gal/Eva Saurova
(Carmen), Laurence Dale/Howard Hensel/Julian Pike (Don
José), Véronique Dietschy/Agnès Host (Micaëla), Carl Johan
Falkmann/John Rath (Escamillo), and Jean-Paul Denizon, Alain
Maratrat; assistant director, Maurice Bénichou; musical
director, Marius Constant; design, Chloé Obolensky.

1982 Brook's discussion/lecture at the Donmar Warehouse, London.
September/October: short European tour of revival of *L'Os*
(including 16 dates at the Almeida Theatre, Islington, London);
cast including Malik Bowens, Mireille Maalouf, Bruce Myers
(Moussa), Abel Aboulitan, Clément Masdongar; percussion,
Toshi Tsuchitori; directed by Malik Bowens.
November: revival of *Carmen* at the Bouffes du Nord.

1983 March: revival of *La Cérisaie* at the Bouffes du Nord; same cast
except for Guy Tréjan (Gaev), Martine Chevallier (Varia), Irina
Brook (Ania).
Release of three film versions of *La Tragédie de Carmen* with
original casts: photography by Sven Nykvist, design by Georges
Wakhévitsch: co-produced by Micheline Rozan, Antenne 2,
Channel Four Television, Bavaria Atelier Munich and Alby
Films.
November: *Chin Chin*, Théâtre Montparnasse, Paris:
co-directed by Maurice Bénichou (with Natasha Parry and
Marcello Mastroianni).

1984 Release of *Swann in Love*, a film by Volker Schlöndorff:
screenplay (from Proust) by Peter Brook, Jean-Claude Carrière
and Marie-Hélène Estienne (with Ornella Muti, Jeremy Irons,
Alain Delon).

1985 July 7: *Le Mahabharata*, adapted from the Sanskrit original by
Peter Brook and Jean-Claude Carrière: *La Partie de Dés, L'Exil
dans la Forêt, La Guerre*: première at the Festival d'Avignon, in
the Boulbon quarry near Avignon: cast including Ryszard
Cieslak (Dhritarashtra), Andrzej Seweryn (Duryodhana),

Matthias Habich as Yudhishthira, Vittorio Mezzogiorno as
Arjuna, Maurice Bénichou as Ganesha/Krishna, Alain Maratrat
as Vyasa, Bruce Myers as Karna, Yoshi Oida as Drona/Kitchaka,
Mallika Sarabhai as Draupadi, Mireille Maalouf as Gandhari,
Georges Corraface as Dushassana, Sotigui Kouyate as
Bhishma/Parashurama, Mamadou Dioume as Bhima and Tapa
Sudana, Pascaline Pointillart, Clovis, Andreas Katsulas,
Jean-Paul Denizon, Tam Sir Niane, Clément Masdongar,
Josephine Derenne, Douta Seck. Designed by Chloé Obolensky:
lighting by Jean Kalman, music by Toshi Tsuchitori: produced
by Micheline Rozan.
September: short European tour (including Athens, Barcelona,
Frankfurt).
October: *Le Mahabharata* at The Bouffes du Nord, Paris: until
May 1986.

1986 September: revival of *La Tragédie de Carmen* for tour to Japan.

1987 Summer: beginning of world tour of English-language version of
The Mahabharata, translated by Peter Brook: première in Zurich,
then Los Angeles, New York, Perth and Adelaide Festivals in
Australia, India and perhaps London in 1988.

1988 February: *The Cherry Orchard*, Brooklyn, New York (with
Natasha Parry).

The Theatre of Disturbance, 1962–1966

King Lear

LAMDA Theatre of Cruelty Season

The Screens

The Marat/Sade

US

'He who hath to be a creator hath first to be a destroyer, and break
values in pieces'

(Nietzsche)

'The theatre has one precise social function – to disturb the
spectator'

(Brook)

King Lear: A New Crossroads

In 1962, at the ripe old age of 37, Peter Brook was already established as one of Europe's most talented theatre luminaries, with almost twenty years of professional experience behind him. As one of the governing triumvirate of the newly re-christened Royal Shakespeare Company, one might have excused his feeling that he had arrived. In over forty productions, he had staged eight Shakespeare plays and seven major operas (including an explosive reworking of Strauss's *Salomé*, with 'scenery, costumes and special effects by Salvador Dali' in 1949: he was a precocious Covent Garden director at the age of 22). He had managed to juggle productions of major European voices (Cocteau, Sartre, Anouilh, Genet, Dürrenmatt) with works by seminal modernists like Eliot, Fry and Miller. He had worked in overtly commercial forms: boulevard comedy (Roussin's *The Little Hut*), musical comedy (*Irma la Douce*), television drama (including four plays from his own pen) and three major films. All that had remained constant were the abrupt changes of gear – between forms, styles, themes, working processes. Later he described this hyperactive period as a conscious process of immersion in as many different forms as possible, following 'a dialectical principle of finding reality through opposites'. Here was someone driven by an overriding passion for experience, in a search for a theatre language of and for our times. He hadn't arrived: he was only just beginning . . .

The development of Brook's experimental concerns is reflected to some degree in the evolution of his approach to Shakespeare. As the youngest director in the history of the Shakespeare Festival at Stratford, the Boy Wonder (as he was then known, affectionately or otherwise[1]) deemed it necessary to abandon his set model and blocking plan on the first morning of rehearsals for *Love's Labour's Lost* (1945): nevertheless

---

[1] Much of Brook's work even during the Sixties was to be treated by startled but patronising critics as the strange fruit of an over-active adolescent imagination, licensed by his status as precocious '*wunderkind*' or '*enfant terrible*' – epithets he only really left behind in his late forties.

he provoked fervent acclaim for his elegant treatment of Shakespeare's text. Rejecting any notion of obligation to period accuracy, Brook elaborated bitter-sweet images of billowing satin dresses and Harle-quins: a *fête champêtre*, indebted visually to Watteau and atmospherically to Molière and Marivaux. Anachronism was freely embraced: here Constable Dull was a Victorian bobby, with helmet, truncheon and a string of sausages. Scandalous to some, a breath of fresh air to others: all was wistful luminosity and movement, colour and silken conceits. A world deliberately and radically separated from the everyday gloom and dowdiness of post-war Britain: an escape into lyricism and dreams, a 'theatre of images'.

Eleven years later came the miracle of his production of *Titus Andronicus* (August 1955, Stratford). Salvaging it once and for all from the scorn of academics and purists ('one of the stupidest and most uninspiring plays ever written', according to T. S. Eliot), Brook trans-formed a grotesque neo-Senecan melodrama of primitive bloodlust – violent death and cannibalism abound – into a rite of authentic passions and suffering, by *suggesting* a horrendous reality with simple stylised eloquence. When Lavinia (Vivien Leigh) appeared, 'her hands cut off, her tongue cut out, and ravisht', the stumps of her arms trailed long ribbons of scarlet velvet, her mouth was veiled with blood-red silk: the scene as a whole was underpinned by Brook's own barbarously amplified 'musique concrète'. The effect was more than haunting or startling: every evening saw fainting spectators carried from the theatre. The times had changed. Brook was now looking towards a theatre of darkness, a forum for confronting modern sensibilities: a theatre of direct event in which what occurred on stage could no longer be a separate reality: it would have to appeal to the eyes, ears, heart and viscera of the spectator's imagination.

Brook's production of *King Lear* seven years later marks a major crossroads in his career, as resonant in many ways as *A Midsummer Night's Dream* in 1970, and his subsequent abandonment of British theatre and its prevailing limitations. *Lear* signals the culmination of Brook's seventeen-year period of collaboration with Paul Scofield: the end of romantic fantasy and decoration of any kind, of lighting effects and fixed set designs (Brook's own design for *Lear* was almost entirely abandoned in the last week of rehearsals). At the same time, a new beginning: the genesis of ensemble concerns, work on the actor as supreme creator, the primary source in an empty space: starkness and provocation, clarity and visibility at every level: the uneasy fusion of Artaud, Beckett and Brecht in search of a prismatic density of expression and form, a truer reflection of the spirit of our age. *The theatre as disturbance* . . .

'A play must leave you in a more receptive mood than you were before. It isn't there to "move" people. That's a ghastly idea. You cry, you have a bath of sentiment. You come out saying you've had a lovely time. I prefer the notion of disturbance . . .'

(Brook in 1964)

D. W.

Lear Log by Charles Marowitz

Charles Marowitz compiled this log while serving as assistant director on Peter Brook's 1962 production of King Lear *at the Royal Shakespeare Theatre, Stratford-on-Avon. The log is not a day-to-day account of rehearsals, but rather 'salient excerpts which reflect the problems and curiosities which emerged during the rehearsal period'. The 'Log' first appeared in* Encore; *the 'postscript' was written especially for* Tulane Drama Review.

Early talk with Brook

For Brook, Lear is a series of intellectual strands which only performance can tie together. Far from being an 'unactable play', he believes its full meaning can only be comprehended existentially – on a stage. He sees it mainly as a play about sight and blindness.

Gloucester, who does not see Edmund's villainy, loses his eyes. Edgar, who does not see his brother's covetousness, loses his freedom. Lear, who does not see the corruption and rancour that seethe within his family and state, loses his senses and ultimately his life. Everywhere one looks, one sees only the facades and emblems of a world and, ironically, as characters acquire sight, it enables them to see only into a void.

Lear-Beckett-Brook

Fable: A blind man, resolved to die, is led up a steep mountainside by one he takes to be a naked lunatic. The steep mountainside is, in reality, a flat field; the naked lunatic, his son. Arriving at what he takes to be the topmost point, the blind man leaps into what he takes to be a fathomless chasm, and falls in a faint two feet away from where he stood. His son, now disguised as a passing peasant, revives the blind man, wards off the treachery of a would-be assassin and leads him to temporary safety, but not before he has had a wild encounter with a distracted king dressed in weeds and nettles.

The plot is as Beckettian as anything out of *Molloy* or *Malone Dies*; the scene, a metaphysical farce which ridicules life, death, sanity and illusion. This (Act IV, Scene 6) has been the germinal scene in Brook's production of *King Lear*, and it has conditioned all the scenes with which it connects.

In discussing the work of rehearsals, our frame of reference was always Beckettian. The world of this *Lear*, like Beckett's world, is in a constant state of decomposition. The set consists of geometrical sheets of metal which are ginger with rust and corrosion. The costumes, dominantly leather, have been textured to suggest long and hard wear. The knight's tabards are peeling with long use; Lear's cape and coat are creased and blackened with time and weather. The furniture is rough wood, there is nothing but space – giant white flats opening on to a blank cyclorama.

Walk through Kensington Gardens in search of Edgar

Met Brook in Kensington. He asked me what, in practical terms, I thought to be the play's greatest problem. I told him that for me it was the character of Edgar, who, after three short scenes as a sober, not very bright or demonstrative young man, transforms into the madly-capering Bedlam beggar, Poor Tom. In all the productions I had seen of the play, the change had never really worked and I concluded that this was an awkward inconsistency attributable to Shakespeare for which one had to compensate by directorial ingenuity.

Brook confessed that he too had been preoccupied with the problem of Edgar but would not accept the theory that it was simply a fault which one could write down to Shakespeare. He believed the play had such a hard inner consistency that everything must be there for a purpose and it was necessary to discover Edgar's place in the scheme of things.

We mulled it over as we walked.

Edgar, legitimate son of Gloucester; perhaps twenty-four or twenty-five years old. Something of an introvert; perhaps a bookish type. One senses that Gloucester prefers his bastard son Edmund; is prepared to believe his illegitimate son Edmund (who has been out of the country for seven years) sooner than his own son Edgar who has lived with him at court. Gloucester's affection for Edmund seems based on the fact that he is a lusty and ambitious youth, possessing the same traits of zeal and flattery that probably raised Gloucester to his high court position. Compared to his brother, Edgar is something of a vegetable. It is true that in his last scenes he emerges as a fearless avenger, but by that time he has been a renegade, a madman, a faith-healer, and a provocateur. Enough has happened to him to have forged an entirely new character.

Why, when he finds himself a hunted man, does this sober, well-behaved, court-educated youth choose the guise of a half-naked, Bedlam lunatic? 'Whiles I may scape I will preserve myself and am bethought to take the basest and most poorest shape that ever penury in contempt of man brought near to beast.' Why should he be so bethought? And how is it that he carries it off so well?

In terms of the text, Poor Tom has more definition (and more scenes) than the original character of Edgar. Where is the consistency in this transformation, and if it is deliberately inconsistent, how can one perform it without forfeiting either Edgar or Poor Tom?

Three times around the Kensington Pond, peering distractedly at model boats, prams and kite-fliers, over two hours of speculation and conjecture: no Edgar in sight.

First reading at Stratford

Brook spoke of the play as a mountain whose summit had never been reached. On the way up one found the shattered bodies of other climbers strewn on every side. 'Olivier here, Laughton there; it's frightening.' Describing the enormity of the task before us, he gave one of the aptest definitions of the rehearsal process I've ever heard: 'The work of rehearsals is looking for meaning and then making it meaning-ful.' To illustrate the extent of this search he related a short oriental fable about a man whose wife had suddenly disappeared. A neighbour came upon the man sifting sand on a lonely beach, and asked what he was doing. 'I have lost my wife,' he explained. 'I know she is somewhere and therefore have to look for her everywhere.'[1]

The day was devoted to a straight read-through of the play. ('Of course it's useless, but it does make everyone feel they have the same work in common and besides, one has to start somewhere.')

It was a reading full of conventional verse-speaking; at times robustly acted; at other times, dully mouthed by actors torn between study of the text and performance. Paul Scofield (this was the first time he and the company had met together) used the reading mainly as a study-session – struggling with the verse like a man trapped in clinging ivy and trying to writhe his way free. One was immediately aware of the actor's resolve and caution. Scofield circled Lear like a wary challenger measuring out an unbeaten opponent, and it was apparent from the start that this challenger was a strategist rather than a slugger.

Third reading

Yesterday and today were devoted to readings, stops, analyses and discussion; Brook pointing out the pattern the play makes in space, dropping provocative but inconclusive hints about character, saying just

---

[1] A story of Majnun and Leila from Attar's *Conference of the Birds*: Brook clearly knew the work almost twenty years before his stage version at the Avignon Festival in 1979. (D.W.)

enough to force an actor to reappraise his entire conception of a role but not enough to supply him with an alternative.

Motives for Lear

'Why,' I asked, 'at the height of his power, obviously still robust and energetic, does Lear decide to apportion out his kingdom and step down?'

Brook threw the question back at me and I began to improvise an elementary psychological explanation. 'You can't apply psychoanalysis to a character like Lear. He does it because he's that type of man. Like de Gaulle or Adenauer or Citizen Kane, he has battened down all the hatches of his power. He has been the supreme ruler. Only one thing now remains greater than actually commanding, and that is the knowledge that your aura will do as well as yourself.'

Unconvinced, I explained that motivation doesn't have to be merely psychological; it can be mythic, epic, or poetic. This was acceptable to Brook who, I find, has a terror of the pat psychological interpretation. I put the question to Scofield, who felt the text supplied all the necessary answers. 'He is getting on and wants to, as he says, put the "cares and business of the state" on to younger people; and also, he wants to make sure he leaves a balance of power behind him.'

Although all this is true, I cannot help feeling it is only part of the truth and that a subtextual reason has got to be found to set the tone of the opening scene.

The crucial insights into any play, Brook believes, will be found by the actors themselves. 'The greatest rehearsal factor is fatigue. When you get so thoroughly exhausted from grappling with a certain problem and you think you can't go on – then – suddenly, something gives and you "find something". You know that marvellous moment in a rehearsal when you suddenly *find something*.'

Rehearsal of Scene One

A rash of verse-speaking broke out today. Brook made a short speech. He pointed out that it was necessary to find the stress of the verse because that led to the discovery of its sense, but once found, it was fatal merely to yield to the verse-rhythm, as that produced only Shakespearian music. 'A line should have no more than one or two stresses. If it is given all the stresses inherent in its rhythm, it becomes metrically correct and dramatically meaningless. In verse which is properly spoken, each character plays his own rhythm – as personal as his own handwriting – but what often happens in Shakespeare is that everyone shares a generalized rhythm that passes impersonally from one to the other.'

Fifth day of rehearsal

Brook relies heavily on the actor's sense of movement. It is the fifth day and everyone is moving freely and experimentally. Nothing has been 'set'. On several occasions, I have pointed out glaring inconsistencies between an actor's moves and his lines only to discover that Brook was entirely aware of them. 'If they don't find it for themselves in a week or two, I'll just say "speed it up" or "slow it down", but while there is a chance of the actor discovering it for himself, I prefer to let it go.'

Brook's production approach is relentlessly (and at times, maddeningly) experimental. He believes that there is no such thing as the 'right way'. Every rehearsal dictates its own rhythm and its own state of completion. If what is wrong today is wrong tomorrow, tomorrow will reveal it, and it is through the constant elimination of possibilities that Brook finally arrives at interpretation.

'My analogy is with painting,' he said. 'A modern painter begins to work with only an instinct and a vague sense of direction. He puts a splodge of red paint on to his canvas and only after it is on does he decide it might be a good idea to add a little green, to make a vertical line here or a horizontal line there. It's the same with rehearsals. What is achieved determines what is to follow, and you just can't go about things as if you knew all the answers. New answers are constantly presenting themselves, prompting new questions, reversing old solutions, substituting new ones.'

It is amusing to see Brook's experimental approach at work with actors and technicians who are used to quick, expeditious, black-and-white decisions. One such person, after describing what he took to be the two alternatives for a certain design problem, was more than a little taken aback by Brook's 'I don't know' – the phrase which Brook uses more than any other. As time went on, this person found that *he* didn't know either, and out of this burgeoning ignorance and constant questioning, twenty alternatives emerged instead of the initial, arbitrary two.

Problems with the Gloucester brothers

The actor playing Edmund tends to casualize the verse; the cunning formality of the character becomes obscured in a genial kind of anti-Shakespearian naturalism. Edgar, on the other hand, suffers from a kind of inner stiffness which makes the physical change to Poor Tom an even greater problem than it is textually.

Brook asked me to devise some improvisations that might treat both problems. The first of these was to give Edmund (who shams with one character after another) a sense of playing many different roles; to enable him to impersonate unlikely people in disguises of relative formality. Edmund was made a Franciscan friar to whom Edgar had come to confess. During the course of the confessional, Edmund, using theological arguments and the pious determination of a clergyman, was to persuade Edgar to forfeit his lands for the good of his soul.

In a second scene, Edmund as clergyman listened to Edgar recounting a series of hideous nightmares which kept him awake. Edmund interpreted the dreams in such a way as to indicate that Edgar had been chosen by divine providence to murder his father, the Duke of Gloucester.

Results were partial but a sense of relationship sprang up between the brothers which had not existed before and, as so often happens in improvisation, the gains that were made were not the ones being sought.

A later exercise in which Edgar put his Poor Tom speeches into the third person, prefacing all the lines with 'he said', succeeded in distancing the character of Poor Tom from that of Edgar. Another exercise with a mask attempted similar ends. Here the actor clapped the mask on when Poor Tom was speaking and whipped it off when Edgar was either making an aside or simply reacting silently.

During the course of the improvisations, another actor from the company entered and observed. When the scenes had finished, we all spoke about the benefits and dangers of improvisation. The older actor listened politely but was not convinced. 'What's the point of it? You've got everything in the text.' We pointed out that this was certainly not the case with Edmund and Edgar, the relationship between Lear's daughters, and the background of the Albany-Cornwall feud. One of the benefits of improvisation was that it provided supplementary material when needed. Through improvisations properly conducted and rigorously monitored, it was possible to create those missing dimensions which made the difference between partial and total characterization. (Brook explained afterwards that for certain actors – he cited Scofield – it was not only unnecessary but wasteful. 'Paul is already struggling with what is essential in Lear. For him, improvisation would only be a diversion of energy.')

One senses in the company an ingrained resistance to improvisation or any other experimental device during rehearsals. Apparently past experiences along these lines have been disastrous as actors have been coaxed into improvisations which were not relative to the problems of the play. With those actors who understand the potential benefits of improvisation, there is a genuine enthusiasm for extra-textual work. Those who object remember painfully the uselessness of past experiments and simply do not see the point. The resistance to improvisation is not in itself worrying, but it is part of a general apathy towards experiment, which is frightening. The overriding preoccupation is with verse-speaking, and there is a tacit (sometimes explicit) assumption that if the verse can be made to work, proper interpretation will automatically follow suit. Both Brook and Hall and the other directors are planning to combat this tendency in the newly-formed Stratford Studio.

Fool: demon and jester

Brook sees the Fool as an inspired zany; someone who serves as a medium through which wit and intuition express themselves. His fundamental quality is *ethereal*; his capers must be airborne and suggest helplessly brilliant improvisation.

It struck me that the Fool is also Lear's conscience; a kind of personified stream of consciousness giving a babbling accompaniment to Lear's weightier pronunciamentos.

Difficulties with the Fool stem from the fact that the actor playing the role is a highly organized individual; entirely in control of himself, making conscious choices which then get polished up and dispensed. Urging him, through exercises, into areas where spontaneity might replace conscious organization, we encountered resistance. At present, he is giving a bright, crisp, thoroughly professional reading of the Fool, but it is without that necessary demonic touch.

Last night we set him an improvisation with Cordelia in order to establish the Fool's off-stage character. 'He is a worried man and terribly tired of all the desperate foolery that he has to carry on all day long,' the actor explained. In the scene that followed, we saw the Fool with Cordelia as she was preparing for the Court occasion which is the first scene of the play. An easy, banteringly affectionate, thoroughly credible relationship was built up between the two characters. The Fool tried out some new material on Cordelia. He teased her about her royal suitors, and one sensed that the prospect of Cordelia's marriage and subsequent departure was painful to him.

The second improvisation was set in Cordelia's chamber after the play's first scene, in which she was disowned by Lear and paired off with the King of France. The Fool, unaware of what has transpired, enters to find Cordelia preparing to leave. He quickly realizes that he is about to lose his only friend in the palace; the only one with whom he can afford the luxury of a private life. The pathos was there, but the scene ended amiably and lightly. (In a British fashion, I thought.) Still it was useful in compelling the Fool to play without prearranged material. But again the great gain was unlooked for. It became clear that the character of the actress playing Cordelia was radically different from the Acting-Self she adopted for the role. The problem now is to get the actress in control of her own reality in such a way that it begins to nourish the character.

Thunder and tumult

Today, for the first time, we saw the rusted thunder-sheets in action. For weeks the designers have been trying to surface them with rust. They had been left out in the rain and allowed to rust naturally, but the effect was not convincing. Experiments with texturing and paint have now produced the right degree of corrosion; they are just ginger enough to have an artistic hue and just worn enough to look genuinely rotten.

Each is fitted with a small motor which enables it to vibrate. This morning while trying out the vibrations, one of the motors went haywire, shook off its mooring and sent a thunder-sheet swooping down on to the stage. It clanked down only inches from where Brook and key members of the lighting crew were standing. The actors have been wary of the sheets ever since, and the storm scenes have gained an element of real apprehension which is all to the good. This afternoon they were used in the run-through.

As Lear rides off 'in high rage' and everyone else slinks off to take shelter from the oncoming storm, a solitary Gloucester stands centre-stage peering upward and listening to the distant rumble. The sound of thunder swells and then three rectangular slabs, like rusty tongues, poke downward from the flies and begin to vibrate. As Gloucester rushes off and the thunder grows even louder, Kent and the Gentleman, whipped by unseen gusts of wind, are flung on from opposite sides of the stage and begin to mime the storm. Cunningly, the entrance of the thunder-sheets coincides exactly with a stylistic change in performance. No sooner does the three-slabbed symbol appear than the acting becomes starkly non-naturalistic. The shape of the mime between Kent and the Gentleman has been virtually choreographed – mainly by the actors themselves – and the scene exists as a clear heightening of the action which paves the way for Lear's entry on to the heath. Worked out in precisely the same detail is the correspondence between Lear's speeches and the electronic storm; each orchestrated with the other so that the thunder serves as an accompaniment to the poetry rather than a dumb, relentless opposition. Scofield uses 'Blow winds and crack your cheeks' as a sound weapon against the din of the thunder rather than a conventional cosmic challenge. This is an effective opening gambit, as it immediately establishes the combat between man and the elements, but as the scene progresses, Scofield tends to gabble away the remaining speeches using them more as defenses against the storm's onslaught and less as articulated poetic ideas. That is always the dilemma in this scene; how much of the verse to use in battling the storm and how much to play in its own right.

Although the charged atmosphere is usually captured in the opening storm scenes (mainly as an involuntary acting-response to the clamour), it is invariably lost in the Hovel scene which follows and which is supposed to be played in pelting rain. It is in scenes like these, where the poetry must be married with a sense of interior reality (what does a storm feel like, what happens to the body in driving rain?) that performance falls down most noticeably, confirming my earlier impression that the company needs to be trained in feeling as well as in prosody, and that in those scenes where Shakespearian intensity is greatest, the truthfulness of the emotion counts more than the scansion of the verse.

Rowdy knights and broken chandeliers

Morning devoted to the Hunting Scene; to creating the reality of Lear's knights; the dusty outdoors, the feel of hard saddle-leather and hunters returning after a long, sweaty ride. Each knight chose a name for himself and brief interconnecting relationships were sketched in.

After Lear's boisterous entrance into his eldest daughter's castle, Goneril appears to admonish Lear about his unruly retinue. Incensed by her words, Lear overturns the dinner-table and storms out. This is the cue for general pandemonium as the knights, following their master's example, tip chairs, throw plates and generally demolish the chamber.

The scene was being played with a false bravado, sustained by 'rhubarb', and in no way suggested the barbaric period in which the play is set. After what amounted to a pep-talk from Brook, the knights, swaggering with a new-found aggressiveness, replayed the scene. On Lear's cue,which begins 'Darkness and Devils', one could almost see a dozen acting missiles rev up for the blast off. As Lear overturned the table, the stage exploded and sent shrapnel flying in a dozen different directions. Tankards whizzed through the air hitting actors and ricocheting into the laps of the stage-managers below; set pieces were smashed over up-ended bits of furniture and a chandelier above the rehearsal stage was splintered into a thousand pieces which came raining down on the full company. The destruction was followed by a gale of nervous laughter that released whatever energies had not been worked off in the scene. The stage-manager spoke very soberly to the actors about artistic control and deportment. Brook smiled an Oriental Cheshire-cat smile, and the rehearsal ended with the kind of satisfaction that always follows the untrammelled release of secret tensions. (Ironically, once the mechanics of the smash-up were fixed, the scene never recaptured the turbulence of that morning rehearsal, although it remains the one moment in the production which is dangerously unpredictable.)

Catharsis, bitter or sweet

One of the problems with *Lear* is that like all great tragedies, it produces a catharsis. The audience leaves the play shaken but reassured.

To remove the tint of sympathy usually found at the end of the Blinding Scene, Brook cut Cornwall's servants and their commiseration of Gloucester's fate. Once the second 'vile jelly' has been thumbed out of his head, Gloucester is covered with a tattered rag and shoved off in the direction of Dover. Servants clearing the stage collide with the confused blind man and rudely shove him aside. As he is groping about pathetically, the house-lights come up – the action continuing in full light for several seconds afterwards. If this works, it should jar the audience into a new kind of adjustment to Gloucester and his tragedy. The house lights remove all possibility of aesthetic shelter, and the act of blinding is seen in a colder light than would be possible otherwise.

At the end of the play, the threat of a reassuring catharsis is even greater. I suggested that, instead of the silence and repose which follows the last couplet, it might be disturbing to suggest that another storm – the greater storm – was on the way. Once the final lines had been spoken, the thunder could clamour greater than ever before, implying that the worst was yet to come. Brook seconded the idea, but instead of an overpowering storm, preferred a faint, dull rumbling which would suggest something more ominous and less explicit.

First run-through on stage

All the inevitable hitches; as erratic and tentative as it had to be but, as Brook remarked afterwards, 'All the bones are there.'

After the run, Brook talked to the cast about continuity. 'We've spent all our time structuring individual scenes and have necessarily lost sight of the whole. Now we must begin looking at one scene in relation to the next. And you must all beware of the Law of Falling Inflections. Each time you make a downward inflection, the rhythm of a speech comes to a halt. What is happening now is you are ending your last speeches with a downward inflection and so the play seems to be coming to a halt after every scene. You must keep in mind that when your particular scene is finished, the play still goes on. You must keep the ball in the air being passed from one to the next without a fumble.'

Instead of conventional shorthand terms like 'more pace', 'break it up', 'faster', 'slower', Brook takes the time to describe an overall theory of continuity and structure. Once this is understood, the shorthand terms appear and then have a greater pertinence.

Apart from finding the play's innate rhythm (which is the main problem), Scofield's Lear still seems deficient in characterization. It is overridingly reasonable but lacks the epic quality the play demands. It is still without the weight and age of the crumbling monarch. One bystander in describing his performance used the word 'bourgeois', which is curiously apt. But this is mainly due to his appearance which, with its *fin-de-siècle* beard and close-cropped hair, is more debonair than doddering. The run-through was followed by one of those elongated private confabs between Brook and Scofield which invariably produce transformations.

First dress rehearsal

Serious costume problems. All the expensive, carefully made leather costumes look like plastic from the front. The white, elegantly-finished furniture clashes with the rust metal set-pieces. The stage has the look of a medieval castle furnished by an up-to-date Swedish department store. There is only one short week in which to texture the leather and break down the wood. There is no panic – only, on Brook's part, a resolve not to be hurried into expedient decisions.

Scofield's Lear has slowly begun to emerge. His method is to start from the text and work backwards. He is constantly testing the verse to see if the sound corresponds with the emotional intention. It is a peculiar method which consciously prods technique so that instinct will be called into play. The Method actor starts with feeling and then adds the externals of voice and movement. Scofield uses externals as a gauge with which to measure the truth of any given speech. He frequently stammers his lines, openly testing inflections and accents, discarding conventional readings not because they are predictable but because they do not tally with an inner sense of verisimilitude.

His concentration is a model to the rest of the company. He even asks for a prompt in character. Only when fumbling for a line does one glimpse the disparity between the man and the character, and then what one sees is a man winding himself painfully into a Shakespearian fiction. Underlying all the rigour of creative application, one discerns the gentleness of the man himself. Under stress imposed by a tardy prompter and his own fierce struggle to master the verse, he never loses his temper. The harshest thing he has ever said was, when prompted with a line that had already been scrapped, 'That's cut. You should know the cuts.' It was neither petulance nor spleen, but a firm admonishment which shamed others by suggesting that their diligence was not up to his own.

When Scofield is sure of his reasons and his text, he is firing on both pistons and Lear soars. When he is not, he falls into a studied, wilful, over-reasonable rendering of the verse. I pointed out some of these passages to Brook; complained that they were dry and monotonous, virtually unacted. Brook explained: 'When Paul finds his reasons he will shift from low gear into high, but anything he is not sure of, he will simply mark out drily as he is doing now. He refuses to throw himself into something he does not feel and cannot answer for.'

Lear's cloak and the roving camera

During tonight's dress rehearsal, there was an electric moment of high drama that Shakespeare would have appreciated. Brook had done away with the usual preview performance and so, apart from technical staff, the auditorium was empty. But a photographer was shuttling from one side of the stalls to the other taking shots of the performance. In the Hunting Scene (Act I, Scene 4), where Lear becomes more and more riled by Goneril's discourtesies, Scofield seemed more agitated than usual. After overturning the table and ordering his knights to horse, Lear comes downstage and proceeds to intone one of those blood-curdling Shakespearian curses which freeze the blood and are supposed to bring retribution crumbling down over everyone's head. In the middle of the speech, Scofield crossed down-stage to the apron and hurled his hunting-cloak at the photographer whose camera had been clicking an accompaniment to Lear's speeches. 'Please get that thing away from here,' he growled in the voice of the furious Lear, and then immediately continued to berate Goneril. One could almost hear the entire auditorium catch its breath. John Goodwin, the press representative, said: 'I suddenly felt myself sweat. It was a horrifying sensation.' It occurred to me afterwards that this is precisely what the production was lacking:

moments so charged and taut that one's insides suddenly ground to a stop. One observer confided afterwards: 'It was so exciting I felt like saying, keep it in!'

Afternoon canter

With the first night performance six hours away, the company was asked to give an easy, underplayed rendering of the play so as to conserve their energies for the evening performance. The result was astounding. Actors who had been belting out the verse since the first readings were suddenly giving scaled-down, unfussingly true performances. Basic relationships, so long obscured during erratic rehearsals, suddenly became crystal clear. A host of textual misconceptions loomed large on the stage like elusive bacteria suddenly caught in a microscope slide. Those performances which were organically rooted and internally-based were revealed in a bright, non-Shakespearian clarity. Those which lacked foundation from the first emerged as the loosely-drawn sketches they were.

Surprisingly, despite the fact that all the actors were saving their voices, the entire performance was thoroughly audible from every part of the house. Even Scofield, whose low-keyed storm scenes were competing with clamorous thunder effects, was both intelligible and moving.

Brook was hypnotized by the effect. 'You see how little you really need in order to capture the reality. If only theatre audiences listened to plays with the same intensity as concert audiences listen to Oistrakh, the performance of a play would be so much richer. But the level of concentration in the theatre is terribly low; there's always coughing, muttering, crinkling and shifting about. But in a concert hall there is a taut silence; everyone is listening for *and* perceiving subtleties. You see this level of acting,' he pointed to the stage where modern-dress actors were moving easily through the Hovel Scene, 'in thirty years this is the way all Shakespeare will be played.'

He mentioned the alleged intimacy of the Elizabethan playhouses and speculated that Shakespeare, in the very writing of his plays, had combated the rhetorical tendency of the Marlovian theatre. This connected with my view that the most influential acting teachers were always the playwrights; that the upsurge of straight-from-the-shoulder realistic acting in England during the past six years was due more to John Osborne, Arnold Wesker, Harold Pinter and Brendan Behan than anything propagated in the acting academies; that if the actor really wanted to learn his craft he had to be tutored by those writers whose plays were banishing the clichés and stereotypes on which 'old acting' was fed.

Brook wondered whether the same applied to Shakespeare, and whether a proper use of the verse could induce in actors an understanding of truths which were, in fact, beyond them. Earlier he and Michel St Denis had spoken about 'being taken by the poetry'. At the time it sounded like a mystical concept, but the more I study the text, the more I find areas that elude rational analysis and logical translation.

Coda

We open in fifty minutes. In the Green Room, everyone is talking about something else, pretending the monster play doesn't exist. In three hours we'll know whether it does or not.

Fait accompli

I have been told that because I helped shape this production, I do not possess the necessary objectivity to appraise it. I don't really believe this, but whatever esoteric knowledge I may possess that invalidates my judgement, certain things I will know better than any outsider. For instance, what goals were set by the production and how close they came to being reached. What problems were strategic and to what extent they were overcome. And of this, I would like to make only three points:

1. My initial reaction to the production was that it was more cerebral than moving; more brilliant as a set of choices than persuasive as an unfolding action. But I now suspect that the removal of *sympathy* and *identification* is the price we must pay for epic objectivity; that, in forfeiting our conventional empathy for the poor old geezer tossed out on a stormy night by two cruel daughters, we prepare ourselves for the profounder emotionalism which comes from understanding the merciless logic of the play's totality; the realization that the tragedy is not Lear's but ours.

2. For me, Scofield has delivered only about fifty per cent of Lear. Lear the ruler is there, as is Lear the madman; but Lear the father and Lear in those supreme final moments where the play transcends itself, is only sketched out. Scofield is probably the most intelligent actor working today. What intelligence can achieve, he has achieved. But his wilful approach to the verse has rattled together more than it has pieced out. Scofield, in a gesture that befits the great actor he is, forces the verse to adjust to his patterns of delivery and as a result, great chunks of it are

distributed wholesale instead of being individually packaged. It is the magnitude of his presence and the intensity of his application which diverts us from lapses in the interpretation.

3. Beneath performances rich in timbre and deep in conception, I still discern the absence of internal life. It is not widespread, but there is enough of it to nullify at least one-third of the play. The epic truth of Shakespeare's tragedy is, for me, subverted by half a dozen little white lies which belong more to the traditions of English acting than they do to any one company.

It remains for me to say only that, out of what may be a perverse preoccupation with shortcomings, I have harped on the failings of this production; others, better situated to judge, have elaborated its virtues, and, lest I seem to be too peevishly humoured, let me say that I agree with most of them.

Postscript

As I write, Peter Brook's production of *King Lear* is coming to the end of its London run. In four weeks' time, it will play in Paris and then it will begin a world tour.

Obviously, anything I feel about the production now is so far from the event that it can have no bearing on the rehearsals or the first performances. In one sense, all that is to be said about it has been said. And yet, I am dogged by a feeling of incompletion. Changes are still taking place; the monster is still shedding its skin and letting out strange new growls.

Every play, once it has accustomed itself to the rhythm of its run, returns inevitably to the earliest rehearsals. Certain ideas thrown out casually during a tea-break or parenthetically during someone else's scene, suddenly return and assume an enormous importance. It is the richness of this backlog in *Lear* which accounts for its endless variety, and, to an extent, persistent unevenness.

It was my task to cut twenty minutes out of the production for the Paris run. Before I set out to do this, I thought it would be a relatively simple task; instead, I found it agonizing. It is not so much that the play is so organically conceived and fluently written that it can bear no deletions. I find with Shakespeare, the reverse is true. It is *so* organically conceived that one can cut out great chunks and still not impair its essence. The difficulty I encountered was that scenes now existed as living acting-matter and their removal necessitated the kind of surgery which is so delicate one usually decides not to risk it. The *performance*, that breathing, daily-tended, nightly-experienced organism, had, in an almost Frankensteinian sense, taken on a life of its own. One could cut the text of scenes easily enough, but the moods and actions which had informed them lingered behind like spectres.

Coming as I did, with my cruel scalpel in my hand, I was obliged to look dispassionately at the performance, and what I found was a new solidity and a new depth. But not everywhere! The opaque performances of the early run had changed only in iotas, and not for the better. But Scofield had become one with the role. The shape of his reading was in almost every particular the same, but it now existed as the topmost round of a series of concentric circles which wound down through the actor's nature into Lear's *données* and then looped firmly around that base which is the mind of William Shakespeare. It was the kind of integration which sometimes takes place in affairs that have gone on for eight and ten years. What was external had not become internal, but the consolidation of intention and technique had produced a fusion which is certainly the next best thing to subconscious inspiration.

After three months, my admiration for Scofield and Brook had quadrupled, but I couldn't disguise a sense of disgust over what had become, not only a 'hit' and a *succès d'estime* but a historical event in English theatre. Tickets for Lear were being sold on the black market. Everyone I ever knew was asking me to get them seats. Every discussion about the theatre soon became a paean of praise for the production and a probe of how its effects were achieved. All niggles of criticism were quickly swamped in pious praise for this 'greatest Lear since Wolfit's' – although nine out of ten of the rhapsodists had never seen Wolfit, and probably never been to another Lear. The show had become not an imaginative, brilliantly-executed, somewhat flawed and erratic Shakespearian production, but a 'milestone'.

'Milestones' get my back up, frankly. For myself, I still see *Lear* as a series of well-made choices, some of which work and others of which fail. My new admiration for Scofield is offset by my contempt for the static, unchanging mediocrity of some of the lesser performances. My enthusiasm for Alan Webb's Gloucester grows as steadily as my disappointment with those actors playing his sons. My respect for Irene Worth's Goneril exists in the same perspective in which I continue to abhor the external musicality of Cordelia and the over-sumptuous staginess of Regan. For me, the Fool is still too urbane to be simply loved by his childlike master, and the ensemble of knights and servants still lacks cohesion with the central action.

I love the theatre most when it openly celebrates its legitimate triumphs. For me, the curtain call is always the catharsis no matter what the play. But I resist the impulse to make an occasion out of a deep-rooted desire to have one. It is this attitude which has made the New York drama critics so ridiculous in the eyes of intelligent theatregoers, and it is this same attitude which, in the long run, subverts and demeans the integrity of the theatre. Much as I would like to throw my hat in the air and do a jig, I feel I serve my sensibility best by scotching that temptation. *Le cul sur la chaise et la tête claire* is still the best posture for the appreciation of art.

Tulane Drama Review, Volume 8, No. 2,
Winter 1963.

King Lear: A Review by Kenneth Tynan

Kenneth Tynan's ecstatic review in the Observer *signalled Brook's
indebtedness to Beckett: Brook had successfully unearthed an absurd
metaphysical farce from Shakespeare's text.*

Lay him to rest, the royal Lear with whom generations of star actors have
made us reverently familiar; the majestic ancient, wronged and mad-
dened by his vicious daughters; the felled giant, beside whose bulk the
other characters crouch like pygmies. Lay also to rest the archaic notion
that Lear is automatically entitled to our sympathy because he is a king
who suffers.

A great director (Peter Brook) has scanned the text with fresh eyes
and discovered a new protagonist – not the booming, righteously
indignant Titan of old, but an edgy, capricious old man, intensely
difficult to live with. In short, he has dared to direct *King Lear* from a
standpoint of moral neutrality.

The results are revolutionary. Instead of assuming that Lear is right,
and therefore pitiable, we are forced to make judgements – to decide
between his claims and those of his kin. And the balance, in this uniquely
magnanimous production, is almost even. Though he disposes of his
kingdom, Lear insists on retaining authority; he wants to exercise power
without responsibility, without fulfilling his part of the feudal contract.
He is wilfully arrogant, and deserves much of what he gets.

Conversely, his daughters are not fiends. Goneril is genuinely upset
by her father's irrational behaviour, and nobody could fault her for
carping at the conduct of Lear's knights, who are here presented as a
rabble of bellicose tipplers. After all, what use has a self-deposed
monarch for a hundred armed men? Wouldn't twenty-five be enough?
We begin to understand Regan's weary inquiry: 'What need one?'

Such is Mr Brook's impartiality, so cool the moral scrutiny he applies
to the text, that we can laugh at Lear's crazy obtuseness without
endangering the play's basic purpose, which is tragic; but generally
tragic, not individually so. Mr Brook has done for *Lear* what he did for
Alec Clunes's Claudius in *Hamlet* some years ago: he has taught the
'unsympathetic' characters to project themselves from their own point of
view, not from that of the inevitably jaundiced hero.

Writing about this incomparable production, I cannot pretend to the
tranquillity in which emotion should properly be recollected. To convey

my impressions, I prefer to quote a slightly revised version of the programme notes I scrawled in the Stratford dark.

Flat white setting, combining Brecht and Oriental theatre, against which ponderous abstract objects dangle. Everyone clad in luminous leather. Paul Scofield enters with grey crew-cut and peering gait; one notes at once the old man's trick of dwelling on unexpected vowels and lurching through phrases as if his voice were barely under rational control . . . Brook means us to condemn his stupidity, and to respect the Fool (Alec McCowen) who repeatedly tries to din his message into the deaf royal ears . . . The knights are tight, and Goneril (Irene Worth) is right to be annoyed; but won't this wreck the scene in which Kent takes his revenge on Goneril's uppish steward? . . .

Later: Kent certainly loses his laughs, but the scene reveals him as an unreflecting bully who is unable to give a coherent answer to Cornwall's patiently iterated question: 'Why art thou angry?' This is the alienation effect in full operation: a beloved character seen from a strange and unlovely angle . . . Gloucester (Alan Webb), so often Lear's understudy and rival moaner, has taken on a separate identity: a shifty old rake and something of a trimmer, capable of switching his allegiance from Lear to Cornwall and back again . . .

Spurned by his daughters, Lear loses his wits purely in order to punish them: 'I shall go mad!' is a threat, not a pathetic prediction. 'Blow, winds' is an aria of fury, the ecstasy of vengeful madness; as Scofield howls it, three copper thunder-sheets descend behind him, rumbling and quivering . . .

Top marks for his drained, unsentimental reading of the lines about 'unaccommodated man'. (Lear by now is a rustic vagabond: cf. the classless derelicts of Samuel Beckett, and especially the crippled hero of *Endgame*.) High marks, too, for Brook's decision to stage Gloucester's trial in the same hovel where Lear has recently arraigned his daughters.

The blinding of Gloucester could hardly be more shocking. 'Upon these eyes of thine,' says Cornwall, 'I'll set my foot': and Brook, responding to the ghastly hint, gives Cornwall a pair of golden spurs with which to carry the threat into literal effect . . .

Am baffled as always by Edgar's inexplicable failure to reveal himself to his blinded father; Shakespeare is here milking a situation for more than it is worth . . .

And suddenly, greatness. Scofield's halting, apologetic delivery of 'I fear I am not in my perfect mind'; sightless Gloucester, sitting cross-legged on the empty stage while the noise of battle resounds in the wings; and the closing epiphany, wherein Lear achieves a wisdom denied him in his sanity – a Stoic determination, long in the moulding, to endure his going hence . . .

But even Brook is defeated by Edmund's tangled liaisons with Regan and Goneril: mainly because James Booth handles verse with the finesse of a gloved pugilist picking up pins, but also because the minutiae of sexual jealousy seem puny beside Lear's enormous pain . . . Lighting deliberately bright throughout, even during the nocturnal scenes, as in the Chinese theatre; and no music except towards the end, when the text demands it . . .

This production brings me closer to Lear than I have ever been; from now on, I not only know him but can place him in his harsh and unforgiving world.

Last month, reviewing Peter Brook's bleak and beautiful production of *King Lear* before it moved from Stratford to London, I stressed its moral neutrality: the way in which, by presenting Lear as a cranky old despot who deserved a come-uppance from Goneril and Regan, Mr Brook had balanced the scales, so that the characters were neither 'bad' nor 'good' but equally entitled to our attentive concern.

They were not doomed by vice or predestinately driven; they were merely people, varying manifestations of 'the thing itself'. Not much nobility was permitted them; often they took the stage kneeling, grovel-ling, stumbling, squirming, wriggling about like worms, forced into graceless postures, slumped in the stocks, or shoved on their backs to be tortured.

I see now a clue to the nature of Mr Brook's cruel, unsparing egalitarianism; his production is amoral because it is set in an amoral universe. For him the play is a mighty philosophic farce in which the leading figures enact their roles on a gradually denuded stage that resembles, at the end, a desert graveyard or unpeopled planet. It is an ungoverned world; for the first time in tragedy, a world without gods, with no possibility of hopeful resolution. No Malcolm or Fortinbras is on hand to rebuild this ruined kingdom: Albany, the heir-apparent, resigns his inheritance to be shared between Kent, who promptly rejects it, and Edgar, who responds with a brief and highly ambiguous speech about obeying 'the weight of this sad time'.

Mr Brook never tries to compel our tears, though we may weep if we wish; as when Paul Scofield's growling king shares a bench with Alec McCowen's sniping fool, the latter anxiously gauging how close his master is to madness; or when Lear and Gloucester, respectively mindless and eyeless, meet at Dover and huddle together for comfort.

But in general the tone is as starkly detached as Albany's, on hearing that Regan and Goneril are dead:

> This judgement of the heavens, that makes us tremble,
> Touches us not with pity.

The key to Mr Brook's approach may be found in an essay by Jan Kott, the Polish critic, comparing *Lear* to Beckett's *Endgame*; I have cited it before in these columns, and it is now available in *Shakespeare Our Contemporary*, a collection of M. Kott's essays.[1]

In brief, his argument is that Beckett and Shakespeare have more in common with each other than either has with the romantic, naturalistic theatre that historically separates them. For one thing, they have a sense of the grotesque, of the absurd discrepancy between the idea of absolute values and the fact of human fragility. Tragedy in the cathartic sense occurs only when there are fixed gods, fates, moral principles or laws of nature to which a man's acts can be opposed and by which they can be judged. Where no such absolutes obtain, the effect is not tragic but grotesque. It brings with it no consolation. 'Tragedy is the theatre of priests,' says Kott, 'the grotesque is the theatre of clowns.'

In *Lear*, he insists, the stage must be empty and sterile, a bare space of hostile earth. Gloucester's mock suicide is a tragic situation transmuted into farce; unless the gods exist, it is a comic irrelevance, a sacrifice made to a Godot who shows no signs of arriving. 'In both versions of *Endgame*, Shakespeare's and Beckett's, the Book of Job is played by clowns.' Shakespeare employs a quartet of near-buffoons – a madman, a fool, a blind man and a feigned demon. As for Beckett: 'The two couples – Pozzo blinded and Lucky struck dumb, Hamm who cannot rise and Clov who cannot sit – are drawn from the "endgame" of *King Lear*.'

Mr Brook, reversing the process, bases his *Lear* on Beckett. At times the measurements fail to tally; there is nothing remotely Beckettian, for example, in the Edmund-Regan-Goneril triangle or the battle scenes. But where the concept fits, as it mostly does, the production burns itself into your mind; you forget poor over-parted Edmund (James Booth), and remember only that you will seldom see such another Gloucester,

---

[1] Brook had met Kott in Warsaw in 1957, during the European tour of *Titus*, which Kott admired intensely. Brook read Kott's book in French shortly after its publication in 1962, and subsequently contributed a preface to the English version. Kott later acclaimed Brook's production of *Lear* as revelatory, the first to expose the play's 'combination of madness, passion, pride, folly, imperiousness, anarchy, humanity and awe.' (D.W.)

and never such another Lear. Nor are you likely to emerge from a theatre with a sharper or more worrying sense of mortality.

The Theatre of Cruelty

'Painting fifty years ago and music too made the discovery that has only just hit the theatre: that bourgeois art = academic = complacent = safe = dull = lifeless = middle-class: so it cannot be the vital art of the twentieth century'

(Brook in 'Search for a Hunger', *Encore*, 1961)

In January 1964, in collaboration with Charles Marowitz, Peter Brook directed a Royal Shakespeare Company experimental group in a five-week season at the tiny eighty-seater LAMDA Theatre's Donmar Rehearsal Rooms. In homage to Antonin Artaud, the season was entitled the Theatre of Cruelty: the project was largely funded by the Gulbenkian Foundation. The three months of private research culminated in limited public performances of 'work-in-progress'.

Brook was trying to push the actors towards a reassessment of the limitations of uniquely naturalistic acting techniques. He aimed to bring to light an awareness of the barriers to creative self-expression through momentary perceptions of vast untapped resources within themselves: 'We were denying psychology, we were trying to smash the apparently water-tight division between the private and the public man – the outer man whose behaviour is bound by the photographic rules of everyday life, who must sit to sit, stand to stand and the inner man whose anarchy and poetry is usually expressed only in his words' (*The Empty Space*).

D.W.

Private Experiment – In Public by Simon Trussler

Simon Trussler interviewed Marowitz and Brook in Plays and Players *during the preparation for the private workshop. What was the relationship to Artaud's writings in this work?*

INTERVIEWER: The title of the experimental programme Peter Brook and you are devising, *the Theatre of Cruelty*, comes, of course, from the manifestos of Antonin Artaud. How do you interpret 'cruelty' as Artaud used the world?

MAROWITZ: I think that the most important thing to be said is that it doesn't have to do simply with physical cruelty being represented on the stage. But it does have to do with a certain kind of rigour in expression and a certain kind of formality which, when it connects with a certain kind of experience, produces a result which is *more true* than the conventional ways of expressing that experience could be.

INTERVIEWER: Artaud has been described as a link between the Dadaist and Surrealist movements and the modern Theatre of the Absurd. Will such a link be traceable in the content of the programme?

MAROWITZ: I think so, because as it's planned now the programme is divided roughly into two parts, and the first part shows the historical basis of the Theatre of Cruelty – what Artaud did, Jarry's *Ubu* plays, and so on – while the second part is going to concentrate on what you might call modern surrealist developments, and will include things by John Arden and Ray Bradbury. Another thing we have in the second part is a surrealist free-style adaptation of *Hamlet*, which in every case uses the Shakespearian material, but redistributes it so that scenes are linked up not logically and progressively as they are in the play, but in a surrealist way, so that one has certain aspects of the character of *Hamlet* made concrete by rearranging the lines and the scenes. It's an attempt to open up the play from the inside – to redistribute all its elements, and try to see if one can present the play free from conventional narrative and still give the essence of what it's about.

INTERVIEWER: How much of all this is in fact derived from the theories of Artaud?

MAROWITZ: Well, Artaud himself didn't really make his theories work ... but his thinking about the theatre can be found exemplified in

29

certain works of Genet and Ionesco. Certainly, the whole avant-garde movement in France in the last 10 to 15 years bears the stamp of Artaud. But what ought to be made clear is that we are not trying to re-create the theatre of Artaud, or trying to take his own old formulas and make them work as he himself failed to do. We're just using him as a kind of springboard into new areas which we feel ought to be explored. And it's ironic that the person who last thought of exploring them was this guy who was a madman and died about 20 years ago. Nobody has really picked up the ball since then.

INTERVIEWER: One gathers that this is in fact a preliminary experiment to the work the Aldwych is doing later this year, which includes Genet's *The Screens*, Strindberg's *Dream Play*, which Artaud once directed, and *Woyzeck*, of which he thought very highly. Do you believe that this kind of experimental work is valuable in building up a coherent approach to the later full-scale productions?

MAROWITZ: I not only think that it's valuable – I think that it's the *only* way one can approach a play like *The Screens*, which is the most ambitious of the plays for the future, because it requires a kind of formality in approach and a kind of acting style which unfortunately is not taught in the drama schools. So the only way in which we can develop an instrument capable of grappling with a play like *The Screens* is by creating a sort of laboratory situation – trying to discover how the style works in isolation, and then perhaps applying it to exercises, to pieces of material that are related to the work. Then, once one can gradually recreate the means, one applies it to *The Screens*, and it becomes possible to do. But if one approached that play with the conventional acting background . . . well, it would just be impossible. It defies psychology, it would simply not work with the bland British approach to acting: it requires a kind of depth-approach that has to be first learnt and developed in actors, and only after the experience has been *had* can it then be applied to the play. What we are trying to do at this stage is to create such an instrument using these 10 or 12 actors, which once it is developed will be able to grapple with the play.

INTERVIEWER: Mr Brook, what is your attitude as a director towards Artaud's theories?

BROOK: I believe that to make the first attempt by a permanent company at very experimental work, we have to define for ourselves why experiment is needed. I feel that in our theatre it is needed more by the director and the actor than by the writer. The reason for this is largely practical –

the writer shares the privileges of almost all other artists, and to make experiments all he needs is the wish to experiment, imagination and very cheap materials – pencil and paper for the writer, sketchbook and pencil for the painter, or piano and a pair of hands for the composer. The writer of plays is largely in the same position of absolute freedom – if he wishes to make an experiment he can sit at home and turn the theatre of his mind into a semi-realised form on a scrap of paper that he can then discard. Now of course for this to become concrete, that writer should be working with actors and directors and his vision should take concrete form.

This is the ideal situation. Actually, at this moment there are in existence in England, in France, in America, a lot of texts by writers who have gone a considerable way in tackling problems *on paper*, which they have partially resolved from their end, but which no theatre company in the world is yet truly qualified to resolve from *their* end. Let's take for an example Genet: he is very much an avant-garde experimental writer, but he's not as utterly and completely way-out as a writer like Vautier, who has reduced language to monosyllables and has written plays that are like ballets and symphonies – just the making of sound patterns. Now Genet has evolved over the years a very complex dramatic technique which calls upon all the resources of many different and often conflicting theatre traditions, from the Japanese theatre to naturalism – and there are aspects of all these in that particular many-levelled form of writing.

INTERVIEWER: This kind of synthesis is very far from Artaud's belief that the whole Western idea of theatre was wrong, and that we should return to the Oriental concepts . . . ?

BROOK: I don't believe that there is a possible theatre today that is *not* a theatre of synthesis. To me the direction of the theatre and the direction that I want to explore is one that in one way or another has always interested me – something that I was exploring a long time ago, in *Salome*, and in different forms in *Titus Andronicus* and in *Lord of the Flies*. It is a field in which ritual and what one calls outside reality completely overlap: and this is the world of Genet. He is a symbolic and poetic writer, yet in *The Screens* he is writing a play that is at the same time an epic about the Algerian war. He creates (in the same way that John Arden or Samuel Beckett created) a stage image – a structure of stage behaviour and attitudes whose meanings can be read off continually in different and complementary and contradictory ways. *Hamlet*, too, is more than anything else a stage *construction*, which can be read and re-read in performance and always yield new meanings, yet never in itself changing – which is, I think, the essence of a structure and the essence of a ritual.

There are very few actors anywhere in the world qualified to understand how, within a virtually naturalistic framework which passes at times into what one can call an epic framework, there can suddenly take place an Artaud-like ceremony. Few actors exist who can take that in their stride, and certainly no group of actors each one understanding what the others are doing and being able to respond in shifting styles.

INTERVIEWER: Within this framework, then, the actors are going to have considerable freedom of approach?

BROOK: Well, I'd like to start in a negative way by saying what I'm *not* doing. There have been a number of attempts to make the actor completely flexible, and he's given a variety of work in different styles for this purpose – so that if he plays with a mask in eighteenth-century costume, every part of his body takes on the appropriate stylistic qualities.

Now we are putting the actor in situations where, for instance, he has to take his first impulse and turn it maybe into pure sound like an Artaud cry, maybe into formal gesture, maybe into a leap, maybe (as in *The Screens* itself) into rushing up to a sheet of white paper and attacking it with paint. What we are *trying* to bring about is for the actor, in making his choice, to make it as an independent, responsible creative artist. Instead of turning his impulses into one of the many forms that are already there (so that his choice fits into the form that he has learnt to appreciate and assimilate), here his responsibility is to transcend his first naturalistic impulse, and then he has to manifest the best expressive choice, in a way that he can afterwards defend as being to the limit of his consciousness. Funnily enough, what the actor first wants to do in an improvisation is only superficially his first idea: when he realises this, in a Zen-like way he can find an even quicker expression, one in which he is operating as an *artist*, not in accordance with his trained reflexes.

To relate this to one other thing: I think it's our job today to discover how we can make any contemporary theatre event as bold and dense as an Elizabethan event could be, facing the fact that the blank-verse device which the Elizabethans used no longer fits, and that we have to find something else. We're exploring what can take the place of blank-verse in the theatre: that is really the simplest summing-up of what we are doing.

INTERVIEWER: Artaud believed that this boldness and density could only be achieved by a complete involvement of the audience in a total theatrical spectacle. One recalls his vision of a theatre in which the audience was surrounded on all sides by the action. Are you going to explore this kind of solution?

BROOK: Yes: all I can say is that what we want to do in the course of the evening is to reopen the question from *all* the points of view that strike us at the moment. Some attempts have been made. In one respect I've been experimenting myself a number of years to try to bring *musique concrète* into the theatre. And there are the attempts to use still or moving projections – mostly, to me, disastrous attempts! But they have all been trying to find a twentieth-century language that can expand the single moment, so that more can be packed densely into it. The element of staging exists purely in relation to reopening these questions.

By *asking* the questions, we hope to weld the group of actors into a special fighting force. Our main hope in this particular experiment is that it will have the right sort of provocative *professional* effect – and this is different from what Artaud was doing. His aim was infinitely larger, and would relate to something that we can't attempt to get to at once, which was to have that effect on *life*.

INTERVIEWER: But would you accept this as an *ultimate* aim?

BROOK: I think that everything has to develop organically in its own way, and I can't believe that in 1964 organic development in the direction we are taking will end exactly where Artaud left off. Actually, I think that the nearest thing to an Artaud theatre we have had was the Brecht theatre – its achievement was certainly often quite different from Brecht's own analyses of it. What he was actually doing in his best work as a director was creating forms and rituals, and in his most remarkable work you can read off many levels of meaning. Like any great realistic work on life, there is obviously a strong social level: but Brecht, by being both writer and director, could also create a completely formal structure, which had as complete an existence as a play of Shakespeare's has on the printed page. The contradiction that was thrown up at Edinburgh between the Committed Theatre and the Theatre of the Absurd is a false one, based on the minor figures of both sides: but the proper theatre represents the true creative area where the two become one and the same thing.

Plays and Players, February 1964

Notes on the Theatre of Cruelty by
Charles Marowitz

The following account of the experimental group's research is based on co-director Charles Marowitz's notes from that period, as well as reflections after the event.

The auditions

Since we weren't casting any particular play and therefore weren't on the lookout for any *types*, and since our main concern was to find actors who were open, adaptable, and ready to rush in where rigid pros fear to tread, it was necessary to devise a completely new audition technique. I decided to do away with those murky soliloquies where a single actor pulsating with suppressed but crippling hysteria gets up and reels off the same speech he has been carting around since drama school. The auditions were collective; anywhere from eight to ten actors working together for at least an hour. The audition was broken up in the following ways:

Disrupted set-piece

The actor is asked to perform his two-minute set-piece in his own way, without suggestions or interference. Once he has done this, he is given a new character and a new situation and asked to play these, still retaining the text of his original speech. (An actor who comes along with 'To be or not to be . . .' is asked to play King Lear in the death scene or Romeo in the balcony scene *through* the Hamlet text.) The task is for the actor to throw himself into a completely different set of circumstances (to improvise) and yet to retain control over his original text (to operate formally). Once the actor has managed to create a smattering of the new character and the new situation, he is given yet another character and a different situation (a barrow-salesman on a market-day, a political candidate standing for re-election), until he has three balls to juggle at once: 1, his original choice; 2, the first variation; 3, the second variation. The actor is then given cue-words which refer to each of his characters, and he is asked to switch rapidly among the three different situations without breaking the flow of his original text.

Text and sub-text

The actor is given a piece of nonsense-text. There is no discernible character or situation. The actor makes of it whatever he can, but he is obliged to use the given words. (This enabled us to discover how the actor, on the most elementary level, coped with language – where his natural instincts led him. It is like a Rorschach test with words instead of ink-blots.)

Object associations

An object is thrown out on to the stage – a toy shovel, for instance. The actor proceeds to build up a scene (in mime only) using the shovel. When something has begun to develop, when the actor feels he is finally *on* to something, another object, entirely unrelated (a briefcase, a shoe-horn, a telephone directory, a plant) is thrown out and the actor is obliged either to create a completely new scene or develop a bridge between the unrelated objects.

Discontinuous improvisation

An actor performing a simple, recognizable action (digging, golfing, wall-papering, exercising) enters. The others choose actions which relate to that actor's choice and a scene (with words) develops. A enters digging with a shovel; B mimes a pneumatic drill ; C grabs a wheel-barrow; D becomes a works-supervisor checking his stopwatch. Then a new actor enters performing a completely unrelated action (making lyrical knee-bends), the other actors adapt to the new action as quickly as possible. (One begins to *plier*, another, Martha Graham-like, rolls his body into a ball; a third begins marking time with a stick.) As each new situation is perceived and developed, another one, as far removed as possible, is begun. Eventually, three separate teams are chosen – each with its own built-in changes – and these three groups, working simultaneously, weave among as many as twelve different situations. The cleanliness of the changes is what counts, also the rapidity with which actors cotton on to the changed situation. The scenes themselves are, of necessity, superficial, but the object is not to create substantial, well-sinewed improvisations, but merely to follow up dramatic leads as quickly as they present themselves.

The first company

Out of about fifty actors, a dozen were selected, and then presented to Brook for approval. (Ironically, there was a slight hassle only in the case of Glenda Jackson, over whom Brook took some convincing. She turned out to be – along with Alexis Kanner – one of the two most resourceful members of the group.)

The average age of the group was twenty-four. Only one member was over thirty, and most were just over twenty. The backgrounds were television, drama-school, a minimal amount of repertory, no West End experience to speak of. The general formation was naturalistic – a grounding in Stanislavski techniques as attenuated and distorted by English drama schools. I felt the need to start from scratch, to plunge the whole company into elementary Method exercises before totally demolishing the Stanislavski ethic. Brook disagreed. He felt the level of proficiency was high enough to tackle the new work directly. I thought this a mistake because Stanislavski was the grammar out of which we were going to build a completely different syntax and I wanted the basis to be sound before shifting it. It is difficult to say, in retrospect, whether we were right or wrong in plunging a group of twelve young actors and actresses into the swirling waters of Artaudian theory, but, of course, there was the time-factor. We had only twelve weeks for training and a preliminary workshop performance. We worked in a small church hall behind the Royal Court Theatre in Sloane Square; a bare, wooden room littered with Brownie posters and the relics of ancient whist-drives. It was a long day, beginning at 10 a.m. and ending at 6 p.m. Each night Brook and I consulted by phone about the objectives of the next day's session, then I sat down and devised the exercises which made up the next day's work. My notes of these sessions are not chronological, and so what follows is in no particular order.

Introduction to sounds

On the very first day of work, before the actors had properly met each other and without Brook or me delivering any orientation-lectures, the actors were handed objects: boxes, bangers, scrapers, vessels, sticks, etc. Each actor had something or other to bang with, and something or other to bang on. They were then asked to explore the range of their *instrument* (the sound the thin end of a ladle made on a tin can; the sound the tin can made against the floor, muted with one palm, held suspended, in two hands, tucked inside a sweater, rapped with the knuckle instead of the ladle, with the forehead instead of the knuckle, the elbow instead of the forehead . . .) Once the range of the instrument had been explored, a series of rhythms were rapped out. Some of these were then varied while others remained the same; some were accelerated while others were slowed down; there were combinations of twos and threes; dialogues between broomhandles and empty crates; scenes from *Romeo and Juliet* played out between metallic tinkles and bass percussions; mob violence with soap crates and pitched battles with tennis rackets.

Eventually *rhythm*, a generalized and over-used word in the theatre, got redefined in exact, physical terms. Not only did actors experience the basic changes of rhythm – slow, fast, moderate – but the endless combinations and counterpoints that rhythms were capable of. Shortly, the same attitude the actors had taken to their objects was applied to their voices and bodies. This was a tortuous adjustment, and one was always fighting the primordial instinct in English actors that believes the voice is the medium for *good speech*, *projection*, and *resonance*, the carrier of the theatrical 'message', and the body a useful but secondary adjunct. Little by little, we insinuated the idea that the voice could produce sounds other than grammatical combinations of the alphabet, and that the body, set free, could begin to enunciate a language which went beyond text, beyond sub-text, beyond psychological implication and beyond monkey-see-monkey-do facsimiles of social behaviourism. And most important of all, that these sounds and moves could communicate feelings and ideas.

Sound and movement similes

Exercise: You come back to your apartment after a hard day's work. Enter, take off your coat, hang it up, pour yourself a drink and sit down at the table. On the table is a letter which you suddenly notice. You put down the drink, open the letter and begin to read. The contents of the letter are entirely up to you; the only condition is that it contains news which puts you into a highly emotional state of one sort or another. Express this state using only a sound and a movement.

The moments in the exercise leading up to the final beat are entirely naturalistic, but the final beat is an externalized expression of the character's inner state and totally non-naturalistic. At first, all the choices were commonplace. People jumped for joy, fell into weeping, bolted upwards with surprise, stamped with rage. When none of these simple expressions was acceptable, the actors began to realize the nature of the exercise. With all their naturalistic choices dismissed out of hand, they had to go in search of a more stylized means of communication. Eventually, the choices became more imaginative. Sounds were created which had the resonance of wounded animals; of prehistoric creatures being slain by atomic weapons. Movements became stark and unpredictable. Actors began to use the chairs and tables as sculptural objects instead of functional furniture. Facial expressions, under the pressure of extended sounds, began to resemble Javanese masks and Zen sculpture.

But once the actors realized what we were after, some of them began to select an arbitrary sound or movement, effective in itself but unrelated to the emotional state growing out of the exercise. Very quickly, frighteningly quickly, actors became as glib with non-naturalistic sounds and movements as they were with stock, dramatic clichés. One wondered if Artaud's idealized theatre ever were established whether, in five or ten years, it too would not become as practised and cliché-ridden as the present-day Comédie Française, or the West End.

Discontinuity

One of the main objects behind the work was to create a discontinuous style of acting; that is, a style which corresponded to the broken and fragmentary way in which most people experience contemporary reality. Life today (I am not philosophizing, merely trying to illustrate) is very much like the front page of a daily newspaper. The eye jumps from one story to another; from one geographical location to another; from one mood to another. A fire in Hoboken; an election in Paris; a coronation in Sweden; a rape in London; comedy, passion, ceremony, trivia – all flooding one's consciousness almost simultaneously. The actor, however, through years of training and centuries of tradition, moves stolidly from point A to point B to point C. His character is *established*, his relationships *develop*; his plot thickens and his conflicts resolve. In short, he plods on in his Aristotelian way, perpetuating the stock jargon of drama and the arbitrary time-system of the conventional theatre.

To break the progressive-logical-beginning-middle-and-end syndrome, one uses improvisation (personal and organic material rather than theatrical *données*) and uses it simply as rhythmic matter.

Exercise: The life of a character is built up. X is an out-of-work writer.

   Scene 1: His landlady asks him for rent which is months in arrears.

   Scene 2: His girlfriend wants to know when they're going to get married.

   Scene 3: His father urges him to give up writing and take a job with the firm.

   Scene 4: His pub-crony exhorts him to come out, have a drink, and forget his troubles.

   Scene 5: His schoolfriend drops in and wants to re-live old times.

   Scene 6: An insurance salesman persistently tries to push an unwanted policy on him.

Each scene is built up independently for five or ten minutes; just long enough for it to have a little meat, but not long enough to develop any real sinew. Then X is placed in the centre of the room and each character – on cue – resumes his scene with him. The scenes, all unrelated except that they all centre on the same main character, follow hard upon each other. With the addition of each new scene, X quickly adapts to the changed situation, the different relationship. Eventually, three and four scenes are being played at once. Soon all are being played simultaneously. At a point, the exercise becomes unbearable and impossible, but before that point, X and his fellow-actors have experienced a frantic sense of discontinuity that just begins to convey the complexities to which any, even the simplest, sensibility is prone.

A collage *Hamlet*

A couple of years before the Royal Shakespeare Experimental Group, I had invited Brook along to a play I was doing at the In-Stage studio-theatre at Fitzroy Square. It was a short play by Lionel Abel called *A Little Something for the Maid*. Originally intended for radio, it consisted of a series of short, discontinuous scenes in which the female character became, by turns, everybody in the male character's life: wife, sweetheart, charlady, male-employer, secretary, mother, etc. Discussing it afterwards, Brook had said it would be fascinating to see Hamlet played that way, reshuffled like a deck of familiar cards. A year and a half later, Brook's idea still knocking around in my head, I sat down to restructure Shakespeare's play.

The idea of the LAMDA *Hamlet* was to condense the play into about twenty minutes, without relying on narrative. This was on the assumption that everyone knew *Hamlet*, even those people who hadn't read or seen it; that there was a smear of Hamlet in everyone's collective unconscious and that it was possible to predicate a performance on that mythic smear.

The play was spliced up into a collage with lines juxtaposed, sequences rearranged, characters dropped or blended, and the entire thing played out in fragments which appeared like subliminal flashes out of Hamlet's life. In every case I used Shakespeare's words, although radically rearranged.

Of all the discontinuity exercises, this had the firmest foundation, as all the actors knew the original play and therefore had an emotional and narrative frame of reference. The first version was essentially a clever exercise in Burroughs-like cut-ups. In the later, expanded eighty-five-minute version which played in Germany, Italy, and later London, the style was better assimilated, the play had more intellectual content and was at the service of a clear-cut interpretation.

Contact

The building of company-sense demands the construction of those delicate vertebrae and interconnecting tissues that transform an aggregation of actors into an *ensemble*. A protracted period of together-ness (at a rep, for instance) creates an accidental union between people, but this isn't the same thing as actors coiled and sprung in relation to one another – poised in such a way that a move from one creates a tremor from another; an impulse from a third, an immediate chain-reaction. Contact doesn't mean staring in the eyes of your fellow actor for all you're worth. It means being so well tuned in that you can see him without looking. It means, in rare cases, being linked by a group rhythm which is regulated almost physiologically – by blood circulation or heart palpitation. It is the sort of thing that exists between certain kith and kin; certain husbands and wives; certain kinds of lovers or bitter enemies.

Group interview

Exercise: A is a social outcast who has spent some time in jail. He has now been released and is being interviewed for a routine job by an inter-viewer for a large firm who knows his background but is prepared to consider him for employment. A needs the job, hates the idea of being patronized, and is torn between ingratiating himself and venting his hostilities. The rest of the group (sixteen actors) are personality-adjuncts of A. One represents his social hostility; Two, his economic need; Three, his attempt to conform; Four, his rebellious nature; Five, his innate cowardice; Six, his suppressed social ambition; Seven, his fantasy-image of himself as a Great Man, and so on. None of A's personality-extensions initiate any material in the scene. They speak only as and when A replies to the Interviewer's questions, and their response is determined entirely by what A actually says and what they glean from the way he says it. Depending on those replies, one or another of A's personality-adjuncts takes prominence. But with every response, all sixteen actors pick up, echo, modify, or extend A's replies in the scene.

> *Interviewer.* Do you think you would be happy in this job?
> A. Oh yes . . . I think I'd like it very much.
> B. *viciously.* Who wants to know?
> C. *pleadingly.* Just try me out for a week, you'll see.

D. *imperiously.* I'll be sitting behind that desk in a month's time.
E. *tentatively.* Could I wear a suit like that, I wonder?
F. *fretfully.* I wonder whether I'm going to be kicked out of this office.
G. *aggressively.* I'd love to put my fist in your eye.

The exercise musters an agonizing degree of attention and, as each actor must speak simultaneously with A, compels actors to grasp implications and innuendoes instead of responding mechanically to word-cues. In other words, it forces actors to cope with sub-text, and to recognize top-text only as a kind of tackle that leads down to the underwater world where all the essential action lies.

Improvs and essentials

There was a good deal of conventional improvisation (built up on actions and reducible to beats), but the more useful work came from variations and extensions of the stock Method approach. For instance: after a scene was played, the actor was asked to divide the improv into three units, and to give a line-title to each unit. Once this was accomplished and it was generally agreed that the line-titles were appropriate to the situation just played, the scene was replayed in its entirety with the actors using only their three line-titles as dialogue. Then the actor was asked to choose only one word from each of the three line-titles, and the scene was played a third time with the sound components of those words serving exclusively as the dialogue. Then (and only then) the actor could choose a sound which accurately reflected the main quality of his scene and play the scene for a final time, using variations of that sound. The playing in sound invariably prompted a non-naturalistic use of movement, and it was fascinating to see how, once the situation had been ground down to basic impulses, the movement graphically expressed the true intentions behind the scene.

Example: Scene – A wants to break off long-standing affair with his girlfriend, B. He now realizes he does not love her, and it would be lunacy to marry. B, however, has become helplessly attached to A and cannot bear the idea of parting. She tries desperately to maintain the relationship.

Scene breakdown in terms of line-titles: 1st replay.
    Boy 1. I want to break off this affair.
          2. I want to be as kind as possible.
          3. I won't be persuaded to change my mind.

Girl 1. I want to keep my hold on A.
      2. I want to reason with him so as to change his mind.
      3. I refuse to be hurt.

Second replay: Essential words.

Boy: Break
      Kind
      Won't
Girl: Keep
      Reason
      Refuse

Third replay: Sounds.

Boy: Ey-ayeOoghn
Girl: Eey-zoohz
(The sounds are fluid and free, merely *based on* the vowels and consonants of the essential words.)

Stanislavski and Artaud

Having been brought up on Stanislavski and the idea of inner truth, it was a major adjustment to discover there was also *surface truth*, and that in certain contexts, the latter was more persuasive than the former. An even more difficult adjustment was to realize that artifice and downright artistic fraud could create a plenitude of truth for an audience and was therefore, according to the pragmatic laws that govern acting, legitimate. The Method argument for inner truth holds water only if its main contention is true: that is, that the spectator experiences feeling to the same degree the actor does. But we all know this is not always the case; that there are hundreds of instances of turned-on actors splitting themselves with inner intensity communicating nothing to an audience but effort and tension. It is equally true that an actor who is almost totally turned-off but going through the right motions in the right context can powerfully affect an audience – almost involuntarily.

The Method actor's test for truthfulness is the intensity and authenticity of his personal feeling. The Artaudian actor knows that unless that feeling has been shaped into a communicative image, it is a passionate letter without postage. Whereas pure feeling can be mawkish or leaden, a pertinent stage-image – a gesture, a movement, a sequence of actions – is a statement in itself which doesn't require the motor-power of feeling in order to register, but when emotionally charged is many times more potent.

There is no fundamental disagreement between the Method actor and the Artaudian actor. Both rely on consciousness to release the unconscious, but whereas the Method actor is chained to rational motivation, the Artaudian actor realizes the highest artistic truth is unprovable. Like certain rare natural phenomena that defy scientific analysis, they *can* exist – and the actor's task is to conjure them into being.

The Artaudian actor needs Stanislavski in order to verify the nature of the feelings he is releasing – otherwise he becomes merely a victim of feeling. Even Artaud's celebrated actor-in-trance is responsible to the spirit that is speaking through him. A seance where nothing is communicated but atmosphere is not half as rewarding as one in which messages are received loud and clear. The very state of trance itself is arrived at methodically. The medium's secret is knowing when to let go of the mechanisms that have produced it, in order to transcend them; the same is true for the actor – any actor – who uses either intellect or instinct to bring him to an important jumping-off point.

Changing gears

Three actors, A, B, and C, are given cue-sounds (a bell for one, a buzzer for the second, a gong for the third). When A hears his cue, he initiates a scene, and B and C, adapting themselves to A's choice, enter into the situation as quickly as possible. After two or three minutes, when the scene is either approaching a high point or running down because of lack of invention, B is given his cue. B suddenly leaps into a completely new situation, entirely unrelated to the one preceding; A & C adapt themselves immediately. Short development, then C is cued, another unrelated scene, the others adapt again, etc., etc., etc.

As important as the actual material thrown up by the scene is the moment chosen for breaking it and beginning another. There is a moment in almost every improvisation where things reach a head and are moving quickly towards a resolution. If one can trigger off the new scene just at that moment, the actor's emergency-equipment is instinctively brought into play. Improvisations like these feed on (and sometimes are destroyed by) their sense of danger. There is an inescapable imperative forced on the actors. They must think and act with lightning speed. They know that within a seven or ten minute period, they have to devise as many as five or six different situations, and they soon discover they cannot cheat by planning ahead, because a prearranged choice is immediately apparent – as is the instinctively appropriate choice which could not have come from anywhere else but the given circumstances. It brings into play a quality that actors tend to think they do not possess: the ability to associate freely and without regard to fixed character or logical consistency. For me, the great eye-opener in this exercise was how, under the pressure of changing gears, actors who never heard of surrealism were able to make the most stunning surrealist choices; and actors who claimed to have no sense of humour, suddenly found themselves dipping into deep wells of fantasy and absurdity that lay on the threshold of their consciousness. Choices which, if actors had time to deliberate over them, would never be made, or would be doctored or modified, leaped out with astonishing clarity and boldness.

Actors and actors

The hallmark of a good actor is his attitude towards change. Most actors make their decisions in the first stages of rehearsal, chart the shortest distance between two points and then proceed in a straight line. For these, the rehearsal period is a tunnel with light at one end and light at the other, and a great stretch of darkness in the middle. Another sort of actor retains the ability to re-think and reorganize his role throughout. He follows every lead and yields to every permutation, and isn't put off by detours and secondary routes. He may take longer to arrive but when he does, he brings a better-rounded result.

This attitude towards change almost distinguishes two separate breeds of actor, and in England today these breeds intermingle in almost every company. It is too sweeping to designate one *traditional*, and the other *modern*, but there is a grain of truth in that distinction – those actors who have passed through the Royal Court, Theatre Workshop, and the ferment of the past ten years tend to have a more open attitude than can be found among the academy-bred, rep-orientated actors of an older formation. Each of these types almost has a vernacular of its own.

Trads	Mods
Let's get it blocked	Let's get it analysed
Fix inflections and 'readings'	Play for sense and let inflections take care of themselves
Block as soon as possible	Move freely for as long as possible
Play for laughs	Play for contact
Final decisions as soon as possible	Final decisions as late as possible and always open to reversal
It was a bad house	It was a bad performance
I take orders	I give suggestions

Am I being masked?	Am I important at this moment in the play?
Can I be heard?	Are my intentions clear?
I'm getting nothing from my partner	I'm not getting what I expected, so I shall adjust
Just as we rehearsed it	As the immediacy of the performance dictates
Let's get on with it and stop intellectualizing	Let's apply what reason we have to the problems at hand
More feeling	More clarity of intention so as to produce more feeling
Hold that pause	Fill that pause
Everything's in the lines	Everything's in the sub-text
I'll play this role symbolically	I can't play concepts; only actions
I am the villain	I refuse to pass moral judgements on my character
My many years of professional experience convince me that . . .	Nothing is ever the same

Speak with paints

Exercise: You have just come out of your flat, locked the door, and put the key in your pocket. You walk over to the elevator and ring. Casually you look through your newspaper as you wait for the elevator to arrive. On a sound-cue, the elevator arrives, the doors slide open and in the elevator you discover a completely unexpected person towards whom you have a strong, specific attitude of one sort or another. (The actor decides background beforehand.) At that instant, you rush to the easel and immediately express that attitude in paints.

As in the similar exercise with the Letter, the most delicate moment in the exercise is the one in which the actor confronts his stranger and moves to express his attitude. If you can organically link yourself to the next, the result is clean and communicative. If there is even a second's hesitation, the result is self-conscious, unnatural, and merely *illustrated*. A later version of this exercise, which proved more successful, was for the actor to play out an improvisation with the stranger in which the chosen attitude was actually manifest, then to have an interim scene inside the flat, followed by the exercise-situation. Otherwise, the actor is working too exclusively from a mental frame of reference.

At first, the paintings were sloppy and crude. On the third and fourth repeat, they were almost artistic, in that they were meaningful, impressionistic blotches which *did* suggest an internal state, interpretable by the other group-members. The paint exercise was used directly in Artaud's *The Spurt of Blood*, by author's direction in *The Screens*, and in a more sophisticated version in *The Marat/Sade*. (The red, blue, and white paint sequences in *Marat/Sade* stem from a similar effect in Brook's production of *Titus Andronicus*, where Vivien Leigh used an unfurled red ribbon to symbolize the flow of blood.)

Reforms: One must assume that Artaud's 'fragile, fluctuating centre that forms never reach' refers to states beyond the reach of *linguistic* forms, but accessible by other means. Otherwise it is soapy mysticism. The potential superiority of an Artaudian theatre – compared even to an overhauled and much-improved realistic theatre – lies in the fact that its language is not yet discovered, therefore not yet tarnished and empty. The danger is that a backlog of five centuries filled with verbal debris may never enable us to hit bedrock. Or to put it even more pessimistically: the actor's social and psychological conditioning is both the main obstacle to be removed, and the one factor which is immovable.

Theatre of Cruelty

The first showing of the group's work unfortunately was titled Theatre of Cruelty and ran a scheduled five weeks at the LAMDA Theatre Club in London. It was never intended as a *show*, but merely a demonstration of work-in-progress, of interest, we assumed, to the profession. The press were not invited in the usual way, but letters were sent explaining that if they felt like coming along, they were welcome, but that we were not particularly desirous of reviews, as this wasn't strictly speaking a show. All of which was a kind of self-delusion that both Brook and I swallowed whole. Only after the event did the obvious truth of the situation strike us. Any presentation, call it what you will, that is done before an audience, invited or otherwise, becomes a show and is judged according to traditional criteria. This is not a harangue against the critics. On the whole, we got interesting, up-beat notices, but the point was that we weren't really intending a theatrical performance, and the overriding point was that it seemed impossible, in London, to present anything short of one.

The programme consisted of two short nonsense sketches by Paul Ableman, similar to our sound-exercises; a production of Artaud's three-minute *Spurt of Blood* (played through first in sounds, then as Artaud wrote it); a dramatization, in movement only, of a short story by Alain Robbe-Grillet; two collages by Brook, one (*The Public Bath*) a splicing-together of newspaper accounts of the Kennedy funeral and the Christine Keeler testimony; the other (*The Guillotine*) made up from original sources; three scenes from Genet's *The Screens*; an anti-Marceauvian mime-sketch called *The Analysis*; a short play by John Arden, *Ars Longa*, *Vita Brevis*, and the collage-*Hamlet*.

There were two sections in the evening which were deliberately marked out as 'free'. One, the improvisations, the forms of which changed every evening with the actors never being forewarned; and two, a section towards the close of the second half, into which we inserted whatever 'specials' occurred to us. On the first night, Brook used this section to rehearse a scene from *Richard III*. Another night, the section was used for a spontaneous exchange between Brook and myself in which we questioned the audience's motives in coming to the theatre, and the whole point of what we were doing there. Early in the run, on the night John Arden was in the audience, without warning we asked him to come forward to justify his short play, and for the occasion we set against him one of the actors from *Ars Longa*, *Vita Brevis* who hated the play and what it was saying.

For the improvs, which I supervised from the stage, I tried to invent new and different challenges every night. On one occasion, we played the Changing Gears exercise entirely in sound; on another, entirely in musical phrases; on another, using only animal-noises. The audience was incorporated every evening and, very much like The Premise, actors worked from suggestions thrown out to them on the floor. The random factors maintained a degree of freshness almost to the end of the run, but their main point was not simply to keep actors on their toes, but to break the hypnotic effect of continuous performance, and to unsettle the myth that grows up once a performance has begun a run. No two audiences saw the same show, and so no two people from different audiences could recount exactly the same memories. Towards this end, roles were swapped (frequently at the last moment); bits altered or dropped, and one piece (written by Paul Ableman) completely unstaged and unrehearsed, played out each evening as the spirit happened to move the actors. Some nights, this was disastrous; on others, after it seemed that every possible interpretation had been tried, startlingly new moods would appear. The playing of this particular dialogue was greatly enhanced by the fact that the two players, who were sometimes required to play quite lyrically with one another, hated each other's guts. The tensions that charged, disfigured, and enlivened the piece prevented it from ever becoming dead material.

It is to the everlasting credit of Peter Hall and the Royal Shakespeare Company that it was understood from the start that this work required total subsidy. There was no question of making money or breaking even, for that matter, and it went without saying this was unrecoverable money (therefore, seats were deliberately cheap – five shillings each). There was no balking after the event, when accountants would solemnly point out £5000 had gone down the drain in a matter of twelve weeks. The drain, in this case, led to a very interesting cellar where certain rare wines were being colled, and even if it should turn out they had all gone sour and had to be dumped, no one was going to burst a blood vessel or demand an official investigation.

Tulane Drama Review, Vol. II, No. 2, Winter 1966.

Cruelty, Cruelty: A Review by Tom Milne

Tom Milne's Encore *review confronted the problem of experiment in theatre, and its interest and relevance to an audience.*

The Theatre of Cruelty's first programme at LAMDA's intriguing little theatre gets off on the wrong foot by waving Artaud as a banner (and Artaud at his woolliest, at that). The programme thus opens with a trio of items which stoutly fight battles which have already been fought and won. There is, for instance, a sketch illustrating Artaud's audition with a theatre manager who asks him to go and sit on a chair: Artaud responds by running, jumping or crawling in frenzied torment before coming to rest on the chair, finally flouncing away, after three attempts to convince the puzzled manager, with a 'Well, if it's realism you want, adieu!' As performed, the actor's gyrations are amusing, but rather less meaningful than if he had simply walked forward and sat down: realism may not be everything, but when a simple gesture is called for, no amount of stylistic decoration or interpretation adds anything. If, on the other hand, non-realistic interpretation is called for, then it would seem self-evident that the theatre today has progressed far enough to provide it. As an example, one may recall the scene from Roger Blin's production of *The Blacks* when Dieudonné Village re-enacts his rape of the white woman, calling on his audience to listen to his singing thighs ('*Ecoutez chanter mes cuisses*'). Here Blin used a perfect non-realistic, physical interpretation in his actor's slow, high-stepping-horse progress across the stage, hands flanking his thighs in a gesture suggesting the skimming of a stone on water.

Similarly, there is in the first part of the programme a short playlet in which a number of masked actors prance about the stage, communicating in an assortment of cries, groans and screams. To me, the effect of this item was simply of a number of actors prancing about the stage uttering an assortment of cries, groans and screams which weren't particularly meaningful. I see no objection on principle to the proposition that such cries *can* be as meaningful as words; but they must *be* as meaningful. Artaud talked glibly enough about the Oriental theatre from a nodding acquaintance with it, and anybody who has watched even part of a Kabuki or Noh play, for instance, is liable to fall prey to the same enthusiasms. But one should not forget, not only the years of

49

training which go into the making of an Oriental actor, but also the fact
that every stylised sound and gesture has an exact meaning which is
known to the audience. If your audience doesn't know what your sounds
are intended to communicate, or can only follow them in so far as they
suggest pain, anger, frustration, etc., then you might as well present a
simple melodrama in which the words are only shorthand for simple
emotions. The other factor which apologists for an Oriental-style mime-
and-gesture theatre tend to overlook, is that most of these theatres
(certainly it is true of the Indian and Japanese theatres) are intensely
traditional – they have to be, because extreme stylisation does not readily
permit innovation, and certainly precludes avant-garde work. The Noh
theatre, for instance, couldn't have its *Waiting for Godot* or its *Les Nègres*.

The premise behind such experiments seems to be the argument,
which has been around for some years now, that language is no longer
adequate as a means of communication. I find this an unproved case:
artists have gone on refining or broadening language in order to express
increasingly complex visions, and a writer like Beckett, for instance, has
been able to communicate with great subtlety through language the
extent to which language fails his characters as a means of communication. What is obvious (and undisputed) is that there are certain things
which can be expressed more completely through other means than
language. One remembers Chekhov's symbolic 'far-off sound of a
snapped string, dying away, mournful' which appears in Act II and at the
end of *The Cherry Orchard* (and which I have never heard rendered so
that it encapsulates as Chekhov intended, the whole play); or one
remembers the terrible, feral cry of Jeanne Moreau at the end of Peter
Brook's *Moderato Cantabile*, which is so much more than a simple cry of
grief as to be indescribable unless one starts analysing the whole of the
heroine's experience in the film. Here, in the relationship between
language and sounds, and the way in which one can illuminate the other,
there is a whole field of experiment waiting.

So far, so critical. But Artaud wasn't always woolly, and the Theatre
of Cruelty programme wasn't always kindergarten. *The Theatre and Its
Double*, which apparently *is* Artaud to many people, is mainly apocalyptic, sometimes frenetic, and pretty vague. Elsewhere, however, Artaud is
both clear and precise. In a manifesto for the Théâtre Alfred Jarry, for
instance, we find the following:

The theatre must present this ephemeral world, truthful but only
tangential to reality. It must be this world, or else the theatre will
have no hold on us.

There is nothing more puerile, and at the same time more sinister and terrifying, than the spectacle of a police manoeuvre. A society reveals itself in such *mise-en-scène*, which reflect the ease with which it disposes of its people's life and liberty. As the police prepare a raid it is almost like a ballet. Policemen come and go. The air is rent by shrill whistles. A kind of painful solemnity emanates from every movement. Gradually the circle narrows. Movements which at first seemed aimless can now be seen to have a purpose: their pivot, the point they were aiming at, appears. It is a nondescript sort of house. Suddenly the door opens and a file of women troops out, like a herd of cattle on their way to the slaughterhouse.

The plot thickens. The trap was not set for some shady gang of crooks, but simply for a few women. Never has such a beautiful *mise-en-scène* been crowned by such a denouement. The whole operation is really a show, and it epitomises our ideal theatre. This anguish, this sense of guilt, this triumph, this relief – these are the thoughts and feelings with which the audience must leave our theatre. They will be shaken and upset by the inner dynamism of the spectacle, a dynamism which springs directly from the troubles and preoccupations of their own lives.

This seems to me a brilliant defence and illustration of the art of the theatre, and it was perfectly realised in the most exciting item in the Theatre of Cruelty's programme – Peter Brook's *Public Bath*. To the accompaniment of whistles, cries and seedy night club jazz, a girl (Christine Keeler figure) enters and performs a striptease, while behind her a judge intones her sentence, and in front a succession of disting-uished gentlemen are introduced to her for purposes of fun and flagellation. The striptease over, she descends to the forestage, is bathed in a hip-bath under the stern supervision of three wardresses, hair inspected for lice, and re-clothed in prison garb. As she enters her cell, humiliated and deprived of her human dignity, the tone changes, and we slide imperceptibly into a realisation that we are watching an eager, public revel in a private grief. She becomes Jackie Kennedy, and the same distinguished gentlemen are introduced, now offering condol-ences. As she kneels before the coffin (the bath) before it is slowly borne away, the effect is shattering. Brilliantly acted by Glenda Jackson, and brilliantly directed by Brook himself (especially in his use of space – the striptease and trial kept at a cool distance, the intimacy of grief brought right into the audience; and in his use of movement – the slow, methodical striptease and prison routine, prefiguring the inexorable stripping down to naked emotion ending in the funeral procession), this sketch perfectly telescopes two scenes and our feelings about them to produce a devastating image, a complex mixture of shame and exhilaration, anguish and exorcism. *'Cette angoisse, ce sentiment de culpabilité, cette victoire, cet assouvissement, donnent le ton et le sens de l'état mental dans lequel le spectateur devra sortir de chez nous.'*

Encore, March/April 1964

The Screens

At this point in their research, Brook felt some dangerous and explosive material was needed to prod them ever further towards new discoveries, as well as to provide some focus to the work. In May 1960, he had directed the first French production of Genet's *Le Balcon* at the Théâtre de Gymnase in Paris: at that time, he had suggested Genet's was 'the most prophetic theatre of the twentieth century'. The link between Artaud and Genet, he believed, lay in the latter's oriental taste for perfection and gravity, his demand for artistic rigour and formality, his search for an unrealisable beauty.

So it was *The Screens*, written in 1961, that was chosen as the climax to the group's period of collaboration. With its starting point in French involvement in Algeria, Genet's play both aestheticised and transcended the political reality. Considered virtually unstageable with its cast of just under one hundred characters and its scenic mobility, it would be an enormous challenge.

One of the training exercises during this period found its way into the performances of *The Screens*, providing moments of disturbing intensity. As in certain 'happenings', the actors were asked to improvise emotional expression using coloured paints and chalks: the aim was for Rorschach-like abstract action paintings, through a short-circuiting of the gap between inner creative impulse and external expression (as in the 'artless art' of Japanese calligraphy). To represent the burning of the orchard (tableau x), the 'arabs' frantically splashed flames on to the screens, while others created the sounds of crackling flames, at the same time twisting and crushing pieces of bright orange paper in their hands. In another scene (tableau xii), images of violent disembowelment, rape, murder and expressions of fear were drawn rapidly, until the whole surface of the screens was covered with the scribblings of evil: a catalogue of horrors in a frenzied dance of death.

D.W.

53

Notes on *The Screens* by Charles Marowitz

An extract from Notes on the Theatre of Cruelty

The work on *The Screens* could be an essay in itself. The early exercises continued, and were gradually adapted to the specific needs of the play. The crucial production problem, apart from perfecting a style that would cope with such a monumental structure, was to communicate both the poetic and political tremors in the play without veering too far in one direction or the other. The Artaudian exercises had prepared us for Genet's metaphysic, and we now began to apply a Brechtian approach to get at the play's political bedrock, and also to define for ourselves precisely what each of those extravagant little scenes was about.

The early rehearsals were spent in reading, discussion, and translation amendments. After rehearsing each scene, key characters were asked to tell the story of what had just happened: 1, as a factual news report; 2, as a policeman summing up before a magistrate; 3, as a fairy tale ('once upon a time . . .'); 4, as a horror story; 5, from the Marxist point of view; 6, from a Freudian standpoint; 7, as it might be described by a highly poetic sensibility, etc.

Brechtian titles were employed as epigraphs for each scene.

SAÏD RELUCTANTLY GOES TO MEET HIS NEW WIFE

THE COLONISTS DISCUSS THEIR POSSESSIONS

SAÏD'S MOTHER INSISTS UPON BEING INCLUDED AT A FUNERAL

Sometimes the work-sessions threw up more material than we knew what to do with, and eventually the problem became one of discarding highly interesting but irrelevant insights. More and more, we concentrated on the text: its colouration, its timbre, its weight and feel. As with Shakespeare, one began to test the truthfulness of every moment in terms of the ring of the words in their context. We found that every moment of naturalism, even the most obvious and unquestionable, benefited by being knocked off balance; by being winged by a metaphor, or studded with a stylization. *Ritualistic* may be a critic's cliché when writing about Genet, but it becomes a directorial Rosetta Stone in rehearsal. Even the crudest situation, three soldiers farting a farewell to their dead Lieutenant (Scene 15), becomes both more comic and more

54

understandable by being acted ceremoniously, instead of in a loose, naturalistic manner.

Like *The Blacks* or *The Balcony*, *The Screens* appears to be about some great social topic (the Algerian War) but is essentially a private fantasy couched in convenient social imagery. Saïd's salvation through progressive degradation is portrayed with all the relentlessness of a thesis-playwright laboriously proving his point. As a play, it proliferates incidents without opening up new ground, and keeps winding back on itself like a badly-wrapped package which becomes fussy without becoming any firmer. Which is not to belittle the genius of certain individual scenes; nor the breadth of the conception; nor the grandiose lunacy in the character of Saïd's mother; nor the hypnotic other-worldliness of the scene where Madani is transmuted into the Mouth of the murdered rebel-leader Si Slimane; nor the easy, unpretentious shuttling between the worlds of the rebellious living and the settled dead; nor the black, urinal comedy between the Arab hooligans and the Algerian Cadi; nor the stunning scene where Arab rebels paint their atrocities on to a series of ever-multiplying screens. But on studying the entire play Brook felt, and I concurred, that the first twelve scenes contained all the gnarled genius of the work, and the remaining two and a half hours held only endless out-riding variations.

One last observation on *The Screens:* in the work of no other writer is the external life of the play quite so essential. In the last weeks of rehearsal, *The Screens* looked murky and gauze-covered in spite of many weeks of trying to cut sense and meaning into the scenes. Then, using Genet's own colour suggestions, Sally Jacobs's stark designs, and Brook's faultless eye for surface-effect, a great wave of colour was spread over the entire play. In the space of four hours (the hours during which costumes and design were added), the play was transformed into something bold, brazen, aptly rhetorical and hieratic, as if the arrival of objects and colour seemed to coincide with the arrival of Jean Genet. One part of me rebelled at what I took to be the spreading of dazzling camouflage, but another was entirely swept up by the camouflage itself. I am not simply describing the extra-dimensionalism dress rehearsals bring to a production. No amount of fancy surface can obliterate a faulty foundation, but in the case of *The Screens*, the costume and decor produced – in one day – two-thirds of the truth, only one-third of which had been evoked in six weeks of rehearsal.

Still, for me, *The Screens* was never an organic production, but a sub-structure and an overlay with a vital middle layer missing. The production made a kind of stark, physical sense in spite of, not because of, our work, and the intellectual uncertainty of cast and producers, the unresolved ambiguities in the text, left an inner fuzziness which a longer run would undoubtedly have revealed.

Tulane Drama Review, Winter 1966

Reflections on *The Screens* by Tom Milne

Tom Milne's review in Encore *vividly described Brook's treatment of* The Screens, *which used an armoury of theatre techniques to provide the audience with a kaleidoscope of startling images.*

Theatre, we are always told, differs from the other arts in that it is incomplete without an audience. But in these days of longer and longer runs and glossier and glossier production techniques, this grows less and less true. The theatrical performance is an attractive package displayed for sale – you pays your money and you takes your choice. If you don't put your money in the slot, the brand is withdrawn; if you do, the mechanism springs into operation and deposits your purchase in your lap. . . .

Jaded palate, one would be inclined to say, but along came the Brook-Marowitz production of Genet's *The Screens* to restore one's faith in a theatre which excites, which really matters, and which *is* only in collaboration with its audience. Whimsy perhaps, but I felt that the production would have been poorer by my absence: certainly I left the theatre elated and at one with the performance. Which, if one cuts the metaphysics, is I suppose a way of throwing one's cap over the windmill for the vitality of a play and production which effortlessly achieved the quality of cruelty which remained so obstinately absent from the recent LAMDA experiments: but it also reflects something peculiar to the good fringe production – the fact that *the* audience (as opposed to *an* audience) is really necessary.

The performance took place in the Donmar Rehearsal Rooms – behind the Cambridge Theatre in shabby Earlham Street – some sort of vast converted warehouse. Not really vast at all, but enormously tall bare walls and tiny high windows give an impression of space and freedom. (Genet asks for an open-air production for *The Screens*, and one sees why. Most theatres are too enclosed; and the remarkable four-level action of the last scene absolutely demands space.) At one end of the room, tiers of rough planking crowded with chairs for the spectators; at the other, the acting area, dotted with tall white screens on castors. A full house, mainly of actors, writers, and so forth, not so very different from an ordinary audience, yet somehow composed of individuals, and not so obviously waiting to be fed. In what followed one could still feel the live breath of creation (this is not a question of roughness, of under-rehearsal or uncertainty – *The Screens* was none of those things – but rather of a subtle alchemy between play, actors, theatre and audience, which must inevitably be lost when a production is subjected to *vernissage*, moves into the anonymity of success, and needs seat-buyers rather than an audience).

Stagehands in white-cowled, Arab-style robes, hidden behind the screens, roll them silently into place; in front of a screen painted with a single palm, Saïd, the young Algerian hero, enters, dressed like a doll or a character from a child's picture-book in 'green trousers, red jacket, tan shoes, white shirt, mauve tie, pink cap'; and Genet's extraordinary Chinese box of fantasies is under way. Each time one strips away a fantasy, another is revealed, then another and another, until underneath one discovers, not Truth, but an image. Martin Esslin has described Genet's work as a 'hall of mirrors'; but unlike Bannister in *Lady from Shanghai*, desperately trying to aim his gun at the real Rita Hayworth from an endless series of mirror reflections, it is not necessary for us to try to divine which is the real one, which is reality out of a series of fantasies, for there is no difference. A truer image for *The Screens* would be a kaleidoscope, which creates patterns containing their own evocative power and beauty, independent of the raw material used to produce them.

As the screens glide swiftly and silently about the stage, sometimes blank, sometimes decorated with vestigial suggestions of scenery, sometimes painted by the characters themselves to represent an object or an emotion, and clashing their unreality against the hard actuality of the few three-dimensional properties, one feels that Genet has created a world in flux, which may (and does) halt at any moment to reveal a naked, visionary flash. What one retains from the play, overall, is a kaleidoscope of shifting scenes, enclosing splashes of brilliant colour, darts of pain and longing, shafts of crude filth and misery, forming and re-forming to make new, pressing patterns. More particularly, one is left with a series of shattering images: as two Colonists chat cosily about the aesthetics and economics of their plantations, Arab terrorists creep stealthily in to draw tiny flames on the screens behind them: then more Arabs, more flames, until the action seems to dissolve in a sheet of fire. Or, in a scene which adds three-dimensional overtones to the Black Queen's tirades calling the black hordes to her aid in *Les Nègres*, the 'La Marseillaise' of the revolution, Kadidja, calls evil to her: and the Arabs come, swiftly drawing their murders, their rapes, their fear, until her screens are covered with scrawled images of evil. The result is electrifying: naked hatred is present on the stage. In both cases we are presented with an image apparently derived out of fantasy but which, like Picasso's *Guernica*, is a poetic distillation which contains a truth more bright than reality.

The Screens, in a sense, is a potted history of Algeria, with its fabled national heroes, its story of oppression, degradation, rebellion, and, after a fashion, victory. On the one side of the play are the colonialists and the military, deliberately presented as crude caricatures (like Sir Harold, with his false nose, rabbit teeth and imbecile chatter; or Blankensee, armed with a padded belly and behind to make himself more imposing), but they are also presented as the symbols of power which they imagine themselves to be and as they are imagined by the Arabs. The gigantic dummy literally covered with medals and ribbons which stands starkly on the stage, or the huge glove imbued with his spirit which Sir Harold leaves in the fields to keep law and order in his absence, are at the same moment absurd and primevally powerful. On the other side, opposing them, are the Algerian rebels, burning, killing, fighting for their freedom, and presenting their victories to Kadidja in the shape of crudely childish drawings. Two fantasies are opposed, and the clash between them is suddenly, shatteringly focused in one of Genet's most viscerally disturbing scenes, here brilliantly evoked in both the production and in Sally Jacobs's décor. The faces of the Europeans – 'an Academician; a Soldier; a Vamp, with her cigarette-holder; a News Photographer; a Widow; a Judge; a Banker; a Little Girl, wearing a communion dress; and a General' – peer from the top of a screen, behind cut-out figures painted to represent period costume, exactly like coconuts on a shy. They chatter. Below sit the Arabs, darkly silent. A shot rings out and the faces disappear, the frightened Arabs vanish, and darkness falls, out of which looms the monstrous, threatening figure of the bemedalled military dummy.

Between these two opposed fantasies lies the path of Saïd, the Genet hero, who stands apart from both to act out his lonely private fantasy in the shadow of national fantasies: the poor man who embraces abjectness and squalor, marrying the ugliest girl in the village, deliberately choosing to become a thief and traitor, and achieving in his total degradation a sort of reality denied to the others. But in so doing, he becomes a fantasy himself: in the last scene of the play, as he returns from his lonely Odyssey, watched by both the living and the dead, Saïd dies, shot, to be enshrined in song as a legend, robbed of his hard-won reality.

What makes *The Screens* so extraordinary, and such an advance on Genet's previous essays along the same lines (enriched progressively through *Les Bonnes*, *Le Balcon* and *Les Nègres*) is the extreme complexity of the levels of fantasy (or reality) spread out in the play. In one scene, for instance, the Arab men feel the stirrings of rebellion as they talk to the whores Warda and Malika; the whores scoffingly retaliate by telling of the legendary hero, Si Slimane. Here the stirrings of rebellion are a dream; Si Slimane, who appeared 'on his horse in sixteen villages at the same time' is a dream; even the whores, empty shells with rotting teeth, gloriously painted and bejewelled, and robed in dresses which protect their fantasy with a massive weight of lead in the hems, are a dream; which leaves the Arab men themselves – are they a dream too, or are they the only reality? In one sense everything in the play is false: the valise of gifts which Saïd and his mother laboriously carry to his wedding turns out to be empty; Saïd's ugly wife – so ugly that she has to wear a mask all the time – whom he cherishes as a symbol of his abjectness and misery, may under her mask be beautiful; the clock which Leila steals is merely a painted image; and even death is simply an easy leap through a paper screen. But behind the falsity lies the naked impulse, and old words like hatred, fear, misery, oppression, even aspiration, take on a new, disturbing power in Genet's mirror images.

Encore, July/August 1964

The Marat/Sade

'If a play does not make us lose our balance, the evening is unbalanced'.
(Brook in 1965)

Since the late Fifties, Brook has been convinced that the central problem facing contemporary theatre is in attaining the richness of the works of Shakespeare and the Elizabethans, complex totalities so dense in experience as to reflect the nature of life itself. At the beginning of 1959 in an article for *Encore* ('Oh for Empty Seats'), he expressed his disillusion with the theatre, in particular bemoaning its lack of vital and urgent material. Theatre had reached

> a catastrophically low level: weak, watery, repetitive, drab, and silly. Why are there no plays that reflect the excitement, the movement, the change, the conflict, the tragedy, the misery, the hope and the emancipation of the highly dramatic moment of world's history in which we live? Why are we given the choice between colour and poetry in the classics, or drab prose in contemporary drama?

Where could he find a play that would awaken and surprise, that would act like Lorca's 'conscious rocket of dark light, let off among the dull and torpid'? When a copy of Weiss's *Marat/Sade* came into his hands, he quickly recognised it to be 'an extraordinarily daring and complex vision', a multi-faceted work uniting instinct and intelligence. This was what was needed to shock the ailing theatre back into life: the raw material of a 'total theatre' in which all the elements of the stage can be made to serve and sustain the play. Weiss had come close to a 'theatrical language as agile and penetrating as the Elizabethans' (Brook in his introduction to the published text).

Weiss has said that he was trying to write a 'thinking' play to be performed in a 'feeling' way, and indeed his juxtaposition (rather than synthesis) of Brecht and Artaud, implicit in the shortened version of the title, is startling. The play is an ideal vehicle for a realisation of Brook's conception of theatre: 'Theatre, like life, is made up of unbroken conflict between impressions and judgements – illusion and disillusion cohabit painfully and are inseparable' (Brook's introduction). Weiss's eclecticism, which Brook more than matched in production, was 'a complete assimilation of all the best theatrical ingredients around'.

Weiss has said that 'it is a Marxist play. Marat should be the victor; if Sade wins the debate, that is bad' (*The Times*, 19 August 1964). If there is a victor in Brook's production, clearly it is Sade. (And yet, as Marowitz reports in his review, Weiss considered Brook's production of his play to be definitive!) In Brook's version, Sade relishes the final cataclysmic outcome of the play, while the paranoid who plays Marat merely adds his weight to the chaotic battle, just one of many lunatics taking over the asylum. There is a switch of emphasis in Brook's version: to a certain extent, Weiss's play is depoliticized by an aestheticisation of the issues presented. And for Brook, much of the play's value is in its non-dogmatic structure. Although firmly on the side of revolutionary change, it never imposes a single moral or political viewpoint. The constant shifting of positions and reassessment of reality allows it to remain open, alive, compelling.

However, the success of Brook's production (without which it must be admitted Weiss's play might well have sunk without trace) stems from his actors' liberation of the spirit of the work: a revolution in theatre in terms of stylistic experimentation, challenging sensibilities rather than ideologies. This is the fundamental story of Brook's work throughout the sixties. Like the Surrealists, he seems to have been suggesting that a revolution in aesthetics and perception of human experience in its totality would have to precede any political reappraisal.

D.W.

The Marat/Sade: An Account by J. C. Trewin

J. C. Trewin describes the rehearsal process and The Marat/Sade *in performance, with reference to its thematic content and its historical background.*

Back from the United States and the *Lear* opening, Brook got down to a project which put to better service the discoveries and the techniques evolved during the workshop months. Towards the end of August he staged at the Aldwych a play called, in English, *The Persecution and Murder of Marat as Performed by the Inmates of the Asylum of Charenton under the direction of the Marquis de Sade*:[1] a title that would be shortened, inevitably, to *The Marat/Sade*. Its author was Peter Weiss who combined, as Brook said later, Jewish family, Czech upbringing, German language, Swedish home, and Marxist sympathies. One had to realize, as a beginning, that between 1787 and 1811, Monsieur Coulmier, liberal-minded, pre-Freudian director of the Charenton Asylum for lunatics on a ridge near the confluence of the Seine and Marne, established regular theatrical entertainments in his clinic: it was a part of his enlightened therapeutic treatment of the inmates. The Marquis de Sade, now over sixty and with a life of stormy excess behind him, was an inmate of Charenton from 1803 until he died in 1814; he wrote and directed many of its entertainments, and it became fashionable in Paris to visit the asylum, as much as to observe the *louche* behaviour of the lunatics as to watch the performance. The plays were acted on a specially built stage; facing this was a box reserved for the director and his friends; and on each side were stands for selected patients who had to bear the scrutiny of the fashionable Parisian crowd in the stalls. From this rose Peter Weiss's play, set within the communal bathhouse, the hydropathic department of the institution . . .

Eventually the experimental group, numbering seventeen now, was fused with the larger company needed for *The Marat/Sade*. Certain ideas used in the Theatre of Cruelty workshop entered the Aldwych production, the bath-tub and guillotine imagery in particular. For most people

---

[1] *Die Verfolgung und Ermordung Jean Paul Marats dargestellt durch die Schauspieltruppe des Hospizes zu Charenton unter Anleitung des Herrn de Sade*. A deliberately undramatic and pseudo-academic listing of the play's contents. Hence a running gag at the time: 'I haven't seen the play but I've read the title.' (D.W.)

63

it proved to be a tumultuous and stimulating spectacle; Brook, in the heat of his rehearsal methods, had had the cast with him for two strenuous months ('The work of rehearsal is looking for meaning, and making it meaningful'). He said at once that he had no time for traditional prettified or melodramatic stage madness. Personally he had expert advice from his brother Alexis, a consultant psychiatrist, and he also visited asylums in London and Paris. During a television programme that autumn 'in the course of talking about acting, he managed to say things about insanity that a qualified psychiatrist might have taken years to arrive at' (Jonathan Miller). He told the cast to study paintings by Breughel and Hogarth and etchings by Goya; articles on mental illness were read together; the company saw two French films (*Regard sur la Folie* and *Le Maître-Fous*) that studied various aspects of madness; and, for two weeks before any script was disclosed, Brook worked with the players severally, trying to get them to 'dig out the madman' from themselves, and to find personal expressions of madness that – while remaining true to the piece – could be sustained for two and a half hours. At first he required the players to create ('We were all convinced that we were going loony,' Glenda Jackson said); then, when they tired, he produced his own ideas, never losing his temper, his eagerness, or his capacity for work. He believed that the only directing method to give results was a fusion of several different methods, all aimed at getting the actor to contribute more and more: every rehearsal became a living process.

As he told Weiss, he approached the play from the Artaudian and Brechtian angles. Herald (Ian Richardson), speaking in octosyllabics, was announcer and satirical commentator; there were signs and placards, and an expository singing chorus of four grotesques. On the other side, the production offered a frightening variety of Artaudian shocks, everything from hallucinations, paroxysms, executions, and whippings, to cries and moans, an infinity of sound variations, and a startling use of make-up. In a preface to the text when it was printed in America, Brook said:

> Weiss not only uses total theatre, that time-honoured notion of getting all the elements of the stage to serve the play. His force is not only in the quantity of instruments he uses; it is above all in the jangle produced by the clash of styles. Everything is put in place by its neighbour – the serious by the comic, the noble by the popular, the literary by the crude, the intellectual by the physical: the abstraction is vivified by the stage image, the violence illuminated

by the cool flow of thought. The strands of meaning of the play pass to and fro through its structure and the result is a very complex form: as in Genet, it is a hall of mirrors or a corridor of echoes – and one must keep looking front and back all the time to reach the author's sense.

Unwillingly released by Brook from rehearsal, the play reached the Aldwych on 20 August 1964: Geoffrey Skelton's English version adapted into free verse by Adrian Mitchell. Mild first-nighters discovered that they represented simultaneously an early nineteenth-century audience and their twentieth-century selves. In a few hours of punching, kicking, dousing and assessing, Weiss imagined Sade's presentation of a subversive play on Charlotte Corday's murder of the extreme social revolutionary, Jean Paul Marat, at the height of the Terror. Alan Brien described the setting in the *Sunday Telegraph* (23 August):

> A towering windowless silo walled with tiny bricks and booby-trapped with sunken pits. Among the inmates with their padded clothes and sunken faces, the devil-worshipping priests and burned-out whores, the lecherous ex-aristos and the lethargic ex-rebels, the childish voluptuaries and the aged virgins, move the black-eyed nuns and the muscle-bound warders.

Bamber Gascoigne said in the *Observer* on the same day:

> The lunatics in their shapeless white tunics and strait-jackets make a bustle and swirl somewhere between Breughel and Daumier. Probably the most stunning scene of all is a guillotine sequence, complete with metallic raspings, buckets of paint (red and blue), and other techniques which seemed self-conscious and false in the Theatre of Cruelty isolation at LAMDA.

Dramatically, the play was a debate between the paranoiac Marat (Clive Revill), prophet of the totalitarian state, and Sade (Patrick Magee), the cold voluptuary, the anarch, apostle of unbridled individual liberty.[1] But what most people remembered, shuddering, was the visual impact, the 'debris of souls from some private hell' (Milton Shulman), the chalky clothing, the writhing limbs, the hysteria, the grimacing, the lolling heads, the whirr and thud of the guillotine, the buckets of blood, the schizoids and cretins, eroto-maniacs and manic-depressives, the

---

[1] Brook has pointed out that the only person they were able to use as a concrete equivalent to Sade was Ezra Pound (D.W.).

faces peering from the hidden baths, and Charlotte Corday's use of her hair to whip the naked Sade (Charlotte acted by a somnambulistic lunatic expressed agonizingly by Glenda Jackson). Then the end, for Brook saw that the close of a production crowned all: the moment when the entire company, advancing towards the edge of the stage, fell to fighting, and to smashing up the bath-house. On a signal, all went quiet. The audience applauded, whereupon the cast replied with the sudden irony of a slow hand-clap. ('If we had conventional curtain-calls,' said Brook, 'the audience would emerge relieved, and that's the last thing we want.') An Aldwych audience, shocked and battered, never emerged relieved. According to a famous mental specialist: 'It was hard to credit that the actors had not been coached by someone who had worked in chronic mental wards for many years, so resolute was their acting.'

After such an experience, exhaustive and exhausting, some of us felt that we could never face again the conventionally stylized lunacies in the relevant scenes of *The Duchess of Malfi* or *Peer Gynt* (neither of them plays that Brook has yet directed).

From *Peter Brook: A Biography*, 1971.

The Marat/Sade: A Review by Albert Hunt

Albert Hunt, writing in Peace News, *details the multi-faceted complexity of Brook's production, its portrayal of the violence latent within society and ourselves. He believed the production to be of 'extreme urgency' in confronting the darker aspects of human reality.*

The Second World War presented a mirror to the human condition which blinded anyone who looked into it. For if tens of millions were killed in concentration camps out of the inexorable agonies and contradictions of super-states founded upon the always insoluble contradictions of injustice, one was then obliged also to see that no matter how crippled and perverted an image of man was the society he had created, it was none the less his creation . . . and if society was so murderous, then who could ignore the most hideous of questions about his own nature?

What the liberal cannot bear to admit is the hatred beneath the skin of a society so unjust that the amount of collective violence buried in the people is perhaps incapable of being contained, and therefore if one wants a better world one does well to hold one's breath, for a worse world is bound to come first. . . .

Norman Mailer, The White Negro

Weiss's *Marat/Sade* play seems to be centred around a debate about the nature of man. The protagonists are Marat, who believes that changing society can change human beings, and de Sade, who sees individual man as evil and violent, and can therefore no longer believe in political action.

The debate is wordy and inconclusive. Moreover, it is conducted almost entirely in abstract terms. By far the most coherent statement is made by Marat, when he goes a long way towards explaining the failure of the French Revolution by exposing its bourgeois origins. This analysis is so lucid that Marat's itchy skin and de Sade's reflections about man seem irrelevant. But if this is what Weiss intended, it conflicts with the presentation of de Sade, who draws the audience's sympathy, and with his speech at the end (written into the English version with Weiss's approval) to the effect that any meaning or none can be drawn from the play. This seems to me an intellectual evasion. It amounts to saying, man is evil; there's nothing to be done; so nothing matters.

In Peter Brook's production, which is the first, triumphant product of the experiment that has been going on at the Royal Shakespeare Company, this debate becomes an at times irritating incidental. This is largely because of the way Marat is played. All the other characters are lunatics *playing* at being important people; but we never have the sense that Marat is anybody but the real French politician. And this is confusing, for the true content of this production is not debate but charade. Just as, last year, Joan Littlewood used a pierrot show to tell the story of the First World War, Brook now uses the theatrical games at Charenton to explore the theme of violence. The result is a communication that would be impossible in any other medium.

The sense of imprisoned violence is present even before the play begins, in the set which Sally Jacobs has given Brook as his raw material. It faces you as you go into the theatre. The stage is huge, and almost bare, surrounded by grey, sickly walls. In the centre there is a huge circle of wooden gates that are shut down over baths sunk into the ground. At the front there are two other gated holes, which later become sewers into which heads roll, and through which blood is poured, red and blue. Inside the circle is an object covered by a sheet; this turns out to be Marat's bath.

On to this bare stage, with the house lights still up, wander the inmates of the asylum, more than a score of them. They are dressed in pale, sickly grey, ragged uniforms. Some are bandaged. Some are cripples or have twitches. One has his arms bound in a strait-jacket. Amongst them are one or two warders in darker uniforms. The inmates instal themselves slowly on the stage, as if allowing themselves to begin to feel at home. They are completely self-absorbed with none of that 'look at me' quality which characterises most bit part acting in Britain. Brook slowly allows their presence, their simply being on the stage to create its own image of imprisonment, loss and bewilderment.

This grey sickness is splashed here and there with colour and gaiety. It is supplied by the director of the asylum and his wife and daughter, who sit elegantly at the side of the stage as spectators; by a herald in a blue uniform, who acts throughout as a master of ceremonies; and by four singers in coloured sacks, comic red hats, and clown-like masks. They, together with the leading 'actors' are presented by the herald in couplets full of elegant banality, and labouredly ingenious rhymes. Ian Richardson, who plays the herald, is gay and detached, so that the violence and the terror are constantly thrown into sharp focus.

This initial contrast – between colour and greyness, gaiety and torment, elegance and horror – introduces at once the method of the play. Everything that happens springs from the basic truth that we are seeing major historical events faithfully portrayed – by lunatics. The result is a constant shifting of levels. Thus, at one point, the patients re-enact the guillotine. Using old tin cans for sound effects, and red and blue paint for blood, they line up one by one by a hole in the ground and leap in. As a climax they throw in a dummy covered with decorations. We see violence distanced, as if in a game. Only the players of the game are themselves violent: the macabre, comic scene ends with an outburst from the patients themselves, who run screaming about the stage.

Or again – there is at times a complete contrast between the situation as we see it, and the roles the patients are playing out. So Charlotte Corday has a lover, strictly platonic. He is young and noble and has to talk romantic love. Only we can see that he is in fact obsessed with Corday's body. As he expresses his purity, his hands reach uncontrollably for her skirt or neckline, and he has to be held back by warders. At the climax of their love affair, he advances towards her with a romantic gesture – and is held back by chains which clank from his wrists. The play is full of such images: Marat is crowned as a premature Bonaparte – he stands like an emperor, and scratches under the white sheet. The girl who plays Corday – activist, assassin – is a patient who suffers from sleeping sickness and spends much of the play asleep on the stage. (She is superbly played by Glenda Jackson, the Keeler of the Theatre of Cruelty.)

In the same way, there is a shifting of time, so that past and present become interchangeable. The patients re-enact a procession by the poor of Paris, a revolutionary demonstration. 'We want a revolution – now!' they sing – only as they sing the 'now' spills over into the present, and they become prisoners demanding their liberation. Whenever, throughout the play, the director of the asylum complains about the subversive quality of the work, the herald always points out that the play is about events in the past; that society is now much better ordered, much more civilized, and that what is described is remote. As he says this, we see warders fighting with patients, and a man in a strait-jacket rolling about the stage.

This element of charade is not just a stage gimmick, like the mimes in *The Royal Hunt of the Sun*. It is essential to Brook's – and Weiss's – vision of human experience. Their concept of reality emerges from the dramatic form of the play.

From *Peace News*, September 1964.

The Marat/Sade: A Review by Charles Marowitz

In The Village Voice, *Marowitz expressed profound reservations about Brook's 'modish showmanship'.*

Brook has never been so prolific or eye-catching. He doesn't so much illuminate the text as set off illuminations upon it. There's always something happening on the stage, if not always in the play itself. The play-proper is intellectually lightweight and says little in its own right, which would not be a serious objection except that its circulating themes – the Revolution, merciless individualism pitted against passionate social purpose, the mind versus the senses – seem to imply a viewpoint and an attitude, but closer scrutiny reveals them to be so many strands criss-crossed as in cats-and-cradles.

Reduced to basic components, the play is a series of marvellous 'happenings' interspersed with polemical dialogues, mainly between de Sade and Marat. The 'happenings', authored mainly by Brook, employ a squadron of loonies in full (strait-jacketed) regalia, having fits of the tics, the shakes, the heebie-jeebies, and other assorted paroxysms (a real ball for the actors, who, for once, are encouraged to indulge themselves to excess). But after three or four of these theatricalist explosions and a couple of elongated polemical discourses, the ordering mentality of an audience tries to collate the shocks and the sense, only to find that they don't really go together; that, in fact, the intellectual dialogues are themselves a kind of theatrical effect. And at the very moment when we are silently raising these objections, along comes the playwright, now in the guise of de Sade, and tells us: the play can be about any number of things; about the sane being mad, or the mad, sane; the times being changed or the times never changing; the mind being supreme or the senses irresistible, etc., etc. – in fact, we can take away any meaning we like or, if we prefer, no meaning at all. Which I take to be sophistry of the most preposterous sort because in that no-nonsense zone of our hearts which feels that people talk because they have something to say, we want to believe that Peter Weiss, the author, possesses some kind of under-lying attitude of his own and that it explains (let alone justifies) the particular texture of his play and the sequence of its events, because if he has written it only to spread gunshot and ricochet ideas, we don't need him for that, and, as Goethe pointed out, if someone has an opinion, let him couch it in positive terms, 'as I have enough problematic stuff of my own.'

The West Berlin production of the play (it was first presented at the Schiller-Theatre earlier this year) was much tamer; compared to Brook's, even flaccid. The director, Konrad Swinarski, a Pole, obviously saw the play as a kind of political tract in which the great lesson was that the naïve democracies of the French Revolution only paved the way for reigns-of-terror and the crowning terror of all, military dictatorship. Therefore, in the last moment of his production, the back of a squat, Napoleonic figure in high cloak and three-cornered hat appears from nowhere, then suddenly turns to the audience to reveal the visage of a death-head. In the last moment of the Brook production, the massed lunatics, wildly singing, begin a menacing procession toward the audience. These are really the two productions' concepts in miniature; to Brook, an essay on violence that should assault its audience; to Swinarski, an epic about fascism that should point up the lethal idiocies of revolution. Neither 'interpretation' quite tallies. Weiss preferred the Brook production, which he takes to be 'definitive'. It was the more successful, the Berlin one having prompted several reservations among critics. However, the Schiller-Theatre *Marat/Sade* is in many ways a more accurate rendering of the text. Perhaps that is why Weiss disowns it. Left to its own devices, the play doesn't stand very tall. But jacked up and made to prance (as it is by Brook), it can pass for an elaborate profundity – which it is not!

Having said all this – and one is really pressed to say it because the critics' reaction has been so rhapsodically obtuse, being blinded by production-effects and backing away from the play in a deference born of non-comprehension; having said all this, one must also say that despite its intellectual slitheriness, it manages to combine the best elements of the Brechtian and Artaudian theatres. It tells its tale, *à la* Brecht, with signs, slogans, and anti-illusionary devices; at the same time, it plumbs its psychic interiors, *à la* Artaud, with wild bouts of violence and cruelty. Its best writing is in the purely descriptive passages, where Weiss lovingly elaborates the minute dismemberment of a revolutionary victim, or Charlotte Corday minutely contemplates the stabbing of Marat. The English production has a marvellous ensemble feeling and some spectacular solo performances – mainly Glenda Jackson's Charlotte Corday and Ian Richardson's Coulmier. But the Berlin production has a much weightier de Sade in Ernst Schroder and a more febrile and fanatic Marat in Peter Mosbacher.

The great thing about the Weiss success (even in Berlin it is the hit of the season) is that the theatre about which Artaud had such eloquent hallucinations is slowly evolving, and the madman – if indeed 'madness' is the right word for whatever it was that sent Artaud's sensibilities sky-rocketing – is gradually coming into his own. Maybe we are gravitating closer and closer to his kind of extremity, or perhaps we simply enjoy peering into the peepholes of the padded cell. Although I don't think it is as simple as that.

Artaud's theatre has two great fascinations for us today. First, it is – despite his aesthetic harangues – *more* realistic than the current theatrical output – by which I mean, closer to the genuine feel of violence and hostility which nourishes our contemporary behaviour and ambitions and second, it contains the seeds of a new and viable aesthetic, an alternative to the low-keyed copy-cat styles which glut our plays, films, and television programmes. The madness of the world (I mean madness in both senses, the anger as well as the imbalance) is making Artaud's wildest pronouncements appear curiously appropriate. The social spleen in his work is already firing the minds of certain writers, and its resemblance to traditional radicalism makes this quite understandable. Before long, his aesthetic ideas, which have no such antecedents, will also take hold, and then the revolution of form will have begun in earnest.

The Village Voice, November 1965

US

'Do we know where we stand in relation to the real and the unreal, the face of life and its hidden streams, the abstract and the concrete, the story and the ritual? *What are facts today?* Are they concrete, like prices and hours of work – or abstract, like violence and loneliness? And are we sure that in relation to 20th century living, the great abstractions – speed, strain, space, frenzy, energy, brutality – aren't more concrete, more immediately likely to affect our lives than the so-called concrete issues? Mustn't we relate this to the actor and the ritual of acting to find the pattern of the theatre we need?'

(Brook: 'From Zero to the Infinite', *Encore*, November 1960)

In October 1965, at the Aldwych, Brook conducted a public RSC reading of *The Investigation*, Weiss's play about Auschwitz.[1] The dialogue, a catalogue of horrors, is taken from the actual testimonies of both victims and accused at the Nazi War Crimes trials. After the reading, Brook was forced to conclude that factual enumeration of atrocities served only to anaesthetise the spectator or listener: as with media accounts, the crimes soon become almost acceptable, even boring. Yet a work such as Picasso's *Guernica* touches us profoundly thirty-five years after the events it records. For a more direct communication of an actual and extreme reality, seen by Brook as one of the prime responsibilities of a living theatre today, different forms would clearly have to be found.

In October 1966, after fifteen weeks of rehearsal, the ambiguously titled *US* was presented at the Aldwych. (It came a month before the New York première of Megan Terry's *Viet Rock*.) Described as a 'group-happening-collaborative spectacle, it had been created to try to approach directly a burning question: 'If I say I care about Vietnam, how

---

[1] Similar readings and a number of productions occurred simultaneously in seventeen cities around Europe, including both East and West Berlin; Piscator's full production was staged at the Freie Volksbühne in West Berlin.

does that influence the way I spend my time?' The group studied, and built improvisations around, newspaper articles and interviews, official reports, happenings, American myths in comic strips and popular songs, and Vietnamese folk stories. The improvisatory period churned up a mass of material from which a collage combination of art and politics was forged. With only a limited amount of scripted structuring by Denis Cannan and Charles Wood, constantly reassessed and rewritten during the performance period, the emphasis was on 'contact with the audience through shared references' (*The Empty Space*).

As in the Theatre of Cruelty season and *Marat/Sade*, Brook was aiming at a theatre of 'confrontation', comprising abrupt tonal transitions and jarring clashes of style, to create the impression of a continually shifting and mutable reality:

> I want to see outer realism as something in endless flux with barriers and boundaries that come and go – people and situations forming and unforming before my eyes. I want to see identities changing not as clothes are changed . . . but as scenes dissolve in a film, as paint drips off a brush. Then I want to see inner realism as another state of movement and flux – I want to sense the energies which, the deeper one goes, become stronger and clearer and more defined. I want to feel the true forces that impel our false identities: I want to sense what truly binds us, what truly separates us.   ('Search for a Hunger', *Encore*, 1961)

For example, a scene of American GIs discussing the morality and methods of torture in an official interview suddenly switched to the provocative image of three soldiers beating, kicking and humiliating a Viet Cong prisoner: almost instantly, the writhing victim and his cries of pain were transformed into the cavortings of a pelvis-thrusting rock-singer, wailing through a song about the delights of napalm ('Zappin' the Cong') to a chorus of screaming fans (see extract from *US* text below). Often the movement was towards the comic, inevitably so for Brook: 'We were continually moving into burlesque and farce as being perhaps the only way that one can deal with extreme horror.'

The counterpointing of comedy and intimidating horror, part of a general assault on the spectators' emotional detachment, was a direct continuation of the earlier work of this period, as were the experiments with paint. In *US*, Brook's investigations of the theatrical expressiveness of the techniques of action painting were further developed through a close group study of 'happenings', phenomena initially generated by painters. Brook admired the anarchic spontaneity and poetry of the best of the happenings, but he recognized the absolute need here for something more disciplined and tightly structured.

In the early scenes, a brief pageant of Vietnamese history in the style of the Chinese theatre, Vietnam itself was represented by a semi-naked individual undergoing torture. (Compare the treatment of Cieslak in Grotowski's version of Slowacki/Calderon's *The Constant Prince*, reflecting the abject abuse, torture and ultimate crucifixion of Poland.) For the division of Vietnam into two parts, there was a heavily ritualized scene of marvellous visual power and imagination: the top half of the actor's body was painted one colour, the bottom half another. He was further flicked and sprayed with a variety of colours, leaving him with a violently lacerated appearance. Finally he writhed in pain on a sheet of paper which was then torn in two: the graphic dismemberment of a nation (see text below).

The ending was a typically Brookian *coup de théâtre*: it continued the theme of burning in a sinisterly poetic manner. White butterflies were released from a black box to flutter into the auditorium. (One of John Cage's musical 'happenings', entitled Composition 1960 no. 5, had simply involved the setting free of a single white butterfly.) Then with ceremonial slow-motion, an actor reached into the box to pick out another. With evident overtones of ancient rituals of sympathetic magic involving the use of a 'double', he proceeded to burn it with a lighter. Inevitably certain members of the audience reacted strongly at this point, something Brook relished: for the sacrificed butterfly was in reality no more than a crumpled piece of white paper. Make-believe *did* have the power to make people stand up and protest if it succeeded in pricking subconscious nerve-endings.

Among those who worked with the group during the rehearsal period were Susan Sontag, Joseph Chaikin (taking a break from rehearsals of *America Hurrah* in New York) and Jerzy Grotowski. The Polish director's blurring of the division between the ethical and the aesthetic has left a lasting impression on Brook's work. During the preparation for *US*, the emphasis was on a continuous and vigorous process of self-research, a daily reassessment of oneself and of one's art, of the relationship between theatre and everyday life. Brook demanded that the actors strive incessantly to 'go beyond themselves'. Brook always attempts to pursue a *via negativa* in the creation process, a stripping away of falsifying accretions. But Grotowski's ascetic monasticism, as suggested in his quasi-religious choice of terminology, is at the opposite pole to Brook's sensuality.

For Brook, repetition and representation almost inevitably signify sterility, ossification and death. With *US*, 'the fixing was the beginning of a slide towards the deadly – the liveliness of the actors waned as the immediacy of the relation with their public and their theme lessened . . . Something was lost in playing it even through a London season of five months. One performance would have been the true culmination.' (*The Empty Space*)

D.W.

US: Narrative One by Albert Hunt

Albert Hunt, one of Brook's collaborators, recorded the first four weeks of US rehearsals. He now considers this section to have been written 'too much in Peter Brook's shadow: and he thought so too'. Nevertheless it provides a fascinating insight into techniques and exercises, aims and concerns.

In an article in *The Times* a few weeks after *US* opened, Irving Wardle, suggesting that the second act of the play negated everything that had been said in the first act, asked how far the members of the team that made *US* had been aware from the first of Peter Brook's strategy. The implication was that Brook himself had a master plan; that from the beginning he knew clearly and precisely what he wanted to say; and that he only collected around himself a number of talents in order to manipulate them for his own purposes.

The argument is, at first sight, plausible. It was certainly true, as Irving Wardle knew, that some of the members of the team felt that the play's final statement was not what they had originally intended. But to suggest that Brook planned this from the beginning is to misunderstand the whole process of work through which *US* was made. *US* was, above all, a search. It was a collective search by a group of people who wanted to say something true and honest and useful about a subject we all felt was very important – the Vietnam War. The statement that was eventually made in the Aldwych Theatre on 13 October, 1966, may not have satisfied all of us. But it was a statement that had grown out of a process of work, and not one that had been conceived in Brook's mind before the process began. And the possibilities opened up by the process are more important than the limitations of the show that was finally produced.

For me, the process began at a meeting between Brook, Reeves and myself at Brook's house the previous December. At that meeting Brook talked of two subjects which were very much on his mind. The first was the Vietnam War – not so much the war itself as what we, in London, could do about it, and how an awareness of the war could affect our lives. He talked about this in direct, practical terms. If you said you cared about Vietnam, how did this affect the way you spent your day? He talked of a well-known actress who, he said, rationed her day out – so many hours for rehearsal, so many hours for writing to MPs or newspapers, or helping in demonstrations. Was this an adequate way of

77

responding to what was happening in Vietnam? If not, what would be adequate?

The other question that was in Brook's mind that night was a very simple one from the *Bhagavad Gita*: 'Shall I fight?' Apparently simple, that is. For it was easy enough to give, in the abstract, a negative answer. But the fact was that, in Vietnam, people were fighting. Simply to wash one's hands of this and utter moral precepts seemed to all of us a useless gesture. And yet the question was there and had to be confronted. Brook wanted to create a show in which this question would be raised in terms of the war in Vietnam.

He felt, too, that the show would have to be made in a new way. Reading through the scripts that came into the Royal Shakespeare Company, he was brought up against the fact that no individual playwright, working alone, seemed able, at the moment, to handle a direct statement of this size. Brook said that perhaps the conditions were not right; that a Shakespeare could only have emerged out of a situation in which groups of actors and writers had established a common language. Our job was not to produce a *King Lear* but to start on the work of forging a language. The theatre ought to be able to speak about a subject as central as the Vietnam War; no play existed that was in any way adequate; in working together we should try to create circumstances in which such a play could be written. (It is important to realize that even in this early stage it was fully understood that we should be heavily dependent on a writer. A writer of some weight would, we hoped, be involved in the process from the start – taking part in our discussions, working over material we should provide him with, later sitting in with the actors and finding material in rehearsals) . . .

We began to read all we could lay our hands on about Vietnam. By far the most useful documents we found were the records of the Fulbright Committee Hearings on Vietnam and China. There was a striking phrase by one of the key witnesses, Dr Fairbank: 'Great nations on both sides are pursuing their alternative dreams.' We began to see the war as a collision of dreams. And there was a piece of dialogue from the hearings that increasingly summed up our response to this material:

SENATOR FULBRIGHT: None of us has an answer. I am afraid not.

GENERAL GRIFFITH: I am afraid I do not have.

SENATOR FULBRIGHT: None of us has an answer.

What emerged above all from the Hearings was the awareness, in the United States, that the administration had drifted into a situation which most people bitterly regretted, but that nobody could see the way out. In these circumstances, to stand on a stage and simply demand American withdrawal seemed both impertinent and inadequate. We had somehow to confront the real, complex situation. The question was: how? . . .

July 4

Brook began by restating his belief in a theatre that could speak directly about contemporary issues. The theatre ought to have a voice that could be listened to seriously. The trouble was that people found it only too easy to dismiss what they had seen as just another theatrical success. He talked about *The Marat/Sade*. The audience, particularly in London, had been able to avoid the play's political implications. If a man like Harold Wilson had seen it, he would have been able to take refuge in describing the play as theatrically exciting. We needed to make a statement that a Wilson or a Johnson would not be able to shrug off in this way.

At the same time, we must be aware from the start that we were not trying to make a documentary about Vietnam. We were going to examine our own attitudes, to ask ourselves as totally as possible how the Vietnam War affected *us*. Brook went on to talk about an image that had clearly been haunting him – the image of the Buddhist monk who had poured petrol over himself and burnt himself to death as a protest against the war. What, asked Brook, could drive a man to such an action? How could we begin to understand the totality of his commitment? As Brook described this burning, vividly and with great intensity, the actors suddenly became very intent. The subject had clearly taken root in Brook's mind as one of the central images of the play.

Brook stressed that the actors were not going to write the play. He explained the working process; the actors would improvise on material which we would offer them, and a playwright would take and shape what the actors produced. Brook also invited the actors to bring material of their own which several of them did.

Towards the end of his talk, Brook commented that *The Marat/Sade* had meant more politically in New York than in London. In New York people had referred it much more directly to the political crisis they were caught up in, of which the Vietnam War was one symptom. He asked those actors who had been to New York to say how they felt American life was different from that in England.

Very hesitantly, the actors began talking. Once they had started, they began to generalize wildly. They all said that they felt America was more violent than England, but the examples they gave were not very convincing. They talked about taxi drivers who shouted, and about the violence they felt on the streets at night. But there was nothing specific, and certainly nothing more violent than one can see in the streets of a northern town like Bradford. One felt only that outside the theatre the actors had never had much experience of violence . . .

After lunch

The improvisations were, some of them, amusing; but when the actors were questioned on who they were, the replies were very vague. Simple details, such as the age and background of the characters they were playing, had failed to come through. Later, an approach was made on the level of popular myth. The actors were asked to model themselves on film stars and play out typical situations. Frank Sinatra tried to pick up Debbie Reynolds in Central Park. Henry Fonda, as father, and Dean Martin, as son, arrived home drunk to find the door locked. Martin tried to break it down; Fonda asked for a hairpin. John Wayne waited for his daughter to come home late at night. He ordered the boy who had brought her out of the house, and when the boy had left, snarled at the girl, 'There y'are. I told you he had no guts.'

These scenes were much more accurate than the earlier ones, and it was clear that the actors were more at home with the myth than with their superficial glimpses of American life. At the same time, one felt that there was a faintly patronizing quality about the work. If we were going to come to grips with what was going on in American society, we should have to look at this culture in much more depth . . .

July 5

We tried to analyze the connection between the society that had produced happenings, and what was going on in Vietnam.

But at this point we were stuck. Apart from the obvious statement that both happenings and the war were the products of American society, there seemed to be very little to say. And then Mike Williams suddenly demonstrated the kind of theatre language we were looking for. He found an image which made the connection in concrete terms. He put a chair on a table, crumpled some paper and took a match. Then, speaking very simply the words of the letter about the butterfly piece, he climbed on to a chair, and pretended to drench himself in petrol. As he reached the words 'Isn't it wonderful to listen to something you normally look at?', he struck the match.

The image suddenly pulled together the two worlds, so that they commented on each other. It did not say simply that happenings were trivial, and that the real Happening was to burn yourself to death. The words revealed the immolation as a dramatic event – and the action placed the words in a wider context. It was this kind of revelation that we were looking for when we placed the material about Happenings in the middle of a discussion about burning in Act Two of the finished production. But I don't think we ever in the end achieved anything as clear and penetrating as this very early, suddenly discovered act.

July 6, 7, 8

In the first two days, our search for a language had developed in three main directions: exploring American life through naturalistic improvisations; investigating American popular myths; and looking at the intellectual world of the Happenings. During the rest of the first week, these directions were developed.

The exploration of American myth took the form of more improvisations from movies, an attempt to play out advertisements, and a study of horror comics. The difficulties were apparent. The actors were used to thinking in terms of character. Asked to put on a propaganda advertisement against smoking, all of them elaborated so that the point of the advertisement was lost in a welter of irrelevant detail. The technique we were asking for was the exact opposite of the one they were accustomed to using. Normally, they would take the bare bones of a text and fill it out with character. Now they were being asked to strip away every detail that would distract from one clear, central statement.

Similar problems arose when we turned to horror comics. The actors were asked to turn themselves into monsters. After several days' work, Ian Hogg was able to transform himself into a creature called 'the Sinister Sponge'. His body swelled out, his head was thrown back, the veins on his huge neck stood out, his arms were taut and he uttered a long, wordless cry. The image appeared twice in the final show – during the 'Zappin' the Cong' number, and later, in the air-raid.

The need to discover a new language of acting was dictated by the form we were reaching towards. We had felt all along that the material was too complex to be developed in conventional terms of story and character. There were too many elements; we had to be able to take in the world where political decisions were made, the cultural pressures behind those decisions and the effects of those decisions on anonymous people far away – and to make thematic links between these different worlds. It could only be done through a flow of imagery, with actors who could move rapidly backwards and forwards between several different styles. But since the training of actors in British theatre is limited, and largely centred on 'character' acting, the actors had to begin slowly and painfully at the beginning. What we were to do was phenomenally difficult. We were trying to discover images from the work of actors, and yet the actors had to learn new and basic techniques before the images could emerge. Two actors spent several hours on one Brecht exercise. They went through 'Good King Wenceslas', singing alternate lines – each moving quickly from Sinatra to Caruso and then to Mick Jagger. While they were struggling with this song, other actors were trying to discover ways of reacting to physical violence, without being struck.

The work on Happenings produced the most finished piece of work that week. A group played out a number of New York intellectuals trying to stage a Happening. They never reached the Happening, and in their failure they caught at an image, a group of people struggling with their own ineffectiveness. It was a superficial image, and unfair to the creative energy that goes into a successful Happening, but it was true, true in so far as it reflected a sense of impotence and in-group isolation. But the limitations were ruthlessly exposed as soon as Brook asked them to turn the scene into an English drawing-room on Sunday afternoon. The result was broad, unfunny cliché.

While the actors were struggling with these initial difficulties, we were facing a new crisis of our own. Charles Wood had so far not been able to come to any of the rehearsals. Soon, he was to drop out completely. From now on until the first act had already been shaped up, we were without the experienced writer on whom so much had initially depended. This, rather than any 'master plan' of Peter Brook's, had a determining effect on the final shape of the show.

July 11

The problems that had been apparent in the early work on pop culture were thrown into even sharper focus when Brook suddenly turned to the war and invited the actors to improvise their response to an air-raid. The actors crawled across the floor of Bourne and Hollingsworth's ballroom in various attitudes of pain. Some scrabbled at the floor, some dragged useless legs, some were blind. One girl had a dead baby in her arms.

After some time, Brook stopped the exercise and began again. The actors created a Vietnamese village. They found work to do. Brook threw a chair – it was the signal for the air-raid to begin. The actors dropped their work, and cowered on the ground, whimpering. When the raid was over, they began to crawl across the floor again.

One small incident suddenly called attention to the thinness of the work. At the start of one of the raids, the chair thrown as a signal nearly hit one of the actors. He reacted spontaneously, flinching instinctively from the *real* threatened pain. Then, when the chair missed, he became a Vietnamese villager again, simulating a wound.

For me, this exercise raised a whole set of questions that were never, I think, answered. Brook had said, again and again, that we must somehow find a language of communication that went beyond our deadened responses to the newsreels and television documentaries. Yet how could these actors begin to compete with those shots of the children whose faces had been turned to crust? All we had to offer in this show was ourselves – ourselves in London, not being burnt with jellied petrol. We – or rather the actors – could not convincingly simulate bombed villagers. They could only confront a particular audience on a particular night with their own, unblistered bodies. Whatever was communicated finally would come, not through a skilful imitation of pain, but through that confrontation. To this extent, each performance would be a Happening. The flinching from the thrown chair said more to me about Vietnam that morning than any of the tortured gestures of the actors. It was this quality of immediacy that we should have to look for.

In an attempt to avoid the need to create a 'real' air-raid, Brook tried framing the exercise between two screens, in a theatrical situation. He asked the actors to pretend that they were people from Vietnam who had come to a village to spread propaganda. They were trying to call the villagers to action against the Americans. Each actor was allowed to make just one point, through a gesture, about the air-raid, in the time he took to cross from one screen to the other.

The screens formed a little stage, maybe six feet across, and the actors crossed this in a line, one by one. They crawled, moved blindly, whimpered. But none of them could find the one clear gesture that could serve as a call to action. They were still too close to actors simulating 'real' wounds – and the problem was exactly the same as that which had confronted them three days earlier when they were trying to make advertisements.

July 13–19

For the first time, Brook showed the way in which his mind was working towards a collage of different elements. He began with a horror comic scenario Mitchell had written, *Zappman*. He worked through the story in very short scenes, then began to inject other elements into it. First, the group were Americans improvising a happening; then they moved into the exercise showing air-raid wounds; then into the first scene of the comic strip. At the end of this scene, Ian Hogg, lying on the floor as a dead GI, did part of Johnson's Great Society speech as an old man. Then the scene went back to wounds again, and then into the second comic strip scene, with Bob Lloyd zapping the Cong, and then turning into Kennedy . . . This mixing of elements was to become part of the pattern of *US*.

But there was still one major problem that we had scarcely touched. How were we to say anything about a peasant culture when none of us knew anything about peasants? Were we simply to ask the actors to imitate Vietnamese peasants rather badly? And was not this pointing once again to the basic truth that our real material was *these* actors confronting *that* audience in the Aldwych Theatre – and that our language would have to be based primarily on this existential fact?

July 20

In an attempt to approach the problem of depicting the Vietnamese, the actors had already done a little work on a Vietnamese legend – the Story of the Mosquito, about a hard-working farmer whose lazy wife is seduced by a rich man and then turned into a mosquito. The actors had tried to present the story in simple mime, but the result was both clumsy and coy.

A Chinaman, Chaing Lui, who had had some experience of Chinese theatre, was invited to come and watch the actors tell the story.

He began by correcting some basic errors. This, he said, is how the wife would cook rice, this is how she would sweep the hut, this is how the husband would say goodbye. He showed the actor playing the husband how to climb a mountain, how to depict the sunset. He showed the wife how to walk and bow.

For the actors, this was a most alarming experience. In the first place, Chaing Lui was fat and round and big, yet he danced lightly and gracefully every time he moved. He seemed to be able to leap gently into the air, and almost float from one step to the next. The much less heavily built actors moved gawkily beside him.

Even more disturbing for them was the precision he demanded and the way he obtained it. The actors had been working through free improvisation, searching for gestures inside themselves. Chaing Lui came and put their hands and feet into the correct position.

Some of the actors complained that the method was restrictive. But in the afternoon, when they tried to repeat the exercise for other actors who had not been there, they found themselves unable to communicate. There had been too many gaps in their basic observation.

Somewhat chastened by the experience, they all ended the afternoon by working at a basic Chinese exercise. They tried in pairs to imitate the scene from Chinese theatre in which two people travel on a sampan. The actors found this extremely difficult. It was interesting that they approached the problem by trying to pretend that they were on a sampan, and by working out logically what happened to the boat. I felt that a group of students tackling the same problem would have started from a rhythmic dance and worked in the opposite direction. For actors used to working inside a naturalist framework, even a Chinese exercise was seen, instinctively, as a 'realistic' problem.

July 21

If we were to find a language to communicate to other people, we must first be able to look honestly at ourselves. Throughout rehearsals, this proved to be very difficult. We all of us – the actors included – had a number of easy responses to the material we were studying. How to get through these responses until we were confronted with what we *really* experienced?

July 25

Brook talked again to the actors, summing up the work of the previous three weeks. He pointed out that every fragment was self-contained and that the putting together would come later. At the moment, they must apply themselves seriously to each separate piece of work. Such a method would go on for several weeks before they began to see anything taking shape.

The actors must be aware that they were trying to create a new language of acting, by collecting bits and pieces from everywhere. The actor must dig inside himself for responses, but at the same time must be open to outside stimuli. Acting was the marriage of these two processes . . .

What had been achieved in these first four weeks? The rudiments of an acting style had been created – the actors were now able to move much more flexibly from one mood to another. A language of theatre, based on a bringing together of many different elements, was being tentatively formed. And most of the material that was to go into the first act had been thrown up in rehearsal at one time or another.

What was still lacking was a sense of disciplined control by the actors, either physical or emotional. What was needed, after all the exploration of different styles, was a tight concentration on one particular area.

This was what we were hoping for from Grotowski when this first period of rehearsal came to an end. The work he was going to do with the actors would inevitably determine the way the material we already had would be shaped and organized.

The actors were ready for the next step in the process of searching.

US: Narrative Two by Michael Kustow

Michael Kustow's account continues from Albert Hunt: impressions from the final two and a half months of US *rehearsals, from Grotowski's workshop to first night.*

Monday 1 August

At this point in rehearsal, having conducted a first foray into the company's knowledge and images of America, Vietnam and Asia, Brook decided to shift the focus inwards for ten days. Jerzy Grotowski, director of the Polish Teatr Laboratorium at Wroclaw, had been invited to work with our actors, putting them through an intensive course of the exercises and training with which his own actors have reached great physical and spiritual skill. Grotowski arrived with Ryszard Cieslak, one of his leading actors. We were all very intrigued by what Grotowski would do. Some of us had seen his explosive and blasphemous production of Marlowe's *Doctor Faustus*, and had witnessed the taxing exercise and stern, almost monastic discipline of his 'theatre-laboratory' in Poland. All of us recognized a remarkable authority in this pale-faced man, dressed in black, habitually wearing dark glasses.

What followed in the next ten days is difficult to describe, because it took place on such a private, naked level, because it was in every sense a workshop, a consulting-room, a confessional, a temple, a refuge, a place of reflection, but reflection conducted not only with the mind, but with every fibre and muscle of the body.

Brook wrote an article for the Royal Shakespeare Club newspaper, *Flourish*, which summed up Grotowski's impact on all of us at this stage:

> Grotowski is unique.
> Why?
> Because no one else in the world, to my knowledge, no one since Stanislavski, has investigated the nature of acting, its phenomenon, its meaning, the nature and science of its mental-physical-emotional processes as deeply and completely as Grotowski.
>
> He calls his theatre a laboratory. It is. It is a centre of research. It is perhaps the only avant-garde theatre whose poverty is not a drawback, where shortage of money is not an excuse for inadequate means which automatically undermine the experiments. In

Grotowski's theatre as in all true laboratories the experiments are scientifically valid because the essential conditions are observed. In his theatre, there is absolute concentration by a small group, and unlimited time. So if you are interested in his findings you must go to a small town in Poland.

Or else do what he did. Bring Grotowski here.

He worked for two weeks with our group. I won't describe the work. Why not? First of all, such work is only free if it is in confidence, and confidence depends on its confidences not being disclosed. Secondly, the work is essentially non-verbal. To verbalize is to complicate and even to destroy exercises that are clear and simple when indicated by a gesture and when executed by the mind and body as one.

What did the work *do*?
It gave each actor a series of shocks.

The shock of confronting himself in the face of simple irrefutable challenges.
The shock of catching sight of his own evasions, tricks and clichés.
The shock of sensing something of his own vast and untapped resources.
The shock of being forced to question why he is an actor at all.
The shock of being forced to recognize that such questions do exist and that – despite a long English tradition of avoiding seriousness in theatrical art – the time comes when they must be faced. And of finding that he wants to face them.

The shock of seeing that somewhere in the world acting is an art of absolute dedication, monastic and total. That Artaud's now hackneyed phrase 'cruel to myself' is genuinely a complete way of life – somewhere – for less than a dozen people.
With a proviso. This dedication to acting does not make acting an end in itself. On the contrary. For Grotowski acting is a vehicle. How can I put it? The theatre is not an escape, a refuge. A way of life is a way to life. Does that sound like a religious slogan? It should do. And that's about all there was to it. No more, no less. Results? Unlikely. Are our actors better? Are they better men? Not in that way, as far as I can see, not as far as anyone has claimed. (And of course they were not all ecstatic about their experience. Some were bored.)

But as Arden says: For the apple holds a seed will grow,
                      In live and lengthy joy
                      To raise a flourishing tree of fruit,
                      For ever and a day.

Grotowski's work and ours have parallels and points of contact. Through these, through sympathy, through respect, we came together.

But the life of our theatre is in every way different from his. He runs a laboratory. He needs an audience occasionally. In small numbers. His tradition is Catholic – or anti-Catholic; in this case the two extremes meet. He is creating a form of service. We work in another country, another language, another tradition. Our aim is not a new Mass, but a new Elizabethan relationship – linking the private and the public, the intimate and the crowded, the secret and the open, the vulgar and the magical. For this we need both a crowd on stage and a crowd watching – and within that crowded stage individuals offering their intimate truths to individuals within that crowded audience, sharing a collective experience with them.

We have come quite a way in developing an overall pattern – the idea of a group, of an ensemble.

But our work is always too hurried, always too rough for the development of the collection of individuals out of whom it is composed.

We know in theory that every actor must put his art into question daily – like pianists, dancers, painters – and that if he doesn't he will almost certainly get stuck, develop clichés, and eventually decline. We recognize this and yet can do so little about it that we endlessly chase after new blood, youthful vitality – except for certain of the most gifted exceptions, who of course get all the best chances, absorb most of the available time. The Stratford Studio was a recognition of this problem, but it continually ran up against the strain of a repertory, of an overworked company, of simple fatigue.

Monday 15 August

Over the weekend, Brook, Hunt and Reeves have gone through all the material we have explored, and decided (certainly influenced by the fiery commitment which Grotowski had succeeded in drawing from our actors) that BURNING, the act of burning oneself, could become the central image of the play's action. They discussed ways of working outwards from this naked act, bringing in history, politics, communications, all the other facets of the war. On Monday, Brook spoke to the company. 'We are now entering the third stage of our work. In the first, you opened up as many fields as you could, ranged as widely through our knowledge and ignorance and images as you could. With Grotowski, you explored deeply and intensely a very focused, tight, personal area of commitment, your own bodily commitment as actors. Now in the third stage, we shall broaden our scope again. But the intense personal exploration will continue – I don't want anyone to feel that the last ten days' work with Grotowski have been a summer school, a refresher course having no direct contact with our subject. No, this personal search – and I know many of you have found it painful – will continue. So once more I say that if anyone wants to pull out now, they can do so.' Nobody did . . .

Tuesday 30 August

In the tiny back room at the Donmar Rehearsal Theatre were: Brook, Hunt, Reeves, Mitchell, Kustow, Cannan and Mark Jones. A very delicate exercise was about to take place, based on the situation of Cannan's proposed final scene. 'You are in Grosvenor Square,' said Brook to Mark Jones, 'with your petrol-can and your matches. You have come to burn yourself.' Mark started to make preparations. Along came Cannan, working off a clipboard of questions. He stopped Mark in midstream, and probed the reasons for his action; the effect he hoped it would have, what he thought of other people and their capacity for change. It was a sustained, John-Whiting-like assault on man's (and Mark's) presumption, using harsh anecdotes and Socratic dialectic to try to undermine Mark's resolution. But it didn't connect with the pitch of utter decision which Mark had achieved, the dogged, almost animal-like honesty with which he held to his choice. Against this impervious sincerity, even the sharpest flints of Cannan's arguments could not pierce.

Mitchell then tried to sway Mark. 'Can't you see that it's self-sacrifice? Have you really tried every other possible route?'

Hunt read Mark a list of the many people who had committed suicide by fire in Britain over the past two years, for reasons that were pathetic, foolish, mad, or just plain inexplicable. Mark's reaction was that however others cared to interpret it, he knew his motives, and in that sense at least was untroubled.

Brook sat down on the floor with Mark. Very close to him. 'Look me in the eyes. What is cruelty? Unlimited exercise of power over others. Do you have power over other people? Do you have power over yourself? Aren't you being cruel to your own flesh by setting it on fire? Aren't you alive? What is you? There is something called life and it's there in you. Have you the right to destroy it? What you want to do to yourself is what the world is doing to itself. You want life for the world, why don't you allow yourself to live? If you stop now, one less act of cruelty has taken place. It takes more courage to face the situation than to burn yourself. It takes the same kind of courage for the super-powers involved in this war to back down from their prepared positions.'

Mark put his head in his hands. There was silence for five minutes. The exercise had lasted nearly two hours. We all sat still. I was very aware of the different kind of contact Brook had made with the actor compared with the others. Brook's questioning had been much more physical, much closer to a confessional.

We tried to discuss the results of this exercise afterwards. Hunt feared the sense of a soothing catharsis which such an intense trial-by-fire-and-argument would generate. Brook said the silence at the end must be 'an open mouth, not a shut eye'. 'Commitment is a changing relationship, like a love affair; not a deal, like a bad marriage. And let's not overestimate the potential effect of the show. An analyst has one person on the couch for maybe twelve years: we have a thousand people on the equivalent of Waterloo Station for three hours. We must work like acupuncture: find the precise spot on the tensed muscle that will cause it to relax. If we succeed, we won't end the war or anything drastic like that, but one person out of our thousand might act differently because of what they experienced in the theatre that night.'

Wednesday 31 August

Into Donmar back room with five actors: Mark Jones, Michael Williams, Robert Lloyd, Glenda Jackson, Clifford Rose. Another very difficult and taxing exercise, relating to the problem of how to act self-burning.

BROOK: 'I want you to start by searching deeply for the idea of being dead. It's nothing to do with imagination or the idea of having been; just try and get as close as you can to the problem of being nothing, now.

'Next; you're no longer dead, you're alive. Listen deeply to what, in the quietest sense, is the feeling of being alive. What is the smallest difference between that nothingness, that emptiness, and being alive. Listen to it.

'Now you have just one possibility: you may place beside you one person, one person who is breathing with you, the person who is closest to you. So you are now in a coma, but alive and aware that you are alive, with one person very close to you. That's all. There are no other elements available to you.

'Now you have a possibility of choice: you may have one of your faculties – speech, sight, touch, movement, sex, taste. But you can only have one. Listen deeply to the life in you. Move towards the person you need most. Let that one chosen faculty flower. Test your choice – is it satisfying? Can you find complete life in that one choice? Is this better than death? Is this a possible existence? Explore with the person beside you.

'Now you have another possibility: you may only bring to life one point of your body – your head or hands, or fingertips, or arms or legs or genitals. Bring life to this point. Make it quite precise; which fingertip? Reach for the other person with this chosen point. Centre yourself on this point, move around it, caress it.

'Now a new possibility: you can live with your whole body – but only in a small closed room. Seek the things and people you need to live. What is the *least* you need to live? How many things? How many people? Throw out anything or anyone not strictly necessary. Check every object minutely. You may have to live with them for a long time.

'Now come out of the room into the outside world. As you put your hand on the doorhandle, decide on the one thing in the outside world that makes you want to go out – an experience, a light, a sound, a colour, people.'

The actors moved around the room, one leaping, one playing with levers on the wall, one swinging hips, one quietly wandering. The exercise lasted ninety minutes.

After a break, Brook set up five benches, and did the entire exercise in reverse. We called it privately 'walking the plank'. Each actor had to take six steps which would lead him to the end of the bench and off. But each step could only be taken after the actor had:

discarded the world and why it mattered
discarded the closed room with precious possessions
discarded the one living point of the body
discarded the one living faculty

discarded the one needed person
discarded the feel of being just alive, accepted death.

Each time the actor made one of these choices, he was to perform the action of stripping off a layer of skin. Most of the actors got to step four, Bob Lloyd got to step five, and stuck. Mark Jones had the greatest difficulty in making any of the steps, got to four, stuck, and then moved off the bench.

For the members of the team in the room it was also a pretty shaking experience. After a break, Brook talked to actors about the particular kinds of burning they were being asked to portray through their allotted character – an aged Buddhist monk, a young Buddhist nun, Norman Morrison, a desperate American avant-gardist, a young Englishman. He then asked them to do homework – to try and find a line through the many facets of the war we were presenting, a line that would concern their final decision to burn. In other words, to look back through all the material we had been assembling, and work out their attitude to each segment of the kaleidoscope . . .

Tuesday 4 October

Continuing the painstaking run-through on stage of the entire show, we reached the end of Act Two. Peter had asked the actors at the end of the run to come downstage, sit on the floor, and try to encapsulate their attitude to the war, and to taking part in this production, in as succinct a form as possible.

This would be the third time over the fifteen-week period of rehearsal that the actors had been asked to express their personal attitudes. The progression with each new statement – or attempt at a statement – had been gradually away from glibness, involving a greater and greater effort to assert.

There follows a summary of what the company said that morning, sitting clenched and concentrated on the Aldwych stage, breaking into speech after periods of heavy silence. Intrinsically, these statements may not seem startlingly original or acute, but the committed effort which each statement cost, the pressure of each individual to relate everything he had done throughout this long rehearsal period to himself as he felt at that moment, was what made the exercise impressive:

1. My mind is a dark cave. There's something red and horrific in it.
2. It's been worthwhile being outraged and informed by the show because through my increased knowledge, the war's become almost more enjoyable.

3. I feel confused and helpless but happier.
4. I am much more concerned about the possible escalation and its effect on me than I am about the Vietnamese people.
5. (One of the actresses was almost crying.)
6. I believe that man is a predatory species. No glib pros and cons will ever change that. This show only scratches the surface of what we are.
7. There's nothing safe and short I can say.

Later, when Peter told the company about the burning-butterfly ending, he asked them to perform this same self-questioning each night – 'What do you feel about the war and this show tonight, at this moment, after this particular twenty-four hours?' It is remarkable that most of the reviewers and many members of the audience, spoke of the actors' 'accusing stare' at the end of the show – when all they were doing was communing with themselves. A case of the guilty eye seeing judges everywhere? For the time being, Brook thanked the company for making a great effort – those who didn't speak as much as those who did.

Tuesday 11 October

Run-through of Act One. Because we were late starting, the actors were asked to keep their own rehearsal clothes instead of wearing costumes. Seeing them from out front, both Peter Brook and Sally Jacobs felt the reality of these fifteen-week-familiar clothes, and thus, forty-eight hours before the opening, we cut all the costumes from the show.

Friday 14 October

Company meeting in the Aldwych the day after the first night.

PETER BROOK to the actors: 'The experiment we have been making since the start is, what is the relationship between theatre and everyday life? Grotowski offered one answer: he wanted to make it a complete and full-time way of life. And he does, in his small Polish provincial town, in that Communist/Catholic country, he can make it monastic. But here we are in London, with all the difference that implies. I myself am not prepared to give fifteen hours a day for the next ten years living with all of you. [Laughter.] I am not prepared to surrender all the outside world. So what are our possibilities?

'The last few years have thrown up possibilities for young actors to make their name very fast. This is as it should be, but it has a negative side: they can easily mark time, and after two or three years doing the same kind of work, what was originally hailed as exciting gets stuck in a rut where it either stays in the same place or goes downhill. Only a handful of actors have the God-given freedom and drive to continue to open up and question. That's the self-renewing life you see in someone like Scofield.

'Now playing this show night after night on the stage poses the same question to everyone – and it is a question of inner burning. Each of you can cheat or not cheat. No one can tell whether you are going to be completely absent or present on stage. But if first one and then another of you start to shut off, the end result will be the total loss of the quality of the group's work. The seeds of destruction are already there.'

ACTOR: 'Why?'

BROOK: 'Because the whole thing is a process, and a process can always go two ways, go into reverse. Acting depends on bringing something all the time, otherwise it can turn in on itself and crumble. No amount of goodwill can keep it fresh – the only way is by bringing something constantly to it. This is the true question: whether you are interested enough to take the experiment further. In which case you will reopen daily the relationship between your work on stage and your daily life. Trying things out constantly.

'Have we compromised what we learned from Grotowski by playing in a large theatre and in the style we have found? I think not, if we keep it growing. His work is deep but narrow: our work here in London is more fragmented but possibly richer. What I am offering you is a technique. It may not interest you. But if it does it seems to me the only way of continuing. It seems a pity to settle for a casual relationship with what you are playing.

'How can you keep the life going? It is inevitable theatre-myth that the second night – tonight – is always a let-down from the first. But need it be so? Certainly, wishing it otherwise won't alter anything. Remember, when we had the critical arguments about the end of the play? Asking for something to redress the balance at the close, we implied disappoint-ment at lack of a solution, at our failure to change the world. We imagined that we were falling short of something positive. But that something was there all the time. It is in the life, the degree of burning, you bring to the performance. People leaving at the end weren't crushed. All of you, sitting round Glenda, aren't crushed by the experience of going through all this. This is the point of the end: you sit there collectively taking the opposite attitude from either not caring or not worrying. This very quality puts Glenda's corrosiveness into perspective.'

US: Extracts from the published text

From Act I

VIETNAM *is stretched between four actors, who paint him one colour above the waist, another below the waist.*

MARJIE: The Geneva Conference. At the Geneva Conference, the French and the Viet Minh agreed on a provisional demarcation line at the 17th Parallel. Elections were to be held within two years.

VIETNAM *is grabbed at one end by* PADDY, *at the other by* LEON. *The actor-audience is starting to divide into two separate groups, while the girls divide into two teams.*

MARJIE: ⎫ In the North, the Democratic Republic of Vietnam, led by
GLENDA: ⎭ Ho Chi Minh!

URSULA: ⎫ In the South, the Independent State of Vietnam, under the
PAULINE: ⎭ Premiership of Ngo Dinh Diem!

VIETNAM *writhes, while* JOHN *holds up a yellow flag described in the next speech.*

URSULA: Regrouping. In accordance with the Geneva Agreements, nearly a million refugees, most of them Catholics, headed south, carrying with them a yellow and gold flag displaying the Pope's tiara and the keys of St Peter's.

PADDY *and* MARJIE *strike poses of fond farewells, while* LEON *prepares to grab* MARJIE, *and* VIETNAM *writhes. By now the actor-audience is cheering and booing the rival statements made.*

GLENDA: Marriages. In accordance with the Geneva Agreements, 90,000 Viet Minh Freedom Fighters left for the North. Thousands married before they left, believing that they would be separated from their wives for at the most two years.

VIETNAM *writhes on the truck while the two teams of girls shout at each other.*

PAULINE: Land Reform in the North! Most of the landlords were executed, and the land given to the peasants. Unfortunately, many grave errors were committed, and many peasants were wrongly classified as landlords. It is estimated that between twelve and fifteen thousand innocent people were killed!

MARJIE: Democracy in the South! Mayor Wagner of New York described Ngo Dinh Diem as one of the great statesmen of the twentieth century, and his government as a 'political miracle'. It is estimated that under Diem four hundred thousand people were tortured and one hundred and fifty thousand killed!

The actors start to spread and flick paint on VIETNAM.

URSULA: Infiltration. Urged on by the aggressors in Hanoi, and in contravention of the Geneva Agreements, many subversive elements infiltrated from the North into the independent state of Vietnam. To counter this, the United States sent military advisers to the South.

The actors are rolling VIETNAM *up in a white paper from the floor of the truck. They tip him over the side, and he disappears.*

GLENDA: Resistance to American Aggression. The people of Vietnam did not lie down before the American aggressors. In 1964, sixty-five thousand troops supported by one hundred thousand irregular guerillas and ten thousand volunteers from the North, carried the resistance to the outskirts of Saigon itself!

During the next speech fighting almost breaks out. The words are drowned by shouting.

PAULINE: Defending the Free World! The United States Government did not lie down before the Communist aggressors. The rapid increase in US military strength from forty thousand in May 1965 to three hundred thousand today was a major factor in defeating the Viet Cong offensive.

The actors step forward with the paper that VIETNAM *was wrapped in . . . it is streaked with paint from his body . . . an 'action painting'. They rip it in half.*

....

The sequence of the torture school moving into the song, *Zappin' the Cong*, grew out of a number of elements. First, there was the work done on torture during the first weeks of rehearsal; second, a film showing an army school in the United States where young recruits are subjected to

Viet Cong tortures to prepare them for the real thing (one sequence showed a young soldier having his head bashed against a pillar, while someone poured tomato ketchup down his head to make him think he was bleeding); third, there was a long interview, printed in *Dissent* and *Peace News*, in which American psycho-war experts condemned physical torture for its effectiveness.

Brook wanted to explore, in theatre terms, the connection between physical and mental torture. He used again the technique of moving suddenly from one mood to its opposite: at the moment of the greatest physical violence, everything was suddenly frozen, and a group in the middle of the stage quietly quoted the interview. At the end of the discussion, the physical violence suddenly returned, and the sequence moved into the song.

A director like Joan Littlewood would probably have made her point in this scene by having her actors change hats. Brook relied above all on the ability of his actors, built up through weeks of work, to change gear very quickly, while retaining their own inner consistency.

The actors suddenly break back into the torture session, the torture groups start. BARRY, PADDY *and* MORGAN *grab* MIKE, *beat him, kick him, and put a dog chain round his neck to drag him round.*

PADDY: You VC? Charlie . . . you VC?

MORGAN: You Viet Cong, you VC? Are you VC? What are you?

BARRY: You're a worm.

MORGAN: You're a worm. What are you?

PADDY: You're a slopehead!

The music starts, and MIKE *starts hitting out and kicking at the three. He is in a frenzy, and the three encourage him.* MORGAN *sticks a microphone down his belt, which* MIKE *pulls out like a sixshooter. The sound of screaming fans comes over the loudspeakers. The other actors will join in the chorus, miming, shooting and bayoneting a small group of 'Viet Cong', forcing them progressively downstage, to the audience.*

SONG: ZAPPING THE CONG

MIKE: I'm really rocking the delta
         From coast to coast.
         Got em crawling for shelter
         Got em burning like toast.

And the President told me
That it wouldn't take long.
But I know I'm in heaven
When I'm zapping the cong.

EVERYONE: Zapping the cong
Back where they belong
Hide your yellow asses
When you hear my song
All over the jungle
Up to Haiphong,
I'm crapping jelly petrol
I been zapping the cong.

Between each verse MIKE *staggers away from the microphone, is rubbed down by* PADDY, MORGAN *and* BARRY, *and swoops back to the microphone for the next verse. He gives it the full pop treatment, and the three behind him form backing group of dancers and singers.*

EVERYONE: ZAPMAN!

Everyone settles down and reads coloured comic books, while IAN *roars and swells, into evil comic monster, grabs her and carries her off up the ladders in the garbage.* BOB *stands up, arms to the sky, announces he is* ZAPMAN, *and goes up the other side of the ladder, kills the monster with an invisible death ray, and* PAULINE *and he hug each other on top of the ladder. The others throw their comics away, cheering as* IAN *slides, dead, down the ladder.* GLENDA, URSULA *and* MARJIE *crouch over* MIKE, *lying exhausted on the floor. They sing into the microphone which is sticking up out of his belt.*

GIRLS: I had a dream about going,
With Ho Chi Minh.
But I'll only be crowing,
When I'm zapping Pekin.
Be spreading my jelly,
With a happy song.
Cos I'm screwing all Asia,
When I'm zapping the cong.

EVERYONE: Zapping the cong,
Back where they belong.
Hide your Yellow asses,
When you hear my song.
All over the jungle,

> Up to old Haiphong.
> Been crapping jelly petrol,
> I been zap, zap, zap, zap,
> Zee, Ay, Pee, Gee, Eye, Ar, Ell
> Is
> ZAPGIRL!

Everyone freezes. HENRY *interviews* HUGH.

HENRY: You said Mao isn't really what he thinks he is. Is that true of the other men who are in line to succeed him? Are they what they think they are? And do we know what they think they are or are they really something other than what they think they are?

HUGH: As a historian, I have a jaundiced view. I don't think we are what we think we are.

HENRY: As a historian you tell us.

HUGH: I think we are all acting in a long stream of history with historical ideological influences in our mind influencing us, whether or not we realize it. It is awfully difficult to be self-conscious completely and understand why you are doing what you do and why you tick the way you do and why you believe in what you believe. We have our own pattern and they have theirs. As a historian, of course, I am a pessimist about human nature.

HENRY: As a politician, I join you.

MIKE *whirls around with the microphone, and leads everyone in a last chorus.*

EVERYONE: Zapping the cong,
> Back where they belong.
> Hide your yellow asses,
> When you hear my song.
> All over the jungle,
> Up to old Haiphong.
> Been crapping jelly petrol,
> I been zap, zap, zap, zap . . .

There are 20 'zaps', ending in 'Zapping the Cong', and everyone freezes in mid-karate chop . . .

From Act II

GLENDA: We could live together and be poor and happy. We could paint the walls ourselves, and make furniture out of boxes . . . We could drink cheap wine, eat pasta, and read *The Brothers Karamazov*. We could make love three times in a night and buy a record player and find we both like Mahler. Until the mistake that is not quite a mistake makes me pregnant. We will talk about this at great length and read Simone de Beauvoir. We will marry in a Registry Office and send up the ceremony by going in jeans. We will say, we don't feel any different being married, let's pretend we're still living in sin. Quite forgetting that when we *were* living in sin we defiantly said we weren't. We will read paperbacks on child psychology and have the baby in a progressive way. You will take a job for which you have to apologise, and another baby will come and to avoid feeling merely bourgeois we will read the entire output of the Olympia Press and know people who take LSD. You will make more money and we will move to a house with a garden and buy a Mini and have serious conflicts about education. We will change over to stereo and get an au-pair. We will own five beds, twenty blankets, fifteen pairs of sheets, one automatic defrosting refrigerator, one electric mixer and pulveriser, one washing machine, one spin dryer, one vacuum cleaner, one Polaroid camera, two pairs of skis, fourteen assorted brushes, mops, buckets and brooms, five hundred and sixty boxes, pen trays, ash trays, ornaments, implements, toys, garments, labour-saving apparatuses and comic novelties, nine hundred books, forty square yards of Wilton carpet with foam underlay and seventy-two records, as new, scarcely played. We will decide we ought to go out more. We will dress up and go to the theatre – choosing, of course, some experimental controversial leftish sort of show. And as we leave the theatre, we will say, not exactly what we really feel, but the proper sensitive intelligent things that everyone else is saying. We will begin to talk always from books and films and plays, and never from ourselves. We will become afraid of words like 'good' and 'bad'; so when we're in doubt we will call the latest thing 'interesting' – to hide our uncertainty. We will be so easily embarrassed by any natural feeling that we will put it in inverted commas, or say it in a funny voice. And at our parties everyone else will be doing the same, so life will really be quite comfortable – apart from occasional exercises of conscience, over something like Rhodesia or Vietnam. You will die before me, because women live longer. The children will put me in a home or build me a bungalow. There's a nice English seaside town where so many old people live alone that philanthropists have issued them with whistles and little cards reading 'Help'. When they feel death coming, they are supposed to blow the whistle and put the card in the window . . .

So you end the war in Vietnam. Where's the next one? Thailand, Chile, Alabama? The things that will be needed are all ready in some carefully camouflaged quartermaster's store. The wire, the rope, the gas, the cardboard boxes they use for coffins in emergencies.

I WANT IT TO GET WORSE! I want it to come HERE! I want to see it in an English house, among the floral chintzes and the school blazers and the dog leads hanging in the hall. I would like us to be tested. I would like a fugitive to run to our doors and say hide me – and know if we hid him we might get shot and if we turned him away we would have to remember that for ever. I would like to know which of my nice well-meaning acquaintances would collaborate, which would betray, which would talk first under torture – and which would become a torturer. I would like to smell the running bowels of fear, over the English Sunday morning smell of gin and the roasting joint, and hyacinth. I would like to see an English dog playing on an English lawn with part of a burned hand. I would like to see a gas grenade go off at an English flower show, and nice English ladies crawling in each other's sick. And all this I would like to be photographed and filmed so that someone a long way off, safe in his chair, could watch us in our indignity! Everyone who doesn't care *what* goes on – so long as it's out of sight – wants it to go on; because if it's being done to someone else, they think it won't be done to them; and if someone else is doing it, that's better than doing it yourself. Every man whose spirit is dying, wants it to go on, because that sort of dying is better if everyone else dies with you. Everyone longing for the day of judgement – wants it to go on. Everyone who wants it to be changed, and can't change – wants it to go on. It doesn't matter that the world will be ash – if your life is ash, you'll want it to go on. And that is why it goes on. And why it will get worse. And why the catastrophe will come.

I want it. You want it. They want it. Like lust, it goes on because we want it. And as with lust, we suspect most of all those who shout loudest, 'No!'

She collapses. IAN *wakes up and shuffles across the stage.*

IAN: We may well be living in the time foretold many years ago, when it was said: 'I call Heaven and Earth to record this day against you, that I have set before you life and death, blessing and cursing; therefore choose life, that both thou and thy seed may live.'

He stops suddenly, staring out at the audience. BOB *enters, carrying a small table with a black box on it. He wears black gloves. He opens the lid of the box, and releases several white butterflies. They fly out into the auditorium, and over the actors. He reaches into the box and takes another one or two butterflies and throws them into the air. Then he pulls out a lighter from his pocket, lights it, takes out another butterfly and holds it in the flame. We cannot tell if it is real or false. As it stops burning he freezes, as do all the actors. The house lights have come up. The actors stay immobile until everyone has left the theatre.*

THE END

US: The Critical Reception

Although enthusiastically acclaimed by many critics, including Jean-Paul Sartre, *US* was heavily attacked by a number of others, including Brook's former collaborator Charles Marowitz, and Kenneth Tynan; their areas for concern were similar to those in *Marat/Sade*. In this treatment of the Vietnam crisis, Brook was accused of childish simplification, vulgarisation, sensationalism, shallow pessimism, emotional cliché, ideological incoherence. Others felt the play to be unfairly anti-American.[1] Clearly the writers were guilty of selective use of fact in their material; for example, any references to Viet Cong atrocities were omitted, considered irrelevant to this work's central concerns. Martin Esslin felt it should have been retitled 'The Persecution and Assassination of Uncle Sam and the English Liberal as performed by the inmates of the RSC under the direction of Peter Brook' (*New York Times*). He found it pretentious, sentimental and self-indulgent; not so much a 'theatre of fact' as a 'theatre of self-pitying fantasy'.

Perhaps an aesthetisation of reality is inevitable in the very nature of an undertaking combining the techniques of Brecht and Artaud, or The Living Theatre. Originally the group had felt that they were starting from 'a classic Berliner Ensemble blueprint' (Reeves in *Plays and Players*, 1968). The wording of Geoffrey Reeves's description of their intentions is significant:

> We outlined the problem to ourselves in the Berliner manner by saying: we are a group of people in a particular society, we exist *now*: the function of our theatre is to take serious issues which concern us and deal with them *in terms of our art*.

[1] Questions were asked in Parliament. On 3 November 1966, Sir Knox Cunningham (UUMP for South Antrim) demanded the withholding of the payment of the RSC subsidy from public funds; he described *US* as 'full of poisonous anti-American propaganda'. Miss Jennie Lee, Under-Secretary of State for Education and Science in Wilson's government, replied: 'It would be a very bad day for this country when the arts and the theatres began simply to reflect whatever happened to be the policy of the government, or, even, the prejudices of the honourable gentleman or myself'. (*The Times*, 4/11/1966)

An essential quality inherent in Brook's approach to all his work *as an artist* is his refusal to impose any single polemical viewpoint on a complex living situation; quite simply he believes that it can never be persuasive in the theatre. Rather than providing the desired and much needed affirmation, it merely rings hollow. Artistically, perhaps any conclusion means naïvety, fixity and death: 'When the theatre is healthy, it is never the expression of a single point of view'.

In this case, he considered all demands for a clearly black-and-white document from a specific political '*parti pris*' to be an idealistic simplification of the issues involved in this 'collision of dreams': 'In the twentieth century, you can't teach anyone anything in the form of a proclamation, a declaration. You can only ask people questions, and open your ears to their questions'.

For someone like Marowitz, Brook is irresponsibly anachronistic in the 'romantic liberalism' of his vision of the role of theatre.

In a critique of the film version of *US* (released as *Tell me Lies*), Boleslaw Sulik of *The Tribune* wrote of how Brook had shown the impotence of decency, pacifism and liberalism when confronted with something as important as the Vietnam situation. He concluded: 'Peter Brook goes no further, offers no solutions. Perhaps he doesn't believe in solutions.' Of course, in such a performance there could be no solutions. As with *Marat/Sade*, Brook's aim was rather to force the spectator to reassess his own position and its validity, and to re-examine his own possibilities of action: 'It is better to face honest bafflement than pseudo-clarity.'

D.W.

US: A Review by Charles Marowitz

Charles Marowitz finally fell out with Brook over US, *a production he disliked fiercely, for its ideological incoherence, and its sensationalist preoccupations with physical cruelty.*

The artistic failure of the Royal Shakespeare Company's Vietnam documentary *US* has been largely obscured by the controversies it has wittingly and unwittingly aroused. In London, at the present time, it is possible to convert almost any lukewarm entertainment into a box-office success by stirring it in the press. In the case of *US*, one had a subject which was already incendiary, and so it was relatively simple to work up the requisite hoopla. This is unfortunate whenever it happens, because it gives an audience the added difficulty of having to disentangle legitimate intentions and actual results from distortions perpetrated by the mass media. But in this case, Peter Brook's production, devised collectively by the Company, is no innocent victim of circumstances. It seemed predisposed to vulgarization; almost intended for tabloid exploitation. Sensationalism – that is, the desire to shock beyond a play's power to shock legitimately – was one of its ingredients.

Intended to goad and disturb, to prod the conscience and pique awareness, the production actually comforts the bourgeois public by restating what it already knows and feels but succeeds in outraging the more discerning and critical. It has won the groundlings and lost the intellectuals, which wouldn't be all that sad if it weren't originally intended for the intellectuals. The Bourgeois Public (BP), confused by the welter of information and misinformation spawned by the Vietnam war, derive comfort from the fact that even Royal Shakespeare intellectuals are as helpless and confused as themselves. Of course it's all terrible, says the BP, I always felt that, and these nice, committed actors think the same.

I have always contended, says the BP, that the situation in Vietnam was highly complicated and practically insoluble, and now these nice, Royal Shakespeare intellectuals have come to the same conclusions. How comforting to find that all great minds do move in the same channels. The 'other' audience who walked into the Aldwych in exactly the same emotional state but equipped with more background and already disturbed beyond the powers of theatrical provocation, were appalled to find muddled thinking and emotional cliché joining to deliver a limp rabbit-punch. The implicit assumption behind *US* is that we, the audience, neither know the situation nor feel strongly enough about it, and it is this basic misconception that has utterly destroyed its effect. The act of artists underestimating the capacities of their audience has glaringly revealed their own incapacity.

The real test of any play about Vietnam must be an ideological one. Before we ask how well it is done, we have to concern ourselves with where it stands and what it sets out to say; and ideologically speaking, *US* cancels itself out. It says – in word and effect – that Vietnam is a nightmare of contradictions; we can never disentangle all its threads. It goes on to say – illogically – that we must come to terms with its complications because the responsibility is ours, and in a contemporary power-struggle there is no such thing as a non-combatant. If the *double entendre* of the title means anything, it means the Vietnam war, which is to say organized and accidental mass-murder, systematic torture, brazen deceit and chronic duplicity, is *us* rebounds on *us* is answerable to *us*. In short, the play tells us nothing that is not already being said day in and day out on news broadcasts, in films, TV and the press. It does not presume to press home a personal viewpoint, although even the fairest assemblage of facts cannot help but indict American Far East policy. It thunders its righteous indignation but never wells up into a genuine protest because it takes refuge in the very disorder and contradiction it has been made to indict.

The evening is a long one. The first act lasts two hours and, when I saw it, was crammed with sloppy, demonstrational acting and familiar extracts from Vietnam folklore, ancient and modern. The poverty of imagination and gaucheness of execution in the play's first two hours are staggering when one considers: 1, the director is Peter Brook; 2, rehearsals were in progress for over four months; 3, the company had the services of Jerzy Grotowski from Poland and Joseph Chaikin from New York.

Like *Marat/Sade*, units of the play open and close like a series of fluttering umbrellas, but unlike *Marat/Sade*, there is no style or thrust to any of these sections. In the early stages of the run, the first act ended with actors, their heads wrapped in supermarket bags, grunting and groaning in some kind of torturous symbol of the maimed and wounded, stumbling into the audience and flailing their arms for assistance. As one cynic remarked: why should I come to the aid of perfectly able members of the Royal Shakespeare Company? This mishap of a 'happening' has already been excised from the script, but it is a grim indication of the sort of thinking that has gone into the show.

The second act improves in one sense, because it stops trying so hard, but deteriorates in another, because the argument dwindles into a kind of romantic liberalism. Finally, accepting the fact that it is not a revolutionary happening but a rather old-fashioned Living Newspaper, it proceeds to concentrate on the spoken word, and on depicting social attitudes to the war. (The entire production is wedged into the framework of one of Adrian Mitchell's better poems about Vietnam, and, to its credit, the production never sounds quite so natural and unstrained as when it stops circumlocuting imaginary theatrical heights, and returns to Mitchell's simple and direct verse-structure.) In the second act, Glenda Jackson (an oasis in the desert) gives a vivid rendition of the bourgeois argument against Vietnam sacrifice and then launches into a knobbly attack on those of us who derive obscene satisfaction from the fact that human desecration is taking place thousands of miles away and therefore beyond our emotional frame of reference. This leads to an imaginary reconstruction of what havoc Vietnam would wreak in a peaceful English society. This is the strongest writing to come out of the evening (author: Denis Canaan) – or is it only Glenda Jackson's acting that makes it seem so?

The production is preoccupied with cruelty – particularly the immolation of Buddhist monks and Quaker pacifists – but it is an aesthetic rather than a political preoccupation. One even suspects it of being kinky. For here, in the midst of the most unlikely material, we have yet another essay in Theatre of Cruelty; replete with Artaudian effigies and theatrical stylizations, and studded with dazzling little thefts from old happenings and contemporary destructivist exercises. The play ends with the burning of a live butterfly and then, to demonstrate its fierce Brechtian integrity, the full cast sits on the stage refusing to finish so that the decision to leave the theatre belongs to each individual spectator.

Devices which could be theatrically stunning appear gimmicky and unconvincing because they do not reinforce any developing, ideological point. What should have been the evening's *coups-de-théâtre* become self-conscious, chosen 'moments'.

In an evening devoted to contradictions and ironies, the crowning irony is that the play winds up proclaiming the situation futile, and the need to do something about it overwhelming. However, the task of dramatizing, as opposed to merely positing, information, has not even been tackled – let alone solved. Despite innumerable theatrical swipes, the evening is theatrically limp and relies heavily on a dramatic predisposition on the part of the audience; i.e., a preoccupation with the

Vietnam conflict. Instead of elucidating the issues and arriving at a viewpoint, it merely dumps the whole kaboodle of conflicting evidence into the audience's lap and demands they sort out what the show's planners have not managed to think out.

With a show like *US*, one's state on leaving the theatre is almost more important than the time spent at the performance. Leaving the Aldwych, I felt leaden and put-upon; a victim of an aggressively More-Committed-Than-Thou approach to life. The futility of the Vietnam crisis seemed even more intense (if that is possible) than when I entered the theatre. I was angered and irritated by this show and have said so publicly and privately, but the underground swell against this production is so great that one begins to shift position to redress a balance. On hearing even fiercer put-downs than my own, I would counter with: but isn't it better to do something about Vietnam than nothing at all, and although I push that viewpoint in private conversations, I no longer believe it; I feel now that if one has no overriding conviction to express on the Vietnam war other than it is horrible and insoluble, it is better to say nothing; that to reiterate clichés of commitment only subverts the efforts of constructive arguments.

Throbbing behind the entire controversy (and at this writing – November, 1966 – there is one in London) is the realization that we are not disputing aesthetic theories but a theme for which *real* American soldiers, and *real* Vietnamese people are *really* dying. The fact of *really dying* while one stages a theatrical performance on the subject, enforces a mammoth responsibility. If this play were about the Korean War or the war in Indo-China, it would somehow be easier to cope with, but being about *the* war of our time, a war whose moral and political implications are greater than even the Spanish Civil War's, one absolutely demands lucid thinking, unimpeachable integrity, and the removal of all the arty-farty tactics associated with conventional theatre. The RSC's production goes no further than bristling sincerity. It isn't enough. We all know that the worst acts in the world are produced by sincere people. In a project of such dimensions, intellectual perception and artistic persuasion count far more than sincerity, and there isn't enough of either.

I had come to the theatre – as so many people will come – out of a hunger to do something, see something, say something which cuts a path out of the chaos. One doesn't need a theatrical performance to explain that we are at an impasse. The role of the theatre in times like today is to elucidate and give a positive lead. A conventional play may end up in a state of fascinating ambiguity, but a social document dealing with a red-hot contemporary crisis cannot take refuge in artistic ambiguities, or else it becomes only another cinder in the eye.

A century ago, the theatre's task, according to Chekhov, was to ask questions. This has been superseded by a world situation in which, if the theatre is to pull its weight, it must – at such times and on such themes – begin to supply answers.

Confessions of a Counterfeit Critic, Methuen, 1973

The Aldwych Liturgy: A Review by the Bishop of Woolwich

One of few reviews publicly deemed a valid response by Brook and Reeves, the following piece by the Bishop of Woolwich (from the Guardian*) compares* US *to church liturgy.*

In all the words that have been spilt over *US* at the Aldwych, I have noticed none that seem to me to have placed it in its real category. There is debate whether it should be classified as 'theatre of fact', a documentary, journalism, 'vicarious psycho-drama', or indeed as a play in any sense at all. Irving Wardle in *New Society*, correctly fastening on the statement 'only an act that is beyond words has any meaning', has recently concluded that it is music. I believe that it is liturgy.

The function of liturgy, as the Church has understood it, is to involve its participants in the saving acts of their redemption. It re-enacts. It overcomes the gulf between what happened 2,000 years ago and the believer's life and action in this world now. It is a remembrance of Christ's passion – not in the sense of reminding Christians of past events outside them, but of internalizing and making present those events in and through them. It breaks down the barriers of time and space so that they are 'there' with Him and He is here in them.

It is this liturgical function of annihilating distance by involvement that *US* is primarily concerned to accomplish. The very ambivalence of its title makes the point that the American action in Vietnam is not just something going on the other side of the world, on some green hill, or rice paddy, far away. What is presented is not in any strict sense 'theatre', a spectacle of a world with no continuous relation to real life into which we can be taken 'out of ourselves' for two and a half hours.

Like liturgy, but unlike a play, it has no author. As the programme notes insist, it is a corporate presentation, a con-celebration, in which the whole company, director, designer, script writers, effects men and song writers, have a shared responsibility. And the audience are equally implicated in the action. There is nothing separating stage from stalls, sanctuary from congregation. Uniting the two, above the proscenium is suspended, in the place of the rood, a monstrous, obscene figure, which we eventually make out to be a dead man – a US soldier.

Then when the action starts we are exposed in bewildering succession to all the elements and arts of liturgy. It begins with an anamnesis of

Vietnamese history, a representation of it, partly by recitation, partly by re-enactment, in which the central figure is a half-naked man representing his people in their sufferings, torn apart, daubed and despised of men. There follows a kaleidoscopic succession of readings, songs, refrains, antiphons, dialogue, preaching, confession, intercession, ritual movements, and recurring symbolic actions and images, particularly of fire and burning.

Above all, everything is done to insist that this is not just, as liturgy so often becomes, play-acting in a separated time and separated space. The rood doesn't stay there impassively to be looked at. It descends threateningly to engulf both actors and audience. The son of man is among them – is them. The players mingle gropingly and disconcertingly with those sitting comfortably in their stalls, and at the end, instead of the actors walking out on the audience to hand-clapping applause, they remain motionless on the stage till the last of the spectators have slunk away.

The reiterated theme is of a reality too painful to be evaded and too profound to admit of any verbal or rational solution. It can be resolved only in action which is itself suffering, and in suffering which is itself action.

The whole thing reminded me more than anything else of Holy Week liturgy. It is not specifically Christian: far from it. It spoke of confession, but not of absolution, of fraction but not of communion. It judged, but it did not pretend to save.

Nevertheless it was a renewal of dedication as the caring community of an intensity that condemns what so often passes for liturgy in our churches. This was a 'liturgy for Vietnam' in the sense that the Church's much-praised 'liturgy for Africa' (with nothing distinctively African about it at all) never begins to be.

I attended it after sitting through two days of Convocation arguing (oh so Christianly) whether we should say 'we offer this bread and this cup' or 'we give thanks over this bread and this cup.' In the end we compromised by permitting either. I cannot dismiss the need to start liturgical revision from this end. But when is the Church going to commission someone like Peter Brook to show us what it might look like begun from an entirely different end altogether – from the secular crucifixion of our time, in which, as Bonhoeffer said, 'Christians stand by God in His hour of grieving'?

Guardian, November, 1966

II

Towards Celebration and Internationalism, 1968–1970

Oedipus National Theatre Company, 1968

The Tempest Théâtre des Nations, 1968

A Midsummer Night's Dream RSC, 1970

'When I hear of a director speaking glibly of serving the author, of letting a play speak for itself, my suspicions are aroused, because this is the hardest job of all. If you just let a play speak, it may not make a sound. If what you wish is for the play to be heard, you must conjure its sound from it.'

(*The Empty Space*)

Oedipus

'The contemporary event touches raw nerves, but creates an immediate refusal to listen. The myth or the formally shaped work has power, yet is insulated in exact proportion. So which in fact is more likely to be useful to the spectator? I want to find the answer.'

(Brook in *US*, 11, 1968)

Brook has long been fascinated by the challenge of presenting ancient tragic themes on the modern stage. In 1965, he had commissioned the American poet Robert Lowell to translate Aeschylus' *Prometheus Bound*, a myth later to be treated in *Orghast*. In 1968, when approached by the National Theatre for a production of Seneca's *Oedipus*, he was furnished with the possibility of attempting to directly affect a secular twentieth-century audience through myth and ritual. With no coherent communal religious beliefs binding modern society, would these ancient themes be devoid of innate value? Was it possible to create what Grotowski called a 'secular sacrum' through the presentation of collective archetypes, if these could be found? What was the relationship between such mythical archetypes and the realities of the modern world? Brook wanted somehow to overcome the modern rationalist spectator's instinctive self-preservation when confronted with timeless and subliminally disturbing themes. Could he strip away the insulation imposed by time and culture to release a powerful and immediate life?

He felt that the text he had been given by the National Theatre, a translation by the BBC radio producer David Anthony Turner, needed to be honed and somewhat revivified. Therefore he asked the poet Ted Hughes to produce a version which would 'release whatever inner power this story, in its plainest, bluntest form, still has, and to unearth . . . the ritual possibilities within it' (Hughes's introduction to the published text of *Oedipus*). The result was a vividly direct poetic text charged with a physical barbarism and viciousness, and an almost unpalatable bestial imagery. Brook considered it to be 'miraculously powerful', and Turner, the original translator, acknowledged that this liberated version was far superior to his own: 'In place of good, serviceable prose, there was inspiration, fire, elegance, poetry. All was magic' (Turner's preface to *Oedipus*).

Clearly Hughes had succeeded in capturing in a fresh and modern fashion Artaud's vision of Seneca. Like so many of the Elizabethans, including Shakespeare, the French visionary had seen him as the greatest of all ancient tragedians. (In 1934, he had intended to produce his own adaptation of Seneca's *Atreus and Thyestes*, entitled *Le Supplice de Tantale*; the text has never been found.) The immediacy of the cosmic and mythical themes and the 'metaphysical cruelty' he had perceived in the very language of Seneca had led him to write in a letter to Jean Paulhan in 1932:

> One cannot find a better written example of what is meant by *cruelty* in the theatre than all the tragedies of Seneca . . . I cry when I read his inspired theatre . . . Under the words I feel the atrocious transparent boiling of forces of chaos . . . Primordial forces resonate into a spasmodic vibration of words. And the words that designate secrets and forces, designate them in a 'trajectory' of these forces, and with their power to tear apart and pulverise.

A strikingly similar view of the spirit of Senecan writing informed the very heart of Brook's production. Like Artaud, Hughes saw the work as an expression of elemental and primeval cruelty, a pre-moral world of instincts in which the protagonists are 'only Greek by convention; by nature, they are more primitive than Aboriginals. They are a spider people scuttling among hot stones. The radiant moral world of Sophocles is simply not present here' (Hughes's introduction to *Oedipus*).

The monstrous excess of the subject matter was lightly politicized, and made more contemporary through echoes in the text of parallel realities in Vietnam, particularly the slaughter of the recent battle of Hué and the Tet offensive: in addition, rehearsals took place during a national epidemic of foot and mouth disease, when hundreds of cattle had to be butchered and burnt. However, none of these references became specific. Speeches laden with images of carnage and extreme horror, like those in Weiss's *The Investigation*, were delivered as epic rhetoric in a dispassionate monotone. As will be seen in the accounts that follow, savagely ominous stasis and ceremony were offset by the use of complex choral material, largely devised during the ten-week re-hearsal period by Brook's associate director Geoffrey Reeves. The collective investigation of the vocal possibilities of the group as a unified entity, with its aim of maximizing tonal variety, came as a result of

Brook's encouragement to treat Hughes's text as a musical score or libretto, to warp and extend the words beyond the merely referential. Eventually they were fragmented into component sounds, further augmented by abstract vocal expressions of terror and horror unearthed in improvisation. Hieronymus Bosch's nightmarish visions of hell were used as a stimulus to innovatory, non-naturalistic excess in this 'exploration of the ugly'. Through a closely orchestrated web of sounds, rhythms and above all breathing, a sort of Artaudian 'tangible music' was sought. The production aimed to induce states of affective excitement in the spectators through sonic rather than physical explosions of movement.

The chorus was both onstage and scattered throughout the Old Vic auditorium, engulfing the audience in a swirling stereophonic vortex of physical sounds. (Artaud had suggested placing the public in the middle of the action, 'encircled and furrowed by it'.) Through repetition and overlay, phrases were echoed or counterpointed both with primitive percussive rhythms, hypnotic shamanic incantation and with Peaslee and Brook's angular electronic 'musique concrète'. Each line denying the existence of the gods was accompanied by a bitterly ironic and stylised rhythmic laugh from the chorus. The overall effect was that of a bizarre primitive opera, a *Rites of Spring* from prehistory: Ronald Pickup later described it as a 'barbaric mass'.

Although critical response to this aspect of the work was generally adulatory, Brook seems to have been guilty once again of removing theatrical representation from any lived experience of the audience. The series of effects that made up these invented rituals were so controlled and musically scored as to lack the human immediacy of their sources. Like *Orghast* three years later (the ultimate fruit of this area of research), for many it could only ever be a purely aesthetic experience.

There are clear affinities between this production's concerns and the work of other practitioners at this time, notably The Living Theatre, the Open Theatre and Jean-Louis Barrault. Indeed a number of critics felt that Brook had created an ingenious but flashy and sensationalist compendium of secondhand, hollow, avant-garde clichés for the consumption of a West End audience. However, the direction of experiment is consonant with work undertaken since the Theatre of Cruelty season: and it is worth noting that this group included Reeves, Hughes and Irene Worth, all of whom were later to travel with the C.I.R.T. to Persepolis for the Shiraz Festival (see *Orghast* below).

D.W.

Oedipus: An Extract from Ted Hughes's text

A Choral Ode from Act I

CHORUS: Thebes   you are finished
the countryside around is empty   the farmers all
dead   the workers all dead   their children all
dead   the plague owns everything

what's happened to your armies   Thebes   all
those brave men of yours   they've gone under the
plague   they're finished   they marched so
bravely away out   eastward   past the last frontiers
victory after victory   right away on to the world's
rim   leaned their banners against the sun's very
face   the conquerors   where are they?
everybody ran from them   the rich nations of the
rivers   the marksmen of the hills   the horsemen
everybody ran   towns empty   scattered   but
not any more Thebes   where are your armies now
Thebes   they're finished   the plague touched
them and they vanished   finished   rubbished into
earth

look at the streets   what are the crowds doing
black procession   they're going to the graves and the
fires   Thebes is a funeral   Thebes is choking
with corpses   why don't the crowds move   there
are too many corpses   graves can't be dug fast
enough   fire can't burn corpses fast enough   the
earth's glutted   death's glutted   and the piles of
corpses rot

the plague began with the sheep   it began with the
grass   the grass was suddenly poison   the air was
suddenly stench

a bull at the altar   massive animal   the priest had
hoisted his axe steadied his aim   in that second

before the axe fell   the bull was down   was it
touched by the god   it was touched by the plague

I saw a heifer slaughtered   her body was a sackful
of filthy tar   filthy bubbling tar

everywhere cattle are dead in the fields   dead in
their stalls   on silent farms there are bones in
cloaks   skulls on pillows   every ditch stinks
death   the heat stinks   the silence stinks

a horseman coming breakneck past us   but the
plague caught him up   it caught his horse   mid-
stride   head over heels   full tilt   down
the rider beneath it

everything green has withered   the hills that
were cool with forest   they're dusty ridges
deserts of brittle sticks   the vine's tendril is white
it crumbles when you touch it

Oedipus Complex: A Review by Martin Esslin

Martin Esslin in Plays and Players *reviewed a production which set out to recreate some unnamed and imagined primitive rite: but, Esslin asks, is ritual even possible in contemporary theatre?*

Why the *Oedipus* of Seneca and not the far greater, far more famous *Oedipus Rex* of Sophocles? Seneca's tragedies, admittedly, had a direct impact on Elizabethan drama; Shakespeare did not know Sophocles, he did know Seneca. But Seneca, whose plays were probably never performed in his lifetime, who wrote them as a scholarly exercise, is a far worse dramatist and an infinitely inferior poet. His construction is clumsy, his sensibility coarse, he indulges in frantically sadistic descriptions of bloodshed and torture . . . but this, precisely, is the reason why, in the age of pop art, the Happening, the so-called Theatre of Cruelty, Seneca should have come to seem more immediately relevant to an experimental producer like Peter Brook. (Jean-Louis Barrault has just done the *Medea* of Seneca at the Odéon – great minds think alike, and the spirit of the times is as active in Paris as it is in London.)

Brook's production of the *Oedipus* of Seneca is far more than a mere conventional play production. It is, in all senses of the word, a *Happening*, total theatre, an attempt to fuse Brecht and Artaud, an experimental production the importance of which transcends such trivial considerations as the immediate success of the first night, or the satisfaction of audiences.

The production is Brechtian in the sense that the acting is distanced – *verfremdet*. The cast list merely contains the names of all actors in alphabetical order: that is, none of the actors is *identified* with a character, although each of the protagonists only speaks the lines of one character (Gielgud – Oedipus; Irene Worth – Jocasta; Colin Blakely – Creon; Frank Wylie – Tiresias, etc.). But they do not wholly enact that character's actions: for example, while Ronald Pickup delivers his masterly rendering of the horrifying report of Oedipus' self-blinding in the character of the Messenger, Sir John Gielgud quietly sits on stage, his face averted, and listens to the speech. When it is over Frank Wylie, the blind Tiresias, hands him his dark glasses – symbols of blindness. Nor do the costumes suggest either the historical epoch of the action or the character's rank or appearance: the dress throughout is contemporary – dark slacks and dark brown pullovers for most men and women;

120

only Oedipus himself wears a kind of jacket over his pullover, and Jocasta a dark dress. The producer suggests that a company of actors has assembled for a *recital* of the play, on the lines of a concert performance of an opera, rather than an enactment of it.

Brook's production is a *Happening* in so far as he uses the whole of the auditorium in a most original manner: members of the chorus are among the audience, leaning, as the public enters, against the pillars of the stalls, dress circle and galleries, and emitting strange, inarticulate, ritualistic sounds, wails, hums, hisses; the audience is literally encircled by the chorus, trapped in the meshes of the tragedy, deeply involved in what is essentially a strange and frightening ceremonial of human sacrifice and shamanistic obsession. Peter Brook has derived the archetypal sounds of this ritual from a close study of recordings of the voices of shamans and priests of primitive tribes, but he has developed them on his own and blends them with wholly contemporary electronic *musique concrète*.

Antonin Artaud, the great obsessional genius to whom Peter Brook owes so much, believed in the magical power of these primeval sounds, the roar and wail and screeching of the gods and of priests possessed by gods and demons. But Brook is the first to have used this storehouse of primitive emotion in a successful production in the theatre.

The whole production thus becomes a primitive rite. There is no interval (how could there be an interval for a smoke and a drink inside a religious ceremony?) As the play opens an immense cube of gold revolves on the stage, the chorus produces the rhythmical drumming that precedes the trance of a voodoo session. The great epic descriptions of horrible sacrifice, terrible visits to the underworld and gory self-torture are delivered in tones of mounting obsession: Colin Blakely as Creon begins to whirl round like a spinning top, like a dancing dervish, as he tells of his encounter with the battered, bloodstained ghost of Laios; Louise Purnell, as Tiresias' daughter, writhes on the floor as she describes to her blind father the ghastly content of the slaughtered animal from which the soothsayer tries to learn the truth about Oedipus' crime.

And Irene Worth, as Jocasta, in the enactment of the mode of suicide Seneca has prescribed for her (she stabs herself through the womb; Sophocles' Jocasta merely hanged herself) performs the ultimate in ritual symbolism: she has to suggest that her suicide is an act of deadly intercourse with the sword on which she impales herself, a terrifying, but unforgettably archetypal, image. Here we are very near the rituals of human sacrifice of primitive cultures.

It is, on the whole, brilliantly done. The question remains: can the emotion engendered by ritual in societies deeply imbued with the beliefs, the holy terrors, the taboos, which rituals embody, be recreated for an audience which merely comes to the theatre for entertainment or mild thrills? Is ritual possible for sceptics, unbelievers? I doubt it very much. The only sphere of primeval awe and primitive emotion left to twentieth-century mass man is sex. That is why all this ritualistic theatre nowadays has to veer towards sexual shocks and images. Brook is no exception here. He ends his production with the sudden, unexpected unveiling of a huge golden phallus (most realistic in shape in spite of a certain stylization) bang in the centre of the emptying stage. There we have what ought to be the only still potent and active and awe-inspiring symbol, the last remnant of a whole Pantheon of primitive godheads. But even this last remnant of primeval awe merely produces titters and nervous giggles in a modern audience. Why? Because the symbol of this deity, in real ritual, would emerge at the height of a deeply stirring, deeply vital religious experience. Here it comes at the end of a very moving *aesthetic* experience. It still has the power to stir the emotions – but merely the emotion of embarrassment – because its terrors, its greatness, its metaphysical significance have been repressed in an age of shallow emotions and mechanised pleasures.

Ritual is only the outward form of the deepest spiritual experience. Can mere theatre evoke such experience? Or should we rather be seeking for the experience itself, i.e. a genuine spiritual awakening before we can validly seek an expression for it in ritual and in theatrical ceremony? Or – can the theatre itself *produce* a spiritual awakening? Perhaps – but only through the greatest, the deepest poetry. This play is no more than an archaeological curiosity, a pretext for technical exercises. Where is the great archetypal poetic drama of our time? In Genet? In Beckett? Where else?

Plays and Players, May 1968

Oedipus: A Review by Charles Marowitz

In The Village Voice, *Charles Marowitz once again questioned Brook's showmanship, his penchant for shallow 'coups de théâtre' at the expense of profundity of content.*

As you enter the theatre, for Peter Brook's *Oedipus*, you find actors in roll-neck sweaters and slacks perched all over the auditorium. They cling to the pillars like birds awaiting migration-orders. They are remote and preoccupied. They are droning out one note, varying its volume in relation to signals being passed from one to the other.

On a cue, the actors turn over the cubes on which they have been sitting, and begin to beat out a tattoo which steadily increases. When it reaches its highest point, the drumming cuts out sharply and the play begins. Or, one might say the oratorio begins, for what Brook has done is to treat the Senecan text like a richly-textured piece of music, with syncopation, parallel harmonies and counterpoints. The sound components of the words have been carefully organized to create a maximum degree of tonal variety. Actors hiss, throb, vibrate and intone throughout the evening. Individual speeches are constantly invaded by group-sounds, frequently mickey-mousing narrative descriptions, occasionally providing a subtle counterpoint to speech.

There is a certain physical excitement in the sounds themselves and the incessant drumming and droning makes frontal assaults on an audience who traditionally expect the auditorium to be a sanctuary from the drama. On the second night, several people filed out wincingly. They were disturbed. Brook set out to disturb them. The whole production is, in one sense, a calculated affront to conventional audience sensibilities. But they were disturbed on a social rather than an artistic plane. There was too much grating noise and too many jarring auditorium effects.

There is a lot to be said for disturbing the equilibrium of the spectator. Especially when he comes to be reassured, but is there really much to be said for provoking physical responses by physical means when no dramatic purpose is being served?

What Brook has created in this newly-adapted version of Seneca's *Oedipus* is an extremely clever and extremely different production. In *The Marat/Sade*, the ingenious externals with which Brook swamped the play were more fetching than the play itself. One didn't complain. Also, in the Weiss, there was a theatrical context (inmates performing a play) which justified the most extravagant theatricalist happenings. In *US*, he once again grafted a production on to a theme. In that case, the disparity between production-style and actual content was painfully evident and the film *Tell Me Lies*, based on that production, revealed its ideological paucity even further. Now again, Brook has devised an ingenious theatrical overlay, the principles of which belong to his own aesthetic rather than the need or purposes of his text.

In one sense, Brook always gives us the same production. Violent imagery couched in the boldest theatrical language, drawing on the full potential of the physical powers of the theatre. Actors operating as spatial components in a formalist design, relying on dynamics rather than characterization. It is often a fascinating experiment in pure formalism; it is rarely the outward expression of the play's inner meaning. It is almost always the eclectic result of Brook's current theatrical philosophy, the present one having germinated during the Theatre of Cruelty season, and recently spiced up with happening-experiments in America, and vocal innovations in Poland.

Brook has gradually become the purveyor of avant-garde clichés to the mass audience. *Oedipus* is thinly disguised Open Theatre techniques, Grotowski-tactics and lifts from The Living Theatre. Plagiarism doesn't enter into it. All theatre-workers borrow from each other all the time. The new anti-traditional theatre is a gradually evolving language being shared and simultaneously discovered in exactly the same way in which Renaissance English came into being. But what in Grotowski or the Becks appears to be an inevitable expression of personally-arrived-at discoveries looks, in Brook, like elaborately camouflaged second-hand goods. The National Theatre Company wears Brook's production like an extravagant Carnaby Street outfit bought off the peg. It's splendid but doesn't quite fit.

The daily reviewers, who are almost totally oblivious of experimental techniques unless they 'transfer to the West End', tend to be bowled over by effects which, to the initiated, are known to be current theatrical vernacular. In this way, Brook is like the liaison between the true avant-garde and the bourgeois public and critics. It is interesting that the people who most railed against *US*, a re-jigged Living Newspaper experiment, were all knowledgeable pros: Tynan, Esslin, Pinter, etc.

It may sound contradictory to go on to say that this production despite (or perhaps because of) its outsize dimensions has some powerful moments. Oedipus blinded is John Gielgud being fitted with two black eye-patches. In the last moments of the play, after blind Oedipus and his dead mother are led off, a glittering veiled carriage is brought on, the coverings slowly removed to reveal an enormous golden phallus. Women in the front rows bowed their heads, whether out of respect or embarrassment one couldn't say. A moment later, the cast, now caparisoned in glittering gold costumes, dance on accompanied by a Dixieland band playing 'Yes, We Have No Bananas' (musical phallic symbolism, no doubt). The audience caught up with the driving rhythms of the jazz join in the festivities and the tragedy of Oedipus is banished in a bout of contemporary jollity. It is an effective finish and, in typical Brook tradition, prevents any chance of catharsis setting in. But in his last two choices, the phallus and the jazz, his strategy stands revealed. It is the overplaying of the hand that puts everything else into perspective.

During the course of the evening, he has applied every sound-gimmick he could muster to keep the verse-heavy Senecan tragedy bristling and alive. And in this, he has certainly succeeded. The moments of blinding and suicide take care of themselves. (Death in the theatre always earns its passing respect no matter what the context.) Now, just in case his other devices haven't worked, it is necessary to have some trumps up one's sleeve; the final *coups de théâtre*, the self-applauding maniacs of *Marat/Sade*, the immolated butterfly of *US*, and so out comes the shocking phallus and the all-demolishing jazz. No doubt there are sound rationalizations for each of these moments. The phallus is a stock Roman prop and connects, supposedly, with the fertility myth ingrained in the play. The jazz, one imagines, is intended to induce that sense of ritual celebration which also was indigenous to the Roman theatre. The fact remains that both choices have been hauled in as safety devices and although they create a *frisson*, being unexpected and incongruous, one is more conscious of the motivation which produced them than the rationalization needed to justify their existence.[1]

[1] Brook's ending for *Oedipus*, although theatrically startling, met with a predictable barrage of criticism and a wall of incomprehension. Such a release of tension is of course consistent with the structure of both Roman and Greek tragedy (and Japanese Noh, with its attendant knockabout Kyogen). Here, with Priapus given rather Freudian overtones, it proved to be something of an absurdity. Although the phallus remains one of the few potent and recognisable symbols of a primeval, pre-rational world, press coverage of this climax meant that very quickly 'shock dwindled into shlock' (Simon Trussler). It is perhaps best understood as a first, and rather clumsy, movement towards a communal celebration of life, the positive implicit in the negative darkness of the production. It was to be another two years before Brook was able to perfect the element of celebration with his astonishing airborne version of *A Midsummer Night's Dream*. (D.W.)

As with *US*, one eye has been cocked on public-reaction and, along with the legitimate motives of production, there was the conscious or unconscious bid for controversy. On a superficial plane, the production dazzles and seduces us with novelty, but a lingering dissatisfaction quickly banishes these virtues. One clings to the idea that a production must be the expression of a play's integrity, and not a demonstration of vivid or fashionable techniques, even when those techniques are superior to the material on which they are being imposed. However effective theatre may be, some part of ourselves demands to know we are being overwhelmed for some reason greater than a director's desire to overwhelm us.

D.W.

King Lear, RSC 1962. Irene Worth as Goneril, Peter Jeffrey as Albany.

Paul Scofield as Lear, Alan Webb as Gloucester.

The Screens, RSC Theatre of Cruelty Season, 1964.

The Marat/Sade, RSC 1964. Patrick Magee as de Sade, Glenda Jackson as Charlotte Corday, Ian Richardson as Marat.

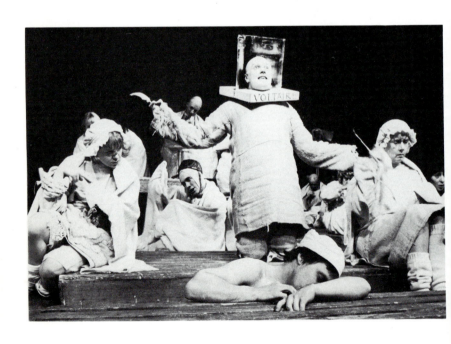

The Marat/Sade.

Two scenes from *The Marat/Sade*.

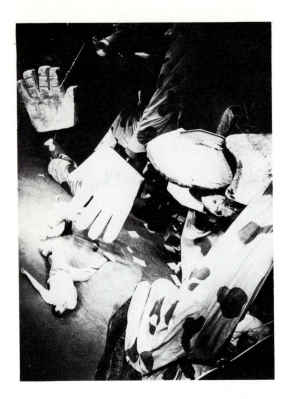

US, RSC 1966.

US, 'The burning of the butterfly'.

Oedipus, National Theatre 1968. John Gielgud as Oedipus, Irene Worth as Jocasta.

A Midsummer Night's Dream, RSC 1970. Alan Howard as Oberon, John Kane as Puck.

Orghast, Persepolis, Iran 1971.
Part II: the ghost of the daughter Krogan murdered.

Orghast. Part II: Furorg, with the Chorus behind him.

Exploration of the Ugly: Brook's Work on *Oedipus* by Margaret Croyden

An interview with the actor who played Creon in Brook's Oedipus, *originally published in Tulane Drama Review: Colin Blakely describes the rehearsal process to Margaret Croyden, a leading journalist who has championed Brook's work to the present day.*

CROYDEN: What was the most interesting aspect of your work with Brook?

BLAKELY: Well, I learned a lot about the actor's craft. We used none of the usual theatrical tools – facial expressions, character development, movement. We had to find other things to do. We were left standing on a bare stage with no movement and no punctuation. There was no punctuation in the script at all. And we were not allowed to finish a sentence. The big speech that I have lasts for something like 15 minutes; I had to do it in terms of pacing and rhetoric and in terms of different tones of voice.

There were no characterizations actually in the play before we did it (it was done only once before, in Paris); it was looked upon as an unactable play and as a reading exercise. Had we done it in the normal way, it *would* have proved unactable. So we had to find new techniques, but the techniques were far from self-evident. That's why we finally ended up with a very plain and simple method of delivery.

CROYDEN: Did Brook impose his own concept, or did he rely on you to come up with something?

BLAKELY: He obviously had his own concept, but we were allowed to experiment. In fact, he said he would tell us nothing but would only tell us what *not* to do. So we just rummaged about within ourselves, and in ten weeks came up with something to suit our requirements, and, ultimately, his too.

You see, he too was looking for the answer of how to do it, but we didn't know consciously what to look for. It all happened as we went along. For instance, we connected the speeches to a deliberate type of breathing, not normal – the kind one uses in voice exercises. This idea grew out of our listening to recordings from various primitive tribes. We found that in certain primitive societies they used certain peculiar breathing methods and certain noises for ceremonial purposes and for the worshipping of their gods. All of this fits in perfectly with Brook's idea of Theatre as Ritual. We had that to begin with but we didn't want to copy a native ritual; so we made up our own rituals. Breathing was our beginning.

CROYDEN: Irene Worth (Jocasta) and John Gielgud (Oedipus) both had mask-like faces at the moment of their catastrophes. How did that come about?

BLAKELY: Well, we talked about masks. In the Roman theatre they used masks: we tried to find out *why*. The Romans used masks because there were, in fact, no characters involved. Every person stood for humanity in a very communal sense. Hence, you'd be at a loss to delineate characteristics of personality, really. The characters were just tools for the author to put his message across. They put on masks, therefore, to blot out any human colour that might appear when the person said his lines. We tried to do that with costumes; we all wear the same brown costume – brown suits and black turtle neck sweaters. Putting on actual physical masks didn't work, because *they* imposed a personality. So we ended up with our own faces, but completely unmoving. We didn't want it to look like a mask, it must be a human being saying the lines – and yet we didn't want it to look like a person either. We couldn't put on a rigid expression which would convey a specific personality, and we couldn't enliven our faces. That, too, would give distinction to our characters.

CROYDEN: When Irene Worth, as Jocasta, kills herself, her eyes and mouth were completely mask-like . . .

BLAKELY: Yes, Jocasta and Oedipus were the only two people that anything happened to in the play. They had to find some method of showing they were blind or dead. They made their faces into 'active' masks. John Gielgud put two patches on his eyes to denote blindness and an open mouth for agony. Irene Worth also used the open mouth. Those were their own creations. Peter Brook did not select them as far as I know.

CROYDEN: In your characterization of Creon, then, you did not have to use this device?

BLAKELY: No, because Creon's an enigmatic figure. He's a catalyst. He makes other things happen, but nothing actually happens to him. He's the middle man.

CROYDEN: How were the rehearsals conducted?

BLAKELY: We discussed things for weeks (the script was being re-written until half-way through rehearsal) and, at first, we didn't discuss the actual play but rather our thoughts and ideas evoked by the play – ideas on destiny, obscenity, cruelty, and barbarism.

CROYDEN: Did Brook emphasize the violence in the play?

BLAKELY: The play is such a violent vehicle in itself that the problem, if anything, was to play it down. However, to play it down would be dishonest as well. If you listen to the play – blood, torn eyeballs, torn insides, and torn gizzards are mentioned about every five seconds for two hours. Death, disaster, plague, sickness, horror are the main ingredients of the play . . . In fact, I wondered whether it was right to perform this in front of people. In one of the speeches – the one in which the slave describes Oedipus' tearing his eyes out – people in the audience became physically ill, and the St John Ambulance Brigade was always on hand ready to carry people out. It happened quite often . . . I don't think that's what theatre is for – to make people feel physically revolted.

CROYDEN: Did Peter Brook want to achieve this end?

BLAKELY: No. He wants to achieve something else by showing the horror. His movie on Vietnam, *Tell Me Lies* (a violent, bitter work as well), was meant to eschew violence in the end. I don't think violence is the message in this play. To my mind, it is about destiny, about people's ability to grasp the fact that they're going to die sometime soon; it describes the courage with which one sets about dealing with this situation.

CROYDEN: If that's the meaning of the play, what's the purpose of the giant seven-foot golden phallus that is wheeled on like a monument at the end of the play?

BLAKELY: They play 'Yes, We Have No Bananas' (which is probably a phallic melody as well) and they all dance around the 'maypole'. I didn't want to do it, and as Creon, I didn't have to . . . I didn't particularly agree with the idea of the phallus anyhow.

CROYDEN: What's the idea behind it?

BLAKELY: In Rome, in Seneca's time, this play would have been per-formed or recited during a festival, a feast; after a tragedy one always had comedy. In fact, a Bacchanalian orgy. Brook recognized in this the common human need for release after an intense experience. The phallus was meant to embody lustful pleasure; the cast, dancing around and satirizing through mime various moments in the tragedy, served to topple the intense, formal, concentratedly tragic world which had occupied the threatre for two hours, onto its reverse side – abandoned, formless, disrespectful, comic. A marvellous idea and a very sound one. Theatrically it was staggering. It didn't, however, succeed totally for two reasons. One, the release which was engendered in the Roman feast involved the whole community: audience and participant were one. Now – although great pains were taken to involve the audience by actually moving into the auditorium, jazz band and all, and in some cases by evoking spontaneous gestures of enthusiasm from individuals – there was still a gap between those on stage and our captive passive audience. We perform, they watch; we need to perform, they don't need to watch. Theatre doesn't spring from a communal need now. However, Brook is probing to find a valid need for what we do which we can share with the audience. To get a response even from one or two people, as we managed to do, is a giant stride forward.

The phallus itself I personally found confusing. The play was over yet here was the cast worshipping a theatrical prop. It was formalized where it should have been a happening. Brook realized very well that he couldn't force a happening – therein lay the anomaly. The phallus also seemed to state more than it should have done. Of course, it got quite a reception, from guffaws to tuts, from boos to feet-stamping applause, and it was very funny and courageous, a stunning *coup de théâtre*. What was it about, though? What it said to me was:

1. You've just seen a load of cock.
2. In olden days the Romans used to do this after the play.
3. You see what can happen when you fuck about?
4. Don't go to bed with your mother.
5. Don't take it too seriously, now you've been through hell, forget it, you can deal with it.

Number five is valid. The rest is unfortunately belittling.

CROYDEN: Did Brook want mostly to work physically in order to get away from the verbal?

BLAKELY: No. If we used our bodies at all, we were to use them in the most unobtrusive and economical way possible. We ended up, in fact, standing very still.

CROYDEN: In the ten weeks of rehearsals, did you all do these exercises together?

BLAKELY: Everybody. Everybody did everything in the play. Everybody else's part.

CROYDEN: What was the point of that?

BLAKELY: So that it would be a communal experience; this was the target of this particular production. First, the cast should have a community of feeling and be on the same wave length – able to respond to each other immediately. Also, the cast were positioned all over the house and the audience had to be attuned to them as well.

CROYDEN: Was it a kind of group therapy?

BLAKELY: No. I would have walked away if it had been that.

CROYDEN: I'm interested in some of the other exercises. Could you give more examples?

BLAKELY: We tried to recreate in ourselves the horror of the story. If anybody had his own horrific experiences, he drew on them. Not all people have had an ultimate horrific experience, but those who had told of sights they'd seen, things like street accidents and so forth.

CROYDEN: You acted them out?

BLAKELY: First we just talked about them, and then we had to describe them without the use of words: sometimes without body, but with voice, sometimes without voice but with body, and sometimes without either.

CROYDEN: What do you mean, without either?

BLAKELY: Well, just with an extraordinary inhalation and exhalation [*he illustrates: a groan*]. We also used as a starting point a picture by Hieronymous Bosch, his vision of hell. We had to describe this, without words, to a blindfolded actress – as if we were dumb and she were blind. All we could make were sounds and we had to express to her the horror in that picture. We came up with some dreadful sounds.

CROYDEN: What was the result of this improvisation?

BLAKELY: The outcome is apparent in the actual production. At one point, the raising of Laius' ghost is suggested as the only way of getting rid of the plague that's afflicting Thebes and forcing Laius to say who murdered him. But they say they've got to open hell to raise his ghost. Everybody is aghast at this. At this point, the chorus start making noises, such as we did in connection with the Bosch picture.

CROYDEN: Was the plucking out of the eyes done without words?

BLAKELY: This was done using various techniques: sounds, movement, but no language. You could get a team from St Bartholomew's Hospital to take somebody's eyes out on the stage, but it wouldn't be art, you see. And if someone had enough drink or mescalin to get him to tear his own eyeballs out, it still wouldn't be art. So, we were discovering in rehearsals what, in fact, art is – or why put on horror like this on the stage.

CROYDEN: What did you discover?

BLAKELY: I don't suppose anyone will find the ultimate answer, it's just a search towards the ultimate answer. The simple answer to the question of art is that art is the essential of things ... We found various movements crystallized tearing out of eyeballs better than others, without becoming messy and horrible in themselves. A certain twist of the hands.

CROYDEN: Was Brook trying to set some image of the body and some sound of the voice that would say more than language?

BLAKELY: That's what we were trying to do, so that when we got to say the actual words, we'd already been able to do it without the words. The words themselves could only narrate what was happening and they wouldn't be imbued with the usual clichés.

CROYDEN: What other exercises did you do?

BLAKELY: We had 'obscenity rehearsals'. They'd go along every Saturday morning and be obscene.

CROYDEN: What did they do at these obscenity rehearsals?

BLAKELY: I wasn't there, but I think they worked on various movements in the play: Oedipus killing Laius, Oedipus copulating with Jocasta, etc.

CROYDEN: I can't quite visualize Irene Worth and John Gielgud doing this sort of exercise.

BLAKELY: They didn't. This was the members of the chorus. The point was at the end of the play: this whole obscenity business was to send up the story, part of the same credo that brought on the phallus and 'Oh, Yes, We Have No Bananas' – it was all to give the impression of a bacchanale.

CROYDEN: How did the acted out copulation help this improvisation at the end?

BLAKELY: They were meant to go through the stages of the play.

Oedipus' first big mistake was that he killed his father so they did an improvisation of the meeting at the crossroads. Then the second big point in the story is that he goes to bed with his mother, marries her and has children by her, so the act of copulation was therefore brought into improvisation, so that at the end of the play, that item could be sent up [satirized].

CROYDEN: You were telling me before that there was another exercise with snakes.

BLAKELY: That was to make the body more expressive. First, one had to be a snake with your whole body and imagine a story for yourself as a snake in the jungle. It starts to rain, or somebody comes to prey or there's a fight, etc. And without moving, with the rhythms of your body, one had to show a snake wriggling away, or biting, or being lazy basking in the sunshine. We did this with parts of our body: our little fingers being a whole snake; then one finger was a snake, and another finger on the other hand was another snake. We would be the snake charmer, and our hand would be the snake, and we would get it to come out of the box. It was a very useful exercise – to try to get your mind to do two things at the same time.

CROYDEN: As an actor who has done classical work, how did you feel without the use of words?

BLAKELY: You always, I think, start from the premise that you should be able to do a play without the words. If you can do a play without the words, and get some emotional meaning, then you know you really have understood the play.

CROYDEN: What other interesting exercises did you do?

BLAKELY: We did chants. We had two guys from Australia with us and they knew authentic Maori ones. We listened to records of native rites in order to get the equivalent of the oracle. The native witch doctor and the oracle of *Oedipus* have a lot in common. We listened to the pattern of their sounds and the pattern created by the use of hands and feet, and the extraordinary things the witch doctor did with his voice. Brook talked a lot about what was the common root of *Oedipus* and the primitives. It was rhythms and the use of the voice to engender excitement. We also did things with Karate.

CROYDEN: Do you think there is any philosophical value behind all this?

BLAKELY: Our job is to make bones out of philosophy, to give it a life. It's growing away from philosophic terms to animal ones, and rooting things in instinct rather than in reason and in logic.

The Tempest

Strange and several noises
Of roaring, shrieking, howling, jingling chains,
And mo diversity of sounds, all horrible . . .

(*The Tempest*, V, i)

1968 was a significant year in European theatre. It saw the publication in English of Grotowski's *Towards a Poor Theatre* and of Brook's *The Empty Space*, two of the seminal theoretical texts for modern theatre. Two key performances in the development of contemporary theatre occurred in this same year: The Living Theatre's *Paradise Now*, premièred at the Avignon Festival, and Luca Ronconi's *Orlando Furioso* in Milan. It also marked the beginning of Brook's move away from the English theatre.

In May, shortly after the opening of *Oedipus* in London, Brook accepted an invitation from the director of the Théâtre des Nations, Jean-Louis Barrault, to work in Paris with an international group. Initially, they planned to produce a version of Genet's *Le Balcon*, which it was felt offered a grotesque reflection of the revolutionary turmoil of France at that time. This project was soon abandoned in favour of Shakespeare's *Tempest*, a version of which was to be performed before invited audiences for one week in July.

The group included a number of actors who would later form the nucleus of the C.I.R.T., including Natasha Parry, Bob Lloyd, Sylvain Corthay and Yoshi Oida from Japan. Brook was eager to discover whether 'all that we had developed within one regional pattern could and should extend itself on to an international scale: whether, in fact, internationalism could be something that would strengthen rather than weaken theatre work' (Brook in *Orghast at Persepolis*, p. 23). This project proved to be the birth of Brook's primary concerns in the theatre to the present day: the search for a direct and living theatre language through the increased human resources offered by an international group.

This was Brook's third involvement with *The Tempest*. The first was at Stratford in 1957, with Gielgud as Prospero: the second, in 1963 again at Stratford, when Brook had acted as Clifford Williams's co-director.

He considers it to be the most complex Shakespeare play of all. Thematically highly charged, it would be ideal material in this situation, affording endless possibilities for an international group to investigate. As with Marowitz's earlier collage *Hamlet*, the aim would echo that of those Dadaists who dismantled clocks, reassembling them to create entirely new 'objets'.

The work was directly linked with those experiments commenced in *Oedipus*: the investigation of word and text, of collective vocal expression and its relationship to physical movement, and particularly of the spectator/actor arrangement. Originally, when it had been their intention to perform in the massive Mobilier National in Paris, they had wanted to stage something involving simultaneity of action in different areas. In such a situation, the spectators would have needed to move around the space: they would have been made responsible for making their own choice as to what they would see and hear. However, the move to the acoustically excellent Round House in London meant a slight change of emphasis, a movement towards an investigation of the nature of space.

The environment created by the designer Jean Monod deliberately sidestepped all fixed stage/auditorium conventions, allowing the performance to reflect Brook's view of the complexity and movement of Shakespeare's text, and to constantly redefine and mobilise both space and the individual's viewpoint. The fragmentation and distillation of the text led to accusations from certain RSC directors of 'raping' Shakespeare. As can be seen from the two accounts that follow, Brook was still groping towards a realisation of Artaud's 'spatial poetry': a web of sculptural physical movements and images exposing the kernel of a dense text.

D.W.

Peter Brook's *Tempest* by Margaret Croyden

An eyewitness account originally published in Tulane Drama Review

Peter Brook's 'experiment', as it became known, was originally launched by Jean-Louis Barrault in Paris in May, 1968, under the auspices of the Théâtre des Nations, and later performed in London. Barrault had invited Brook and the Royal Shakespeare Company to organize a company of international artists – actors, directors, scenic designers (including Joe Chaikin, Victor Garcia, and Geoffrey Reeves) – to examine and experiment with some fundamental questions in form: what is theatre, what is a play, what is the relationship of the actor to audience, and what are the conditions which serve all of them best? As a frame of reference for this research, Brook decided to work on ideas from *The Tempest*. The play appealed to Brook because, according to him, it had always appeared on the stage as something sentimental and pallid. Among other things, he wanted to 'see whether *The Tempest* could help the actors find the power and violence that is in the play; whether they could find new ways of performing all the other elements which were normally presented in a very artificial way . . . and whether the actors could extend their range of work by using a play that demanded this extension.' But most important, Brook hoped that by commingling foreign artists, he could achieve a synthesis of style relevant to our times, which could obviate the conventional passivity of bourgeois audiences.

The experiment was performed in the Round House in London, formerly a nineteenth-century station house for the end-of-the-line trains, and currently a centre for Arnold Wesker's working class theatre group, Centre 42. The Round House is a circular building with an enormous round dome; one has to climb a steep flight of old wooden stairs to reach its entrance . . . The 'theatre' appears to be a huge gymnasium; no stage, but enormously high ceilings, from which Brook had hung a circus-like white canvas tent. The only other 'scenery': a number of low Japanese-type wooden platforms of various dimensions, jutting out into the open space. Stationed right, left, and diagonally are several giant mobile pipe scaffoldings with wooden planks, on which actors and spectators sit. At various moments, these scaffoldings, complete with passengers, are 'rolled' or 'flown' into the open playing area. Otherwise, the audience sits on three sides: on boxes, benches, stools, and folding chairs; five musicians (drums and percussion) sit parallel to the platforms. Most of the time the lights remain on – at full blast and very white.

Spectators can sit anywhere, and many choose the scaffolding – especially the highest planks. Before the performance, people mill around the arena: actors and audience are indistinguishable. But soon the actors vocalize, dance, play ball, do handstands, turn cartwheels, and limber up.

Finally a group appears in the centre of the open space: they arrange themselves in pairs, stand perfectly still for a moment, and then begin the 'mirror' exercise.[1] This is combined with a low hum that grows louder and louder as the audience becomes quieter and quieter; we know the play is about to begin. Suddenly the actors 'break the mirror', and run on to the platform. What follows is not a literal interpretation of Shakespeare's play but abstractions, essences, and possible contradictions embedded in the text. The plot is shattered, condensed, deverbalized; time is discontinuous, shifting. Action merges into collage, though some moments are framed, then, as in a film, dissolve and fade out.

The actors wear work clothes. Ariel, played by a Japanese actor, wears his native kimono; Prospero, played by an English actor, wears a white Karate suit. Both are thereby set apart.

Having broken the ritual of the mirror, the actors face the audience and display archetypal masks (made with their facial muscles) and correlative physicalizations. Accompanying these are animal sounds, grunts, moans, howls, whispers, intonations, and gibberish – attempts to find a correspondence between the facial, the physical, and the vocal. The 'masks' are those of the people aboard the ship, just prior to the tempest; they mean to be essentially social as well as archetypal. (According to one actor, the masks were derived from a study of the seven deadly sins. Later, someone suggested the actors study the seven deadly virtues so that they could assume a mask-on-top-of-a-mask, as people do in life. The difficulty of creating contradictory masks is obvious: there was so much distortion that no mask was really clearly

[1] As Innes points out in *Holy Theatre* (Cambridge University Press, 1981, p. 137) the mirror exercise is for Brook an image of the ideal relationship between actors and spectators; an action evokes a corresponding reaction which in turn is fed back in to inform the next action. This is also the ideal interrelationship between performers in an improvisation of the sort the C.I.R.T. group performed in Africa. (D.W.)

delineated.) While part of the group plays the passengers, others play the ship itself; the remaining enact the altercation between Prospero and his brother. Meanwhile, Ariel has been evoking the storm: he uses the sleeves of his kimono as wings with which he calls forth the spirits; his voice (a combination of Japanese and non-verbal sounds) and powerful Noh foot movements evoke the wind, rain and thunder. As the storm increases, the shipwrecked crew moan: 'Lost, all is lost,' counterposed to the sounds of those in lifeboats, the crash of the ship as it sinks (the percussion instruments help), and the rest of the cast (a chorus) who echo key words. Meanwhile, Miranda and Prospero converse: she intones the Shakespeare lines – using no end stops. As she speaks, she jumps, runs, skips, climbs the scaffolds, and once appears on the runway on top of the tent about 60 feet up. The Shakespearean lines are delivered ametrically, the object being to imagize or abstract the driving force *beyond* the symbolic word – gesture and sound are central.

The crew land on the island half-dead and half-blind. Miranda and Ferdinand meet, fall in love; as innocents, they touch, look (part of the mirror exercise), and make love in the rocking position. This is homosexually mimicked and mocked by Caliban and Ariel; other members of the cast in turn mirror Ariel and Caliban. The possibility that Ferdinand and Miranda themselves embody monster characteristics appears to be the implication here. (The 'mirror' exercise is essential to the meaning of the performance: every image used in the production is either contradicted, counterposed, or mocked by the 'mirror.')

The awakening of the near-dead crew is a fascinating sequence. They stir blindly. As if in 'The Garden of Delights', they touch, smell, look, feel, and copulate – to the echoes of 'brave new world' and 'how beauteous is man'. The islanders revel in sensuality, a primitive microcosm. But soon the forces of darkness are unleashed upon the 'good' – Caliban is born. He and his mother Sycorax represent those evil and violent forces that rise from man himself regardless of his environment. The monster-mother is portrayed by an enormous woman able to expand her face and body to still larger proportions – a fantastic emblem of the grotesque. Running to the top of the platform, she stands there, like a female King Kong, her legs spread. Suddenly, she gives a horrendous yell, and Caliban, with black sweater over his head, emerges from between her legs: Evil is born.

Prospero tries to contain Caliban by teaching him the meaning of 'I', 'you', 'food', 'love', 'master', 'slave' – the last two words unleashing Caliban's apparent rebelliousness and innate brutality. Helped by the percussion instruments and the 'flying' scaffoldings, he escapes Prospero, climbs the scaffolds, jumps to the platforms, rapes Miranda, and tyrannizes the whole island, only to be captured and imprisoned in the 'caves' (openings between the platforms). The percussion, accompanied by atonal music, begins again. Ariel moans, 'Ah, ah, brave new world'; the chorus moans (or mocks), 'how beauteous is man'. Caliban escapes; the takeover of the island begins.

The islanders become monsters; the slave, Caliban, is now monster-master; he and his mother dominate the scene, enacting a wild orgy, mirrored by the company's fast and fluid sexual configurations. Caliban, large and fat, but somehow acrobatic, stands on his head, legs spread; Sycorax (also large and fat) stands behind him, her mouth on his genitals. Then they reverse positions. The others follow suit: fellatio, cunnilingus, and other variations of anal and oral intercourse convey a monster-sexuality, a Dantesque phantasmagoria: the 'Garden of Delights' has been transformed into the 'Garden of Hell'. The entire cast forms a giant pyramid on the scaffoldings: Caliban on top, Sycorax on the bottom, holding Ariel prisoner. 'This thing of darkness I do acknowledge mine' is the leitmotif echoed by the group as they prepare to kill Prospero.

Prospero is pursued and captured. He is wheeled in on a table, and then thrown to the floor. Now the group seems a pyramid of dogs: they are on top of him, they bite him, suck him, and chew him. The leading image is homosexual rape, Caliban and Prospero locked in each other's arms. All at once, there are loud obscene sounds – gulping, swallowing, choking, defecating, and farting. For a moment, everything is post-coitally still: the 'dogs' lie spent at Prospero's stomach and genitals.

The tension is broken by Ariel's arrival; he brings ribbons, costumes, gay clothing – material things – to bribe the dog-pack. The group breaks into game improvisations, and the scene dissolves into Miranda's and Ferdinand's marriage ceremony, performed in Hebrew-Hippie-Japanese rites. On some nights, the rites are discarded for the Hokey-Pokey dance. The wedding over, Prospero says: 'I forgot the plot.' Each actor stops where he is, thinks a moment, then someone begins the lines from the epilogue: 'And my ending is despair'; another picks up, 'Unless it be relieved by prayer'; a third, 'Which pierces so, that it assaults / Mercy itself and frees all faults.' The verse is spoken in various rhythms, inflections, intonations, and phrasings – all of which mix until the sounds fade out, leaving the audience in stillness. Only the echoes of '. . . ending . . . despair . . . relieved . . . by prayer . . .' are heard in the distance. The lights do not go off, there is no curtain, the empty space remains quite empty . . .

Tulane Drama Review,
Volume 13, No. 3,
Spring 1969.

Actors at their New Exercise: A Review of *The Tempest* by Irving Wardle

The programme consisted of a linked series of exercises deriving from *The Tempest*, presented in a circus ring equipped with mobile steel scaffolds and a pair of jutting wooden platforms – an environment designed to encourage free physical expression and to provide multiple acting areas. What the company presented was less a rearrangement of the play (on the lines of the Marowitz *Hamlet* collage) than a series of physical explorations of key passages: the idea of the brave new world, the master and slave relationship, the quality of sexual delight and sexual misery.

Lines, often reduced to a couple of words, were delivered in a dehumanized chant and then taken up and explored by the company in movement and choric speech: sometimes in the form of mass action, and sometimes broken down into smaller relationships. One preoccupation which ran through the programme was the question of power; how a single actor can impose his will on the rest of the company; or how a pair of actors, swapping identical lines, can match their separate strings. The other preoccupation was with isolation, shown – whenever ensemble contact broke down – by detached figures pursuing solitary ritual transformations into animals and machines.

Compared with Mr Brook's previous experiment the evening showed less interest in musical formality and more concern for the freedom of individual actors – partly no doubt, a result of the unfinished nature of the work. What it demonstrated was his unrivalled capacity for directing the audience's eye to single chosen details in the midst of elaborate spectacle, and for creating potent imagery, such as that of a blind company reaching out their hands to explore the new world of each other's bodies; or the sight of Prospero, swinging by one hand from the top of a scaffold as he thunders his recollection of Caliban's plot. The evening was charged with the sense of talent being stretched beyond its accustomed limits . . .

What the Round House audience saw was a double experiment which investigated a number of general acting problems while seeking a new way of penetrating Shakespeare's text. The key issues were rhetoric and imagery – the most potent qualities of the play, both of which generally evaporate in performance. Brook's way with rhetoric was to introduce a Japanese actor and draw a mesmerized chant from the other speakers; obliterating character with the aim of discovering some form of impersonally emotional delivery uncontaminated by rant. With imagery, his method was to select a highly charged line and expand it into a sequence of actions – as where Caliban flops out of Sycorax's thighs and begins to learn language from Prospero, every fresh word bringing him closer to enslavement. Some of the sequences – such as a love quartet of thin spirit voices vibrating in the air – radiated an unearthly illumination. Elsewhere the troupe fell back into abstract exercises; and strayed over to members of the audience to caress their hair or mew like cats at their feet . . .

The Times, 19 and 27 July 1968

A Midsummer Night's Dream

The Shakespearian theatre: an ideal

'Shakespeare is a model of the theatre that contains Brecht and Beckett, but goes beyond both. Our need in the post-Brecht theatre is to find a way forwards, back to Shakespeare.'

(*The Empty Space*)

In all his work, Brook is looking for a renewed theatre language as rich and alive as that of the Elizabethan theatre in general, and of Shakespeare in particular. Brook has elaborated his own particular, rather romanticized, vision of the works of Shakespeare. Like Leonardo's, for Brook Shakespeare's universe is 'quite simply *the* universe': a microcosm reflecting the macrocosm, a *teatrum mundi*. Taken together, his plays form a 'global vision' of the different aspects of the real world. As such, Shakespeare's work is 'anonymous', 'like the sphinx'. For Shakespeare was what Brook calls 'a completely evolved man', whose strength lay in his personal disappearance behind the body of his writings: they are an expression of an essential humanity transcending the confines of any ego.

Such theatre exists both as permanent challenge and ideal for Brook, largely because of the density and totality of experience expressed, and the intensity of the conception, both of which can only be liberated in a realization born from a 'true meeting' with today's reality:

'The Shakespearian theatre speaks simultaneously in performance to everyone, it is "all things to all men", not in general, but at the moment when it's being played, in actual performance. It does so by reconciling a mystery, because it is simultaneously the most esoteric theatre that we know in a living language, and the most popular theatre.'

(Brook in Trilling's 'Playing with words in Persepolis',
Theatre Quarterly, 1972)

His works are a kaleidoscopic 'pop art' collage in which all that is constant is the free association of images and a mobility of thought which takes us from 'high' or 'low': from 'holy' (that which 'contains all the hidden impulses of man') to 'rough' (his external actions and that side of him which 'admits wickedness and laughter'): from the lusty, popular, vulgar world of the flesh to the introspective, metaphysical and magical world of the spirit.

In Shakespeare's *absence of style*, private and intimate balance epic and public: different elements co-exist discontinuously and painfully, just as we know intuitively they do in real life. Yet here they are in a concentrated form, neither neutralized nor compromised by each other's presence. According to Brook, three hundred years before Picasso, Shakespeare's multi-faceted structures were already 'the cubism of the theatre'. As a result, his plays 'are more realistic than any form of writing before or since: his work can give you simultaneously the surface image in a context, and also tremendously dense information about things unseen and unspoken.' (Brook in *Sight and Sound*, 1963)

Brook believes that the freedom of a totally non-localized stage space remains far beyond our present comprehension:

> 'It means that every single thing under the sun is possible, and not only quick changes of location: a man can turn into twins, change sex, be his past, his present, his future, be a comic version of himself and a tragic version of himself, and be none of them, all at the same time.'   (Brook in *Sight and Sound*, 1966)

With nothing imposed, the resulting impression is of absolute freedom. A constantly shifting viewpoint means that no single authorial voice is forced upon us. The necessary absence of a single style makes the possibilities limitless:

> 'Its purity is its impurity . . . The purity is that of a highly seasoned and grained piece of wood which is pure because it is true to its own texture: the texture the theatre has to be true to is the impure one of the world in which the audience lives.'
>   (Brook in *Parabola*, 1979)

Brook suggests that whenever any single specific form or style is imposed on Shakespeare's work, the inevitable result is a restricted, reduced version of the original. The director's and actor's task is therefore to attempt throughout to 'capture in [their] net the richest amount of contradictory, clashing, opposed, discordant elements that criss-cross these plays'. For the vitality they possess lies in the inestimable quantity of contradictory yet simultaneous experience compressed into single moments, 'often crowding, jostling, overlapping one another'.

However, Shakespeare poses very real problems for theatre practitioners and audiences today. The pressure of empty and thoughtless convention can snuff the life from his work: 'Nowhere does the Deadly Theatre install itself so securely, so comfortably and so slyly as in the works of William Shakespeare'. (*The Empty Space*)

A Midsummer Night's Dream at Stratford

'The stage is a world of marvels and enchantment: it is breathless joy and strange magic.'   (Meyerhold)

When Brook began work on *A Midsummer Night's Dream*, at Stratford in 1970, he was aware that the play had become encrusted with the cloying residue of nineteenth-century Romanticism (as expressed in Mendelssohn's music) and with the memories of such epic production pieces as Max Reinhardt's celebrated 1935 film version. Brook saw the challenge of finding the 'secret play' beneath these accretions, of discovering and uncovering the play's core. It had to be made available and alive to all. He also asserted that 'there is in the theatre a constant and very respectable need for newness for its own sake. The showmanship side of the theatre is very respectable: it must never be boring.'

Many thought that once again Brook would approach Shakespeare's text from Jan Kott's viewpoint, as expressed in *Shakespeare Our Contemporary*. Brook acknowledged the value of Kott's essay in castigating the saccharine sweetness of so many productions which ignore the sensuality within the play, the suppressed fears of its protagonists: yet he rightly suggested that Kott had only allowed himself to see one aspect. A literal production of his reductionist and abstracting viewpoint would lack all joy, sparkle and magic. Shakespeare had balanced more disturbing themes with an atmosphere of enchantment. There is never any doubt that the underlying strain of darkness will be overcome, or at least assimilated.

Brook saw the play as a celebration of pure theatricality, an expression of the liberating joy of 'play', an ode to both actor and the performing arts. For this reason, it would be a release after the darkness and violence of his recent work. In fact, the general tone of the production was of wildly anarchic exuberance, uninhibited physical inventiveness and magical simplicity.

The production's starting point was an attempt to discover what a contemporary notion of magic could be. In what terms could it be meaningful today?

'It is only by searching for a new discrimination that we shall extend the horizons of the real. Only then could the theatre be useful, for we need a beauty that could convince us: we need desperately to experience magic in so direct a way that our very notion of what is substantial could be changed.'

D.W.

A Midsummer Night's Dream

Extracts from two accounts of the rehearsal process of Brook's Dream: *John Kane's essay (*Sunday Times, *1971) details 'the search for the hidden play' while David Selbourne's book,* The Making of A Midsummer Night's Dream *(1982), reveals tensions and incomprehensions concerning the nature of Brook's search.*

When My Cue Comes Call Me, and I Will Answer by John Kane

We began the morning with a series of exercises. At one stage we tried holding conversations without words, using the gymnastics of the circus tumbler as our vocabularies. With a neatly executed cartwheel Barry Stanton (Snug) launched himself into the centre of the ring we had formed. John York (Mustardseed) replied with a sinuous and suggestive forward roll. Barry thought about this for a moment and then repeated his initial statement. In reply, John lowered himself backwards into a crab position and then gracefully lifted his legs over his body, completing a delayed backward somersault. Barry, breathing heavily, performed a third cartwheel, decidedly heavier than its predecessors. As if in mockery, John answered with a perfect cartwheel of his own followed by a somersault and a backward flip. It was like watching the village idiot being cross-examined by a sharp prosecuting counsel.

The stage management produced a bundle of short sticks. These were distributed amongst the company, and we were encouraged to twirl and bounce them as they were passed round the ring from hand to hand. Peter asked us to experiment with them amongst ourselves in the three weeks before rehearsals to acquire a basic dexterity. But their real value lay in the equation of them with words. As we passed the sticks from hand to hand, to the rhythm of drums, over long distances or from great heights, so we were to learn to handle words and speeches, experiencing them as a group.

Some of us walked back with Peter to the theatre during the lunchbreak to look at sketches of the costume designs. On stage, Sally Jacobs, the designer, was discovered experimenting with light reflecting from various thicknesses of wire. She handed me a drawing of a curly-headed character wearing a one-piece baggy-panted luminous yellow jump-suit and a moonlight-blue skull-cap. I found it impossible to relate the picture I held in my hand to any conception I might have had of the part of Puck up to that time.

Peter explained: Recently, he said, both he and Sally had witnessed a Chinese circus in Paris and had been struck by the difference between our performers and theirs. When the Western acrobat performs, his costume emphasises his physique. We not only see the trick being performed, we see the mechanism ticking over. If we applaud, we applaud their expertise and rejoice in the perfection of the human body. The Chinese acrobats hid the shape of their bodies with long flowing silk robes and performed their tricks with delicacy and speed, so that it seemed the most natural thing in the world for them to spin plates or walk on stilts. Sally's costumes were an attempt to impart this uniqueness to the magical elements of the play. It was up to us to fill them with the required assurance.

When we began the eight-week rehearsal period we formed a ring of cushions on the floor; this was to be our usual discussion formation. Peter began by repeating his belief in a 'secret play' to be discovered during rehearsals. Without more ado we began to read through the play. We didn't get very far. Peter stopped us after the first couple of lines to tell us that he didn't want it 'acted'. He wanted us simply to 'read' the play. We listened to him in silence and then, all nodding wisely, began where we'd left off. A few more lines trickled by and again he stopped us. 'Shakespeare didn't write these lines for nothing. All I'm asking you to do is simply read them.' Again we nodded; again we started; again he stopped us.

In times of confusion Peter takes things very slowly. Indeed he takes so long over the occasional word that you begin to suspect he may have a speech impediment. He looks at the ceiling or at the floor. His hands become soft pink pincers moulding ideas like pie-crust. He pokes his head forward as if to propel his thoughts across the distance that separates us. In the silences, we sift his unfinished sentences in our minds, trying to supply the missing magic word that will transform our dullness and re-establish communication. I'm still not sure that I understand what it was he wanted from us at those readings, although I had a solo rehearsal with him one Saturday morning.

During the discussion that began this session, I suddenly decided to confess that I sometimes found the process of repeating performances tedious. I further confessed that I'd always thought of the actor as being fairly low on the creative scale since he is interpretative as opposed to totally creative.

'But why should you feel such despair?' said Peter. 'In India, the actor is considered to be the greatest artist, the most creative.' And as always he suggested an exercise. We sat on the floor of the Studio facing one another. It was quiet and still except for the occasional, muffled clack of wood on wood and the laughter of retired shopkeepers and army men playing bowls beyond the window. Following his instructions, I closed my eyes and repeated the word 'Light' while simultaneously trying to analyse the process that led to the utterance of the word and the changes in its intonation. After a few minutes of this, he asked me to repeat the experiment, this time using the word 'Dark'. After an equal amount of time had passed, he gently stopped me, told me to open my eyes and then to describe the sensations and responses that the exercise had aroused. As best I could, I told him what I had seen with my eyes closed, where the words and the images accompanying them were situated in the darkness and what it was that provoked different attitudes towards the same word, conveyed to Peter by the variety of ways I said it.

Peter listened in silence and then asked me whether or not I thought it possible that such a precise examination of the word might take place during performance; and if it could, how much richer it would prove when applied to words in conjunction with one another as in a sentence or line of verse. Creation and exploration need not and in fact, must not stop on the last day of rehearsal. The actor must always be open to change. 'You must act as a medium for the words. If you consciously colour them, you're wasting your time. The words must be able to colour you.'

Running parallel to this rigorous mental approach, an equally stringent physical programme was started. Each morning began with a 'warm-up' session accompanied by an extended version of the improvised drum-break that opens the second half of our performance. Over the eight-week rehearsal period the Studio filled up with trapezes, ropes, plastic rods, spinning plates, tennis-balls, hoops, paper, string and a variety of musical instruments. For at least half-an-hour every day we exercised with these until they became extensions of ourselves. Peter ran his 'nursery' with a firm hand, and whenever he felt we were using our 'toys' as crutches, he took a grave delight in snatching them out of our sticky fingers and locking them away in his bottomless confiscation-cupboard.

A brief exploration of the text reveals three very different worlds in *A Midsummer Night's Dream*, the Mechanicals, the Lovers and the Spirit World of Theseus/Oberon, Hippolyta/Titania. During rehearsals a fourth world emerged. We decided that if Spirits were omnipresent it would be impossible for them to be confined to the 'Fairy' scenes. They must be available to speak the lines of Titania's fairies, but they could also be around to lower trees for Lovers, carry lumber for the Mechanicals and produce sound effects wherever appropriate. The actress and three actors playing Spirits, were dubbed 'Audio-Visuals' and were given complete licence in the early days.

With the setting of the Mechanicals' scene these Audio-Visuals made a first appearance; from there on the run-through assumed a different character. Most of the company still had their books in their hands which obviously hampered them, but not the AVs. They were free to wander where they pleased and assist or screw up whatever they liked whenever they liked. It soon became obvious that the Spirits that morning were certainly mischievous if not downright malevolent. The forest and its inhabitants exuded a primitive savagery that infected everyone who came in contact with them. As the group feeling grew, a wild gaiety seized the company. With books in one hand and a hoop or a cushion in the other, we whipped the play along like some frantic, bobbing top until it eventually exploded during the Titania/Bottom confrontation in a welter of torn newspaper, cardboard phalluses and Felix Mendelssohn.

As the noise and the laughter died away, we looked around the room and as though awakening from a dream ourselves we realized that we had been possessed by some wild anarchic force, that we had been in contact with elements of the play that no amount of discussion or carefully plotted 'production' could have revealed.[1]

Unseen by us, Peter carefully prepared the ground for these 'revel-ations'. Towards the end of morning in the fourth week of rehearsal, Sara Kestelman as Titania awoke to find David Waller as Bottom transmogrified at the foot of her bed. Don't ask me to recall the events leading up to this, but somehow or other I found myself on top of step-ladders at either side of the stage manipulating a long aluminium

[1] In performance, this scene remained one of the most explosive and controver-sial of the play, on account of its vivacious visual movement and colour and its charged and gross sensuality. (D.W.)

pole as though it were a microphone boom. On the sidelines, Alan Howard was sitting on an empty tea-chest beside Ben Kingsley, who had brought his guitar to rehearsals at Peter's request. The rest of the company were distributed round the room on cushions and chairs.

While the dialogue between the Spirits, Bottom and Titania proceeded, Peter surreptitiously motioned Ben to begin playing. Sara heard the soft chords and as she reached the lines, 'Be kind and courteous to this gentleman,' began to sing the words to a melody that took shape even as we listened to it. I lowered my 'boom' in and Alan started beating out a fairly complicated rhythm on his tea-chest. The AVs suddenly joined in with an unrehearsed but perfect four-part harmony backing to Sara's song; and then from all round the room, the rest of the company added their contributions, complementing the original musical impulse.

Our first response to the Mechanicals' play proved harder to recapture. The Mechanicals had been rehearsing by themselves in the Methodist Hall while the rest of us concentrated on the arrival of the wedding party in the Studio. When they eventually joined us, they were made to wait outside the door and ordered, as though they were tradesmen (which indeed they were) to spruce themselves up before entering the presence of the 'Gentry'. Peter turned the rest of us loose on the costumes from previous productions, and while we put together bizarre outfits for ourselves the stage management lit dozens of candles, which were to be the room's only source of light. We sat down behind the semicircle of candles and ran through the dialogue leading up to the entrance of Peter Quince. On cue, I – now playing not Puck but Philostrate – left the room and ushered the Mechanicals into the presence of Theseus and his court. They had no idea of what was happening behind the Studio doors and of course we had never seen them perform before. They appeared as underrehearsed as Bottom and his colleagues were in the text. Philip Locke as Peter Quince acted as the play's Prologue and its genuine prompter, holding the Penguin edition of the *Dream* in his hand. The court found this very funny at first but as our jokes at their expense grew more desperate, the actual substance of their play, together with the strangeness of our environment, began to work on us and by the time we had reached the death of Pyramus and Thisbe, their innocence had a weirdly moving effect, reducing us to silence.

Alan Howard as Theseus thanked the Mechanicals and delivered the last speech to his Court. Suddenly, at a sign from Peter, the stage-management slammed on the overhead spotlights and we got to our feet blinking in the savage brightness. 'Go on!' said Peter. 'Go on to the last speeches of the play.' I was so stunned by the shock of the lights that I began Puck's 'Now the hungry lion roars' without time to think about what was being said (which is, I suppose, exactly what Peter intended). That speech and the other three which constitute the play's epilogue said themselves and we reached the end of the play understanding the necessary transition from the Court world to the Spirit world by experiencing it.

To understand it was one thing; to reproduce it was another. We had many hours of black despair when we tried unsuccessfully to recapture the sensations we had first felt when we knew that a moment of the play had been 'experienced' properly. Peter could drive us to distraction by his demands for an increase in our self-awareness. He would sit down with us and shake his great head in disbelief that we could have gone so far forward in one direction while taking so many steps back in another.

In the hope of retaining my sanity, I resorted to unabashed escapism. During the eight-week rehearsal period, I got through at least twenty-two English detective novels. My recreation bore fruit. If you want to find one of the sources for the 'stilt sequence' during the Demetrius/Lysander quarrel, I direct your attention to the chapter entitled 'The Scissor Man' in Nicholas Blake's *The Deadly Joker*.

Sunday Times, 13 June 1971

The Rehearsal Process: An Extract from
The Making of A Midsummer Night's Dream
by David Selbourne

Second week, first day

. . . The form of the set was now revealed to the actors. A model of it was carried in by the designer. It had been discussed, she said to me later, as early as January [i.e., six months previously – *Ed.*] The idea, for what looks like a white squash-court or gymnasium, had come to Brook and her together. Neither of them alone was its originator. To the actors, Brook says that the set 'will emphasize every sound, reveal every movement and give every freedom'. Brightly-lit, it 'will provide a white daylight magic'. In it, he warns, 'we must make an effort to avoid every suggestion of the strain of a muscular circus. The aim will be to reveal the moment of coolness.' He adds: 'Everyone will be taking part all the time, without the usual exits and entrances. There will be a continuous round of movement and stillness. All will be present, each taking up the baton from the other.'

'The costumes,' he continues, 'will say nothing.' Only the mechanicals' appearance will emphasize their 'fixed occupation' and its nature, in juxtaposition with that of the court and the courtiers. 'With a white background and a few objects,' Brook tells the actors, 'all the richness will have to come from the performing group.' It will have to 'paint the picture as it goes.' Moreover, 'literally illustrating the action is out.' If Puck 'says he is going', then 'it is sufficient that he says it, and stands still.' And 'when he says he is back, he is back.' Once more, the exploration of the nature of theatrical illusion, and of the role of imagination, including the audience's, beckons.

Now, as if to compensate for the humourlessly (and dangerously) leaden ending to the first week's rehearsals, Brook says, surprisingly: 'We are not going to get bogged down into doing anything too seriously. It's all a game anyway.' He lightly suggests – but does it lighten or increase the load on the actors? – that the rehearsals should begin to explore a 'range of acting-styles', in order to achieve 'different kinds of illusion and presentation', and to discover 'which illusion is the most effective'. Into the white engine-room set, which will have high walls, gangways, rails, cradles, swings and ladders, Brook even threatens to

154

introduce a live rabbit, as Reinhardt did, to create a 'reality' which would outface all the actors' struggles to defy gravity with Shakespeare's words and their bodies.

The actors, who have been gathered around the model of the set – and with which they seem taken – now disperse, energies apparently aroused by the new mood to a new beginning. Brook catches the moment swiftly. A circle forms, to drumming, a baton passing from hand to hand as the circle turns, dancing. Each member of the group takes it in turns to go to the centre, as the circle speeds into a frenzied gyration and a manic exchange of sounds in rhythm. The physical energy seems to express both frustration and hoped-for exhilaration; a longing for action and for even intenser expression. Then Brook, anxious not to lose the electrical charge which has accumulated, says: 'Form as tight a circle, sitting on the floor, as we can get.' He is sitting among them. A complete and uninterrupted rereading of the play is beginning. 'Read the entire play, touching,' he tells them. 'Bring it to life just for us here. See if we can get an experience, now, of bringing the play alive together.' He tells them, too, that they also have a 'simple freedom' to add and improvise.

The experiment is, in fact, sustained for only twenty minutes. But in this time there seems to be established such a closeness of relation and interrelation, commitment and participation, that for the first time an ensemble sense of intimate collaboration is achieved among the actors. During these twenty minutes, it is as if reservations and hesitations, strengths and weaknesses are at last coming to be shared between them. Thus, Hermia's 'I know not . . . how it may concern my modesty, In such a presence here to plead my thoughts' becomes an intimate question, between friends. Yet, like a circus ringmaster, Brook suddenly changes direction, whip cracking, throwing the actors (pleasurably?) off-balance. There is now to be an opening-out of movement, from enforced confinement into the whole area of the studio.

And the new sense of space immediately freed the actors for a wider and spreading invention. Taken back once again to the play's beginning, the actors are physically uncaged, now roaming the acting arena and moving freely in its new-found expanses, the canvas become dangerously boundless. To free rhythms of their own – but under the ringmaster's watchful eye – feelings, voices and gestures seem to have been liberated together. At the same time, voice is hollowed out by the new distance, facial expression and body's detail diminished, gesture expanded (into disorder) and the words' cadences roughened. Now Lysander, in the first scene, paced in time with his words. Helena entered swinging; while, strangely, the new physical intimacy between

Hermia and Helena seemed even closer for the distance which separated them, and which they now had to traverse in order to touch each other.

Third week, fifth day

The actors sat once more in a circle. They held hands, while sounds were exchanged between them. Brook, moments after our conversation, asks them to evoke 'the noises of night'. These noises, he says, 'should arise spontaneously from silence' and 'be communicated around the circle'. Irritably, he demanded that the silence be 'absolute'. And then, with all eyes closed in a deepening semi-trance (or the simulation of it), the first stirrings of sound began to arise from the actors, and gradually grew to a raucous and caterwauling climax. Once more the whole room – and my metal chair – vibrated. Now, Brook asked the actors to form two seated circles. To one group, he gave the word 'moon', and to the other 'sun'. Neither of the words was to be spoken, nor sung, nor 'illustrated'. Instead, each actor or actress was to emit the sound which the word assigned to the group evoked in him, or her. And each group, while making its own sound in chorus, was to listen to the sound made by the other – not to echo it, nor to answer, but 'for mutual awareness'. But this sun shed no warmth, and this moon no light. For they were metaphors of pure sound; and beyond reason.

Sounds are then 'thrown across the room' from one group to the other, as if they were juggling objects, flung arrowing through air. At Brook's instruction, the noise of the builders' yard follows, in a generalized mouth-made chorus. Finally, Brook orders each actor to communicate with a selected partner at long distance, using a chosen sound from the repertoire of the builder, in a mounting discord of shouted brick and metal. And when this is over, the texture of the stage floor for the finished production is announced by the designer. There is talk of hessian, to give the actor-turned-acrobat a good foothold and purchase, while Brook gives his new orders of the day, as well as the further perspective. Those actors who, at any moment, are not taking part in the 'actual spoken story' will drop out of the acting but 'comment on it by their presence'. The next rehearsal stage is to 'make sure the story-line is clear'; while at the end of the rehearsal period as a whole, Brook warns the actors, 'there must be a discipline as tight as a drum'. This discipline, he tells them, 'will not be an external one'. It will have been 'derived from their work' and, as he puts it, be 'self-imposed'; an assertion, such is Brook's authority, which is (paradoxically) beyond challenge.

A Midsummer Night's Dream: A Review by Donald Richie

Donald Richie, in Tulane Drama Review, *highlighted the circus elements of Brook's production.*

At the beginning of Peter Brook's production of *A Midsummer Night's Dream* the entire cast, caped like artists of the flying trapeze, stride to the crash of snare drums through the double doors of their canvas-white trapeze-hung set, smile professionally, mindful of later heights and daring, gesture a grand if impersonal welcome and are off into the wings and about their work. This *Dream* is to be a circus – that best of all dreams for children of a certain age.

The play begins. As at the circus the only colour is the costume – the actor is boldly outlined against the white, looking at times like an oleo, at times like a Kate Greenaway illustration, at times Chinese. Musicians, prop men are visible at the sides, those actors not working look on from above with a professional interest. The guitar player accompanying Helena's monologue gazes at her like a magician's assistant – she is a familiar sight to him, he is perhaps gauging her performance, perhaps not.

Later one understands the distribution of the cast: the lovers are the pony-riders, the jugglers; the fairies are high-trapeze artistes; and the rustics are, properly, the clowns. One also understands that this is one of the grandest and most circus-like circuses that one will ever see – a real dream circus which never existed on sawdust, all circuses rolled into one. There are spinning plates from the Chinese circus, cymbals and drums break and accent speech (Titania and Oberon's first appearance) as in the Japanese, Bottom's ass is very Bolshoi, and Puck – himself from the Neapolitan fairs – confounds the lovers on high French stilts straight from the Medrano.

It was, indeed, perhaps the Cirque Medrano's performance of the play several years ago – and from Cocteau's unrealized circus production, five pieces of Erik Satie's score for which exist – that first gave Brook the idea for this production. Eclectic it is, and eclectic it ought to be for Shakespeare's most eclectic play, the one which Madeleine Doran has called 'a little triumph – one of the earliest of Shakespeare's plays in which things so disparate and so various are gathered up into a single whole.' Yet, the play is also more than this and if Brook's idea had

only been '*Dream* as circus', then it would have been faintly disappoint-
ing instead of, as it is, strongly satisfying. The art of the circus is the art of
pantomime – the enjoyment lies in what is done and not in what is said.
Seeing the *Dream* as a circus, Brook produces a gloss on the play, an
illustrated edition in which every line is underlined, acted out, and the
evocative power of the naked word, of the imagination, is ignored.
When, for example, the fairies' lullaby ('You spotted snakes, with double
tongue . . .') is turned into a polyphonic chorus, no single word understandable, the fairies levitating in their sling chairs, the poetry itself
evaporates. When, for another example, the 'over hill, over dale' passage
is delivered more or less canonically by all the fairies (the fairies
furthermore both arch and patronizing toward their well-worn words),
one realizes that Brook's bending backward from the pretty and the
sentimental has ended him in the equally sentimental stance of the
cynical, and, more important, that – again – the word is no longer there.
As the *King Lear* production (both onstage and in film) indicates, Brook
is no friend to poetry, but one wonders if the kind of evocative theatre he
tries successfully to create is indeed so different from that created by
poetry that he need so avoid the perhaps purple stanza.

Sometimes, too, his illustrations turn into footnote – like interpretive
glosses. When we agree with them we find them charming – all of Puck's
business, his entrances on circus ropes, his smiling irony at his own
language alike. Less charming are those with which we find it difficult
to agree. A coltish, humorously self-deprecating but not yet wholly
disillusioned Helena is made a hoyden to the extent of pinning her
Demetrius under her – a characteristic for which the lines have not
prepared us and a construction which (as is later evident) they will not
support. Hermia is put on the trapeze merely, apparently, to illustrate
her line about puppets, a flouting of the play's own conventions (the
swings belong to the fairies) which adds nothing and proves confusing.

Usually, however, Brook is in this first half of the play faithful to the
circus idea. It is very charming and the first-act finale with its confetti,
its streamers, its dazzle, its snippets of circus-band Mendelssohn,
the clowns philosophically sweeping up during the intermission, is
delightful – a child's-eye view of the magical world under the big top.

The production, however, is also more than this, and here is where
perhaps its greatest interest lies because, in the end, Brook wins back
much of that power of evocation he squandered through disregard of the
perfect word. One becomes aware of this (in retrospect) early in the play.
After the bravura entrance of the artistes the play begins, and we find
that Hermia is not speaking with Theseus, though her lines are directed

to him, but with us. Later, Lysander and Hermia, though conversing together, are kneeling downstage and, again, addressing the audience. Over and over we discover that not only Puck (whose lines are occasionally written for our ears alone) but almost everyone else in the cast (including Bottom) are speaking over the footlights. These are not asides. They are halves of a conversation which the audience is offered and which, in the second half of the play, it takes up.

Brook would believe, along with Björnson, that 'the sense and meaning (of the play) are in ourselves. The play takes place . . . now in you . . . now in me.' He would also hold, along with Meyerhold, that there is 'a fourth creator, in addition to the author, the director, and the actor – namely the spectator.' This he has indicated in most of his productions – *Lear, Oedipus, The Tempest, Marat/Sade* – and this he again indicates in the *Dream*.

Tulane Drama Review, Vol. 15, No. 2, Spring 1971

A Midsummer Night's Dream: A Review
by Charles Marowitz

Charles Marowitz, in the New York Times, *placed Brook's production in the shadow of Meyerhold: directorial imposition at the expense of true dramatic interpretation.*

It being staged by Peter Brook, famed for *Marat/Sade*, it goes almost without saying that this is a defoliated *Midsummer Night's Dream*. Gone from the Royal Shakespeare Company's production are the terpsichorean fairies, the vernal glades, the mischievous woods. In their place: a white, gymnasium-styled quadrangle hung with swings and ropes and surmounted by a metal catwalk from which hovering actors emit sounds, throw confetti, burble, heckle, kibitz and brood.

Brook's starting point seems to have been the contemporary notion of magic. Since woodland sprites and evil fairies no longer convince, on what magical basis can *A Midsummer Night's Dream* be founded? Brook's answer is theatre-magic; a sleight-of-hand composed of scenic tricks and stage illusion, but with the mechanics laid bare for all to see. The herb, love-in-idleness, which drugs Oberon's victims and is responsible for all the amorous confusions of the evening, is here translated as a silver dish magically rotating on a silver rod – a conventional conjurer's trick passed spinningly between Puck and Oberon. The transformations of the night sky, alive with shooting stars, are represented by streamers tossed by actors from one side of the stage to the other. Bottom's transformation is not into the conventional ass's head but into a clown-like visage with button-nose and oversized ears. The instigators of all these transmutations, the aforementioned double-act of Puck and Oberon, spend most of their time airborne, conversing from swings, chasing victims over catwalks or down ladders, or goading their grey-uniformed pixies into wilder and merrier acts of impishness.

This, as has already been noted by Irving Wardle of *The Times*, is out-Meyerholding Meyerhold. Here, almost fifty years after the heyday of Meyerhold in Russia, is his circus-theatre returned with a vengeance, and Meyerhold, despite flirtations with Artaud and Brecht, has always been the most durable influence on Peter Brook. The Show in this *Dream* is not Shakespeare's, but Brook's. He has used Shakespeare's text as a trampoline on which to display some dazzling effects. This is theatre glorying in its theatricality, using every scenic opportunity as a pretext for a theatrical riff.

The shock of dislocating the play is so great, the effect of seeing it reassembled in a bright, hard context free of traditional associations so refreshing, that we are hypnotized by the very 'otherness' of the creation. (It's as if Hamlet were to be played by a one-eyed Negro with a thick Yiddish accent.) But as one flits from one burst of energy to the other, the nagging question persists: is the shattering of an illusion the aesthetic equivalent of illusion? For me, in this case, it isn't.

Peter Hall's straightforward production of this play some six years ago had a clear, contemporary insinuation running throughout it. His lovers were as conscious of their 'lyricism' and false pathos as we were. That tongue-in-cheek production offered a highly sophisticated view of rustic revelry, and the fact that we were all in on the joke (the characters included) displaced the sentimentality of the play. Hall produced his bevy of effects by humanizing the fantasy. Brook, by abstracting it, provides a lot of marginal dividends, but side-stepping the traditional problems of the play doesn't solve them. In their place, he has offered dazzling solutions to other problems which have no direct bearing on the play: i.e., how to produce sharp, telling moments using a theatrical shorthand based on Oriental theatre-techniques; how to shatter stock reactions to overfamiliar material; how, using pure sound, to orchestrate a highly versified text without recourse to conventional musical interpolation.

But chugging along within this highly rejigged framework is the story of *A Midsummer Night's Dream* – the imbroglios of Hermia and Demetrius, the tensions of Oberon and Titania, the conflicts of Egeus and Lysander – and these scenes are played out in a thoroughly conventional manner within the more fanciful context, so that all through the evening the production offers a kind of twin-channel entertainment. 1) Turn one knob and you've got brilliant theatrical effects taking place in outer-space. 2) Turn the other and you're trundling along with Shakespeare's narrative played in a purely terrestrial style. The most one can say for Brook's alternatives is that, in almost every case, they are preferable to the drone of the original material, but the dichotomy between the existential and textual realities doesn't make for unified reactions.

Nevertheless, there are strokes in this *Dream* which no one has ever achieved before. The jubilant marriage ceremony of Bottom and Titania ends in a wilderness of paper plates and confetti as Mendelssohn's *Wedding March* blares in the background – a cumulative effect of celebration so triumphant you feel like throwing rice at the newly weds and jumping up to kiss the bride.

The company, particularly David Waller's Bottom and Alan Howard's Oberon, are steadfast, and their best moments are traditional ones in that Shakespeare, rather than Brook, provides their material. The comic craftsmen are more individually characterized than one has seen them, but much less funny.

Sally Jacobs's forest consists of coiled wires hung from fishing-rods through which lovers tangle and disentangle themselves. The clean, industrial texture works within the rest of the setting but doesn't really serve the dramatic purpose. No matter how cleverly they are manipulated, they never say 'forest', they always say 'wires'. Richard Peaslee's 'score' of interpolated sounds by unfamiliar instruments is one of the production's best inventions. If you're objectifying a Shakespeare play, it works well to have tonal footnotes providing a running commentary.

As part of the trend to escape the stranglehold of the classics, Brook's *Dream* is a bold, breathtaking somersault into another direction, but it doesn't really transcend its basic material or reconstitute it into a completely different creation. This is the *Dream* still saying what the *Dream* always says, but in a much flasher context. Ultimately, one comes to the conclusion that if it is to be hailed as loudly as it is being hailed in England, it must be as a superb example of aesthetic one-upmanship, but not as dramatic interpretation.

New York Times, 13 October 1970

Brook has always been concerned with finding ways of combating the process of ossification that appears to be inherent in the repetition of performances. Theatre representation should be what that word suggests, the making present of something fresh for a particular moment. A production must constantly be jogged back into life through what Brook refers to as a 'permanent revolution' at all levels. During either the run or the tour of a work, both actor and director need to ask themselves repeatedly 'whether this process of sclerosis is inevitable, whether it is part and parcel of nature herself. To understand this is of vital importance.'

To retain the collective vitality of this production during its extensive run in both Stratford and London, and on its subsequent world tour of what he calls 'the glamour circuit', it was evidently necessary to sustain the life of each actor's creativity on a daily basis. As well as periodically re-examining the work, Brook had tried to engage each actor's imagination fully from the beginning. All were encouraged to have their own deeply personal link with the material, which could then evolve and grow during the run, like any valid relationship. In theory at least, the sum of these ever-changing individual visions would always be a work of freshness and immediacy. However, this production was restricted within the rules and conditions of a prestige tour. The RSC were 'condemned to go to middle-class showcases in the major cities, going from comparable slot to comparable slot, rather like carrying Stratford around the world.' As a result, after more than five hundred perform-ances in all, 'for better or for worse, it had to repeat itself. In the end, for worse, because the actors had to do their duty rather than what came from life.'

What had been needed instead was an encouraged evolution of the 'spirit' of the play – the actors' physical, emotional and intellectual relationship with the material. Brook recognized that this could only be allowed to occur by removing a performance from stultifying, fixed forms imposed externally. If it had been played around the world in different conditions and to a wide range of audiences, each time an external form being created afresh from the set of conditions of that specific performance and not from any abstract conception of the play, its life might have been extended. In reality, however, the outer form of the production could never be reassessed within the commercial con-straints of such a tour; eventually it was this same outer form that came to be taken for the inner spirit. In addition, 'the present set-up of the theatre, with its formal institutional apparatus, provides the wrong arena for communication, ceremony and involvement' (Brook in *The Making of A Midsummer Night's Dream*, p. 41). Brook knew it was time he moved on to be free to investigate the 'deeper chain of rules' separating and uniting human beings the world over, to pursue his search for a truly living theatre of 'real international forms'. For him, 'a non-English talent obliged to flower in unconducive surroundings' (Marowitz), such an investigation could not be conducted within these shores; in 1959, he had written:

> 'England destroys artists . . . [their] edge is rapidly knocked off . . .
> No one presses the artist to do anything – all they do is to create a
> climate in which he will only too readily castrate himself'
> ('Oh for Empty Seats', *Encore*)

Within the English theatre milieu, there is 'no conflict, only reassur-ance', resulting in a deadly 'auto-conformity'. So, although at the very zenith of his career with the RSC, he would have to start again else-where. From zero.

III

The C.I.R.T.: Three Journeys, 1971–3

The Aims of the Research Group

Orghast at the Shiraz Festival, Iran, August 1971

Africa, December 1972 – February 1973

America and *The Conference of the Birds*
July – October 1973

'(There is) a need for destruction – not of the present Theatre, because why should we want to destroy it? – but for the destruction of the belief that there is any validity in the present Theatre . . . The Theatre that we know over a long period of time has been the Theatre of the Lie rather than the Theatre of the Illusion – simply because its points of contact with the life around it are almost entirely cut. Cut on a social level, cut on a political level, cut on an emotional level, and cut on an intellectual level . . . The fact that in the whole range of emotions, nine-tenths of them are squeezed out of the theatre means that it is operating in a closed building with a very thin strand of experience. These are the deadly factors which mean that any belief in this form as it stands has to be taken and destroyed'

(Brook in *Transatlantic Review*, 1976)

'Any path is only a path, and there is no affront, to oneself or others, in dropping it if that is what your heart tells you . . . Look at every path closely and deliberately. Try it as many times as you think necessary. Then ask yourself . . . one question . . . Does this path have a heart? If it does, this path is good; if it doesn't, it is of no use'

(Castaneda, *The Teachings of Don Juan*)

The Centre: The Aims of the Research Group

In the final years of the 1960s, Brook had spent much time and energy persuading various bodies to provide him with financial assistance in the setting up of what was to be called *Le Centre International de Recherche Théâtrale* (C.I.R.T.). From 1 November 1970, a group of actors and directors from as far apart as Japan, Mali, Romania, France, Great Britain and the USA conducted private research work within the Mobilier National, Paris. Brook had foreseen that only when commercial and financial aspects of theatrical enterprise were eradicated could any real experimentation take place. Since *Oh for Empty Seats* (in *Encore*, January 1959), Brook had dreamt of being in a position of *total subsidy* which would free him from the crippling exigencies and impositions particular to the 'glamour circuit'. In collaboration with his longstanding friend, the producer Micheline Rozan, he subsequently received unprecedented amounts chiefly from the Ford, Gulbenkian and Anderson Foundations, and, in the first year, from the Iranian government, commissioning a work for the Shiraz Festival of the following year. He also received grants from the J.D.R. III Fund, the David Merrick Arts Foundation and UNESCO. He wanted to 'make a chink . . . by going against the current'.

Indeed, he was now able to turn his back on the conventional channels and forms within which commercial work – the selling of a product to a consumer market – must remain. Such work could only ever be a corruption or compromise of all that Brook felt to be valid and alive in the theatre. He would now be able to work in a wider variety of conditions, to realize his need to look through theatre for a way to 'evolve something up from the seed; not to add things together, but to make conditions in which something can grow'. With no obligation to give regular performances and the 'right to fail', the research group would have time to develop and explore material and forms, the effect on the work of differing performance conditions and the nature of the actor's craft and of theatre itself.

For Brook, the Centre has always had three different but equally important functions to fulfil. Firstly, it has 'a responsibility to theatre-going audiences, remembering that, as a performing group, we cannot survive without a relationship with the people who keep the theatre in existence' (Brook in *Kaleidoscope*, 1978). Western theatre today has rarely been in so grave a crisis; it has become largely 'narrow, parochial, class-bound, closed in style or closed in content to the richness and contradictions of human experience'. At the same time, he firmly believes that 'the theatre in the deepest sense of the word is no anachronism in the twentieth century; it has never been needed so urgently'. It is partly for this reason that over the last ten years Brook has agreed to play to Western audiences in showcase theatres and festivals. However, his deepest convictions lie in the Centre's other two functions, the first of which is a determination to create a relationship with 'the people who would never cross the door to a theatre in a thousand years, by seeing them on their own ground in schools, meeting-places and open-air places' (Brook in *Kaleidoscope*, 1978).

Since the Theatre of Cruelty season, the emphasis of Brook's research had been largely on the preparation of the actor. Around the time of the *Tempest* experiment, there was a noticeable swing towards an emphasis on the actor in relation to the audience in changing environments and conditions, and on the development of a natural relationship with each particular audience. Throughout the Seventies, this was Brook's central concern in his work. Over the subsequent three-year period at the genesis of the C.I.R.T., the outward movement into life (what Brook refers to as 'work-in-the-field') was to take the group on a major journey every year (Iran, Africa, America), supreme exercises in the validation of the research work behind closed doors, as well as an infusion of life through exchange. There were (and still are, to this day), also a number of minor sorties to schools, *'foyers'* for immigrant workers, hospitals and prisons in the working-class areas of Paris and its suburbs. The rejection of normal Western theatre audiences is deliberate:

> 'Unfortunately, the cold-blooded point is that for the research we want to do everyone is equal except people who normally go to the theatre, because all over the world theatre-goers contain a high proportion of those who through going to the theatre accept its crumbling conventions.'

Like Grotowski's paratheatrical activities, such theatre practice is culture for an inverted élite. Much of this work must necessarily take place outside the limiting framework and limited responses of the European theatre-goer in whom Brook detected a certain quality of reticence in the face of lived experience. He felt that this narrow band of society was conditioned towards intellectualization, rather than direct experiencing of a shared event on a human level. The fundamental aim here was to explore 'what the conditions were through which the theatre could speak directly. In what conditions is it possible for what happens in the theatre experience to originate from a group of actors and be received and shared by spectators without the help and hindrance of shared cultural signs and tokens.'

The third function of the Centre concerned

> 'the responsibility of the group to itself and its craft, which means the actor knowing that he must constantly, and with equal care, try to develop himself in relation to others in other ways, through group exercises, which improve his possibilities of serving his craft well, and, at the same time, increase the general understanding of the mysterious nature of that craft itself by trying out things that have not been tried before'   (Brook in *Kaleidoscope*, 1978)

Here the movement is inward, for research must include self-research, a process which can only take place in conducive conditions out of the public eye. Such work is 'privileged, thus private; there must be no concern about whether one is being foolish or making mistakes'. Confidence and trust in the group as a non-hierarchic family and respect for the intimacy of the place of work are essential prerequisites in this 'search for processes, combinations, causes and effects hitherto unknown'. In this way, the elements of theatre can be placed under a microscope, just as Leewenhoek had done with water; in other words, taken down to their smallest forms to be contained and examined in minute detail, to make their true components visible. Research is above all an opportunity to 'clarify, distil, discard'. However, Brook is aware of the madness and danger of believing for a moment that theatre work can exist in the absence of a relationship with an audience. Without 'a rhythm like a pendulum that went in and out of life, the isolation would turn in on itself'. A relationship with a community and a creative role for spectators are the crucial elements in any validation of this private work:

> 'Scientists can work behind closed doors; we must continually throw them open and lock them again'

Above all, training is collective experience in 'the strongest of all drama schools, life'. Yet in order to reassess the discoveries made during the work-in-the-field, they would have to return constantly to the conditions of the laboratory; inner and outer (Baudelaire's *concentration* and *évaporation*) had to be balanced.

The structure of the initial three-year cycle can be seen as a logical development of this notion of a 'rhythm in and out of life', as well as being consonant with Brook's general ideals. During the first year, the group intended to create an intensely hieratic and poetic theatre work, a 'high' work made up of mystical and esoteric vocal and gestural abstractions (*Orghast*). The emphasis in the second year (the African journey) would be on simplicity and naïvety; the aim was to create popular 'low' work, unprepared yet direct. This would necessitate a regression to a zero point, an unlearning of techniques, a return to the very roots of creative expression. According to Brook's Shakespearian ideal, 'high' and 'low' co-exist; therefore in the third year (the journey to America) the aim was to bring the two strands together into a dense totality, a rich experience accessible to all.

With his international group, Brook never intended to synthesize different world theatre techniques into a sort of 'dramatic esperanto'. He did not want his actors to exchange their individual '*trucs*', although the group has inevitably borrowed methods of approach to the opening and preparation of the actor from the individual cultures represented. In this range of very different individuals, who would clearly not normally have been brought together, he saw the potential for a 'strong fertilising experience' based on their diversity and their shared compulsion to work:

> 'What is artificial and natural is transformed by work, work transforms everything; and the moment there is a job to do, then these actors brought together cannot get away from it. They *have* to put their similarities and differences into play. And the work has to be, in this case, the making of theatre material. And in the making of theatre material, the understanding of what theatre material is . . .'

The microcosm of the group combined a range of colours, sizes and skills as rich as that of a commedia dell'arte troupe; in its diversity, it would mirror the real world. It was hoped that creativity could be born from the setting up of a 'difficult friction', so that 'each one's culture slightly eroded the other's until something more natural and human appeared'. For it was found within the group that the popular clichés about each individual's culture were often shared by that individual. Through collective work, he would be able to discover that what was taken to be his culture was merely that culture's artificial mannerisms, accreted ethnic tics, which had inevitably brought about an impoverishment of the original vital impulses at the heart of that culture. His most profound cultural identity and individuality, reflected in something very different, had become disguised:

'To become true to himself he had to shed the superficial traits which in every country are seized upon and cultivated to make national dance groups and propagate national culture. Repeatedly we saw that a new truth emerges only when certain stereotypes are broken.'

In this way they could come together out of life to analyse and reveal common ties and essential differences. By prising off those stereotypes imposed by his own culture, the actor could discover what animated its forms, and perhaps could emerge more himself in relation to it:

'The Japanese becomes more Japanese, the African more African, until one reaches a level where forms aren't fixed; a new situation appears which allows people from different origins a new act of creation. They can create together and what they create takes on another colour. This phenomenon is similar to that of music, where all the different sounds retain their identities, but, joined, they give rise to a new event.'

Eugenio Barba once described his aims with the Odin Teatret in this way: 'Shatter your own circle within the theatre. Then shatter the circle of the theatre.' The growth of the individual within the theatre inevitably necessitates a redefinition of what the theatre is, and a renewed conception of what it could become. Brook considered the C.I.R.T. to be presenting a direct challenge to

'all the elements that in all countries put the theatre form into a very closed bracket, imprisoning it within a language, within a style, within a social class, within a building, within a certain type of public.'

D.W.

Orghast at Persepolis: An Account by A. C. H. Smith

An account of the experiment in theatre directed by Peter Brook *and written by* Ted Hughes. *Antony Smith worked with Brook and the C.I.R.T. as literary adviser on the* Orghast *project. The following extracts from* Orghast at Persepolis *describe the group's work both in Paris and Iran preceding the Shiraz Festival.*

In the 1968 project, leading to the *Tempest* exercises, the group had experimented freely with language. The pressure of having to be linguistically inventive all the time risked drawing concentration away from other areas, like physical gesture and group coherence, and so in 1970 it was decided to restrict the language used in exercises. For a polyglot group, a very small, fixed vocabulary of invented syllables would serve best. Each actor contributed one syllable, and the order into which they were originally put (though they could in theory be used in any order) began *bash/ta/hon/do*, by which name the language was subsequently known.

The myth of Prometheus was the field of experiment for the whole year: an open field, so vast that anyone may make a fresh path into it. It was approached not only through *Kaspar* and *La Vida Es Sueño* but also Seneca's *Hercules Furens* and *Thyestes*, an Armenian play called *The Chained One* (the myth is Armenian in origin), some research into other authors who have used the theme (Goethe, Gide), and other myths concerning the origin of fire; and, principally, Aeschylus's *Prometheus Bound*. The problem with playing Aeschylus in Greek is that no one knows how he sounded to the ancient Athenians. Reeves, who prepared the Greek text for the company, pointed out that 'we don't even know the line divisions, let alone the stressing. From the evidence of performance, it clearly must have been closer to what we know as music than what now passes for acting. As the direct communication of emotion is more powerful through music than through the associative images of language, trying to approach an ancient text through a technique of exploratory articulation and improvisation seemed more promising than attempting to play it in a modern English translation.'

The exploration of Aeschylus's text, however instructive, was only a

172

step in the direction Brook wanted to take. In the Centre he aims to cut through the division in the theatre between those who insist on the primacy of speech or on the primacy of physical gesture. Thus, an exploration of the roots of language must go beyond the verbal into the physiology of speech, and ask another set of questions, which Brook put in *The Empty Space*: 'Is there another language, just as exacting for the author, as a language of words? Is there a language of actions, a language of sounds – a language of word-as-part-of-movement, of word-as-lie, word-as-parody, of word-as-rubbish, of word-as-contradiction, of word-shock or word-cry?'

In an attempt to answer such questions, and find a fresh path into the Promethean myth, Brook asked Ted Hughes for a series of rhythmic syllables, like the Bashtahondo series, except that the meaning of Hughes's syllables would not be arbitrary but 'a small visible portion of a gigantic unseen formation', the impulses that Prometheus aroused in him. They were to be sounds for actors to find their way into, 'a process that parallels the original creative one'. (*The Empty Space*, p. 13)

It needs to be stressed that *Orghast* was a particular language not only to Hughes but also in that it was created for a certain group of actors to perform at a certain place. Like *Oedipus*, for Hughes, and like Brook's earlier communal experiments, it was shaped by 'millions of tiny suggestions', in Hughes's phrase, from the whole company during the work. It is not a text that any other company could make use of. For the same reasons, any written version of it cannot give more than an approximation of what it sounded like when the actors got 'inside' the words, a process that took months of experiment. However English some of the root sounds were, its effect when spoken was very far from English, or any other language of discourse.

The following passage was one of the earliest that Hughes wrote, and was exceptional in remaining unchanged right through to the performance at Persepolis. It was spoken by God-Krogon, the off-stage counterpart to the visible King-Krogon, who destroys or imprisons his sons in fear of being usurped by them. Beneath the *Orghast* text is the translation – scoring might be a better word – which Hughes gave the actors until, in the final stages, it was no longer necessary.

BULLORGA OMBOLOM FROR
darkness opens its womb

IN OMBOLOM BULLORGA
in the womb of darkness

SHARSAYA NULBULDA BRARG
I hear chaos roar

FREEASTAV OMBOLOM
freeze her womb

NILD US GLITTALUGH
rivets like stars

ASTA BEORBITTA
icy chains

CLID OSTA BULLORGA
lock up the mouth of darkness

IN OMBOLOM KHERN FIGYA GRUORD
in her womb I make my words iron

The word Orghast itself was the product of two roots, ORG and GHAST, which Hughes had offered as sounds for 'life, being' and 'spirit, flame' respectively. ORGHAST, then, was the name for the fire of being, the fire at the beginning, the fire at the centre, and so, metaphorically, sun. Closely related were GRA, 'physical fire', and ASTA, 'ice'.

The idea of a group of actors working largely in private is apt to suggest a relaxed, self-confident, even cosy atmosphere. The reverse is more likely, especially at the start. In the conventional theatre an actor has a different audience every night, and can, if he wants, continually allow himself the same evasions and indulgences. In a group, they soon become intolerable, to himself as well as to the others. Yoshi, the Japanese actor, wrote in some notes he made on the work that an actor, 'having come to understand past experience and techniques, must throw them all out, strip himself naked, free himself to look for something fresh, always remain flexible'. At the same time, he is 'opening up his talents for the others to absorb'. Such work is ideally undertaken in a group living a communal daily life: as, Yoshi wrote, the military arts are learned in Japan. Discoveries in the theatre are not attained by a director, but only through such a group. 'The director's job is to say No to habits, not to instruct.' Brook argued a similar point in an *American Theatre* interview: 'One doesn't want the departmentalizing of a drama school. Also, we don't use "experts". With fifteen people we have an enormous reservoir of skills and understandings. Each one can for the day become "fencing master". No one from the outside can have authority but within the group the question of authority doesn't arise. Everybody recognizes the relativity of anything they bring. They show what they can do, which is open to be taken, explored, developed and questioned . . .'

PREPARING THE BODY
Mornings began with nearly half an hour of warm-up exercises, which the whole group, including Brook, did together on the mat in the great hall, following snapped-fingers signals given by one of the Persian actors. After a fortnight, Brook allowed some time at the start of the day,

before the group exercises, 'for each of us to do what he personally has to do to prepare for the day'. For some it was breathing practice, for others acrobatic work on the mattresses and cushions that had been made for the project. 'Acrobatics will come in useful among the rocks of Persepolis,' Brook remarked. His ideal actor, the perfect instrument, would be an acrobat, juggler, singer, dancer and clown, as well as having the more conventional skills.

After the warm-up came, usually, an exercise for the whole group, or for separate small groups, using the sticks in a series of movements ranging from gentle to warlike, carried out with a similar range of vocal sounds. It was usually led by Yoshi. Brook often joined in this one too. I saw him, one morning, throwing his stick in the air and jumping with the effort, his toes pointed, like a little boy's.

Of Chinese origin, like the bamboo sticks, is Tai Chi, which was an end to the day's work. It is a technique of bodily awareness, in which apparently simple movements are carried out, very slowly and grace-fully, in a slightly knees-bent position, which balances all the body's muscles against each other. Brook learned it from a teacher in Paris who had been taught by a Chinese master, and he insists it cannot be learned other than by receiving the impulse from a true initiate. Sylvain Corthay, Natasha Parry and Yoshi were the instructors. Brook does it with careful grace, and demands an attitude of reverence toward the exercise: I was ticked off, once, for sitting at the edge of the room and making notes. (The great hall was generally to be respected as a place of serious work. Brook's four-year-old son was not allowed to play in there, even outside working hours; and Irene Worth was appalled when she found a half-eaten slice of water-melon in a corner.) 'The meaning of Tai Chi is a very profound one indeed,' according to Brook. 'It can be found if the positions are found. The positions are like a formula: if you can get the head, body, stomach, eyes and arms into the right relation, at once something happens which won't happen if the positions are not quite right. In just doing a couple of tiny movements, do they give a suggestion of that or not?' A Persian said she became aware of relationships in her body, 'and began to feel the blood flow'.

A comparable exercise, used occasionally, was one in which two actors faced each other in silence, one performing a sequence of unpatterned movements, the other seeking to mirror the movements as closely as possible, to the extent, at best, of knowing instinctively what would come next.

Finally, among the body preparation can be included breathing exercises. For the most part, they were done individually, under the supervision of Andrei Serban, who took the opportunity to apply techniques derived from ancient Zoroastrian sources. He classified the exercises into four stages, ascending in difficulty as the weeks went by. I will record a few examples, with Serban's proviso that, as with Tai Chi, it would be useless to experiment at random with them, unsupervised by someone who understands their purpose and personal effect. All of them depend, of course, on correct breathing from the diaphragm.

The simple exercise from the first stage is an exception to the proviso not to experiment: indeed, Serban recommends it to everyone three times a day before meals. 'There will be a remarkable change. Your whole life can depend on how you hold your shoulders. We normally use only a third or a quarter of our breathing capacity.'

Stand with shoulders back, arms by the side. Breathe in deeply for seven seconds. Hold the breath for four seconds. Breathe out for seven. Hold it out for four. Continue for three minutes.

From the other stages:

Stand, arms by the side, feet slightly apart and turned a little outward. Breathe in for seven seconds. Breathe out for seven seconds, meanwhile swinging one extended arm, palm facing inwards, clockwise. Continue arm-swinging during next breath in of seven seconds. Hold breath, clench fist above head, bend to touch ground with fist, not bending knees. Straighten up and breathe out fast. Repeat with other arm.

Stand, arms stretched sideways, fingers extended. Breathe in. Sing any 2/4 song andante ['Twinkle, Twinkle, Little Star' was popular], rising on toes on first main beat, going back on to heels on next, and continuing; on first rise bend index fingers in to the palms, extending them again when going down on to heels. Repeat with other fingers in turn, till the breath is exhausted.

Kneel, sitting back on heels, elbows tight against ribs, fingers pointing forward. Breathe slowly in. During exhalation, sing A-O-IM, on the last three notes of a descending scale, in beats of roughly a second. On each A- throw right arm up straight, returning it to the side during O-IM. When the breath has run out, repeat with left arm. Then with both arms together.

Lastly, from the fourth stage, which Serban says 'is quite impossible' – he was the only member of the company who could get right through it, and twice it made him faint. He warned that it would be dangerous to the heart to force oneself through it.

Kneel upright, back and thighs in a straight line, hands together behind neck. Breathe in. Lean forward to touch ground with forehead; while slowly straightening up again, sing a scale. Breathe out. Repeat, leaning backwards this time; then sideways, touching ground with each elbow. Relax. Then go through all four movements in one breath, not singing the scale until back in upright position at the end. Then do all four movements again, this time having breathed out first, and not breathing in until regaining final upright position.

Apart from generally toning up the breathing muscles, the exercises are designed to improve awareness of the breath by changing its direction. The co-ordination of limbs, head and voice is also being trained.

PREPARING THE VOICE
As the company in Paris had explored several languages that they could not understand literally, seeking what meanings could be tapped in language considered as physically expressive behaviour, so the augmented group in Persia worked, week after week, at four languages which are spoken nowhere, but which were to form the language of performance at Persepolis.

In *Orghast*, Brook said, 'all is music, in the contrast of the letters and in the rhythm. We are working in a language that doesn't exist in order to do things we could not do in French, English, Farsi. In them we are bound by literal meanings. We could not utter them freely: to pronounce them in any way we chose would be ridiculous. These are letters made by a poet. Don't regard it as a foreign language. Out of his letters it is possible to develop something that has the meaning of the voice of the vulture.'

VULTURE: HOKKVATTA SCAUN HOANAUN
　　　　take him to the healer

　　　　ESSECKITA GRUUSVA KHERRON
　　　　ask the name of the sickness

　　　　MOARGHUST　　　GLEORGHASTA
　　　　love of　　　　　the vulture

An hour or more would be spent by a small group taking turns at saying just one word, sometimes stretching it to six or seven seconds in exploring all the sounds in it. An instance was HAZAC, meaning 'horror', around which a chorus was built later. Ten minutes was given to just the letter C. 'Keep trying it, like a musician tuning his instrument,' Brook instructed the group, sitting in the circle of cushions on the carpet. 'The last thing in music is to look for the various expressions. Actors are prone to think: I am an actor, I have to act. It is not a matter of acting Ted Hughes, but of discovering what range of sounds is possible within each of his words, and in sequence. The voice is like a mountain with caves. Go into all the different caves there are.

'We practise to make the voice free. Afterwards, all that matters is to find something true between you, not something theatrical. What's true is more dramatic. A crowd chanting slogans in the street is not dramatic, it is mechanical. Vocal exercises are child's play compared with the acting of a word. The most important thing of all is what has happened just before.'

Reeves remarked, 'Peter is using the word "truth" much more this year. He used to talk about "different lies".' This, in a country where truth of any kind is very elusive, and the dignified answer is Yes.

Avesta was introduced into the work through Brook's general interest in Persian culture, and in particular through his and Ovanessian's reading of Zoroastrian hymns. After Alexander's defeat of the Persians, Avesta did not survive in any spoken form; the only evidence of it was a representation on cowhide, the hieroglyphics of which indicated as closely as possible what the tongue and mouth should do to form the sound. The cowhides were discovered at Persepolis in the fourth or fifth century AD and transcribed into a different alphabet. For example:

Zarathuštrô. Spitāmô. Hvô. Nê. Mazdaw. Vaštī. Ashāicha.

It is known that the first two parts of the Persepolis book are in dialogue form, describing myths, and that the other three parts are sacred prayers, but, as with classical Greek, nobody can be sure exactly how the language sounded. A student of Avesta, Mrs Tadjadod (the author of the opening play at Persepolis in the 1970 Festival, which Ovanessian directed), instructed the company in her method of pronunciation by example, the actors constantly repeating the sounds after her, sitting in upright postures on the carpet. At first, she illustrated the shapes of vocalized air with powder sprinkled on stencils.

No phonetic notation can encompass the range of sounds, guttural, nasal, glottal, explosive, compound consonants, seventeen vowels, produced in and around a chanted monotone, the voice moving suddenly from lips to throat to nose, and shifting abruptly in pitch. Although its strangeness naturally caused mirth at first, and the Persians had special difficulty with it, there is nothing grotesque about Avesta; on the contrary, it has a powerful dignity and beauty, and promised a new sort of theatrical vibration.

It proved essential to learn whereabouts in the body the sounds were coming from. 'If the real origin of the sound is not used,' said Mrs Tadjadod, 'Avesta will not communicate as it should.' Like Orghast, it is a language that reveals the body as a map of human experience.

The third language was the Greek of Aeschylus's *Prometheus* and *The Persians*.

The pronunciation used was the Erasmic, giving full value to each letter. It was transcribed for the actors into the Roman alphabet, thus:

CHORUS: *IÓO IÓO PERSÍS AÍA DÚSBATOS.*
XERXES: *EÉ EÉ EÉ EÉ TRISKALMÓISIN*
              EÉ EÉ EÉ EÉ BÁRISIN OLÓMENÓI.

In contrast to the strict practice of the Avesta pronunciation, the company were encouraged to explore every possibility of the Greek, even when they did not understand its meaning, by speaking it conversationally, shouting, whispering, solo, in chorus, face to face, and in a circle facing outwards. Brook, whose whole practice as a director is a continual creaming away of the froth, warned them against 'the pleasure of strumming' – knowing a few intonations and getting monotonous. Against an easy music of imported meanings, he said, must be imposed an anti-music, a return to the vocal properties inherent in every word, the syllables felt and vital. He instanced people speaking on the telephone, who express all they feel in their faces but get little of it into their voices. When the company shouted a passage, he asked that the same energy be channelled into a quieter voice.

Three speeches in Latin, from Seneca's *Hercules Furens*, were also incorporated into the work, passages chosen for their ferocity, in contrast to the blandness of most Latin texts.

As well as the four languages of performance, there was a vocal warm-up exercise, in which Yoshi led the company in producing a samurai's range of semi-chanted sounds, long, short, high, low, rapid, slow, loud, quiet, at the same time taking up different body postures. The voice could discover new possibilities beyond its normal confines.

Apart from the exercises at the start and close of the day, and the improvisation sessions, the company usually worked in small groups, or even singly and in pairs. Brook and Hughes concentrated on Orghast, Ovanessian on Avesta, Serban on breathing and the chorus work, and Reeves on Greek; the groups of actors rotated day by day, so that all the directors had an experience of the Persian actors, and the latter got to know the work of the Paris people. One group worked in the great hall, one in a small upstairs room, and the others in the front and back gardens. Sometimes directors would work in pairs, and often actors would be on their own for a session, either working alone or, more usually, one helping others with a language with which he had already learned some skill: the Persians demonstrating Avesta, the Paris group Greek and Orghast. 'In two hours,' Brook remarked, 'someone can reap the benefit of what took a year's work to discover. It was like that with the LAMDA group. There were eight of them, and their experience was passed on to the sixteen we had in the *Screens* group, and so to the thirty in *Marat/Sade*. A lot of actors in England are scared of losing their personality in disciplines like this, but those who go through it find that a much greater, more precise individuality results.

'When one approaches a new language, each letter carries with it a world of meaning that has been forgotten. In going back to the sources of language, we are returning to the source of meaning. Orghast and Avesta are not just different languages, they carry a different story. To be completely inside these sounds, the voice moves in different rhythms, starts in a different place in the body, and ends in a different place.'

IMPROVISATION

When actors improvise in private, with no audience but their colleagues, they are preparing their imaginations. It is frightening enough to be stripped of prescribed text and movements, and even more so when, as sometimes happened in Persia, character and situation too are taken away. Actors, then, come face to face with an existential void, an empty space, in which it is up to them to find some act that has a communicable meaning.

In some avant-garde groups, improvisation in rehearsal or perform-ance is respected as being so unique to the actor doing it that it is beyond criticism. To reject it would be to reject the actor as a person, a sin akin to mocking someone on a drug trip. Behind that attitude is a syllogism: he is an actor, an actor is an artist, therefore anything he does is art. (Just as the merest blot by Picasso is revered and bought at a high price.)

In Brook's view, that is superstition, 'the first delusion of the under-ground'. Personal expression is not theatre. The subjectivity of actors is not the subject of a play. Improvisation is just one more means of tuning the instrument, the group, in preparation for the performance of something objective, hard and yet open. In *The Empty Space* (pp. 112–13) he wrote: 'Many exercises set out first to free the actor, so that he may be allowed to discover by himself what only exists in himself;

next, to force him to accept blindly external directions, so that by cocking a sensitive enough ear he could hear in himself movements he would never have detected any other way . . . Improvisation aims at bringing the actor again and again to his own barriers, to the points where in place of new-found truth he normally substitutes a lie . . . If the actor can find and see this moment he can perhaps open himself to a deeper, more creative impulse.'

It is true that from an improvisation grow ideas, characters, lines, situations that may be directly incorporated in a performance – a good deal of *US*, for example – but only if the imagination is disciplined by an objective already understood by the group: if not a text, at least a subject matter and shared attitude.

In Persia, improvisation served several purposes. There was the basic job of preparing imaginatively for Persepolis. It was also a way for the Paris group and the Persians to learn to respond to each other as actors. A further idea arose, of making, through improvisation on certain fixed situations, a quite different show, a comic one in the tradition of the Persian *ruhozi*, which could be performed for any audience anywhere, like the shows given to children in Paris. Such work aimed, quoting *The Empty Space* (page 114) again, to 'lead actors to the point where if one actor does something unexpected but true, the others can take this up and respond on the same level. This is ensemble playing: in acting terms it means ensemble creation, an awesome thought.'

Two actors wait while a third comes from behind them with any prop he has cared to pick up. Once he is in front of them, the challenge is to respond to the situation sketched by the third with his prop. Three more actors try it, but this time they are asked to perform in silence.

Half a dozen are distributed around the great hall, at the high interior windows, on the balcony and floor. When the improvisation begins, it is left open for them to define what the setting represents, and their own part in it.

Next, the task is to find out, through gesture alone, who in the rest of the group is acting as your enemy and who as your friend. The form changes again: they work in pairs, learning to speak simultaneously; they advance slowly on hands and knees towards each other, till one succumbs to an impulse to retreat.

All improvisations were done in Bashtahondo, later freshened up by the addition of a few syllables, making about sixteen in all. A 'miraculous gadget', Brook called it. Sometimes there was an accompaniment on drums, or other percussion, used sparingly, at critical moments. With Bashtahondo went a corresponding language of gesture, for a couple of sessions: it was turned into a dance, a song, a competing rhythm between two groups, a voodoo rite in cross-rhythms.

As soon as any situation turned gelid or confused, Brook interrupted with a gong, and in a cool voice introduced some new element: reversing the characters, advancing the situation to two hours later on, asking that all that had just taken twenty minutes be repeated in three, at a heightened rhythm, or simply sending in reinforcements.

Probably because the two groups of actors were still getting to know each other, the tendency at first was always toward broad comedy, basic competitive situations in which lust, violence and grief were projected with Punch-and-Judy unsubtlety. It could be very funny, quick, or dead. Brook laughed, but never praised or criticized at once: to do so would have been to define the improvisation as a performance, not an experiment. Conclusions were drawn only when the whole session was over, and then in group discussion. They were chiefly concerned with what elements could be developed, and what was not worth pursuing. Brook's thumb-nail distinction was that good elements breed variations spontaneously, whereas with bad ones you have to keep thinking up new things the whole time.

After a few sessions, Brook began to structure the improvisations more tightly. He would posit a situation, a field at night, say, in which treasure is buried; or he would suggest that two or three of the company stick to relationshps that had already worked well – jealous master/ oversexed servant, wise guy/stooge – to provide a form within which others could develop something new.

In a good improvisation, he said, the important thing is to sustain the character through contingent moments. 'The whole challenge, as in a sporting event, is the speed at which things happen. If you let it carry you away, you lose control, it becomes accidental, and makes less sense. But if the speed produces concentration, so that you are thinking fast enough to be fully aware of what's going on, then suddenly an atom of energy is cracked open.'

When Yoshi watched improvisation for the first time, in Paris in 1968, he says he wondered how they could do it. Like any creative act, at its best it fascinates, intoxicates and scares anyone watching. One of the kitchen staff came to clear some cups away, and was still there two hours later. That was a good evening. Some evenings were dead, missing the intensity which all the exercises, in various ways, sought through some discipline that, like poetry, imposes restraints to concentrate the energy: 'filters', as Brook put it, 'to eliminate certain rays so that others can be seen more clearly'. After a fortnight's work in Tehran, he remarked:

'Now we know, there are two kinds of actors, those who hate freedom and those who hate discipline.'

Reconnaissance

Brook talked about the 'the rule of luck' in finding the right conditions of performance. 'It is not a process of building, but of destroying obstacles that stand in the way of the latent form. You simply can't say, at the start, what form the work will require. Technicians never understand this process, especially in film studios. They think you don't know your stuff if you can't tell them straight away what you want. They see it as an identification parade: "Why didn't you say from the start it was a small guy with a beard?" When I did *Titus Andronicus* I lay on a beach and made lots of little sketches in the back of a book I was reading. Weeks of rehearsal went by. I happened to open the book one day, and saw one of the little sketches I had quite forgotten, and it was exactly the design, in germinal form, that we were looking for by then. It is the same with costumes: as soon as an actor is given what he will wear on stage, his interpretation of the part is dictated, or at least limited. You have to deny the scenic conditions entirely to begin with, not even think about them until you are well into the work. On the *Dream*, Sally Jacobs was in at every discussion and rehearsal. She supplied props which served a strictly functional purpose, but left every scenic possibility open to the end. In *Lear*, we threw out most of the set at dress-rehearsal stage; there was nothing wrong with it, it just wasn't necessary any more.'

As long ago as 1947, in fact, Brook had done the same thing, thrown out the scenery at dress-rehearsal stage, in his Stratford production of *Romeo and Juliet*. Since his earliest days in the theatre, he has observed his own rule: to 'start each time afresh from the void, the desert and the true question – why clothes at all, why music, what for?' (*The Empty Space*, p. 39).

Brook went on: 'In this work, now, the work of the Centre over three years – it's not practical to envisage any longer period, at present – it's only at the end that it has to make sense. The result we are working towards is not a form, not an image, but a set of conditions in which a certain quality of performance can arise. This sort of work takes a long time, and unfortunately it is in contradiction to the budgets and building schedules of festivals.

'Monod, (our designer), started on the principle: what does one need to do anything at all at Persepolis? A closed space was essential, so he designed an audience box, part of which would be movable, part would stay put, in a consecrated spot. It was a startling design in its own right, but not in regard to the dramatic material. It was scrapped by financial circumstances, and it led to a simpler box, no longer so startling. No one felt excited about this one, but it served to bring the issue to incandescence. The issue is: what is the relation between this dramatic material we have to work with, and the place in which we are to perform it?

'The material is Avesta, the language of Persepolis; Greek, the language of its destroyers; and Orghast, the language of man, written through and for this place, containing the light and dark of Persepolis, as Manichaeism did. The movement of *Orghast*, like Ted's own movement as a writer, is from dark to light, sunset to sunrise.

'As soon as we found three places of stone, simple surfaces against which movement can be dynamic and speech resonant, the idea of a specially built set became an excrescence that just dropped away. When we were told there would be no electricity at Naqsh-e-Rustam, our trained reflexes answered, "We'll get a generator". Then we recognized the self-evident fact: we have found what we've come for. The best we can do in designing and lighting a set turns out to be: nothing at all.'

Later he applied similar principles to the actor's work. 'The process of rehearsal is that of a pendulum. If you follow it, it is very clear. There are always two lines. What matters in the early stages is the energy, not the result. As you clear away the debris, the process gets hotter. Outsiders are astonished, appalled: even the actors sometimes are. Until the moment of incandescence, all forms are theoretical. They haven't been through the fire. So if, for instance, an actor in *Hamlet* decides – as often happens – that Rosencrantz is, say, homosexual, and holds on to that decision right through to the performance, it will stick out as a rigid mental idea, that hasn't been tempered into human terms. In the early stages, anything goes: good ideas and bad ideas must pour out in a shapeless, generous and energy-producing mess. This over-elaboration needs to be encouraged into chaos and confusion. Then bit by bit the excrescence is cleared away and the true shapes, the true lines, that were there all the time, can be discovered. Towards the end of rehearsals I become more interventionist: I seem to give the actors their performances, word for word – but *their* performances, not mine. I'm reminding them of what they know.'

I asked Brook if he would want to generalize his own method of work as the best. 'It's very difficult to say. The traditional method is certainly lifeless; it's schematic, and a scheme is the expression of weakness, not strength. It doesn't allow for growth, and the unexpected. But there is an enormous fascination in the temperamentally opposite method, the capacity to think with such clarity as brings with it a clarity of form from the start – it fascinates me because it's totally outside my reach.

'I work empirically in everything I do. When I write an article, for instance, it all comes out rapidly at first, ideas without form, then I do some editing with arrows, scissors and tape, and suddenly it's there. The exception is when I want to write a strongly emotional piece, but that is rare. In the theatre, for me this dynamic, or empirical, process is a filter, through which a form is found. In films, the same thing is achieved at the editing stage. But I have admiration for a man like Jancso who can plan and find his shot, virtually editing the film in the camera. In cinema, I would like to work in a greater clarity of thought.'

He makes a strict distinction between the personal expression that is a film, or a novel, and the collective expression of theatre. 'A film is the inside of one man's head projected on to a screen. At first sight, there appears to be a relationship between making a film, or writing a novel, and writing for the theatre. Where the crunch comes is that material written for someone else to speak, action in which meaning is to be found, only exists in its inner, objective tensions: the subjective experience of one man's world, however fascinating his obsessions may be, is not enough, because it is always incomplete.'

Thus, he has no time in the theatre for 'authors', the '*petits maîtres* of theatre'; even Artaud he finds 'uninteresting' as a playwright, 'a restricted, obsessional surrealist of his time, using a set of repetitive symbols. If we call "author" a man who projects his own private world, then Shakespeare isn't an "author". From his plays, hardly any autobiography can be culled. He furnishes from his own deep and specific experience certain extraordinarily concentrated and related nuggets from which an infinity of forms can evolve. For this reason there can never be a right "author's" shape to express any of Shakespeare's intentions. Every production is a meeting between Shakespeare and a new group in new circumstances from which a new three-dimensional image of the world is produced. Only Chekhov, by other equally mysterious means, arrives at a similar objectivity.'

The performance of *Orghast* would not represent a 'Ted unity': it was in recognition of that that Hughes was willing to incorporate Avesta and Greek from other writers' minds, on the edge of his own experience.

What Brook wrote in *The Empty Space* about design could as well apply to this argument about writers: 'What is necessary is an incomplete design; a design that has clarity without rigidity; one that could be called "open" as against "shut". This is the essence of theatrical thinking.'

'The ground,' he says, 'is all the time being turned over and prepared for the day when suddenly lightning strikes and out of the mouth or the pen of someone comes the writing that the theatre has not heard for centuries.'

Uzbakhi: the beginnings of the carpet show in the village of Uzbakhi

Brook told the company: 'Improvisation is the moment of truth for good actors. That it can be enjoyable doesn't alter that. The actor goes into the circle to see if it is possible for him, for a short time, to let drop his normal defences, knowing he has no help from someone else's words or text. Everything is put to the test at the same time: Can he believe in the people he's playing with? Can he trust himself? Has he truly any imagination? Courage? Concentration? It is a moment of truth because the answers will be obvious to everyone else. With the confidence of knowing that everyone is searching in the same way, great risks are possible. One goes into an improvisation to make discoveries, not relying on luck. In two hours, an actor may live out a whole life. When the imagination is put to such a test, extraordinary things must appear. We can only reach things of such purity and intensity through trial and error.

'An improvisation has nothing before or after. It is true to itself. Anything outside it, other times, other relationships between the actors, have no place within it. Always, in good work, the people sitting around should be silent, understand the efforts of the people who are working. If there is an unexpected laugh, it doesn't make the people working show off, or try to please, but helps them to double their involvement in their relationship.

'If this large group can begin to find what this exercise means, it could achieve something remarkable. We could go and play improvisations before people, a marvellous enriching of all our work. So our work in the evenings now has a precise aim; something to take out and show other people.'

Brook privately remarked that the Centre could spend all its planned three years on finding some 'philosopher's stone' for improvisation: a set of characters, like the Tarot pack, or some other perfect form of infinite variety. For the present, the form he would use, to tighten the work with a view to performing it elsewhere, was an outline scenario commissioned from Hughes. Called *Difficulties of a Bridegroom*, and based on a previous work by Hughes, the story incorporated situations and characters discovered in the improvisation work so far. The theme was a shy lover's travails. It was an attempt at archetypal comedy. In the first main scene, for instance, the lover meets the family of the girl he has fallen for. They are alarmingly eccentric, and concentrate their appetites upon him. The father challenges the lover to prove himself a man by performing a series of gymnastic feats and indicating, with glares, that the boy should emulate them, which he is pathetically unable to do. The mother instantaneously directs her arch lust at the boy; more demurely, the girl's big sister also wants to grab him for herself. A rival suitor of the girl arrives, a rich young man, and is accidentally killed. Following a folk tale told from Siberia to Tipperary, the corpse refuses to be disposed of. Whenever it is packed away in a makeshift box, one limb flops out again. If you sit on the feet, the head pops up. A policeman takes a keen interest, and is framed into believing that he himself has killed the corpse.

The stages of the plot were laid down, but the details, the narrative texture, were left for fresh invention each time. The characters were fixed, and cast permanently. The only props were the bamboo sticks and the boxes made by Monod. Bashtahondo was used throughout.

This carpet show, as it was known, was worked on intensively during the first three weeks of July. Sometimes the main characters rehearsed privately, away from the rest of the company. Its first full try-out was one evening when the Baghe Ferdous was visited by a company of actors led by Parviz Sayyad, a successful commercial director of modern plays, a weekly television show and films. The *ruhozi* players who had visited the Baghe Ferdous also operate out of Sayyad's company. The evening began with a communal dinner, followed by a drumming free-for-all, wild dancing, and spontaneous improvisation, in which the visitors and the company got to know each other a little. The spontaneous themes turned, as the company's early improvisation work had, on situations of sexual competition. Is that the highest common factor in humanity bereft of language, how we would be if we had never learned to speak? An English actor suggested that the recurrent sexual theme was provoked by the Persians in some false mimicry of what they had heard about avant-garde theatre in Europe.

In the carpet show the boxes were used, far beyond their original purpose, for fantastic, Bosch-like effects: a box walking on one leg, or a box crowned with a forest of groping hands. The visitors made occasional entries into the work, with the sympathetic humour of character actors. Brook enjoyed the 'ludicrous mixture of types' that resulted.

A week before going to the village, Brook spoke to the company about the reasons for going. 'We are not here to learn what we know already.

To make theatre within any familiar pattern will always work to some degree. We know that everywhere in the world theatre related to social problems interests those concerned by them. Such theatre is very healthy, but it is not what we mean by research. There are rare things – pieces of music, certain gestures – that can communicate to anyone anywhere. What we are looking for in Orghast and Greek is whether there are rhythms, forms of truth and emotional involvement, which can be communicated without going through the normal channels. Maybe not. Or maybe we are completely mistaken in the way we're going about it. That is the honest risk in experin.ent. If we were doing a play by Shakespeare, Molière, or an Iranian author, the play could succeed, and should. There would be no point in starting to work so as to make it not communicate. In that theatre, one knows success is possible. In our area, the impression on the audience may be totally different from the effect we aim at. It may give us an uncomfortable moment. But it will teach us an enormous amount about what is pure and impure in communication.

'Exactly the same goes for the village. They will be people apparently as far as possible from ourselves in shared cultural references, yet identical human beings. In theory, communication goes on only through a shared language and set of references. Perhaps so. We may discover no communication whatever. But I would personally believe, in that case, that it was we ourselves who were not free enough to make it. It will be a basic acting experiment for all of us, questioning whether we can be clear and simple with ourselves.'

By the time the actors started with quiet music and singing, some fifty women, grouped together, forty men and over a hundred children had gathered close around the carpet, and other men were watching from a distance. The villagers brought out their own carpets for the non-acting visitors to sit on, and jugs of water. A man with a stick went round shaking it at noisy children, until he was persuaded not to by Azadi, during his introduction to the show. One of Sayyad's group translated the introduction into Turkish. At the end of it, there was great clapping from the audience; and more clapping at the entry of one of the Persian actors in a dress and high heels, at all subsequent new entries, and at any demonstrative gags. The most successful gags were in the silent-film tradition, such as the business with the corpse. The village men laughed openly, though only a few of them found the policeman funny. The women were more reserved, and covered their faces when Azadi observed that the Mother was more interested in the Suitor than the Daughter was. The children seemed scared at first by anything strange, the Japanese groans Yoshi made as a magician, or the sight of the box walking, but were won round by the knock-about. As the show went on, the actors relied increasingly on gestures, and less on what few words of Farsi they allowed themselves.

At the end there was a general dance, in which some of the children joined. One of the Persian actresses had brought sweets, which she threw in handfuls among the audience, where small boys hunted them; this gesture, which had not been planned, Brook thought 'the only lapse of taste', though it was later defended on the grounds that the play ended with a wedding, and they had been wedding sweets. After the show the women in the company, who had throughout sat at the edge of the carpet and done no more than make music, were asked by the village women why they had not joined in the play. Some of the actors were individually invited to drink tea, but as the rest were preparing to leave could not accept.

Lively chatter in the bus going back expressed the release, or at least relief, the company felt. Brook's first reaction was that there had been 'no exaggeration of response in the audience. Thus it was a true, major exercise: all exercises done within the company alone are to some extent artificial.' The show had achieved 'a strong focus, which is often lacking in street theatre work by groups in England'. If anything, he felt it had been done with more than the necessary force, from nervousness; contact in the village, and acceptance, had been reached more readily than the actors realized. 'It taught us the need for crystal clarity. Simple action without a text shows up bad acting habits. In an hour the lesson, if learned, could be a purgation.' Another lesson was that 'it was more natural than any of the Paris shows because adults and children were all mixed together in the audience. There was no infant caste.'

In a company discussion the next day, the Paris group were enthusiastic. One called it the most exciting experience he had ever had as an actor; and Reeves, looking back at the end of the work in Persia, was to find it 'the most successful and most interesting' of all that had been done. It was, he said, a pity that it had not been done sooner, or repeated later: 'Brook is rightly concerned about preparing things properly, but in this particular unknown area the actual experience of playing is worth hours of prior discussion.' In the Paris group there had been some apprehension, and even snobbery, about the village work; but now there was respect for the dignity and finesse of the villagers, in contrast to the tea-house on the main road, 'where we were just sights' said one, and still more to the behaviour of people in Tehran.

The Persians, however, who had been touched by the actual experience in the village, now mostly reverted to the rationalizing scepticism they had felt before it happened. They spent a lot of the discussion in offering evidence that Uzbakhi was not a typical or unspoiled village: a few of the men worked, or had worked, in town; had visited relatives in Tehran; had been to the cinema, or seen television, and recognized Azadi, and were prepared to see women acting; had not only performed in *ta'zieh* but had seen *ruhozi* in a neighbouring village; did not share a room with cows. Brook thought those arguments trivial: 'the fact that foreigners didn't scare them made the situation *more* alive'. Behind the Persians' reservations, an impartial observer remarked, was a resistance to foreign cultures, which threaten the identity of a country tugged between East and West; a protectiveness of their own cultural roots, as exemplified in the village. There was, too, ambiguity about *ruhozi*, which on the one hand they suspected Brook of aiming to steal and, on the other, felt was not good enough as art for artistic actors to take to a village. 'I am asking this group,' Brook said, 'to turn its thinking into something very precise: to propose the elements we would like to see as the future basis for such work in a village. Not just ideas – ideas are cheap – but concrete elements, characters, situations, that can be developed.' But the theorizing went on, and Brook stopped the discussion abruptly.

A. C. H. Smith, *Orghast at Persepolis*

In Triumph through Persepolis by Andrew Porter

Andrew Porter, an opera critic for The Financial Times, *was instrumental in persuading the Shiraz Festival to commission* Orghast *(28 August 1971). The reviews that follow won the rarest of accolades, praised and quoted by fellow critics at Shiraz.*

The sun rose at six. I was at the top of Naqsh-e-Rustam, the sacred mountain behind vanished Istakhr, into whose sheer cliff-faces are hewn the hypocaust tombs of Darius, Xerxes, Artaxerxes and Darius II. Marvellous place at any time, overwhelming as sunrise formed the climax of an experience which had begun twelve hours before, four miles to the south at Persepolis: Peter Brook's *Orghast*, public first-fruit of his International Centre for Theatre Research which had been working for a year in Paris. At the foot of the mountain Man walked a cow to pasture along the path which a little earlier Kings and Heroes had trod. From a dozen crags the Gods were calling and chanting sacred *Avesta* texts in the old magic language of Zoroaster. As light flooded the plain a flock of goats, their bells mingling with the ritual chime from the mountain, passed across the scene: unplanned but ideal close to the drama. The King had been burnt in the fire-temple, Prometheus had been unbound, Salamis fought and lost, and on the Persian plain the people's day began once more, as it had done for unchanging centuries.

Orghast is a drama – opera, ritual, ceremony, theatrical action – with its roots in many things: myth, history, the sites of its performance; Brook's preoccupation with the nature of theatrical communication, his researches into what bodies, voices and lights can achieve when deployed before an audience; his knowledge of contemporary music with its spatial effects, counterpoints of random detail under large-scale control, and free juxtaposition of speech and song (from *Titus* onwards Brook has shown himself an accomplished composer; and a 'concert performance' of *Orghast* would grace an ISCM Festival); also, I think, his experience of Persian *ta'azieh*, which is so profoundly impressive and affecting even when no words are understood. *Orghast* was played in tongues unknown (*orghast*, and that of the *Avesta*) and little known (classical Greek, Latin) to its audiences. Immediate sources were Aeschylus, Calderón, the *Tempest* exercises, and Seneca's *Oedipus* at the Old Vic in Ted Hughes's translation.

To share in the first part we pass through portals and palaces and climb a steep mountain track, flare-lit, to the tomb of Artaxerxes III, a huge open cube cut into the mountain behind Persepolis, three sides and its floor of living rock, the fourth open to the palaces and the great plain. The actors are already disposed on the dim empty platform; we line the sides. High above us Prometheus is chained to the crag. A mystic chant swells from all sides. The voice of Zeus, of Ormazd in Old Persian, rings from the skies. Earth answers deep in the cave. Light, personified, silhouetted against the sky, cries an invocation. Prometheus sends fire to man, and a globe of fierce fire descends from above, past the relief of Ahura-Mazda, past sculputred Artaxerxes upheld by his two tiers of subject races before the fire-altar, to be received by Man below.

But Man, as even Prometheus who loves him admits in Aeschylus's play, is an imperfect creature; fire is at once a boon and a force for destruction. Krogon, the King, advances, and his attendant, Strength, seizes and appropriates the fire for royal power. The tyrant father fears the son who may overthrow him: Krogon's first son is murdered; the mother, a sad, mad shadow of grief and revenge, will pursue him to the end of the play. His second son, Sogis, is caged in a cave (Calderon's *Life is a dream*); grown, he is dragged forth painfully to pursue his destiny. Prometheus lights his reason: in thick animal tones Sogis echoes the Titan's ringing lines, ʻΟ Διος αἰΘηρ. At a feast Krogon, driven mad by light, kills all his current family; recovered, in the light of sanity, he blinds himself.

Winding through the action, leading, coaxing, restraining, cradling the child, freeing the chained youth with a touch of his torch, is Furorg, who seems to personify human instinct, at once tender and fierce, unreasoning. Furorg leads Sogis to the blind father he must kill, but – and this is where *Orghast* departs from the murderous old myths – the youth cannot do it. Krogon stumbles out into the night. The platform grows dark but fires leap up on the lower terrace, and after a silence we feel our way past the actors still sitting or standing there to the plain below.

The rites of *Orghast* are chanted from the *Avesta* in a Zoroastrian language of singing vowels, ullulating portamentos, and sudden sharp cut-offs with a steep rising inflection to a glottal stop. No one could speak it except one scholar, Mahin Tadjadod, who determined a pronunciation and taught it to the cast. Passages from *Prometheus* are declaimed in an open-vowelled ringing, singing Greek (*oo dee-os a-ee-theer*) as if from an opened heart. The Latin of *Hercules furens* (when the family is murdered in madness) strikes a high rhetorical note. But most of *Orghast* is performed in *orghast*, a dramatic language invented by Ted Hughes, an attempt to find the sound most directly communicative of ideas (light, darkness, death) and even of specific objects (skylark, fish, the whirling dust-clouds which are *flota falluttu*), sounds which carry an emotional and dramatic sense even when the listeners do not know the precise meaning of the words.

Hughes and Brook began the work in English. A scene was written, and then the poet found himself blocked by what he called 'literature'. He tried an experiment in syllabic sound, another in which the inter-national cast declaimed charged words for their sense rather than their pronunciation: of *murder* a Japanese actor made a sound in which murderous intent was clearly recognizable though the original word was not. From such research *orghast* was born. Essentially it is a development from English, but an idealized dramatic English, 'clear-eyed, resound-ing, with strong teeth', whose vowels sing clear and true into the night, blaze fiercely, or shine like the steady moon (*luna*, or *moan* in *orghast*) which played over the drama. The consonants are craggy (fire is *gheost*, while *orghast* itself is the sun; agony, *dagon*, acquires that initial stab so that it can be cried out as the English word cannot). *Eorda* is earth, *man* is man, *ladda* is son (Hughes spoke of the Yorkshire influence). When English does not supply evocative sounds, Romance roots are called into play. *Palom* is dove, *narga* is nothing, *ombalom* womb. *Lugh* is light and so *glittalugh* is star.

On paper a little basic *orghast* is easily acquired. *Datta ma ladda lugh* means give my son light, and *bak opp eorda* return to earth. Persians might find it harder, though their sounds are evocative too: *amurdaad* (immortality), *Dadhv* (the Creator), *spandarmad* (holy submission) are names of the Zoroastrian months, not yet *orghast*, though they very well might be. But learning the language is not the point – in fact precisely not the point; the intention was that the audience should respond instinctively, not set themselves semantic puzzles. Hughes suggested a simile of music which had been buried for centuries until all sophisti-cated developments had decayed from it, and only essentials remained. My peek at some pages of the script was unauthorized – and undertaken only after I had seen the piece several times. The 'plot' as outlined above needed no verbal crib (only the proper names are supplied from subsequent knowledge). Response was direct enough to, say, the three different words for darkness: *bullorga*, which is plainly active, teeming darkness, the kind Mark sings of in Tippett's opera *The Midsummer Marriage*; *blott*, the removal of light, blindness; and the *narga* of nothing-ness. On returning to the performances my understanding remained instinctive, for it is not the meaning of the words on the page which matters, but the sense of the sounds in the context of the dramatic action. When Furorg croons over the baby, or sings his *lohorn* song leading Sogis, and in part 2 the pilgrims, into the distance, his meaning needs no translation.

Yet I was not sorry to have seen some of the text in black and white. (Brook often insists that a play exists only while it is being acted, and has no life except that which players and audience together provide: too extreme a view which does not allow for the imaginative reader, of text as of musical score, who can experience a performance – can be producer, players and responsive audience in one – while he reads.) On the simplest level, perusal dispelled some unnecessary etymological mysteries which had been spun. Reading *Orghast*, aloud, proved a curiously stirring experience; pronouncing the lines one could under-stand, sensuously rather than rationally, why they had fired acting of such openness and force. Hughes has a marvellous ear, and here commands a language free from all sound-limitations. Root sounds, stems, syllables, break apart, reshape to make new senses. *Boda kagaock*, *boda scrord*, something laughed, something screamed – and though we may not know the exact meaning of the words we can hear clearly enough what kind of laughter, what kind of scream was heard. Far from Persepolis, beside a sunny Mediterranean sea, I cried *urgith*, trying to fill the word with the meaning I knew it bore. I asked my listeners what it meant. *Death* was the unhesitating, and correct, response.

The sacrifice of normal verbal comprehensibility (to at least one part of a multi-tongued audience) in order to achieve a new openness, a more direct kind of communication, was one object of the research. Another, the effect of this on the performance of an international cast with no language in common, playing to a similarly international audience. Discovering our, and their, changes of response to the four languages, the varying degrees of specifically verbal understanding (following, on this semantic level, none of the *Avesta*, a few words of Greek, rather more Latin, in time a little *orghast*), was part of the endeavour, which became an adventure, a voyage of excitement and instruction, for the playgoers as well as the players. Brook had discovered, he said, that some episodes seemed to 'need' Greek, or Latin, that the sound-pattern of those languages expressed more perfectly, more directly, certain ideas or states of feeling. In early rehearsals other languages and other juxtapositions of idiom had been tried; and in late rehearsals there were some curious fortuitous effects of theatrical interest: as when through the flaming funeral rites there cut Irene Worth's voice in English demanding to know whether the fires were safe, or when, in a visual parallel, an assistant on a bicycle hastened after the Messenger from Salamis to take him the torch he had forgotten.

Naqsh-e-Rustam is a long line of cliffs, part of the mountain bounds which circle the plain of ruined Persepolis, sacked by Alexander in 330 BC, of vanished Istakhr sacked by the Arabs in the seventh century and now buried in desert dust, and of thriving Marvdasht whose industries are powered by the increasing output of the Darius dam. High on the rockface are the huge Achaemenian tombs, cut deep into the mountain; below them, the reliefs of Sassanian triumphs, including Shahpur I's capture of Valerian in AD 260. Over the centuries dust dunes have built up at the foot of the cliff. The Achaemenian fire-temple (let us call it that, though the purpose of the building has been disputed), excavated to its base, rises now from a deep square pit. In preparation for the October Festivities the cliff-foot had been levelled to a huge parade-ground – less picturesque than it was, but a noble setting for theatrical action which formed part 2 of Peter Brook's *Orghast*.

Things began at 4.30 in the morning, so that they should end at dawn. The only light came from huge bowls of fire which blazed on the crags. The audience thronged the site, free to follow the action wherever it moved. From a rock by the tomb of Darius II a Vulture – the Vulture which had rent Prometheus, and dragged Sogis from his cage – screamed a summons; from a fiery pit below, Furorg the light-bearer led *Krogon geblott auld*, the old blinded King, on the last stages of his journey. He felt his way painfully up the rocks, followed ever by the pale, mad, chanting figure of the wife whose child he had killed, long ago. From the distance came a call from the voices of Hercules and Sogis. Sogis's mother heard it too, and came forward to greet the son who was returning. Reunion; and slowly, chanting, singing and murmuring in *Avesta* and *orghast*, the main characters from part 1 made their hour-long pilgrimage down the central path which runs the length of the site.

And the movement of their minds, their memories of deeds, battles and strife, took visual shape and verbal form in an enactment of Aeschylus's *The Persians*, done with violence and much movement, in hectic torchlit chase across the full site, zigzagging across the slow processional path and scattering the onlookers. The two actions coincided when the pilgrims had reached a space below the great central tomb, and joined in the choral invocation:

> King of old days, Our Sultan! Come, appear!
> Stand on your tomb's high crest, King of our King!
> Darius, Father, Lord, Preserver, hear!

When from the darkness of Darius's tomb-mouth the solemn shape stepped forth, the effect was overwhelming, and the impulse to fling oneself to one's knees along with the actors proved hard to master. What could have been just melodramatic became thrilling and awe-ful. Darius chanted his great speech in periods whose pitch rose step by step. (Only later, much later, did the analytical mind recall Hector in Berlioz's *Trojans*, and wonder whether the influence was conscious.) Atossa now joined Krogon to lead him to his final adventure in life, to a deep fiery cleft in the mountain face, an encounter with Mage and Sibyl. And then, while Xerxes advanced with his grief, and the Messenger from Salamis progressed and passed along the full stretch of the site with his long speech, Krogon was carried to rest in the fire-temple amid a counter-point of solemn funeral chorus. Dawn was at hand. A steep path led straight to the top of the mountain, where already the gods were calling. The survivors went upward to greet *orghast*, the sun, irresistibly drawing the more involved members of the audience with them.

Instinct, intellect and genius, months of hard study and sudden late moments of inspiration (faculties of both creators and onlookers made keen by sleeplessness, by the stimulant climate, and by the extraordinary spell of the sites), went into the making of *Orghast*. I saw it five times, under varying lights, from different places, choosing different aspects of the drama: one night never straying from the pilgrims while the actions surged back and forth, another racing to Persian assemblies on the hills and running to meet the Messenger from Salamis. *Orghast* part 2 is, among other things, a 'spectacular', which makes stunning use of cleft and crag, plateau and sculptured platform, and also such chance things as the archaeologists' scaffolding round part of the fire-temple. No light except from fires and flare, and nature's. Electric sound at times, to fill the place with omens, and carry voices from cliff to cliff with strange resonances. The critics who saw only a moonlit pre-performance, with few people there, stressed the visual beauty of the show; but it reached its dramatic climax only on the last morning of the festival, at the single public performance, when the site was thronged.

Part of the Paris Centre's research concerns the interaction of different cultures. Krogon was played by a Japanese, Katsuhira Oida, Noh-trained, samurai film-experienced, with power and passion, jaw muscles of fine-tempered steel, a classical tragedian with a flame of violence whose emotions blazed in face and body. Furorg, Malick Bagayogo, came from Mali, soft-stepping, gentle-fierce, instinctive and beautiful; sometimes a grown Puck, sometimes a grown Ariel, as he carried his torch through this world of dark complex feelings; a deep croon in his tones. Bruce Myers, Sogis, tore thick animal cries from somewhere deep in his body, shaping them to words, and in the arch of his straining back could make us share the agony of a beast-intellect being dragged to the light of wisdom, to accept his destiny.

Irene Worth, Moa, divine Earth-Mother-Wife of the God-King, rang through her deep-based vocal spectrum. Natasha Parry, the voice of Light, shone like a bright star. Paloma Matta, but more eagle than dove, screamed the avian summons in tones which set the scalp pricking. Fahime Rastkar's grave gentle beauty as Moasha, Sogis's mother, brought the element of human tenderness to the fierce tale. And so one could go through the long cast – Michèle Collison's grandeur, of voice and bearing, as Atossa; Robert Lloyd's noble voice in the heavens; Pauline Munro's obsessed mother, following the King like a pale steady flame: Nazar Azadi's clear, heroic Hercules; the *Persians* chorus led by the free-voiced Darius Farhang; many others. Vocally and physically this international company had been brought to a rare degree of expressiveness.

Orghast will never be seen anywhere else. It is 'the product of the work done in Iran, and of the effect of Iran itself on the work'. The musics of its drama, the wide-flung counterpoints of speech, speech-song and song, the elaborate patterns of dramatic and sonic densities, to some extent the language itself, were all dictated by the spaces and acoustics of its sites. The western-based dramatic tongue which Ted Hughes has invented, the Greek mythology, the elements of Greek, Latin and Spanish plays, have all taken new root here, in this drama of darkness and light. 'From Zoroastrian times,' Arthur Upham Pope writes in his *Persian Architecture*, 'the beautiful was integrally associated with light. It was an essential component of the divine personality. Physical light in Persia – intense, palpable, creative – persuasively expounds the role conferred on it by religion.'

Orghast was claimed as no more than experiment, a research-project, 'work in progress'. My surrender to it was not instant, but by the end it was total (except for details, such as feeling that the electrical amplification, recognizable as such, struck a jarring note). The playgoer who entered deeply into *Orghast* passed through fire, and can never be the same again.

The Financial Times (11, 14, 16 September 1971)

The 'high'/'low' dialectic of the nature of Brook's work in Iran and subsequent-ly in Africa is reflected in the two forms of Iranian theatre with which he has had direct contact, and by which he has been most profoundly affected. The intensely hieratic and quasi-mystical poetry and hermeticism of Orghast *mirror the form of the traditional Iranian passion play, the 'ta'zieh' ('mourning'), which Brook had seen the previous year in Nishabur, a remote village in the north-east of Iran. Similar in many ways to the medieval mysteries, these cycle plays are performed to celebrate the martyrdom of Immam Hossein, the father of Shi'ism. The stories are conveyed orally from one generation to the next, to be enacted by the villagers themselves. Spectators participate actively, lamenting aloud or supplying whatever comes to hand to represent sacred relics (e.g. a pencil for Muhammad's finger, a hubcap for his shield). Brook compares this lengthy communal event of epic grandeur to Oberammergau 'without the commercialism'. It taught him that true incarnation in the present moment and communal celebration can only ever be possible* within these forms *within the shared references of a particular group (in this case, the Shi-ites). At the same time, he felt it to have been 'the most moving and miraculous thing I've ever seen'.*

On the other hand, he took as his initial model for the forms to be explored during the African journey the improvised roughness of the 'ruhozi'. At least four hundred years old, this popular theatre form is still performed by strolling players similar in many ways to the European commedia dell'arte troupes. It comprises very fast and energetic improvisations around fundamentally comic human relationships and situations. In Iran, it has often been snobbishly rejected as somehow artistically invalid because of its popularity and its vulgarity. Yet Brook defines three different types of vulgarity in the theatre: first, when the actor's self is suddenly and unintentionally revealed under pressure; second, the exploitative vulgarity of low comedy; and finally, that infinitely valuable vulgarity common to forms such as the 'ruhozi' – liberating, anarchic, Dionysiac, as timeless, international and refreshing as all great comedy from Aristophanes and Plautus to Jarry and the Marx Brothers. To a certain extent, the 'ruhozi' must remain a prisoner of its own fixed traditions, chained within the enforced repetition of certain restricted situations and relationships. Yet its vital energy in performance, the strength, clarity and immediate communicability of its forms carry it free from such limitations. First-hand contact with the 'ruhozi' (and similarly with Habib Tanvir's Naya Theatre later in India) gave Brook an ideal: that of a group of players moving from village to village, improvising in an energetic and direct way accessible to all, using the set of conditions of that particular time and place alone. It was surely here that the seeds of the African journey were sown.

D.W.

Africa: 'In Search of the Miraculous' (December 1972–February 1973)

After the *Orghast* project, the group returned to Paris for fifteen months of intensive research work in private before once again setting out, in December 1972, on a three-month journey in North and West Africa. For a number of reasons, Brook saw Africa as the logical next step in their work. He has long felt the contemporary European theatre to be crippled because it attracts only a very narrow band of society. Characteristically, he turns to Elizabethan society for comparison. At that time, theatre audiences were a truer reflection of a whole society. Brook felt that his actors would be creatively stimulated by being exposed to a wider variety of responses from within a living culture, like that of the Elizabethans. He saw just such a possibility in a journey to Africa, which was structured so that the group would encounter as wide a range of different peoples as possible, (in many ways matching the mixed backgrounds and traditions of those who had come together to form the C.I.R.T.).[1] These consisted of various religious groups, including black Muslims, Catholics and animists, as well as people from a wide range of climatic conditions, from desert to rich rain forest. In addition, the freedom of travelling across country in Land Rovers allowed them to be in the unprecedented position of being able to create 'the kind of work which only begins when you can play where you want, when you want, and where absolutely no set of circumstances lays down anything whatsoever except the self-imposed obligation to do your best work when the time comes.'

Brook's view of an ideal theatre event as a meeting point between different levels of reality is reflected in the somewhat modish romanticism of his conception of Africans (and of Third World cultures in general). For he believes the Africa of village life to be the place where

[1] The journey (December 1972–February 1973) took place at the mildest time of year. Starting in Algeria, the route led across the ultimate 'empty space' of the Sahara, through Niger to Nigeria (for more than one month) and on to Dahomey, where the coast was reached. The return journey took the group back through West Niger and Mali, a different crossing of the desert and finally back to Algiers.

'the intertwining between the imaginary and the real is at its freest; where an imaginative experience is at its most open; where the human challenge is at its greatest.' It offers one of the few remaining cultural situations in which 'the combination of social and religious structures is such that there is a greater width to the possible spectrum, a greater possibility of interrelating the most ordinary and the most hidden levels of experience.' Without a trace of condescension, he compares Africans to children. They exist with access to a free passage between the world of everyday reality in the present and the world of magic and imagination, the past and the future. They animate the everyday with a sort of psychic 'mana', and are in turn animated. Compare this to Lévi-Strauss's view:

> Savage thought is definable both by a consuming symbolic action such as humanity has never again seen rivalled, and by scrupulous attention directed entirely towards the concrete, and finally by the implicit conviction that these two attitudes are but one.'
>
> (*The Raw and the Cooked*)

Brook feels that make-believe is a necessity in their lives; they are natural creative artists in a land where life is permeated by the texture of theatre. They have much to teach the modern European, for example, in the area of play:

> Playing is a natural activity . . . a basic function, like eating, drinking, making love. Out of playing comes exploration of life through imitating it. Out of that come a million forms of celebration and attempts to understand. So all vital forms of theatre are in a sense an extension of a natural activity.[2]

The lives of both children and Africans prepare them in a unique way for the theatre. They are natural audiences in that they fill the creative role demanded of an audience with the richness of their imaginations and the honesty of their responses. At the same time, their freshness of vision offers a direct challenge to the actor's clarity; as Brook told John Heilpern in Africa, 'The eyes of the child are alive.'

In Western life in general, there exists an unhealthy separation

---

[2] cf., Schiller: 'Man only plays when in the full meaning of the word he is a man, and he is only completely a man when he plays' (*Essays Aesthetical and Philosophical*, 1745). Apparently Brook's views owe much to the rather unfashionable writings of Lévy-Bruhl (in particular *Primitive Mentality* and *How Natives Think*): cf., for example, 'In the collective representations of primitive mentality, objects, beings, events can be, though in a way incomprehensible to us, both themselves and something other than themselves'.

between dream and reality, between the poetic and the concrete, between culture and everyday life. Make-believe is no longer deemed necessary. It was when Jung travelled in Africa that he experienced what he considered an enlightenment, recognizing for the first time the dissociation of modern European man from his own profound being. Progress was seen by him as a denial of man's essential relationship to nature and myth. Jung had originally gone to Africa to 'find that part of my personality which had become invisible under the pressure of being European'. In effect, the experience proved to be one of confrontation with his own unconscious, and subsequently with the potential for an intensity of life suppressed in 'civilized' man.

Brook counts his work with children as among the most demanding and informative of his experience in the theatre. Considered the freest of all spectators, children have been used as an acid-test. They are 'the perfect audience. They crystallize things without judging as adults do.' He claims to have learnt more about 'what is pure and impure in communication' from these experiences than from any others. Untainted by aprioristic cultural assumptions and conditioning, therefore having no concern with notions of 'correct' response, they react with a vital and innocent honesty. If their demand for *interest* is not met, they show their boredom, just as the African villager would turn away and leave. (He suggests that, on the other hand, many European audiences expect a certain degree of boredom as an inherent part of any 'cultural' event, blindly accepting and even demanding it.)

Brook still talks with glee of an incident in the Mobilier National, during preparation for the *Orghast* project. An experiment with a children's show ended with an unpredictably violent but honest response, manifesting the true quality of the work created. Unconsciously, the actors had approached the performance with a drop in their level of seriousness and commitment. They had forgotten that 'a simple show for children is as valuable as the most mysterious show for adults'. In their dissatisfaction, the children responded to this patronising lack of respect by physically attacking the actors with the sticks with which they had been working. This moment of open revolt was seen as an educative experience for the actors, prompting a reassessment of their assumptions and a growth in sensitivity. It was hoped that the experience of playing in Africa would offer a series of similar (though less physically painful) shocks to the group.

In going to Africa, he was consciously putting the group in a position of vulnerability. In the absence of the complicity that comes from shared cultural references, an equivalent would have to be found in an essence of what is human in experience. Brook suggests that a great number of European performances fall flat precisely because the performers work from pre-established sets of limiting and divisive assumptions. In reality, yesterday's truth may be meaningless today. Instead, he was asking his actors to begin again every time from as near as possible to a zero point where nothing could be taken for granted. They would have to find a way to coax today's shared frame of reference into being within the heat and action of the performance. So, if the improvisation evolved in accord with the changing tempo of response, every moment would see the birth of a form appropriate to the conditions feeding that moment. If the group approached the work and the relationship to an audience on a level they respected, the audience would respond with respect, but they would not give the actors 'a second glance through respect for theatre conventions'. Evidently, in such a situation, highly prepared and polished work would be both irrelevant and 'anti-life'. In conversation with me, Brook compared it to the preparation of conversation before attending a dinner party.[3] Therefore, in Africa, and indeed anywhere outside the rules of Western bourgeois theatre, *improvised forms* would be absolutely necessary.

'Change and develop with each audience – or we're lost'. According to Brook's extreme pragmatism, any dogmatic approach will be deadly: 'The only rule is that which comes in the instant when something comes towards you.'

As a result of the necessity of improvised forms, Brook was able to continue his quasi-scientific investigation of the nature of improvisation in a practical situation, work which to a limited extent the group had begun in Paris and in villages in Iran. A more extended period of work in Africa gave him the possibility of exploring the *dialectic of form and spontaneity* in particular. Above all, he wanted to research the re-lationship between 'what has to be prepared and what must not be prepared'. In improvisation, an open, non-restrictive form must be found to encourage the free play of the actor's creative energy, a form which at the same time is not so loose as to collapse into inarticulate and anarchic diffusion. 'Too much freedom is a lack of freedom' (Grotowski). He must be able to create a concrete moment of truth between himself and the spectators. This can only be achieved if the actor faces some external requirement, a strict and clear condition,

---

[3] Any 'true performance' must have 'some of the same values as a meeting between two strangers, which is lifeless if it mechanically follows a ritualistic formula, and only has meaning if each time there is a new human variation'.

throughout the work to free himself; the friction of the resulting conflict may give rise to a creative spark.

In the work of Africa, Brook attempted to find an increasingly simple condition as starting point for an improvisation; in general, this took the form either of a simple scenario or of a single object. The scenarios were built largely around universally recognizable relationships, archetypes of conflict and competition painted in very broad emotional tones such as hate, love or lust. The highly physical style of these improvisations suggested a sort of cartoon manicheism of human relations in which forces of good and evil battled together. Almost inevitably, the tendency seemed to be towards the rough comedy of the circus or the silent movie, the world of pratfalls and knockabout slapstick. In general, it was felt that the aims of the work were compromised by the actors' submission to the tempting but false security of the easy laugh, thereby establishing an artificial and insincere complicity. At the same time, moments of great comedy built upon a common human truth were created; at such moments, the response became the shared laughter of liberation and enlightenment, laughter which has its roots in our deepest inner impulses.

Clearly the simple everyday *objects* – a loaf of bread, a stick, a box, shoes, (a door, in similar work in Paris) – were as close as possible to a zero point, as well as being a means of centring, anchoring and focusing collective work, a means of preventing anarchy or the aimless meanderings of self-indulgent fantasy. In such improvisations, the object itself serves as minimal supportive rule, the tightrope-walker's rope demanding respect at every moment, at the same time a source of marvel, a stimulus to the imagination, a raw material for full creative exploration. For example, a box offers an endless possible series of improvisations used as a closed or an open space; an everyday object of great simplicity, it nevertheless possesses infinite creative possibilities. A box appearing to cross the empty space at the centre of a ring of spectators immediately creates an interest and demands development. Similarly, a shoe thrown into 'the glaring vacuum' somehow undergoes a creative transformation; the power of focused attention can breathe life into the inanimate. When an old hag puts on the shoe to become young and beautiful, an element of the magic accredited to the object by the space is realized in concrete terms. In almost all such improvisations, the object was displaced from its normal functional usage. The use of objects in this way has become an integral part of the group's theatrical practice; *Ubu aux Bouffes* (1977) was later to be the clearest and most condensed expression of such work in a full production.

The group continued to experiment with improvisation in *musical forms*. Much of this work was a direct development of openings revealed during the *Orghast* project, when vocal possibilities had been used as subliminally communicative sound, breath or vibration. Here they were to be used to sustain or comment upon an improvisation, or as a means for collective improvisation in itself. This area of the work was conducted largely by the young American composer Elizabeth Swados. It took the form of vocal exercises in non-naturalistic sound and collective choral work. For example, the group would establish a simple theme or rhythm around which a soloist would improvise, often in conjunction with, or in counterpoint to, simple physical movements. The broad emphasis of all such work was on the investigation of the relationship between a rhythmic base and an improvised solo part – the ensemble in relation to the individual – as well as on the development of a group ability to modulate and respond collectively. Vocal expression was augmented by the use of simple instruments. The musical training was not systematic, the aim as always being clarity and simplicity rather than virtuosity.

Yet the simplicity that is concomitant with the desired state of innocence is perhaps the most complex form of expression to create, for it entails the discovery of open, accessible forms that avoid triviality by retaining a full charge of meaning. When Brook refers to Brecht's ideal of a theatre of 'naïvety', he means the concentrated plenitude within simplicity of the 'haiku' or the honed economy of the Zen calligrapher's circle. As I have repeatedly stressed, such immediacy and truth can only be liberated by the constant shedding of external, accreted forms, those lies that come so easily to the surface in any creative process; by a process of refinement down to the direct impact of an *essence*. David Hockney once talked on television of his ideal in art, referring to a Japanese painting of a snail seen from above. After dipping his brush in the paint, the artist had initially formed the spiral of the shell, commencing at its apex, then the snail's head and finally its glistening trial – all *without recharging his brush*. As the trail faded and dried in the snail's wake, so did the paint stroke. This mirrors perfectly Brook's ideal in theatre: the creation of a direct language of simplicity and precise economy in which all that may be distractingly superfluous and excessive is rejected and alien in a spontaneous process of expression.

During the journey, the group were able to experience at first hand the use of rhythm and vocal expression in the ceremonies, dances and songs of various African tribes. They witnessed and participated in a number of traditional festivals and celebrations. In Kano, they saw 'griots' at work – the caste of storyteller-cum-historian-cum-mountebank entertainers whose extraordinarily vital relationship with community audiences has long fascinated Brook. They were present at dances of huge puppets, sacrifices in the forest of Oshogbo (Nigeria) and moments of possession. Many of these experiences offered concrete glimpses of what Brook calls 'holiness'. Apparently abstract forces were fully realized in the here and now in individuals who had truly become 'vehicles for the spirit'. In many ways, the instances of Yoruba possession which they encountered reflected qualities Brook had sought within the theatre. As is not the case with the cruder and more hysterically violent forms of possession in Haiti, for the Yoruba, consciousness is not annihilated when the god enters his body. He remains fully aware of himself, yet at the same time is totally transformed, at one with the god. Therefore, he is at the point of union between the two worlds. Like Brook's ideal actor, paradoxically he is completely 'involved while distanced – detached without detachment'. In addition, the Yoruba's openness and sensitivity nourishes his natural faculty for immediate transformation, for multiple changes of identity, in this critical but necessary form of make-believe that is his spiritual and social life-blood.

The aim of such contact was not to imitate the new forms revealed to the group but rather, through exposure to this richness of life, to force a recognition of how incomplete their own range of possibilities remained, and to challenge the individual to broaden this limited range. Brook was very sensitive to suggestions that the trip was perhaps the ultimate refinement of colonialist plundering, that the *exchange* he posited was in fact sufficiently one-sided (in his favour) to be called theft. He was fully aware that such an enterprise could be interpreted in terms of a sort of cultural imperialism. In reality, he studiously avoided such a possibility by approaching both the work seen and the work done with enormous respect and effort. Only through truly giving up themselves could the actors be felt to have fulfilled their part of the exchange. According to Bruce Myers, 'we gave them our energy and openness. It was a real giving and receiving.' In any event, it is of course impossible to estimate the lasting effects upon the Africans. For Brook's group, on the other hand, it has become evident that this journey remains the most important collective experience to date. It is no overstatement to say that it has left the most profound and visible influence on all their subsequent work.

There were unquestionably areas of failure, of which Daniel Charlot was highly critical in his report to UNESCO. Brook had attempted to

carry over the work on the development of group 'antennae' of awareness into the everyday life of the group. If a community understanding
could be made to permeate all levels of life on the journey, it could only
feed the quality of the work produced. As Brook had written in his
introduction to Grotowski's *Towards a Poor Theatre*, 'a way of life is a way
to life'. According to Charlot and Odimbossoukou, two impartial
observers, however, it was evident that there was a certain lack of
commitment to the group unit outside the work itself. Charlot felt that so
much was taken for granted that it was only the strong personal bond
Brook had established with each individual that kept the group as a unit
at all. Certain improvisations were mediocre, lacking energy and imagination. Just as frequently, there was a sudden loss of dynamism
during the testing moments of transition between one situation or
relationship established within an improvisation and subsequent ones.

Regularly, an actor would lack that essential faculty that Gurdjieff
called 'self-remembering', an objective, critical awareness of self. During an improvisation, he would succumb to the gratuitous and contingent logic of his personal fantasies, forgetting his responsibility to the
other actors and to the particular audience. This led to a lack of clarity
and a cutting of contact with the surrounding life: improvisation for
improvisation's sake. Often the group showed themselves unaware of
the barriers to communication that they set up by taking naturalistic
conventions of illusion for granted. On one occasion, Helen Mirren
limped grotesquely across the space, playing an ugly and crumpled old
hag; Brook remembers that the Africans believed the beautiful young
European to be suffering from a very painful illness. There were
moments of a surprising (if unwitting) tactlessness, even vulgarity; in the
course of the improvized 'bread show', sometimes a loaf would be thrown
around, trampled underfoot and wasted – a mere accessory in a game for
the well-fed actors, yet the very stuff of survival in areas racked by
famine. In addition, Brook's relentless appetite for work, coupled with
fatigue and illness, in some ways had a self-destructive effect. By the end
of the journey, the actors had largely exhausted their imaginative energy,
coming full circle to repetition of earlier work. Perhaps understandably,
this return to 'dead' ideas was a comforting escape from the rigorous
demand for fresh creation. Inevitably their work had never been met
with the exuberantly enthusiastic responses liberated by, for example,
the griots. In general, the interest established by the group's appearance
in a village was born from curiosity and astonishment at the novelty of
the situation, rather than from the work itself. However, Charlot
concedes in his records that of the thirty-four public performances on

the journey only six were disasters, four of those simply because the space was overrun by the pressure of a massive crowd.

Yet this unprecedented journey was surely vindicated by those 'privileged moments' when profound contact clearly was established between the group and their African hosts, particularly in the encounters with the Bororos and the Peulhs. Brook still remembers the innocent joy of the group's first performance in the desert township of In-Salah; at the time he had suggested that it had given rise to 'a feeling of simple and total attentiveness, total response, and lightning appreciation, something that perhaps in a second changed every actor's sense of what a relationship with an audience could be'. On some occasions, a point of contact was created in the revelation of common areas; for example, a number of the sounds produced by the group in improvisation were found to echo exactly vocalizations in the African performances. From time to time, the influence of the living culture of Africa – of what Brook refers to as the Third Culture – brought to light fresh possibilities from within the group.

Brook has described one such experience. Late one night, on the road from Gboko to Ife in Nigeria, a curious chance meeting took place. The group's singing attracted a number of children to their camp. They informed them that a funeral ceremony was taking place in their village near by. The group went with the children to the village and were invited to participate in the ceremony, whereupon they improvised songs and simple dances for the villagers: 'We reached an extraordinary moment of feeling – a feeling of understanding and of clarity. It was something quite exceptional; perhaps it was a *paratheatrical experience*. We were in the pitch dark, with no moon and no light, so that the villagers were like shadows; we never saw them. Finally, before dawn, we left, still having never seen the people. We had met their hearts, but we never to this day knew their faces, nor did they know ours.'

Brook felt that this unique situation had liberated the best work the group had ever done. An innocent celebration of life through collective creation, it had been made possible by the shared experience of the journey. The actors as human beings had fully met their responsibilities to other human beings in a moment of truth and honesty. Together they had consummated 'a marriage of different worlds' (Malik Bowens). Brook knew that the spirit of such moments could not be repeated mechanically; it could only ever be rediscovered. His suggestion that it may have been a 'paratheatrical' experience is pertinent. His description tallies closely with those rare accounts (and with my own experiences) of Grotowski's work since abandoning the theatre that, for him, had become 'a ghost town'. Indeed, much of Brook's terminology in his descriptions of the work of this period draws heavily on Grotowski's own utterances, particularly in the emphasis placed on theatrical event as '*meeting*'. What is certain is that such experiences take the participant far beyond the emotional shallowness and somewhat masturbatory aestheticism of the happenings of the Sixties. Since 1974, when Brook and his group made permanent roots for their work in a theatre in Paris, one of their most important shared ideals has been to try to find a way of feeding such celebratory experiences into work conducted within the theatre.

D.W.

The African Journey by John Heilpern

John Heilpern was invited by Peter Brook to accompany the C.I.R.T. on the African journey. The following account comes from Conference of the Birds: The Story of Peter Brook in Africa. *It offers a rare insight into the day-to-day concerns and obsessions of Brook, and the struggles of his actors.*

> 'Man lives in a state of imagination, in a dream: no one sees things as they are. To him who says to you: "What shall I do?" say to him: "Do not do as you have always done; do not act as you have always acted."'
>
> ('The Lost Key', from Attar's *Conference of the Birds*)

In Salah

The crowd was growing now – 300 or so spilling onto the carpet. A fat and furious schoolmaster was pointing angrily at his watch, lashing out at his truant children. They just dodged away and dodged back again. The village mad woman, an old hag holding a mirror and comb, stopped the show when she decided to jig around on the carpet for a while. Who would have her? She was singing and admiring herself in the little hand mirror. Who would have her? A violent row blew up amid laughter from the crowd, for there were no takers. Then Sylvain Corthay took off on a risky solo, making wild and strange sounds to a basic beat from the group. The audience collapsed with laughter. They were like lightning. The second he made it, striving and straining after a specially meaningful sound, they just roared with laughter. They weren't cruel or anything. They just couldn't help it. 'You see,' Brook whispered to me, 'they've good taste.' Corthay gritted his teeth, ploughing on with the solo in a daze.

Then the group began many improvisations based on some of the archetypes they'd worked on in Paris – a trickster, a king, a giant, a corpse – the first tentative improvisations performed in ones and twos as the white camel was slaughtered in another corner of the market-place, groaning and spitting blood.

Perhaps what followed might strike you as very naïve. Brook met Bertolt Brecht shortly before he died. Brecht said: 'You know what my real term for the theatre is? My term is the Theatre of Naïvety.'

'Quick!' said François Marthouret. 'Give me an idea!' 'Search *me*.'

209

Then he was on the carpet, struggling with a cardboard box. The crowd fixed on the box with total attentiveness. There was a stillness about the people, an expectancy. What's in the box? Another box is in the box. What's in the second box? Marthouret struggled with the box again, a Kaspar character, someone who could not speak, struggling with sounds and objects as if they had just been discovered. He buried himself in the box, head first. The crowd laughed. He emerged with a conch. No sound would come. Blow harder: no sound. *Harder!* He got a sound. Marthouret grinned from ear to ear, as did the audience.

Helen Mirren went on the carpet, blowing on a slide whistle. She talks with the whistle to Miriam Goldschmidt who replies with a flute. Michèle Collison joins them, is lured by them, on to the carpet. She has a flute. The three women talk to each other. Enter a corpse: Lou Zeldis, the tallest corpse in the world, taking a great theatrical bow. The actors laugh but no one else understands the bow. What's a bow? But the corpse is dead on its feet. Bagayogo takes its hand: the hand sticks to him. Myers goes to the rescue: corpse envelops the rescuer. No one escapes a corpse. Zeldis, now an actor, takes another bow. Ah, so *that's* what a bow's for!

What next? Nobody knew. Brook wasn't saying anything either. Enter a void! No actor was moving. Until Katsulas suddenly took off his huge army boots and placed them in the centre of the carpet. Then he abandoned them there.

The crowd stare at the boots. The actors stare at the boots. Everyone in the place is staring at a pair of army boots. It was as if we were all seeing them for the first time. Then Katsulas, who must have been having a little think, approached the boots. What luck! To find a pair of boots in the middle of nowhere. So he put them on, for he hadn't a pair of his own. Then he's in those great boots, and he's feeling really good, and he's strutting around that carpet a new man, a powerful man, a *giant* of a man! Sometimes the boots won't walk where he wants them to. They kick and fight him. But Yoshi Oida decides he wants the boots, confronts the giant, grows frightened, hides in the crowd. Uproar! The giant goes after him, but grabs a child instead. Everyone's laughing now, except the child who's really scared. So the giant, who's a gentle giant, takes off one of the boots and gives it to him. The child doesn't know what to do. 'Blow,' mimes the giant. Marthouret is on the carpet now, blowing into the boot for the child. No sound. Blow harder: no sound. *Harder!* The boot makes the sound of a conch. Swados is blowing her brains out on the conch at the edge of the carpet, and everyone knows this but it doesn't matter. The child's eyes are wide. The giant asks him to try. He blows and blows, and the sound comes. The child just looked at the boot and he looked at the sky, and he couldn't say a word.

Enter Ayansola on one leg. Goggles over the bedsheet round his head, tartan socks tucked into his natty Italian shoes, a terrific sight. Ayansola gets that claw working hard on his talking drum as he hops about on one leg for extra effect. The crowd loves this showmanship and cheers him. SCLEEAAAAH! Katsulas is in there now, screaming, seizing the moment, cartwheeling across the carpet to the surprise and delight of the crowd. Others join him, running, diving, tumbling – acrobatics of a sort, which create their own energy and excitement. A dance begins to drums. Those actors were really enjoying themselves. With all its limitations the show had gradually become an ideal theatre perform- ance. It was an *event*.

Work with sticks followed, exercises in rhythm and timing, audacious patterns and images, at which the crowd often fell still and watchful. They didn't mind when things went wrong. But they really loved it when they went right. When the sticks bent into an invisible circle, something that really needs incredible discipline to make, a perfect circle, slowly building from the ground to the sky, each arching his stick in precise timing with the next until the sticks seem to take life, a life of their own – that can be miraculous when it works and the crowd sensed it, watching in total silence until the invisible circle was made, and applause. A song followed. And that was all that was attempted in the market-place of In Salah.

I don't think I've ever seen the actors of Brook look so happy. That was a very special day. It had been a meeting of innocents: a celebration. But once gained the innocence was to be lost as quickly as the next performance, and never found again.

That audience had seemed reserved and gentle: open. They were totally free of any conventional theatre associations. They hadn't seen an acting group before. The name Brook meant nothing to them. They just received the work in the most open way. They were Brook's 'searchlight' – he often used the term – new eyes that really challenged the actor's sense of clarity and simplicity. This was one of the best reasons for going to Africa: whenever the group performed something obviously dramatic or arty, the audience found them out every time.

Why had the people of In Salah laughed so much when Sylvain Corthay made his strange sounds? I've heard actors make similar sounds in experimental work in Europe and America – and they've passed muster, even been acclaimed. After all, Brook spent a whole year inventing a new language of sounds, Ted Hughes's *Orghast*. But In Salah rejected them, Brook explained, for one very simple reason: they weren't good enough. What the actors and Brook did on such occasions – throughout the entire journey – was in its way equally simple. They began all over again. In this way, the second-to-second vibrant response of the audience was the best teacher the group could have. When the people of In Salah collapsed with laughter at Corthay's sounds, Brook compared it to the moment in Zen teaching when the pupil earnestly asks a vital question only for his revered master to reply by swiping him over the head. For the Zen pupil such a shattering moment might lead to illumination, and set him on the right path.

It's strange: when I asked Corthay what the laughter felt like, he said it was just like being hit over the head.

Tamanrasset

All the joy and innocence of In Salah, the innocence more than anything, was smashed at the next performance.

Two days after the search we reached the bustling desert town of Tamanrasset, famous capital of the old Tuareg empire, and pitched camp among the rocks and boulders of the surrounding desert.

As soon as the actors sat round the carpet, they were ambushed. Brook had made a tactical error – the street was too narrow to hold a huge chaotic crowd that appeared unexpectedly from nowhere. The group tried to keep calm. People were spilling on to the carpet, forcing the actors back against a wall. 'Just keep calm and everything will be *all right*.' As soon as you sat down, ten kids sat in your lap. When you moved them off, twenty more took their place. The crowds were climbing walls, clinging to trees, submerging Land Rovers, shouting, calling, laughing, fighting to see what was going on. Instant Stravinsky was going on. The actors had launched into a little esoteric musical work. But the songs were too hesitant and gentle. Nobody could hear them. 'Keep calm. Just keep *calm*.' Ayansola was sent in with a pat on his back, like a substitute footballer to save the ball game.

He knew he couldn't go wrong. He really had an evil grin on his face as he took his drum and whacked it so hard they could have heard it back in Algiers. Cheers from the crowd! But some of them were ironic. Brook laughed when he heard them, taking the point. 'Now that man can play! That man knows what he's doing!' Swados screamed for a faster number from the group. 'They want action!' But a battered old truck was forcing its way through the audience at the time. We had to roll up the carpet to let it through. It was a sort of interval.

'*Box Show!*' ordered Brook, who seemed intrigued and excited by the chaos. He likes the unexpected to happen. The crowd was growing, buzzing with the flies around the freaks who'd come to town. The village elders gossiped and giggled together at the back. The kids were having a wild time. But the veiled Tuaregs created a sense of distance: bewildered eyes. A tough group of young men in Western clothes stood at the front with their arms folded: critics.

François Marthouret, white in the face, entered the carpet to save the show. Have you ever seen the glazed eyes of a boxer just before he's sent sleepy-time Joe?

Marthouret played The Lost Man born into a world he can't understand. For a split second he glanced at Brook. Brook stared back with eyes of ice. Marthouret was lost, all right. Panicked and confused by the chaos and the noise and heat and flies, he looked desperately at the actors around him. But he must have seen his own face. The others were pole-axed too. They couldn't get to the boxes through the crowd. They couldn't get in them. The precious boxes were piled up behind a tree. The children were sitting on them.

'Oh Christ,' murmured Mirren, staring in disbelief at the carpet. She could see several actors in boxes had made it at last, crashing into each other in the confusion. There was a pile-up in the centre of the carpet. Marthouret was playing the Lost Man as never before. Katsulas looked wild. Zeldis had the giggles, appeasing the gods with a little dance to himself. Then Bagayogo, who's a bit short-sighted, strolled on to the carpet at the wrong time. Brook's face lit up. He was waiting for someone to abandon the boxes and throw the show in a different direction. But Bagayogo decided to stick to the text, squinted at the helpless Marthouret and strolled off again. The story was lost. Jokes fell flat. Scenes were cut, confused, thrown away. The actors didn't know where they were. Brook looked resigned and embarrassed, pouting.

Unable to move freely around the carpet, the actors were forced to wait in a space behind a tree to make their entrance. The tree had become the wings of a theatre. The carpet had become a stage. By accident the group was travelling back in time towards the format of the traditional theatre. The audience was 'out there', and feared. Even the group's fear belonged to the past. Those marvellously relaxed moments of real improvisation were missing. 'Get through it,' they seemed to be saying. 'Get *through* it.' You had only to look at two faces in the group for an expert reaction. Swados – scowl, squirm, cringe, kill. Brook – pout, and in this nightmare, more pout. Brook watches every performance with all the intensity of a laser beam but when he pouts – that's it.

The audience didn't seem to mind too much, though. At least they weren't throwing things. A couple of scenes worked, and they were fun. The crowd was more baffled than anything, like the actors. They weren't what Brook calls 'a natural audience'. A natural audience is one in which both sides – actors and audience – relax to the point where judgement and defence melt into shared experience. For Brook it's what theatre is all about. It becomes a spontaneous event. The last line Bottom speaks in *A Midsummer Night's Dream* is 'The wall is down.' It's the key to Brook's entire approach to theatre. But no walls were down in Tamanrasset, for nothing was shared. That first celebration of innocence at In Salah seemed like a miracle now.

Marthouret looked punch-drunk, exhausted and drained by the heat and tension. 'It's a marathon,' he gasped, as the others did their best to help and turn the tide. A tower of boxes was built. Mercifully, the box tower signalled the end of the show. The actors sang as they built it, a hymn of praise prepared when hopes were high. But the box tower tottered and collapsed, tumbling into the crowd.

People drifted away. No applause.

Perhaps the best thing about Brook's actors is that they never blame anyone except themselves for a failure. The conditions were to get far, far worse than Tamanrasset but I never heard them take it out on the impossible conditions, not really. Yet it was incredibly difficult for them, more difficult than it was for Brook. Brook is in the business of research – opening up questions. If he'd wanted to put on a successful show in Africa he could have prepared and perfected one, and hoped for the best. But this wouldn't have helped him find an answer to what he's searching for. Part of the crippling nature of the work is that the moment anything is a success it must be abandoned. If not, it becomes set and closed – unable to teach anything fresh.

It didn't particularly help the guilt and depression of the actors after the disaster of Tamanrasset, but Brook never went to Africa to 'please' an audience. It's just that he put the emphasis on risking failure, failure in every direction, in the hope of learning something new. But it can be a terrific strain on actors. They understand what's expected of them, yet their natural instincts are to please and entertain. They volunteered for the Brook Experiment but they panic, lose all confidence, go through crisis after crisis, looking back to the good old days when there was such a thing as a well-made play, and a script, with dialogue. It's why Brook's critics often see him as the all powerful master-mind using his actors as helpless guinea-pigs. But I think they might be wrong about that.

Everyone on this journey – Brook, the actors, Swados, the audiences, even myself – everyone was the guinea-pig.

Brook led the conference after the show, more a post-mortem, over warm beer in the fly-blown bar of the local rest house. Nobody blamed anyone or anything. Brook discussed the show quietly, talking in terms of greater urgency and pace. Change direction, switch with the different moods of the audience. It was no use hoping for the ideal audience we'd found at In Salah. There was nervous tension here – noise and movement, demanding speed and action. A far greater involvement was needed, more urgency, more danger. The playing area was too cramped for the boxes. It had been a mistake – but why not abandon them, take more risks, begin again?

'It is our whole reason for coming to Africa,' warned Brook. 'Change and develop with each audience – or we're lost.'

Still, I think Brook may have been privately pleased with the disaster of Tamanrasset. Failure can be more valuable than success, if you look at it the right way. If there was any complacency left in the group, the shock-encounter had finally smashed it. No one could now take anything about this journey for granted, including Brook. For in Paris he thought *The Box Show* a direct and simple piece of theatre. Perhaps an audience schooled in Beckett or the Theatre of the Absurd might have found the boxes a powerful image. Yet in spite of all the chaos and panic, the boxes seemed highly complex in Africa. They seemed presumptuous. They were shown to be no more than what they were – a theatre convention that could have no meaning to people who couldn't recognize the convention. A way must be found to create a direct response. The event had to justify itself totally, living or dying on human terms alone. And so one is forced to create a new language, more powerful ways of communicating than anything these actors had known. But *how*? What is simplicity? Perhaps Africa would tell us.

The Shoe Show II: Agades

After any setback Brook returns to work immediately and keeps moving. It's as if he wills and forces events to take a better turn. In the most extraordinary way imaginable, they were about to.

He organized another show to take place in Agades as soon as possible the next day – the first show outside a market-place. But the villagers in the fields somehow thought we were tourists. Perhaps we were, in a way. They were going to put on a show for us.

And so we became the audience.

We left after dark, planning to light the show with the fluorescent lights from the camp or the film crew's powerful generator. A young boy guided the Land Rovers along the dusty tracks into the fields. Brook had fixed the location during the day: a Tuareg village, farmers, goat men, makers of camel bags and shoes. We hung the lights between two trees, feeding the wires into the car batteries. I couldn't see any homes in the dim light. We were in a field of sand and stone: the empty space.

When we arrived a man and a boy were playing drums and gourds. We thought it a nice welcome.

We shook hands with the village elders, tall and lean in their robes and *cheches*. Veils give such men a sense of mystery: you meet their eyes. We smiled, shook their hands, and sat around the carpet. But the man and the boy weren't stopping on the drums. So we smiled and sat some more. But a group of women joined the drummers now. The women were bunched together in brightly coloured costumes, best outfits, singing and clapping for us. And they weren't stopping either. None of the villagers gathered round the carpet, not even the children. And then of course it dawned on us. We weren't expected to play, but to watch. We were the audience. They must have thought it a bit grand to bring a carpet to sit on.

Brook wasn't sure what to do. Do we begin? Do we wait? The singing might go on for hours. It was similar to American-Indian music, chants, and calling sounds that last through the night summoning the spirits. People do not value what is easily come by, and the spirits take their time. The drumming grew more insistent, the women sang on. They clapped a basic hypnotic pulse round and round a circle as each sang and returned to the pulse. The sound grew louder, building. But as the actors waited on the carpet their eyes began to open. The pulse grew out of the skills of generations. From the pulse, sounds took life. The women were creating a perfect improvisation. The women smiled.

Hesitantly, Swados began to edge towards the women, and joined their music. They weren't offended. They helped her with the strange chants and rhythms, taking her with them.

Others ventured off the carpet to sing with the women.

The rest joined the drummers with their own drums. The Tuaregs were taken by surprise now, shrieking with delight at this unexpected audience participation. Their shrieks sounded like battle-cries.

And to our astonishment, the field was suddenly full of leaping Tuaregs. Without warning the men dashed into the centre of the field and started leaping up and down. It was a *dance*, a jumping-up-and-down dance. They rammed a walking stick into the ground and jumped up and down with such force the earth vibrated. I couldn't believe it. It was as if they were using pogo sticks. They were going crazy! They were taking off! They were FLYING! If a youngster had the nerve to join them, the men charged into the field and knocked the child's stick from under him. 'Out of the way! Let the *men* dance!' And the child scampered off. And the women kept singing. And the Tuaregs kept leaping into the field, jumping up and down on walking sticks.

And it was catching. A few of the actors were trying it out for themselves on the carpet. It wasn't too difficult to learn. But could they risk it? Perhaps it was a sacred dance, not to be tampered with. What the hell! They went leaping into the field, leaping up and down with the Tuaregs. And others were tempted now, high on the chants and drums, jumping so hard their feet were cut and bled through their shoes. HAAAAAAAAAR! The Tuaregs went *wild*. Madness! They were trying to lift the earth. There's madness in the field.

On such occasions, the amazing inscrutable Yoshi Oida is without equal. Very nice, no doubt, to have travelled all this way to leap merrily up and down with the Tuaregs but one couldn't help thinking it wasn't quite the point. 'What did you discover?' people would ask when we got back. 'Oh, you know. Leaping Tuaregs . . .' But without warning in the field of madness Yoshi Oida suddenly appeared with a specially tiny stick he'd found somewhere and was leaping up and down on his knees. Because he was the leaping midget. And the leaping midget was taking cunning little leaps back towards the empty carpet. And the Tuaregs, hysterical with laughter, began to follow him. Instantly, Katsulas sensed what was happening and went cartwheeling wildly round the field in the same direction. The leaping midget and the giant Katsulas were racing for the carpet! And the other actors caught on now – diving, rolling, tumbling, screaming and leaping across the field until the whole village began to follow. *Transformation!*

There's a new audience round the carpet.

'SHOES!' shrieked Bagayogo, holding them up because he was taking no chances this time. People were going to know this show was about *shoes*. When he chooses, Bagayogo can stop the world. 'hey! KARRRRAAAAAAAAH! KARRRAHAAAAAAAAH! TOTOTOTOTOTOTOTOTO! SHOOOOOOOOOOOOOOOOOOOOOOOOOS!' The Tuaregs began to laugh and giggle a bit. But Bagayogo looks as if he'll *kill*. And no one laughs any more, except Brook, who can't really stop. It's something he does when incredible things happen.

And they did happen that night. Through the most unexpected and extraordinary means the audience had pumped new energy and life into the actors. The wall was down. In its place, real exchange, real and precious sharing. Yet in the normal way, actors find this trust in an audience difficult to come by. Often in theatre it's an ambiguous relationship, full of fear and suspicion – perhaps it's veiled hostility. Faced with an audience 'out there', the actor feels judged. In return, he defends himself. It's Brook's favourite illustration for all the stifling tensions and difficulties involved in performing in public. In French theatre, you actually find the expression *se défendre*. The actor defends himself against critical judgement and assumed hostility through the role he plays. He wears it like a suit of armour: a costume. But in Africa the traditional pressures were absent. You could begin from zero. In this relaxed atmosphere perhaps a way might be found to prepare and soften an audience. Little by little, an audience might be brought to the point where a totally natural event takes place. The actor and spectator become partners. For both will have been transformed simultaneously.

And for the first time, something of that very special quality began to happen in the village of the Tuaregs. Brook's urgent pleas and conferences were beginning to reap a few rewards at last. The pace and mood of the actors matched exactly the outward sensibility of their audience. They took it from there. At times it was as if they were playing in a frenzy, switching direction time and again, risking more and more in an effort to catch all the moods and lightning responses of the people. In such a way, an actor conditioned only by traditional theatre audiences is stretched and challenged to discover skills that perhaps he thought did not exist in him. In the most vivid way the true meaning of words such as 'spontaneity', 'danger', 'events' and 'relationship', 'openness', 'meeting', such words, mere words, are seen in a different light.

A meeting with the Peulhs

Brook asked the actors to sing a song.

They sang the Babylon song, our anthem, to raise the spirits. But this was totally and marvellously ignored by the Peulhs. The men just continued admiring themselves in the tiny mirrors.

Brook asked the actors to sing one of Bagayogo's songs as Swados played her guitar. But at the end, the men were still admiring themselves and the women were admiring the guitar.

More songs followed, a total of six, but each was met with the same glorious indifference. The Peulhs weren't moving. They weren't returning the music. How much Brook and the rest wanted it, music that took you into other worlds, told magical stories, music sung for love and joy – *give it*! Show us the secret! The Peulhs carried on admiring themselves in the tiny mirrors.

Perhaps we should give up. What right did we have to be there? Perhaps we should let it be. But Brook decided to take a different direction.

He asked the group to make a sound they had worked on during the research in Paris. He asked for an 'ah' sound – just this one basic sound that was to be extended and developed as far as it could possibly go. It seems an easy thing to do. Yet the group had worked on this one sound for weeks and months. It seemed like an awful moment of truth in Agades.

The group began to make the sound. The Peulhs were still staring into the mirrors. I watched the actors grow hesitant, uncertain whether to continue. But the sound stretched and grew – and the Peulhs unexpectedly looked up from their mirrors for the first time. The sound took life, vibrating. The Peulhs discarded their mirrors and joined the sound. Oh, it seemed miraculous! It was as if the Peulhs were pulling the sound from them. They pointed to the sky.

Just as the unimaginable sound reached its height, or seemed to, no one would venture any further. Somehow it was frightening. The two sides had met and come together in one sound. And yet it was as if they were stunned and frightened by the discovery. Ted Hughes has written of the sounds far beyond human words that open our deepest and innermost ghost to sudden attention. Was this such a sound? For everyone making it, the Peulhs and the actors together, stopped suddenly and would go no further.

But now the Peulhs offered an exchange and sang their songs. And they told Brook something very precious. He knew at last that he was on the right road in the search for a universal language. Perhaps we were only beginning to understand. But spirits speak there, in invisible worlds.

Why is simplicity always so hard to find?

The Peulh music showed us that a universal language might be as simple as one note repeated many, many times. But you must discover the right note first. There's a catch in everything. The Peulhs could vary and enrich the sound, changing it in subtle ways, but the strength behind the sound isn't made through force. Somehow, the strength makes itself. With the Peulhs everything seemed effortless. Even the sound itself seemed to have a wondrous life of its own. When you listen to the Peulh music it reaches the point where the music actually seems to make itself. The Peulhs were like human musical instruments. We were light years behind their 'simplicity'.

And yet the sound that reached and touched the Peulhs from the actors had been no shot in the dark. Both Brook and Swados had talked of the possibility of one note that can become a source, the purest of essence. So much of the group's work was based on this. A sound might somehow be found that encompasses an entire feeling, and conveys it. And there's nothing revolutionary in any of this – as the Peulhs and others prove – but it's why Brook was so excited during the meeting. He was certain at last that he was on the right track, for the Peulh magic cut across everything he's working towards in theatre.

Month after month at his centre in Paris, Brook found that the most powerful expression in sound and movement always comes through shedding more and more outward forms. It's an attempt to make the greatest impact using minimum means, and the Peulhs had mastered it to perfection.

'It's good,' I said to him after another exhausting workshop. 'The research is good. Yet I can't help feeling all this is sort of *hopeless* . . .'

'Then tell me,' he replied instantly, 'if a man wishes to reach his full potential, what's the greatest obligation on him?'

Obligation?

'Who puts it on him?' I asked.

'He does,' Brook replied.

'He doesn't want an easy life?'

'He wants a fulfilled life.'

'Then the obligation', I imagined, 'is to try to fulfil yourself.'

'But why do you say such a thing if you believe all this is hopeless?'

'In the hope that it isn't.'

'Faith,' said Brook.

Innocence and Experience

No more than thirty spectators had drifted round the carpet, and remembering the maxim that Nigerians only move when they sense action Brook at last ordered the show to begin. But the gentle musical section which opened the show fell flat. Yet it seemed okay to us. Then the songs that followed were greeted in silence. What was going on? The actors looked blank, sinking. Swados was vaguely hysterical. 'I've made a discovery!' cried Brook after another song died. 'Music is the least universal language there is . . .'

He meant the group was still rooted in Western culture or the new musical influences of the Tuareg and Peulh. But what matter here? The gulf between the actors and the small silent audience was as wide as a canyon.

'Acrobatics!' ordered Brook, as a captain keeping a stiff upper lip calls for the lifeboats when the ship is about to sink. One of these days, I thought to myself, we're going to hit an iceberg. That's what they thought on the *Titanic*. But as always happened the sudden eruption of life brought the first cheers and warmth from the audience, and expectancy. In such a way events can prove deceptive.

The crowd had now grown to more than a hundred, as if by magic.

The Shoe Show came next as Katsulas the Giant strode confidently on to the carpet. Maybe a gambling man would have shortened the odds of success now. Swados the Witch has a sixth sense about these things, foreseeing doom. But I thought at worst the show hung in the balance. It would go one way or the other, I decided. But then almost without exception everything in the show, every single event and happening, every improvisation, every sure-fire routine, every joke, every trick, everything, everything failed. I couldn't believe my eyes. The show we had thought so direct and simple was greeted with total and horrifying bewilderment. The same show, the universal language show that all of us including Brook had been so confident about, was the biggest disaster of the journey.

For Katsulas who was stuck in every scene, hard though he tried from time to time to make a dignified exit, the experience was shattering. It was to take him literally weeks to recover from it. Stranded on the carpet, it was as if he were living out the worst of all actor nightmares. Every actor dreams about forgetting his lines. He's alone on an empty stage, speechless. It's the same nightmare as the concert pianist playing the silent piano. But for wretched, dying Katsulas the dream had come true. As one scene after another was greeted not with derision or uninterest but with this terrible crucifying silence, he was helpless. Trying all he knew to hold the show together, the only reaction he managed to get from the crowd was the one that finished him. Without meaning to, this huge and gentle man terrified the children. No matter what he did the children always scattered, and ran away.

For a split second Katsulas caught my eye. 'You were *right*. This is a tragedy.' But then in the panic and desperation he did something amazing. He began to use language. Suddenly, he was talking and babbling in non-stop English. Unfortunately, we were in a Hausa-speaking village at the time. But Katsulas had returned to the only safety net that was left: words. In Brook's non-verbal theatre, he had reversed the actor's traditional nightmare. Instead of forgetting his lines, he remembered them.

'Anyone care to join me?' he asked the rest of the actors sitting stunned round the carpet.

As Yoshi Oida tried to help out I glanced in Brook's direction, but he was now in urgent consultation with his son. Simon Brook was about to make his guest appearance.

During the show Katsulas always tried to get rid of the shoes near the end, throwing them away over the heads of the crowd. But one of the actors always lobbed them back. Katsulas would throw them away again, and back they came. This time, Simon Brook would return the shoes personally. Brook was secretly directing him to do no more than walk slowly towards Katsulas and hold out the shoes. He mustn't say a word. Also, he mustn't get the giggles.

Ahead of schedule, Katsulas threw away the shoes. 'I want a wee!' whispered Simon Brook, hopping up and down. 'Well you can't!' cried his father. 'You're *on.*'

Katsulas was looking up at the sky awaiting the return of the shoes. 'They'll be here any second,' he announced. 'Any second NOW.' When Simon Brook made his entrance, 'Oh, no!' cried Katsulas, nonplussed for the moment. 'Not *you*. I can't take any more. Go away! This is your uncle Andreas speaking. Go away and wipe that horrendous smile off your face.' Determined not to speak or laugh, Simon Brook had cemented his face in this vile twisted smile, a smile of pure evil. And the harder he smiled the more evil he became. 'GO AWAY!' But Katsulas fell silent. The young child kept walking slowly towards him, and held out the shoes. Suddenly, the unexpected event began to go far beyond mere charm. It was as if the child wasn't acting. Somehow we were compelled to watch, it was so truthful. And for the first time the silent audience responded and understood. The child in his innocence had done what all the others with their fine acting skills couldn't do. If only for a few moments he had shown us the nature of simplicity.

Then it was lost and he laughed and giggled now and danced in the magic shoes.

What had gone wrong? Like the actors, I couldn't fathom why the show failed so miserably. Everything had seemed right. We'd never felt so confident. The show really did seem to work. Yet when it came to it, the harsh truth to be swallowed was the simple undeniable fact that the audience couldn't understand what the hell we were supposed to be doing. And what now of Brook's universal language? I just couldn't make the failure out. But Brook could . . . Far from being discouraged by the reaction, he was the reverse. In fact he seemed to be fascinated by the entire disaster. It was irritating in a way. Everyone's hit for six except for this one excited little man who's saying, 'But can't you *see*?' Brook knew exactly what had gone wrong, and nailed it.

'Why are the shoes magic?' he asked me unexpectedly. It was the kind of Brook question that you know instinctively goes to the heart of the matter. But it doesn't necessarily help.

'Pardon?'

'Why are the shoes magic?'

'Well, they change people. It's like the Chief says.'

'Yes, but why?'

'Because they change people,' I could only repeat.

'I know,' Brook replied again. 'But *why*?'

And the more I thought about it the more I began to think there's no sane reason on earth why a pair of shoes should change anyone. It was just the answer Brook was waiting for. And at last I understood.

We'd missed the obvious.

Attempting to create a universal language, the show had been built entirely round a theatre convention of the West. This is the convention which takes it for granted that shoes can transform people, bringing luck and disaster, the popular folk reference on which so many children's stories are based. I'd seen too many pantomimes. But the African villagers hadn't, or any form of theatre as we know it. The audience couldn't understand what was happening because it couldn't share the convention. How simple everything seemed now! In spite of all our attempts at directness and simplicity we were still skipping the steps, taking short cuts to dramatic effects that could have little meaning here. We were still trapped in restricted art forms that made sense only to ourselves, which is why the rehearsal of the show was a success and the performance a failure. Offer an audience a theatre convention it doesn't understand and the lie will be given to the convention. It will become what it is, no more than a device: a cliché. And so one begins again.

And exactly the same lesson was true for the actors. An old hag puts on a pair of shoes and is transformed into a princess. It's obvious: the shoes must be magic. But without explanation or the use of language the event becomes a puzzle to anyone unschooled in the make-believe process. Unless the actor can somehow establish something totally honest, real simplicity and directness will always escape him. He can't rely on shared assumptions. He will be forced to do something incredibly difficult: create the assumption for himself. If he can do that, he will have discovered truth.

An actor tries to portray an old man and so stoops, walking with difficulty. We would recognize the character instantly. But the African villager might see something entirely different. Why should he see an old man? He might see someone making an interesting physical movement or imagine him carrying a heavy object. Katsulas portraying a timid man transformed into a giant lunges at the audience, as giants tend to do. But the adults look bewildered and the children scatter. Perhaps they see a stranger in their midst who walks across a carpet and for no apparent reason goes mad. But whatever interpretation you put on the reaction, they can't really understand what's happening. And they're right not to. So the actor must break with his own habits and clichés, and begin again.

Extracts from John Heilpern's *Conference of the Birds:
The Story of Peter Brook in Africa*

America and *The Conference of the Birds*
(July–October 1973)

> 'Theatre only touches us if it's exploring life beyond the clichés;
> there's no fun in clichés. The cracking through the cliché of life to
> something behind it is obviously going towards something finer, so
> that each step in that direction is a step towards the sacred – in
> other words, a step out of the boringly known towards the vast
> unknown, which is magical'
>
> (Brook on BBC 2, 1982)

The journey to America (July–October 1973) can be seen as the
culmination of the C.I.R.T.'s initial three-year experiment. Its aim was
to draw on the experiences of the first two years, to attempt to bring
together the two very different strands of work – the mysterious, dense
poetry of *Orghast* and the rough improvised comedy of Africa – to find
'*a marketplace performance of true seriousness*' (Geoffrey Reeves). Once
again the works of Shakespeare served as model for Brook's ideal of a
poetic complexity encouraging a wide range of responses: a theatre of
simplicity and directness which, in performance, would belie any
artificial barriers between tragic and comic, between mysterious and
popular. The problem of finding material capable of reconciling 'the
high moments of *Orghast* and the tombs at sunset, with the audience
falling about with laughter and the children in the village' seemed to
have been answered in the discovery of *The Conference of the Birds*. The
story of the birds' journey to see the Simorgh parallels legends and
myths of other cultures: the legends of the Holy Grail, Jason and the
Argonauts, Gilgamesh's epic search for the secret of immortality,
Bunyan's *Pilgrim's Progress*, and perhaps most pertinently, Gurdjieff's
search across Central and Eastern Asia and North Africa as recounted
in his semi-autobiographical *Meetings with Remarkable Men*. Clearly it is
reflected symbolically in the group's crossing of the desert in Africa and
their subsequent journey across America. The numerous anecdotes
(almost 150 in Attar's full original) seem to represent individual phases
in the journey of human consciousness in search of enlightenment.

225

Many of the birds drop by the wayside; the process of stripping down to a true self must be relentless.

The coherence with the group's work and ideals is evident. Thematically, the stories of *Conference* (as later of *The Mahabharata*) contain qualities that Brook considers to be fundamental to human understanding. Man as bird is an archetype with its source in a prehistorical consciousness. For Brook it represents 'that intangible something in human beings which want to fly,' man's inner aspirations, his desire to go beyond himself to make contact with transcendental truth. Here lies the deeply poetic, 'metaphysical' aspect of *Conference*. For Brook, it offers the possibility of a true *theatre of myth*.

> '*Conference* speaks in the language of the god, the bird, the serpent. It is the simplest and deepest way of communication, and it cannot be translated. When you say the serpent is a symbol of something, you are not getting more clarity, you are getting less. These images are clear in the sense that they ring true to your heart and stomach'.   (Brook in *Los Angeles Times*, 1973)

At the same time, the story (and Brook's subsequent treatment of it) never becomes lost in the dull and shifting clouds of a pretentious mysticism. For the poem contains 'an essential truth . . . Everyone who hears about those going through Seven Valleys is at once captured. He doesn't know why.' The *journey*, the *struggle*, the *search*: all express a truth far beyond the theatre, a truth in life. Repeatedly, in the public sharing of this essentially human and private experience, socio-cultural barriers have been seen to crumble. Throughout the group's differing versions of *Conference* over the years, a central constant has held fast: 'The techniques differ but the aim is always to deny that foreignness is a barrier.'

Over a long period of time, the work on *Conference* has made great demands on Brook's actors. Constantly returned to during the Seventies (from the first free improvisations in Paris before the journey to Africa to its performance as a scripted play at the Avignon Festival in 1979), it remained a symbol of the work for the group, a focal point for the development of a commitment to their own ideals. Like Shakespeare, Attar's poem proved a permanent challenge in performance, by its very nature rejecting any attempts to structure it finally: 'It goes beyond one's capacity to penetrate it completely. Nobody can completely take hold of it, so that as something to work on it is inexhaustible.'

Until the journey to America, the work on *Conference* had been fairly limited. There had been improvisations in Paris before, during and after the trip to Africa, many built around traditional links between bird behaviour and human types: nightingale as lover, eagle as king, falcon as warrior. The group undertook a close study of bird movement and song, not to imitate them, but to find a fuller expression of that element in the nature of earthbound humanity that wants to take off, to fly and sing. They sought to reflect and convey a state of being, a 'spirit' in sound or movement, just as they had (using different starting points) in *Orghast*. Initially, in Paris and Africa, the actors worked with scenarios written by Ted Hughes. The fable is illustrated by a large number of anecdotes within the central story of the birds' journey. Many of these possess a lyricism and sensuality reflecting that of Hughes's own poetry. Many of the stick exercises and vocal improvisations at the heart of the work in Africa were to become incorporated into performances; so, for example, in these early versions of *Conference*, the crossing of the Seven Valleys of enigma was conveyed through a stick dance ('The Travel Line Dance').

The journey across America, from West to East, began in the Californian mission town of San Juan Bautista, home of El Teatro Campesino. Although they had travelled very different routes, Brook and the founder of El Teatro Campesino, Luis Valdez, had arrived by 1973 at a remarkably similar point in their conceptions of the role of theatre. According to Valdez, the two sides of the Campesino's work ('*acto*'/'*misto*') were complementary, two aspects of the same reality. He reacted strongly to the false divisions established between 'political', 'religious', 'popular', 'spiritual' or 'mythical', just as Brook does.

> There can be no separating an act of theatre into the political, the spiritual, the joyful. There is only *one complete act* which, in its truth, contains all elements. If this is searched for with passion, then everything is struggle, and the actions of performance and the actions of life need to be informed with the same force'
>
> (Brook, *New York Times*, January 1974)

Like Brook, Valdez proposes a union of high and low, holy and rough, in which the *acto* approaches the world through 'the eyes of man' and the *mito* through 'the eyes of God' (Valdez). At the time of Brook's arrival, Valdez and ETC were still actively involved with the farmworkers' cause. They were in the middle of a burning dispute with the capitalist Teamsters' Union, who were brutalising chicanos into abandoning Chavez's union; two strikers had recently been murdered. So ETC had returned to the fields to perform fresh actos in direct support of the workers, as in the early days of 'la Huelga'.

Initially the two groups felt it was very difficult to find an area of common ground. At first the C.I.R.T. group had reacted against what they saw as the 'political' theatre of the campesinos, failing to recognize the similarity in aims and ideals to their own work. For both groups, theatre is only legitimate if it reflects a deeply committed 'search for something real' (Brook) which can be carried over into life beyond the theatre. Yet the diversity of cultural backgrounds within the C.I.R.T. group means that 'they reflect in an extreme way the condition of most urban groups – there are too many issues and too many factors for a political or social consciousness to find its form'. Despite this claim of Brook's, a certain group consciousness *had* been developed through the common experience of the journeys, and through the nature of their relationship to the material. Eventually, through communal life, debate (with, among others, Cesar Chavez), and the exchange of practical work together, the two groups reached a recognition of their shared search through theatre: to make other dimensions visible, to touch man at all levels of his being, to heighten and clarify consciousness, to unify.

One of the highlights of the collaboration, a 'true meeting point' according to Brook, occurred in mid-August in a performance created in response to Chavez's call for a general strike. The two groups jointly improvised an acto-style guerrilla theatre show called *The Fatties and the Shrimps*, performed from the back of a truck to an excited crowd of union members and strikers picketing in Delano. Similar work was also created for 'scab' workers, delivered to them from the ends of the vine rows in the fields. On a number of occasions, these fast, energetic sketches were conducted under the threat of physical violence from groups of Teamsters' members present in the fields.

However, the most profound collaborative successes came in the different fragments of *Conference* performed in theatres, parks and churches. Although initially the campesinos had been reluctant to work on such material, gradually the relevance of Attar's poem became clear. An expression of solidarity was found largely in a recognition of the struggle and search at its heart. The culmination of this area of the work came in a joint open-air version (*Los Pajaros*) before the campesinos in a park in Livingston. For Peter Wilson, who recorded the journey for the Centre, the most striking moment came in the representation of the birds' initial discord in terms of the actors squabbling in different languages (a reflection of the two groups' initial difficulties). Brook has always maintained that it is above all in the intercultural relevance and communicability of this Sufi poem that its extraordinary quality lies: 'translated from Persian to French, from French to English, from English to Spanish, and played by actors of seven nationalities, [it] had made its way across the centuries and across the world to find a new and urgent relevance in the context of the chicano struggle.'

On leaving California, the group's first stop for work was in the chic tourist resort of Aspen, Colorado, where they were the guests of the Institute of Humanistic Studies. From there they travelled to the Chippewa reservation at Leech Lake, Minnesota. At the invitation of the Walker Arts Museum, Minneapolis, they spent a week working with the La Mama-backed Native American Theatre Ensemble. As well as being shown various ceremonies and taught dances and songs by descendants of the once formidable Nez Percés tribe, they continued collaborative free improvisations around *Conference*. As a result of their earlier work in Paris with the American National Theatre of the Deaf, they were able to find fascinating points of communication with the Indians' poetic form of sign language.

The culmination of this initial three-year period of work was reached during the group's three-week stay at the Brooklyn Academy of Music, New York (September/October 1973). Although the group was by now 'at cracking point', their work at the BAM was concentrated and unrelenting. It included contact with a number of other street-theatre groups in different parts of Brooklyn, the development of 'Theatre Day' workshops, and regular evening performances of *Conference*. Brook pursued his determination to find a balance between the loose, high-energy improvisations outside theatre rules (and buildings) and the concentrated intimacy of the work within the BAM. Both sides were of equal importance, the one serving to inform and validate the other.

Brook rightly credits Brecht with having recognized the absolute imperative of actors as human beings to relate themselves and their craft to society and its needs. He suggests that there is a need today for

a much greater sense of responsibility than actors have ever been prepared for. A responsibility towards himself and his own personal search for truth. A responsibility as a social animal. The responsibility of not functioning purely for himself or his group's development, but simultaneously to be true to that and true to his audience. And perhaps one further responsibility, which is for the actual virus that he is injecting into a community's bloodstream through his actions: for what is being brought into the air at that moment, and for what the people who are there take away with them.'

(Brook at the BAM, 1973)

The development of the *Theatre Day*, the core of the work at the BAM, can be seen in these terms. Limited numbers of free tickets had been distributed by the International Theatre Institute, permitting members of the public to spend a whole day with the group. In the morning, the actors demonstrated various exercises, inviting participation. The afternoon session took the form of a joint exploration through free-form improvisation and discussion. Finally, in the evening, different performances of *Conference* were given. Although most of the work done in this way was deemed to have been both useful and rewarding, occasionally a single bad experience – extreme self-indulgence, a clash of insensitive egos, exhibitionist showing-off of technique – proved sufficient to push the whole day off course. In an instant the delicate web of relationships set up through the work would fracture.

Workshops took place with a number of other groups. According to Peter Wilson, one very fruitful day was spent at La Mama with a Chinese group and their director Tisa Ehang. Another occasion united the National Theatre of the Deaf and the Native American Theatre Ensemble, both of whom had worked with Brook's actors before. Both groups were successfully integrated into the evening's performance of *Conference*.

Another day's workshop was conducted at the BAM with Grotowski's Teatr Laboratorium. This was to be the first and last time the two groups were to share anything more substantial than passing contact. Reports of the work vary enormously. For Wilson as passive observer, the non-verbal, non-active nature of the proceedings meant that 'it hardly seemed to happen at all'. Grotowski refused to participate in what he considered to be games; 'one is not obliged'. Gently and tactfully, he rejected the improvisations in general as 'exhibitionistic'. For Bruce Myers, this coming together of 'holy' actors was contrived and disastrous. Despite Brook's (and Grotowski's) emphasis on finding a way of surmounting any imposed myth of self or myth of the actor, Myers felt they failed to meet in any way. Locked within those myths, they collided by merely trying to 'out-holy' each other. It was only outside the work that he felt able to make any sort of contact. Malik Bowens, who had worked with Grotowski in Poland before joining Brook in Paris (indeed it was Grotowski who had introduced him to Brook), found the intensity of Grotowski's approach somewhat stifling. On the other hand, Yoshi Oida, one of the few who appear to have gained from the meeting, talked with glee of a very simple improvisation he shared with Grotowski, in which he responded vocally to Grotowski's flute.[1] This simple exchange illustrated perfectly what Grotowski now concerned himself with, as well as marking the extent of the gap between the two groups. Having moved beyond the theatre, he was searching for something much finer and more delicate than Brook, who remained very much the man of the theatre.

The external work took the form of free improvised street threatre, in yards, parks and at street corners in the more remote areas of Brooklyn, as well as in different enclosed environments: churches, halls, gymns, and community and drug prevention centres. Informed by the energy and directness of the carpet shows in the African villages, the experiences in and around Paris and with the campesinos in California, the perform-ances were a means to find new responses, to reveal the deeper culture of America within the ethnic minorities – Black, Italian, Puerto Rican. After an unannounced arrival, the group would attract local kids with the sounds of their instruments. From that initial arousing of curiosity, contact would have to be retained through an improvisation. With young blacks, they found a freedom and richness of imaginative responses, 'a joy and spontaneity' (François Marthouret) to match that of the African villagers. With other groups, such as immigrant Italians, they often met with a lack of response, even open hostility. However, direct contact with such a breadth of response became an integral factor in determining the differing forms of those last evening performances of *Conference*.

Before leaving for Africa, Brook had told his actors that they would simply be applying the essential practices of a Broadway musical to this rather special material: 'The Broadway musical becomes a reflection of its audiences, because it is evolved on tour, tested nightly by different audiences and rewritten' (Brook in Heilpern, *Session Based on Voice*, C.I.R.T., 1972).

Although by the very nature of his theatical practice at this time (the journeys), Brook had totally rejected this type of theatre: 'on Broadway this is done for the worst reasons because it is serving the false god of commercial success', nevertheless 'the principle behind it is of the greatest validity'. It was only in America, with the different approaches to *Conference* at the very heart of the work, that this could become true. Yet it was not so much a case of the 'evolution' of *Conference*, for the nature of these performances and the flexibility and complexity of the

---

[1] In conversation, Yoshi laughingly suggested to me that the difference between Brook and Grotowski is that the former is a 'sadist' – placing the actor in a position of danger, thereby enforcing exposure and creation – whereas Grotowski is a 'masochist'; in a shared process, he helps the individual to reach inside himself, painfully but gently drawing out the impulses of his inner being.

material made a distinctly different event, a different impression every time. The forms for a particular performance would be chosen by those actors selected to lead that performance; these would be partially determined by the milieu in which the performance was to be given, partially by the 'leader's' own changing interpretation of the poem.

Three performances took place during the *final night*; they are still vividly remembered by all who took part. At 8 p.m., Yoshi Oida and Michele Collison led an exuberantly joyful performance of great energy, spontaneity and life. Here *Conference* was mined for its rough comic ore: the popular celebration of the carpet show. At midnight, Bruce Myers and Natasha Parry led the group back to Attar's text in a direct tribute to him which tried to capture the gentle humanity and delicacy of his original. This was achieved largely through an intimate, ceremonial reading of Attar as 'the Word', 'whispered to the light of candles' (Brook). It was a performance marked by moments of great poetry and sensitivity; it included the use of incense, rosewater (the meaning of the word 'attar' – he had been a perfumer) and a real white dove, as well as soft evocative music, 'the sound of a feather and a clapperless bell' (Wilson). Yoshi Oida remembers it as a creation of true 'holiness' and 'spirituality'. Finally, in a performance led by Andreas Katsulas and Elizabeth Swados which started at 4.30 a.m., the poem was presented almost entirely through ritualistic choral work and energetic abstract improvisations.

At dawn, as the performance came to the end, Brook led everyone back to the carpet. He talked at length to the assembled group about the work; this was the last time they would be together for over a year. He told them that these final versions of *Conference* had reflected a quality of 'true understanding', linking the multiple strands of the three years' experiences; together they had reached a point of clarity that would not have been possible without those experiences. He believed that all three versions had clearly married authentic individual visions of the truth within the poem. From this point, they would need to reassess, to evolve, to move on afresh with an ever-deepening energy: 'If we stay at the same point, we go down.' The group was separating just as their work had reached its finest moment.

A Better Quality of Understanding: An Interview with François Marthouret

François Marthouret was an integral member of the C.I.R.T. during its early years: here the French actor describes the role of improvisation and training in Brook's ideal of 'naïvety'.

MARTINE MILLON: Can you describe that period of the Centre's work at the Mobilier National in the early Seventies, still largely unknown? In particular Handke's *Kaspar*, in which you performed the central role. How do you locate that work in the Centre's history?

MARTHOURET: *Kaspar* was our first work on a written text, Handke's play, but it was also a concrete support for our exercises around certain themes. I remember that Handke defined the character by placing him somewhere between Buster Keaton and King Kong, a description sufficient to set the imagination in motion. The character could only use one phrase to express himself within a framework that's been imposed on him, a sort of living room. As he never manages to express himself with this single phrase (which was 'I would like to be what someone else once was'), he ends up turning everything in the living room upside down. We respected Handke's directions very precisely: loudspeakers guided this character, destroyed his phrase, and gradually helped him to reconstruct a language enabling him to find a relationship with the room's furniture, with everything around him, so as to re-establish the room's order. By doing this, they constructed a language for him permitting him to live and act in this framework. And gradually, this wonderful pupil became increasingly knowledgeable: he could put everything in its rightful place; he began to ask questions to find out who was teaching him this language and order, until the questions become intolerable to those listening and guiding him, and indeed they kill him off.

We worked on the basis of Handke's text, evolving different performances to be given in different places. One day Handke was there, we gave two performances as a sequence: one in the fixed framework Handke had indicated, following his directions exactly, using all the props etc.: the other, our own explosive improvisation and adaptation of the text, with large cuts – we were trying to set up images encouraging the creation of a whole series of relationships between this rather mad clown

233

and the others. Initially these others merely stay behind microphones: gradually the actors intervened in a concrete physical way in the epic poem of a person between Buster Keaton and King Kong, to create images and situations which had not been determined beforehand.

M.M.: The common theme with *Orghast*, it seems, is that of the origins of language and of non-verbal language. To what extent did work on non-verbal elements become of use to you in the work on subsequent texts, such as *Timon of Athens*?

MARTHOURET: Obviously it was useful in as much as the words invented by the poet Ted Hughes for the vocal score of *Orghast* were part of this same area of experimentation: each sound, each word had an existence absolutely connected in an organic way with a body movement: we did not aim to try to illustrate the intellectual meaning of a word; on the contrary, we were trying to invent or discover its organic meaning. A word, even one loaded with meaning or imaginative resonance, had first of all to be embodied in an actor. His imagination had to find a vocal colour, a rhythmic dynamic, and a whole range of things of that kind which were more easily liberated when one wasn't blocked by a desire to signify such and such an illustration of the meaning. To say 'fire', the word invented by Ted Hughes had a certain sonic quality: it provoked physically and in a practical way a mobilisation such that one could convey 'fire' by means of the voice, the body. It's vitally important, because when one confronts a text by Shakespeare, one recognizes the extent to which the imagination of actors is often limited by the mental process of illustrating the meaning. There was an obsessive concern in all this work: to try to rid oneself of this tendency one lapses into when one performs, to try to re-transmit thought. All the artisanal, practical work we did at that time served to test that the actor's task consisted above all of being able to create full gestures, to infuse sounds with life, and effectively, to be able to truly think a thought, to live a feeling or emotion, but *uniquely* through the concrete elements that are one's body and one's voice. We were trying as much as is possible to eliminate those parasitic impulses which cause us to limit ourselves, on a sensual organic level, in the transmission of thoughts and emotions contained within the words. In theatre, it's not enough to make things explicit for them to be living: words must be nourished by an imagination, not only by a desire to demonstrate. One must find the practical means for an actor to be able to inhabit all the musical, rhythmic colours around words, all the facets offered to him within his expressive means: the rhythms of his body and his voice. Words correspond to a score, a musical quality, not only a cerebral meaning.

M.M.: You took part in the journey to Africa, also in that period preceding *Timon*. In your opinion, what were you looking for?

MARTHOURET: It was a question of finding out, given the nature of a particular set of circumstances changed in every new occasion, what the best way of telling people a story is. If they don't understand anything of what you're doing, one can either carry on for one's own pleasure without caring about them, or force oneself to find the simplest and most elementary ways of making oneself understood.

M.M.: You once talked of 'naïve' performance, with reference to *Timon*. Can you describe and develop what you mean by this word?

MARTHOURET: There was something that always struck me in the work of that period, which often emerged during an improvisation. The most traumatic painful moment I always experienced was when I had to take the first step on to the performance area, crossing its outer edge: every actor from Broadway to the Moscow Arts Theatre knows this moment. In some ways it's reminiscent of the toreador's entrance into the arena. In an improvisation, when you are not always entirely aware of what you're going to say or invent, the craziest moment is when you get the impression that you're abandoning yourself, you're leaping into the void: when you cross the edge of the circle, you feel the need to be in a state of intense activity, of much more intense life than just before entering the space. This energy you plug into to get on, you have to feed and sustain with a sort of generosity, which is not only suicidal: every movement will be followed by another to enable you to exist in a continuous manner, to be fully present for a certain time in the circle. At that moment you invest all that you are, you cross the edge with maximum mobilization, or fear, which comes back to the same thing. You hurl yourself into the void, *completely*. This need to commit yourself fully confronts you, at the precise moment you have to invent and create, with something awful at the heart of improvisation: am I going to lie, or am I going to be authentic? Not from a moral point of view, but in the sense that you are either going to crumble into a pile of dust or you will blossom with life, in other words make yourself available to a certain dynamic.

M.M.: You cannot substitute for it by technique?

MARTHOURET: No, because it's a sort of vital challenge. Technique enables you to sustain a form, but not to mobilize what's inside. A naïve actor has the ability to put himself in a certain state of curiosity, of danger at that very moment in the here and now. Naïvety is a way of committing oneself totally to reinventing totally what you're in the process of doing: inventing without cheating: trying to *be*. Technique offers us the possibility of mastering a wide range of means: it does not enable us to experience that state of permanent reinvention we call naïvety.

M.M.: The daily exercises you worked on (I'm thinking of the Oriental ones in particular), did they have as their aim the development and control of this energy?

MARTHOURET: All the exercises we did aimed to bring into play very practical things: the control of a breath, or of a movement. They are techniques. At the same time, in theatre there are no gratuitous techniques. These exercises have never been innocent, they stem from a truth. Not necessarily a precise intellectual or philosophical truth. But if one makes a movement in order to release a sound without its being immediately stifled, that sound is not the expression of any old thing, but of what one *is* at that very moment. Peter gave an example, pointing out that exercising something does not imply that one is indifferent to whatever mobilizes us: he referred to one of his piano teachers who said that there was no reason not to play every single note in an exercise as if it were a concert recital, no reason not to invest in it the totality of what one loves, of what one wants to say through it. Why exercise it passively? Theatre technique has that exciting quality in as much as it brings into play the body and spirit of a human being, and there's no reason for everything not to be invested in the smallest of exercises. There's no point in spending ten years training to put one's right foot behind the left ear, if one's not exercising what's most essential: how to fill this movement with life, how to live it fully. If technically your only concern is to put your right foot behind your left ear, you'll soon exhaust any interest: firstly, because it's a pretty tiring position, and secondly, because it doesn't express anything else. If an actor trains himself to do this movement in order to prepare his body, to make it available, there's no reason for him to do so passively, without him committing the totality of his body, and of his spirit as well.

M.M.: The Oriental exercises you practise, do they stem from a desire to shatter the body's habits, to stimulate alertness?

MARTHOURET: Mainly to extend the horizons of understanding. On a typical working day within this group, we worked for 8 to 10 hours a day, and someone who stayed for a whole day would not have been able to understand what we were doing. Because we would move from futility to the most total concentration, from very rough vulgar exercises to what was apparently something very mystical. We worked with a stick in the same way as a finger, with a sound from the Greek theatre, songs from Japanese Noh or Africa. We were offered the opportunity of experiencing the most diverse of exercises from the palette, the richest there are. Not towards some abstract end. It was linked with a better quality of understanding amongst the actors within the group, and at the same time with a greater understanding of oneself as an actor.

From Martine Millon's interview with
François Marthouret in July 1983, translated by David Williams,
Les Voies de la Création Théâtrale XIII.

Timon of Athens, C.I.C.T. at the Bouffes du Nord, Paris 1974. Bruce Myers, as Alcibiades, confronts the Senators.

Timon of Athens. Malik Bowens, as Apemantus, addresses the audience.

The Ik, Paris 1975. Andreas Katsulas, as Colin Turnbull, with an Ik.

Two missionaries attempt to teach Christian hymns to the Ik.

The Ik. Andreas Katsulas, as Colin Turnbull, (on ladder) with Yoshi Oida as
Atum, an Ik.

The Conference of the Birds, Paris, 1979.

Below: The slave awakens when his mask is removed behind the white cloth.

The masked king aims an imaginary bow and arrow at a real apple on his servant's head.

The representation of the birds. From left to right, in foreground Perrin's parrot, Katsulas's peacock, Bénichou's Hoopoe (with hand puppet). Directly behind peacock, Maratrat's falcon.

Ubu aux Bouffes, Paris, 1977.
Andreas Katsulas as Ubu on
cable drum.

The peasants await the
arrival of Ubu.

Two scenes from *The Mahabharata*, Paris 1985.

Two scenes from *The Mahabharata*, Paris 1985.

IV

The C.I.C.T. at the Bouffes du Nord: 'A Place Marked by Life'

Timon of Athens, October 1974

The Ik, January 1975

Ubu aux Bouffes, November 1977

The Conference of the Birds, July 1979

The Bouffes du Nord by David Williams

Taken from a long essay describing Brook's major productions at Les Bouffes du Nord in Paris, David Williams' account analyses the form of Brook's 'found' theatre and of the first production staged there: Timon of Athens *(1974). The essay was originally published in* New Theatre Quarterly.

'*A theatre is like a violin. Its tone comes from its period and age, and tone is its most important quality.*' (Peter Brook, BBC Radio, 1950.)

The return from the enriching collective experiences of 'work-in-the-field' brought with it a recognition of the unsatisfactory nature of so many theatre events in Europe. Brook knew that the group would have to create something very special into which the spirit and energy of those experiences could be channelled, communicating and authenticating them. The change of name to the Centre International de Créations Théâtrales (C.I.C.T.) in 1974 marked the move from the initial three-year research period to the creation of a permanent theatre for public performances of specific works.

The nature of the group's subsequent work has been determined to a large extent by Brook's discovery of a dilapidated and derelict theatre in the unfashionable tenth arrondissement of Paris, behind the Gare du Nord. Les Bouffes du Nord, constructed as a *théâtre à l'italienne* in 1876 by the architect Louis Marie Emile Laménil, had been a theatre of some prestige and history, but, out of use as a theatre since 1950, it was finally abandoned in June 1952 due to a fire. It nevertheless closely matched Brook's ideals, and to this day has remained largely as it was after the fire. In 1974, the French Ministry of Culture under Michel Guy donated a million old francs (approximately £10,000). This enabled the completion of a programme of most necessary repairs within three months. The Centre only received permission from the local Préfecture to open the building to the public on the day before the opening of the first production, *Timon d'Athènes*, in October.

Externally the theatre is entirely anonymous: there are neither bright signs nor advertising, only a small board detailing the timing of the performances beside a large red door. Although disembowelled and in a state of decay – *une maison en ruines* like Timon's – the spirit of the theatre's past remains. It is above all a place marked by life, unlike modern theatres which Brook believes are constructed according to

241

scientific preconceptions and schema, and *not* according to the demands of the life of a theatre event. Impressions are strangely contradictory, for it appears to be at an indeterminate mid-point between renovation and demolition. Like Timon's Athens, it bears the marks of transition from an old to a new world. The traces of a decadent aristocracy in decline are in evidence in the Bouffes, a world of change. We are witnesses to the death of one kind of tradition and its forms; yet there are visible signs of the birth of another form of life, built from the worn-out shell of its predecessor.

The Bouffes was thus to provide an ideal space thematically for *Timon, Les Iks, Ubu, La Conférence des Oiseaux* and *La Cerisaie*, all of which concern themselves with worlds in transition. Above all, *Timon d'Athènes* is eminently suitable for production in this space – a 'lost' theatre for a 'lost' play. Material and environment are organically coherent:

POÈTE: *Comment va le monde?*

PEINTRE: *Il s'use, monsieur, à mesure qu'il grandit.*[1]

The Bouffes mirrors the leprous state of the society and the decay of human relationships within the play. It also infers a reflection of the state of our own society.

The playing area, originally the front stalls and stage, forms an immense empty space, a *tabula rasa* impregnated with a heightened potential for creation. Non-specific, neutral, and open, it possesses the freedom and infinite transformability of the non-localized Elizabethan stage. As if in an enclosed courtyard, performers and public are bathed in the same 'open-air' light throughout. The full horseshoe shape of the benches (situated on the same level as the playing area) and of the three balconies above gives the theatre the concentration and relationship of direct contact with the spectators that the group had experienced on the carpet within the circle of African villagers – that 'bowl of living human focus in which something can unfold'.

No attempt has been made to conceal the remaining evidence of the theatre's past splendour. At the same time the balconies, with their crumbling rococo decorations and engravings, and the pockmarked walls reveal contradictory signs of a fresh artifice in the limited but unconcealed restoration. The towering back wall, over 50 feet high, is scarred and pitted by the wear and tear of the years, like an aged human

[1] *Timon d'Athènes* (Paris, C.I.C.T., 1978), p. 13.

face, but the only sign of the former stage and its machinery is a wide horizontal band traversing the wall and the dark square stain above, framing the old stage picture, like a Turin shroud for a dead form of theatre. Beneath the wall lies an empty gaping pit, illuminated from below, at once fascinating and disturbing (in most subsequent productions, it has been filled and covered over). On the wall above the chasm hangs a precarious metal catwalk, an echo of the Elizabethan theatre's balcony.

The immediate reality of the setting is simultaneously present and invisible in the double vision of reality that is a performance. The wall itself, rather than creating a barrier cutting theatre off from life, seems to be infused with a life as dynamic as that of the playing space at its foot. It both concentrates and focuses the action in the space, while adding visual depth to the spectator's vision. In addition, as in the relationship between playing space and public, it possesses a curious quality uniting both epic and intimate.

As a whole, the theatre reflects Brook's desired economy of means, his growing asceticism in the move towards a 'poor theatre' in which the actor is free to communicate directly and intimately. The lesson of Africa was perhaps above all the necessity for reinjecting human content into the theatre at all levels, for placing '*human being in relation to human being*'. (Thus Malik Bowens, one of Brook's actors, suggested to me that Brook's ideal since Africa had been to try to replace '*la quincaillerie scénographique*' of most modern theatre performances with '*un décor humain*'.) Before any performance at the Bouffes, actors and spectators mix at the small café next to the theatre; often they enter by the same route. Brook has no time for the myth of the actor or of star systems: his theatre must be tied to and drawn from the life of the community.

Seating within the theatre is purely functional, even spartan – one of the few noticeably reconstructed elements. It comprises simple wooden benches covered in cheap hard-wearing cloth, providing just over 500 seats, over half on the ground floor, the remainder on the three balconies. (There is space for 260 spectators on the unnumbered ground-floor benches; the first balcony has 110 seats, the second 92, and the third 36.) Even for the spectators on these balconies, the actors' presence and visibility as well as the space's extraordinarily rich acoustic qualities are retained: there are no privileged positions, only changes in perspective. So from above the formal shapes and choreographed patterns of the action are emphasized, while for those on the benches below the immediate proximity heightens a performance's emotional force and encourages a more active participation in the action. Normally no distinction in the prices of the seats is made: the set rate is cheap, the economic factor excludes fewer people.

These are all clear political choices on the part of the company administrators, underlining the non-élitist, populist ideals the group had built up during their travels. Brook recognizes the need for a reinvention of *necessary* popular theatre forms, accessible to all comers. His vision of a living culture is perfectly expressed by Thomas Mann's Adrian Leverkühn in *Doctor Faustus*, a composer who had dreamt of an art of 'innocence' that would be 'the servant of a community, a community united by far more than education, a community that would not have culture, but would perhaps be one . . . *an art on intimate terms with mankind*'.

Timon of Athens: An Account by David Williams

The idea of performing a translated version of a Shakespearian text had been in Brook's mind for many years. Despite his overriding respect for Shakespeare's writing as poetry, he has never turned the words themselves into sacred idols. His aim has always been to liberate the spirit of a play by chiselling out what is effective and alive today, presenting this in forms accessible to a modern audience. So, for example, he had been impressed by Akira Kurosawa's film adaptation of *Macbeth* (*The Throne of Blood*, 1957). Taking only the story and its themes, the Japanese director had drawn on Noh forms and Samurai traditions to create a valid and living transmutation of Shakespeare. Very little emphasis was placed upon the spoken word; what words were used were never direct translations of the Shakespearian original. Brook feels the film to be a masterpiece, for Kurosawa had found a way to bridge the gap between the power and vitality of Shakespeare's language and the linguistic archaisms that inevitably set up certain barriers for a modern audience.

Subsequently, in the late 1960s, during preparation for his own film version of *King Lear*, Brook had asked Ted Hughes to 'translate' Shakespeare's text into his own contemporary idiom, as if translating a foreign classic. The results forced him to admit that, in this case, the original had assumed a sacrosanct status: the poetry was simply too well known. Although deemed to be of interest in its own right, Hughes's version made the play less accessible by setting up a field of interference, distracting to those familiar with the original; it merely invited games of comparison. Yet the experience was crucial, for Brook gained a clearer insight into the possibilities and problems of such an approach. Perhaps a lesser-known Shakespeare play could profitably be translated into a foreign language?

In Shakespeare's text, *Timon of Athens* is imprisoned within archaisms, making it accessible only to specialists. Its poetry does not possess a music as vital as that of, say, *King Lear*. In addition, it is not known if the text that we have today represents Shakespeare's final version; although finished in conception, it remains unfinished in form. Jean-Claude Carrière's version for the C.I.C.T., stripped down and

245

polished, has made the heart of the work accessible to a much wider contemporary public.[1] Shakespeare's images, vortices of compressed energy, are conveyed with simplicity, directness, and economy. Deliberately excising any imposed commentary or interpretation of the text in his translation, Carrière concentrated on conveying the story with clarity. To heighten immediacy and tension, he broke down Shakespeare's lengthy sentences into shorter phrases of concentrated force. He transposed successfully the sensual quality of word as sound to be liberated by the group's rich vocal abilities in performance.

Remarkably effective in performance, it was as if the words were invented there and then. In a performance in one Paris school, the lycée Montaigne, the young audience was convinced it was seeing a play by a modern writer. Clearly this freshness was to be a major factor in the play's success. Created for the Festival d'Automne, and opened at the Bouffes on 15 October 1974, *Timon* was awarded the Grand Prix Dominique for the best production of the year, as well as the Prix du Brigadier. All its 112 performances at the Bouffes were sold out.

In 1975, Brook recalled that fifteen years beforehand he had written-off *Timon* as being of no interest to a modern theatre audience.[2] However, any play by Shakespeare is 'like a sputnik, it turns round, and over the years different portions of it are nearer to you, different bits are further away. It's rushing past and you are peeling off these different meanings.' It is dynamic in so far as it is charged with an endless series of meaningful facets 'altering in a mysterious way as the text moves through the centuries'. Suddenly, and for Brook 'mystically', *Timon* had once again become important and alive for the early 1970s.

On a superficial level, the play clearly has contemporary relevance in terms of its thematic content: capital and property, prices, credit, inflation, waste. One American critic described this *Timon* as 'a living

---

[1] Jean-Claude Carrière has been Brook's writer on all the C.I.C.T. productions, writing and rewriting texts in close collaboration with both Brook and the actors. He was one of France's leading screenwriters of the 1960s and 1970s, noted above all for his work with Luis Buñuel, including *Le Journal d'une Femme de Chambre* (1964), *Le Charme Discret de la Bourgeoisie* (1972), and *Cet Obscur Objet du Désir* (1977). Carrière's experiences in cinema have proved invaluable in scripting works consonant with Brook's 'anti-aesthetic' of dynamic montage, prismatic discontinuity, mobility, and immediacy of thought and image – the very qualities he so much admires in the Elizabethan theatre. The broken line of narrative development and the element of surprise in Buñuel's brand of surrealism come close to Brook's stylistic ideals.

[2] *New York Times*, 10 August 1975.

emblem of the West brutally awakened from its paradisial consumer's dreams by the oil crisis'.[3] The nascent capitalism of Timon's Athens is presented by Shakespeare as already in a state of decay, and Karl Marx often referred to *Timon* in his own vehement critique of the role of capital in society. Like Shakespeare, he defended human values as opposed to monetary, material ones. He saw the acquisition of the power of money as the instrument of universal division, in a capitalist society becoming a god-like force alienating man from his fellows and from himself as a social animal; against nature, it corrupts and destroys. The imagery of bestiality and cannibalism running through *Timon* reflects the degradation of a humanity fragmented by the cancer of capital.

Timon's movement is from a philanthropic position of commitment to liberal altruism, through a moment of enforced lucidity concerning the hypocrisy, greed, and egotism of his parasitic flatterers, to the contrary extreme of metaphysical pessimism and misanthropy. Locked within a dream more powerful than reality, then suddenly thrown into harsh confrontation with that reality, he withdraws from society, rejecting humanity absolutely, like an 'embittered hippy'. His failure is in his acceptance of self-annihilation in anarchic despair. Like the birds in *Conférence*, he finds himself faced with the unknown; unlike them, he 'dies in confusion. He has not reached any point of *transcendent understanding.*' For Brook, the fable's universal quality investigates the nature of the relationship of the individual to society, rather than the individual himself. Is our society reaching a point of no return similar to that of Timon's Athens? In our position of crisis and change, what must be saved and what destroyed?

As Brook points out, Shakespeare's Athens is as symbolic as Ubu's Poland. Although it carries echoes here of the generals' junta in the Athens of the early 1970s, at the same time it remains unlocated historically and geographically. This aspect is further underlined in Brook's production by the mixture of styles, traditions, races, and accents. The performance is essentially the telling of a story by a group of actors to an assembled ring of spectators – another echo of the African experience. Initially the actors consciously adopt a storyteller stance, maintaining a certain distance between their roles and themselves. They act as a mirror to the spectators' position; at first seated on cushions to form an inner circle of focus, they listen and watch (in the second half of the play such devices had to be abandoned, the growing tragedy demanding greater identification). There is little separation between

[3] Pierre Schneider, *New York Times*, 3 December 1974.

actor and spectator. During the interval, the spectators are invited on to the playing space. Similarly, the actors make constant sorties into all levels of the seating area, using the space fully. The performance becomes an intimate and luminous event, all present sharing both space and light.

In the first half, the back wall, lit from below, becomes a screen on to which ominous silhouettes may be projected. The sculptural qualities of the figures' spatial location and their flowing cloaks is highlighted in this way. The lone shadow of Timon in the growing darkness of the end of the first half emphasizes his solitude and the fragility of his situation; the void beckons. In the second half, the ragged Timon *clamans in deserto*, the lighting becomes suitably oppressive, a startlingly bright glare pinning him to the ground in this Beckettian no-man's-land. Décor is minimal throughout: relationships and locations are established through the geometric positioning of the actors and their play, their costumes. Virtually the only scenic properties are a number of anonymous sack-like cushions (later used in *La Cerisaie* and *La Tragédie de Carmen*).

Brook recognizes that any approach to Shakespeare must respect and transpose that author's 'naïve imagination', for it is this quality that can give his works the immediacy and accessible universality that exist in those fifteenth-century Flemish paintings which locate the Crucifixion in their own contemporary world. The deliberate quality of naïvety at all levels of performance – the immediacy of the text, the clarity and directness of the forms, the co-existence in counterpoint of different elements from popular theatre traditions – is perhaps most apparent in the child-like simplicity and legibility of Michel Launay's costume designs. The actors' ordinary clothes generally remain visible beneath their costumes, which serve as simplified guides to character, externalizing moral nature or function in the same way as the costumes of the medieval theatre.

As a whole, they form a non-specific jumble of stereotypes; Brook does not attempt to impose a stylistic unity by setting the production in, say, Victorian England. Single elements, metonymic archetypes as is usual in popular theatre forms, were employed to allegorize with clarity an individual's or a group's essence – for example, Timon's gold neck-chain, or the somewhat surreal outsize account books of his predatory creditors. Like everything else in this world, the costumes undergo constant change: initially Timon wears a highly fashionable white suit over a gold lamé shirt; by the second half, the gold has gone and the same suit is in shreds.

As in the theatre of Brecht, often there is a clash between a costume's significance and the words or actions of its wearer. Many are caricatural or satirical, and therefore consistent with the Jonsonian nature of the minor characters in the original. The thieves are clad in black leather jackets and flat black caps, sporting heavy dark moustaches: middle-eastern brigands all. Sartorially, Alcibiades is almost a cartoon, erect in the black, red and gold uniform of a Greek general or South American dictator – all epaulettes, medals, and shining buttons. In performance, the cartoon comes ferociously to life through Bruce Myers's extraordinarily gaunt vocal presence.

Caricature with a similarly sinister twist marks the Athenians surrounding Timon. At the banquets, their flowing, gilded cloaks smack of cheap ostentation and degraded aristocratic pomp. In the second and final banquet scene, Timon's movement away from this society is immediately evident in the contrast between his simple white robe and the luxurious trappings of that society's representatives, the senators, whose flapping black capes suggest crows. There is a certain lack of individual differentiation, even anonymity, in these group identities, for the central individual figures are being contrasted with the collective (and this facilitates their frequent role changes).

Finally, direct evidence of the C.I.R.T.'s journeys is visible in the costumes, notably in the *Thousand and One Nights* visual splendour of the whirling dervish dance (the 'masque' of the first banquet), a frenzy of floating capes and chants. Exotic and exciting, the scene conveyed perfectly a sense of debauchery, waste, and excess: in a flash, Timon's Athens became the teeming casbah of a North African city, or a middle-eastern harem.

The work to liberate the life of the text created certain problems for Brook's actors, all of whom were at that time highly proficient in freer, more improvisatory forms, yet lacked textual experience. This is the reverse of what Brook had found at the RSC – extraordinary response to text, real problems opening up in improvisation. Instead, the shared experience of the journeys had encouraged an opening towards 'areas of sound, rhythm, movement – *the concrete nature of what seems abstract*'.

Brook has always detested the vulgar tendencies in the vast amount of work put in by those actors trained according to the bastardized version of Stanislavski's 'method' employed in many drama schools today. In place of what he considers to be the false profundity of an emphasis on psychological subtext and on creation through the limitations of emotional memory, he proposes an approach of non-interpretation in which what is communicated is above all the direct, *physical* conviction of the actor. Inner motivation in Shakespeare is to be found in the music, rhythms, and imagery of the text. The actor's task is to stimulate a response by freeing the spectator's imagination.

In this case, the life of the text was released by means of the vocal capacities the group had developed on their journeys. With power and amplification, the space was filled, their voices having apparently assumed a physical, corporeal extension. Words became actions charged with their own energy. At the same time, the vocal work never foamed over into the excesses of baroque rhetoric. Constant shifts in modulation and rhythm, infusing the whole with movement, led the performance from the epic grandeur of Timon's universal despair to the 'minor' intimacy of the ironic barbs Apémantus addresses to the ground-floor audience. As in improvisation, an inner dynamic – a certain organic energy – had to be traced and focused by the actors throughout the multiple transformations. Then even in moments of silence, the spatial evolution of the nature of the relationships could create that 'stage moving picture' Brook has always desired.

The Bouffes itself demands an exploration of its three-dimensional possibilities. Used as the site for daily workshops, experimentation, and rehearsal, its spatial potential has been fully investigated by the actors. In *Timon*, the animated spatial poetry was masterful. Like film directors, Brook and his actors concentrate our focus of attention on a single individual, a group, a simple telling detail (the *close-up*), then rapidly expand it outwards to take in the whole, thereby constantly redefining the relationship of part to whole. At the same time, everything appears logical and natural, belying the artifice of the staging.

All possibilities are exploited in entrances and exits (incidentally the only elements fixed by Brook before the rehearsal period). The holes burst high in the wall on either side of the space, at the level of the second balcony, are used by poet and painter in the opening scene. We then move to the hole at the back from which Timon emerges gloriously. At the play's climax, he redescends painfully and slowly, consumed into the bowels of the earth. Sometimes, as here, the hole is charged with the medieval theatre's symbolism of the 'low', the infernal. Sometimes it serves as a purely functional means of access to, and departure from, the playing space. It is never locked within a single frame of reference.

Perhaps we are then taken up on to the metal catwalk on the back wall, which in similar fashion may take on connotations of height, a station of moral superiority and power. So, for example, at the end of the play, Alcibiades – avenging angel in the name of Timon – towers over the quaking senators, Athens at his feet. These connotations reverse those of an earlier scene in which a military tribunal discusses an errant soldier's punishment; all the while, the victim stands motionless high on the back wall, exposed and insecure above the waiting chasm. Above all, the use of this catwalk in *Timon* serves drastically to alter the aesthetic texture of the visual whole for the spectator. It is used as a tool for investigating unexpected perspectives and a cinematic depth of field.

From David Wiliams, 'A Place Marked by Life: Peter Brook at the Bouffes du Nord' *New Theatre Quarterly*, February 1985

Energy and the broken line: A Rehearsal Log by Jean-Pierre Vincent

Jean-Pierre Vincent, assistant director of Timon of Athens, *made a record of his impressions of the daily working process: it was the first time a French director had been embroiled in Brook's approach to an Elizabethan work. These notes were published as an epilogue to the C.I.C.T. text of* Timon. *They draw no final conclusions on the work, stopping half-way through rehearsals.*

August 1: 'Radiant' words

There is a remarkable difference between the Shakespearian phrase and the classical French phrase. The difference is not one of pure form, for the language is the 'material' form that the development of thought takes: we are dealing with another kind of *reason*.

Beyond the particular meaning of words, the French sentence is clearly based on grammatical architecture, a linear progression supplying information in a precise order, oriented towards the end of the sentence (where the accent is placed).

Grammatically, the Shakespearian sentence is much freer: meaning stems from an almost uninterrupted chain of powerful words which radiate and resonate around themselves, reacting and rebounding against each other. As in all constellations, some shine more than others, they determine the colouring of a whole passage, or even permeate the entire play (breath, sun, leprosy, etc.). Others illuminate minor themes, which are none the less incessantly renewed and vital, in the fusion of a process of thought.

These suggestions are not only of linguistic interest: they are essential to the understanding of actions and of the actor's work. In the unfolding of actions, in work on vocalising the text, these radiant words must be taken both in themselves, assumed and lived with the fullest intensity, and at the same time they must be *thought* in giddying succession. They must carry their true weight, and yet through their reciprocal action ensure the life and lightness of the ensemble. In this instance, sensuality and intelligence are more inseparable than ever.

August 12: Improvisations on the beginning

What is immediately apparent is that one must play the relationships written into the text, and not for example the splendour of the location, Timon's immense house: the setting is in the luxuriant savour of the text. Hence Shakespeare's extreme mobility: more effectively even than film montage, it enables instantaneous changes in location, mood, point of view on the action. For example, in Apemantus' commentary on the banquet, one can have both close-up (on Apemantus) and a shot of the ensemble, a depth of field (the material reality of the banquet itself).

We are feeling the need to maintain a certain distance between the characters, to ensure the presence of a certain dimension in their behaviour, to avoid detailed business, a reduced form. But Shakespeare's theatre is built upon the continual oscillation between *natural* and *epic*, never one without the other: the actor's task is primarily to avoid caricature (an external style) *and* naturalism (the attempts of modern psychological actors to work 'internally' can be embarrassing if misdirected). In any case, it seems to be difficult to arrive at an epic energy before mastering the variety and truth of the human content.

August 13

Determining the order and content of sequences written into the text: how the play is constructed from nothing. A poet meets a painter: they discuss the world: where are they? At the North Pole? In London? They tell us gradually, element by element evoking setting, characters, images. They announce Timon's decrepitude, we expect a gloomy tale: but then here comes Timon himself, brimming with happiness and dynamism. He distributes gifts, before becoming lost in intimate thought, and so on. One must always accept the extreme *naïvety* and *unpredictability* that characterise Shakesperian development. On the one hand, on the level of realistic observation, material events are numerous and violently contrasted: but the telling of the story implements continual changes in point of view in relation to the story being told: in this light, the first act of Timon is a gold mine. *Never take into account what happens afterwards . . .*

August 14: The actor's work

Play each image fully, none the less considering it outside any contextual framework initially. Totally infuse oneself with it and commit oneself to it for the duration of its passage through one's head and mouth. The only means of humanly attaining the lofty heights of a text as rich as this: the constant variety of images suggested by the text, then accepted by the actor's imagination, ensures an extreme density in the development of the actor's work, but *a density that evolves in relation to the material* of the text. Substantial difference from our nineteenth-century tradition, within which the character possesses a plausible form of behaviour, and a language reflecting the way in which this plausible creature would speak. In *this* case, the character (and other elements as well) only exists through the succession of words he says. Character and story are constructed from moment to moment, in an unexpected way: in the form of a *broken line* (as Timon himself says: 'Everything in our human nature is oblique. Nothing is straightforward except for direct spite').

September 6: The richness of the second part

On a first reading, the second part of the play may resemble an interminable litany, an almost uninterrupted series of insults that Timon addresses to the universe. Thus the limited favour the play has gained in relation to Shakespeare's other plays. It is often considered to be linear, uniformly aggressive. But by working on the character of Timon and the succession of people with whom he converses using the method elaborated above (radiant words, total commitment to each image, unpredictable development), one uncovers the outlines of an extremely rare variety of philosophical human adventure.

Timon's prophetic ravings, his volley of oaths and curses, initially appear to have been cast in the 'inside-out' mould, a negative image of the first part. In fact detailed and attentive investigation enables considerable differences in attitude to emerge. The play's ending is not a two-act malediction.

September 11

The aim is to sweep from within us the dross of nineteenth-century sentimental tradition and of our Cartesian habits. The text, the concrete element of work, traces the movement of thought, extremely rich thought at that. So the actor who exhausts himself in showing he is thinking weighs down and impedes this movement considerably. In the same way, the 'sub-text' that is necessary when one performs nineteenth-century theatre today is also plainly visible in the text, delivered in front of an audience: so we have to abandon the psychological brakes and buffers of our theatre.

Of course, there can be no question of wanting to perform 'like the Elizabethans'; of course, a contemporary performance of Shakespeare presupposes moments of silence, ruptures in tempo, but one thing remains essential: the current of energy tying all the elements of the play together can never be cut.

It is remarkable to be able to state that with the help of this kind of speed, one understands the text better, inspite of the profusion and complexity of images; from one radiant word to another, the time is briefer and the flux between them is not severed: so the listener is invited to exercise his vivacity joyfully and freely, he is encouraged towards an understanding which does not only call his analytical faculties into play. This being said, it still remains necessary to pursue detailed work in the elucidation of the play's relationships and realities: those are the rules of *this* game.

To unite energy and intelligence, rapidity and profundity, generosity in the moment and rigorous calculation: increasingly this seems to be the basis of our work . . .

Translation by David Williams.

The Ik: An Account by David Williams

Brook's next production at the Bouffes reflected the anthropological overtones of much of his work since the formation of the C.I.R.T. *Les Iks* (presented, like *Timon*, as part of the Paris Festival d'Automne in 1975) was an adaptation of Colin Turnbull's best-selling study of an African tribe, *The Mountain People*. Brook had known Turnbull for many years, and had long been haunted by the tragic story of the Ik, a tribe of hunters and gatherers from Northern Uganda, who had originally existed in the relative prosperity of most primitive communities in their natural state – in an intimate relationship with the land. In 1946 a governmental imposition, Kafkaesque in its arbitrariness, forced the Ik to resettle as farmers in the arid mountains above their former home which subsequently became the Kidepo National Park. The bitter irony of this interference was that no concern was shown for indigenous peoples and their way of life. The Ik's demise was due in part to the 'civilized' world's attempts to impose upon 'primitives' notions of humanity and respect for the lives of others.

Brook saw this material as 'a very rare meeting point between a personal experience, objective facts, and poetic, mythic elements'[1] – the concrete reality of an anthropological study, and a parable vision of our own fallen condition and universal predicament, with Turnbull's personal journey as the point of union. In performance, it became the story of an African tribe told by actors of five different nationalities, for, like all of Brook's work, it is about all of us:

> The Ik survive – at a cost – and so do we. The parallels are alarming. The same sort of situation can be seen in Western urban life. For me, it's the perfect metaphor: something which exists on two levels – real in the sense of life as we know it, and real in the deep sense of a myth.[2]

[1] Brook in *Les Iks* (Paris, C.I.C.T., 1975), p. 97.
[2] Brook in *The Sunday Times*, 4 January 1976.

Brook recognized that Turnbull's 'education', his journey into the 'heart of darkness', had to be the pivotal spring of the dramatic narrative. Philanthropic and scientific values and motives could be sounded in this transplantation of a representative to another continent. Like Timon, Turnbull's initial innocence and naïvely confident approach are shown to be founded in ignorance. Locked within the aprioristic assumptions of his liberal humanism, he willingly accepts the title of *iciebam* – friend of the Ik; and we remember Timon's friends. He is harshly awakened from his post-BaMbuti dream world into a nightmarish reality. His despair echoes the anguish of Lear's 'Is man no more than this?' (III, iv); as one reviewer remarked, as a result his book 'reads like an exorcism'.[3] We see his degradation as something dies within him.

The form of *Les Iks* in performance was arrived at by stripping down and fusing two very different sorts of work. The mass of material spontaneously created during the actors' physical exploration was disciplined within a constantly re-adapted written version, which drew on both Turnbull's original and the actors' improvisations (it was written by Colin Higgins, author of *Harold and Maude*, and Denis Cannan, Brook's former collaborator on *US*, and translated into French by Jean-Claude Carrière). In this way, a honed living event resulted from the synthesis of spontaneity and discipline. Forms and energies were found to communicate directly and physically images of a reality, in a way that is much deeper than the superficiality of most stage naturalism. Somehow a racially mixed group of actors, using their ordinary clothes and no make-up, transcended their appearances to represent (make visible in the present) an *essence* of Ik-ness recognizable to all. After a relentless chipping away of all that was superfluous, what remained was a minimal, evocative framework of the necessary, a bare realism of the kind that Henry James referred to as possessing 'deep-breathing economy of organic form'.

At every level of the performance – narrative, invented Ik language and dialogue, actions and gestures – forms were understated, sparse and flat. The studied simplicity that resulted, almost unbearably stark, was somehow more shocking and traumatic.

Brook considered *Les Iks* to be in a direct line from *US*. Both drew on immediate and burning socio-political realities, lives still being lived, to create very different forms of what became known in journalistic shorthand as 'theatre of fact'. Both projects were viewed as challenges to find forms of theatrical expression of greater power and directness than

[3] *Times Literary Supplement*, 8 February 1974, p. 131.

that supplied by the surfeit of photo-documentary evidence, to which the West has become insensitive through over-exposure; the horror of the reality has become insulated. It is significant that both productions received criticism from the same quarters, and for similar reasons. In this case, Kenneth Tynan attacked in *Theatre Quarterly* Brook's 'shallow and factitious pessimism' and 'amoral misanthropy' in his choice of material and in the depiction of Turnbull's despair (he reaches the point where he wishes for all the Ik to die, leaving no trace).

An interpretation of Brook's *weltanschauung* as one of facile nihilism is indeed understandable in the light of the nature of Brook's thematic material since *King Lear*. He seems to have been fascinated by the belief that in certain extreme situations, civilizing social restraints reveal themselves to be false and shallow, crumbling to unleash the human beast within. From *Lord of the Flies* ('a potted history of man'[4]) to *Les Iks*, his anti-idealistic bent has chosen to portray the death throes of liberal altruism and humanism, the destruction of innocence by experience. Yet such apparent pessimism is surely validated when one reads those accounts of 'respectable' people in concentration camps, of American soldiers in the horrors of Vietnam, even when one experiences at first hand the darker side of any modern city.

As with *US*, the critics of *Les Iks* suggested that the production's pessimism, confusion and despondency merely served to feed the self-righteous concern of liberalism. Ultimately, it was felt that the production comforted the western bourgeois audience. Passively contemplated from a distance, the situation is accepted, as is the conviction of the futility of action reached by Turnbull, the representative of western liberalism in the play. A direct appeal to the masochistic conscience of the West can, these critics suggest, only facilitate a cheap emotional reaction. Purged from the will or need to act, the individual can give himself a pat on the back for being aware and for being shocked, before sinking deeper into his armchair. The story was seen as pandering to the prevalent taste for the vicarious.

A number of critics also questioned the ethics of exploiting a tragic human reality for entertainment, for the fulfilment of a modern theatre audience's needs for aesthetic 'frissons'. Irving Wardle (in *The Times*, Jan. 16 1976) doubted whether this was a legitimate subject for theatrical treatment at all, describing the performance at the Roundhouse in London as 'an event that trembles on the brink of obscenity: a study of total human degradation rehearsed in conditions of subsidized

---

[4] Brook, 'Filming a Masterpiece', *The Observer*, 26 July 1964.

security and now imported from Paris as the intellectual treat of the month'. As in much film-making or photography, the starting point of the actors' work, the treatment of horrific reality as art tends to aestheticize, to beautify. Arguably *Les Iks* had exploited a human tragedy, turning it into an object for appraisal and enjoyment. To a certain extent, perhaps, Brook as director of such a theatrical enterprise was guilty of the formalist attitude Ernst Fischer suggested as character-izing the works of impressionism: 'the attitude of an observer concerned only with his impressions, who does not intend to change the world, and to whom a bloodstain means no more than a poppy in a wheatfield'.[5]

Brook rejected the dogmatism of his socialist-realist critics, defend-ing his production as an honest attempt to confront a splintered and confused reality. Clearly these critics were naïve in treating Turnbull's approach and despair as a full reflection of Brook's own convictions. Turnbull is implicitly criticized throughout, in his reaction to his liberal-humanist dilemma and in his role as recorder, which in itself underlines his acceptance of the immutability of reality:

> although the camera is an observation station, the act of photo-graphing is more than passive observing. Like sexual voyeurism, it is a way of at least tacitly, often explicitly, encouraging whatever is going on to keep on happening. *To take a picture is to have an interest in things as they are, in the status quo remaining unchanged* . . . to be in complicity with whatever makes a subject interesting, worth photographing – including, when that is the interest, another person's pain or misfortune.[6]

In addition, Brook believes the other side of the coin was inferred within the pessimism concerning that particular reality. Brook described the play as 'the image of a world that is betraying its possibilities'. As such, he believes it offers a rare challenge to the limitations of a strictly Marxist analysis. Fundamentally, the pre-'fall' unity of the Ik did not have an economic basis; collapse has resulted from the removal of cohesive spiritual traditions. He sees any interpretation of the situation purely in terms of the imposition of capitalist oppressors as naive. In this situation, it is simplistic to suggest that economic intervention would be effective.

The Ik's story was thus seen by Brook in terms of 'a form of myth about the loss of tradition', about the tragic collapse and destruction, through necessity for survival, of everything that had made their lives

---

[5] Ernst Fischer, *The Necessity of Art: A Marxist Approach*, Penguin 1963, p. 75.
[6] Susan Sontag, *On Photography* (London, Allen Lane, 1973), p. 12.

meaningful: yet even in this descent, there are moments when one is made acutely aware of 'the potentiality, the virtuality that is being missed'. One example in performance was the Ik's arrival at the mountaintop 'place of God' (which, in the Bouffes, meant the actors scaling rungs up the back wall). The momentary re-establishment of a flow of contact was expressed in a spontaneous song of liberation, quickly stifled in response to the presence of Turnbull. In this way, the spectator is a witness to 'the force of tradition through the sense of its disappearance'. In the vacuum left after its disintegration, its life-giving energy is made present and visible. The positive is implied in the negative; the Ik imply the existence of the BaMbuti pygmies.[7]

Seen in this way, it could be argued that *Les Iks* offered a challenge to action on a personal level. Like the birds in *Conference*, initially Turnbull is forced into a recognition of the nature of reality and of the need to act. However, like Timon, his aprioristic moral framework is crushed and discarded, leaving him no possibility of transcendent understanding.

From David Williams, '"A Place Marked by Life": Peter Brook at the Bouffes du Nord' *New Theatre Quarterly*, February 1985

[7] In the mid-fifties, Turnbull had studied 'the forest people', the BaMbuti pygmies of the Ituri rain forests in the Congo. The Ik lacked everything that characterised the gentle 'pre-civilized' idyll of the pygmies: an organic understanding of their environment, social cooperation, a vital family life, a coherent spirituality.

The Ik: A Review by John Lahr

John Lahr's review from Plays and Players *describes* The Ik *at the Round House in London.*

The actors in Peter Brook's *The Ik* prepare their space at the base of the wooden amphitheatre, spilling nut-brown earth from burlap sacks on to the concrete floor. They will enact the story of an African tribe of hunters wedged in the mountains between Kenya and Uganda whose major hunting grounds have been turned into a national park and who have been forced to abandon their nomadic pursuit of food for farming. This parched, infertile soil with only a few grey sedimentary rocks and a handful of wood to break the monotony of the barren landscape are the emblems of what the Ik must now call their world – a society of starving, isolated souls transformed by governmental fiat from a nation of hunters to a band of scavengers. The Ik's world is without hope, without meaning, without community, without ceremony. Nothing can renew them. Social responsibility has evaporated. Life is reduced to a ruthless and unrelenting scrounging for food; and food is the only value. In the Ik vocabulary 'goodness' is the word for 'food'; and a 'good person' is one 'who has a full stomach'. The echoes of this profound selfishness can be heard in our own society. 'We don't know *how* to celebrate,' Peter Brook wrote of Western society, 'because we don't know *what* to celebrate.' Even in our well-being, Brook's fascinating parable has much to show us about why we feel our own world diminished.

The Ik dramatises a shocking and unpalatable fact: there is no such thing as 'basic human values'. This makes the event deeply disturbing and offensive to a bourgeois audience. The Ik have adapted to the cruel rigours of their new way of life in which adulthood comes at twelve and death at thirty. What has evolved is a horrendous inhumanity which survives because it 'works'. Children are thrown out of the family at the age of three. It is a sufficient burden among these mountain people to feed oneself, let alone another. Loveless, the children grow up with no allegiance to their family. In turn, when the parents are old and cannot feed themselves, they are turned out by their children to die.

Brook reconstructs Turnbull's findings in stark, haunting images. He shows a boy ferreting in the earth and swallowing pebbles for nourishment. Later, the same boy is lured close to the fire by his mother who proffers food, then pulls it away so that her son burns his hand on the fire. She laughs, like all the Ik, at the misfortunes of others. The laughter is unnerving but symptomatic of a people who survive at the expense of others. The laughter is double-edged – a small victory for their comparative well-being, momentary acknowledgement that they have cheated death. It is also a barometer of their profound cultural depression. 'A joke,' Nietzsche wrote, 'is an epitaph on an emotion.' And in their mountain purgatory, the Ik's malicious cackle seems an echo of a time now almost eradicated from the cultural memory when the Ik appreciated the beauty around them, their family, and the communal responsibility of a nomadic life.

The Ik rarely mourn. They hardly notice the death around them. In this, they are eerily modern. Isolated by a survivor's selfishness, ritual is totally absent from their life. They are part of a group, and yet cannot coexist as a group and perform those healing communal ceremonies which might revive their society. 'The object of ritual,' the anthropologist A. C. Hocart wrote in *Social Origins*, 'is to secure full life and to escape from evil.' The Ik cannot escape; and they know it. Overwhelmed by poverty and their own spiritual separation from their past, the Ik have no technique for giving life because they no longer have faith in that life. Powerless, the Ik no longer even attempt to control life and transcend it with the magical projects that usually make a community cohere.

Atum, the genial mountain hustler who guides Turnbull through the Ik villages, panhandles medicine and extra food for his wife long after she has died. When caught out, he explains that he buried her – as the Ik often do – in his compound, not only to dupe Turnbull but the other villagers for whom a feast would otherwise be required. It was not always this way for the Ik. The tribe's priest, Lolim, recalls with poetic simplicity the old burial rites where seeds that fed the deceased in life were planted on his grave. 'Seeds grow into plants. To make new life. Death is life in another form.' That sense of sacredness has vanished from the Ik experience; and with it, the technique for honouring spirit and making it visible.

Brook presents Turnbull's documentary evidence in the sparse, selective style of a fairy tale. The information is fascinating; and it takes the place of dramatic tension. Brook and his well-trained troupe do well in not turning the tale into a finger-point Oxfam ad. But the pageant, which has so many profound and disturbing implications, carries a curiously small theatrical blast. The fault lies in the adaptation by Denis Cannan and Colin Higgins, which gleans the high points from Turnbull's book, but never allows him to be more on stage than as Mr

Interlocutor. In fact, Turnbull's encounter with the Ik was stormy, beginning with disgust and depression and turning only gradually over the years to understanding and anger at their exploitation. Turnbull's struggle with the Ik sets up a dialectic between tribal values and the illusion of Western values in the book which is not adequately translated to the stage. This diminishes the debate and shrinks the scope of this otherwise memorable event.

'God gave us hunger,' muses the priest Lolim. 'Not the hunger of today but a hunger that kept us moving in search of food.' Brook's penultimate and finest image shows the Ik hunger of today and how the nobility of the hunter has mutated into the humiliation of the beggar. Three Iks tote famine relief sacks of grain back to their village. They have lied to the authorities about the number of dead in their villages to get more grain. Laughing, they stuff their mouths with dry grain. They vomit. Cram more grain into their maws, then vomit again. 'Better to carry food in our stomachs,' explains one of the Ik. 'When it's in our stomachs, no one can steal it.'

Plays and Players, March 1976

The Ik: A Review by Albert Hunt

In New Society, *Albert Hunt located* The Ik *in relation to Brook's earlier work (notably* Marat/Sade*) and questioned Brook's myopic political vision.*

In 1964, Peter Brook stunned the London theatre with his production of Weiss's play, *The Marat/Sade*. The production was the culmination of several years' work Brook had done with a particular group of actors, under the title of the Theatre of Cruelty. Last month, Brook stunned the Paris theatre with a 'creation' based on Colin Turnbull's book (*The Mountain People*) about an obscure African mountain tribe, the Iks.

The two plays, ten years apart, mark the twin peaks of Brook's attempt to invent, virtually single-handed, a genuinely contemporary theatre. They also reflect the cultural assumptions on which that attempt has been based. I believe that it's important to examine those assumptions with some care. They demonstrate the difficulties facing any individual in our society who is struggling consciously to create new artistic forms.

That Peter Brook is the most talented individual director, in the conventional sense, to have emerged in our theatre for 30 years few people would deny. If he had wanted, he could simply have spent his life turning out one international success after another, as if by magic. But what makes him an important artist is that he's a man possessed by an idea. He's driven by a need to search for ways of exploring the ultimate in human experience in terms of the ultimate in theatrical expression.

This search has led him through Artaud, the Theatre of Cruelty, Grotowski, Japanese Noh plays (as in his brilliant *Midsummer Night's Dream* of 1971); and now the rituals of primitive tribes. Throughout, he has been looking for ways of confronting an audience with an experience so direct, so overwhelming, so *necessary*, that the consciousness of that audience can be disturbed, shaken and, to some extent, changed. Both *The Marat/Sade* in London and *Les Iks* in Paris have provided Brook with material through which to carry out his exploration of the ultimate in experience.

The *Marat/Sade* was, of course, a play in which the inmates of the lunatic asylum at Charenton performed, under the direction of the Marquis de Sade, a dramatic representation of the assassination of Marat. Here, the ultimate was represented by the demented inmates of the asylum, and also by the figure of Sade himself. Describing his interest in the play, Brook once said that he saw in Sade the ultimate expression of tendencies towards cruelty that he recognized in himself, and that we would all recognize in ourselves if we could only be sufficiently honest. In *The Marat/Sade*, he then led the actors to confront the cruelty in themselves, until they in turn were capable of forcing the members of the audience to confront *their own* cruelty. The fact that the central figure in Brook's production was a theatre director, and that the actor, Patrick Magee, played Sade as Brook, demonstrated where Brook's particular interest was located.

In *Les Iks* (now at the Théâtre des Bouffes du Nord) the ultimate in human experience is represented by the mountain people described by Colin Turnbull. He found them to be a people living at the extreme limits of anything that could be described as humanity; for whom the only good is food; who, when they find food, gobble it down secretly in order not to have to share it with members of their own family; who build stockades to protect themselves from each other; who drive their children out to fend for themselves at the age of three; who see giving food to the old and dying as a criminal waste; who will gorge themselves sick on relief grain rather than distribute it to those in need; and whose only pleasure is to laugh at the misfortunes of the weak and the helpless. In the preface to his book, Turnbull tells us how he was driven to say repeatedly, 'How inhuman' – then adds that to say 'How inhuman' is to presuppose 'that there are certain standards common to all humanity.' His book is largely about how he was driven to question that presupposition.

It's not difficult to see why Brook, in search of the ultimate, should be attracted by such material. But there's a further point of affinity between himself and Turnbull, which Brook referred to specifically in a recent interview about producing Shakespeare that he gave in a French theatre revue. 'As in anthropology,' says Brook, 'there are two schools. Certain researchers prefer to go into a far country knowing nothing about it, while others leave only with documentation and after deep study. For me, with Shakespeare, the questions only become strong, hard, interesting when you're inside them. You can approach a Shakespeare text without knowing anything outside.'

Turnbull, in his own first chapter, describes how, for him, the Ik were in the beginning a completely unknown quantity. He didn't even know their correct name. And he sees this as good. 'In this case,' he writes, 'there was all the advantage of an almost completely clean slate.' His approach to this anthropological task was that of Brook's to

Shakespeare: both would like to come at their subjects with virgin minds.

But, of course neither Turnbull nor Brook can do this. Turnbull doesn't bring a 'clean slate' to the Iks. He brings a discipline and a whole set of values and assumptions. But at least these values are openly stated, and the importance of the book lies in the way they're thrown into question by what he observes.

Brook also brings to the subject a discipline and a set of values and assumptions. But in Brook's case, the assumptions *aren't* openly stated. They're accepted without question. In order to discover what they are, it's necessary to go back to the time when they were first formulated; in a series of remarkable reflections first published in the theatre magazine, *Encore*, around 1960.

In these reflections, Brook announces three central areas of interest. First, he is seeking for a theatrical equivalent of the 'revolution that took place in painting 50 years ago.' 'Do you know,' he asks, 'where we stand in relation to the real and the unreal, the face of life and its hidden stream, the abstract and the concrete, the story and the ritual? What are "facts" today?'

Secondly, in relating this to the actor, Brook is searching for a form of acting that goes beyond 'anecdote or characterisation'. He saw elements of what he's looking for in a production of Jack Gelber's *The Connection* – the play about drug addicts waiting for a fix. 'The actors who are portraying these characters,' he writes, 'have sunk themselves into a total (beyond Method) degree of saturated naturalism, so that they aren't acting, they are being.' And he goes on, 'I think it shows that there is a super-naturalistic theatre ahead of us, in which *pure behaviour* can exist in its own right, like pure movement in ballet, pure language in declamation . . . I believe that *The Connection* shows how naturalism can become so deep that it can – through the intensity of the performer – transcend appearances.'

Thirdly, Brook wishes to use these new abstract rituals, and these developing forms of acting, to create images that communicate to us, directly and physically, the realities of our time. Brook quotes two such images. One is Sartre's image of hell in *Huis-Clos* – 'Hell is other people' – which, he asserts, has 'entered into the terms of reference of our whole generation. I think that to anyone who saw the play the word "hell" is more likely to evoke that closed room than fire and pitchforks.' The second example is the woman in Beckett's *Happy Days*, buried up to her bosom in sand. 'Here,' says Brook, 'is the audience (and the critics) at any play . . . which after two hours asserts that life is good, that there is always hope that all will be well. Here is Walter Kerr, and the audience of *The Miracle Worker*, and Ike, and most of our politicians, grinning from ear to ear and buried up to their necks.'

It is, I think, important to note the *nature* of these images Brook cites, and the particular way he sees them. Beckett and Gelber are both, to Brook, images of futility and total despair. They destroy the 'facile optimism' of all of us 'ensconced . . . in our stalls.' Even more important, Brook accepts the truth of these images as a self-evident mirror of our time. This acceptance of the validity of futility and despair affects the meaning he attaches both to *The Marat/Sade* and to *Les Iks*.

In *The Marat/Sade* and *Les Iks*, Brook carries his early ideas about actors 'being' rather than 'acting' to an advanced artistic level. In *The Marat/Sade*, Brook asked his actors not to perform madmen, but to become mad. In rehearsal, he put them in the situation of digging up the roots of madness in themselves; of finding those corners of themselves which could lead towards madness; and of building their behaviour throughout the play on what they had discovered inside themselves. In terms of acting, the results were overwhelmingly successful. Madness became the central reality of the play, against which all the arguments of Marat and Sade, and all the events of the political terror had to be measured.

In *Les Iks*, after ten further years of experiment, Brook has carried the possibilities of 'being', rather than 'acting', to an even more complex level. While rehearsing the play, the actors representing the Iks themselves built and lived in an Ik stockade, and played out episodes in Turnbull's book which were never to appear in the script. The result is that, throughout the two hours of the play, they become Iks.

This 'being' is achieved without the aid of any surface naturalism. They make no attempt, for example, to look like Iks, by appearing naked, or painting their faces in a uniform colour (there are people of many different races and hues in the cast). They wear their rehearsal clothes and keep their own physical appearances. And they don't create, for the most part, any specific characters. They're able to move at will from being young children to very old people. Brook even establishes a non-naturalistic use of language (reminiscent of the invented language of his and Ted Hughes's Persian experiment, *Orghast*). The actors speak gibberish to each other, but offer explanations in French when necessary.

What they do create consistently is the quality of being Ik. The 'being' is revealed in the way the actors behave – in how an old woman falls over shrieking with laughter when she shakes hands with the actor playing

Turnbull (she's so weak with hunger, she explains, that the gesture pulls her from her seat); in how a stockade is built and later destroyed; in how an idiot child picks up a berry from the ground, contemplates it with delight, and puts it into her mouth, only to have it snatched away by another child; in how a man whittles away endlessly at a block of wood. Though the actors show different characters, they always remain *inside* the Iks, throughout the performance (as Brook wishes to remain *inside* a Shakespeare text). Look at this, says Brook. *This* is human experience.

In a universe where all is madness, Sade becomes comparatively normal. And in a universe where all is degradation, Turnbull becomes the image of futile action. Both these interpretations arise directly from Brook's despairing vision of the human condition. But both, significantly, distort the material he is working with.

Weiss's *Marat/Sade* (as distinct from Brook's) is a play about actors playing at being madmen playing at being politicians. The critical intelligence of the actor, his performance as a madman, and his added performance as a madman playing a politician, hold three different realities in balance. Weiss doesn't come down in favour of any of these realities. But he presents them in such a way as to force us to ask questions. Is Marat merely the puppet of Sade? Or does the strength of his arguments put Sade's fashionable psychological rhetoric into question? On the other hand, isn't Sade's analysis necessary to complement Marat's constant manifestos? Weiss holds the contradictions up for our inspection, leaves us to think and to choose.

Brook leaves us no such choice. He overwhelms the contradictions with the reality of madness. Weiss asked: Does the fact that a man has an itchy skin affect the validity of his aguments? Brook asserts political thought and action are futile in a universe where ultimate reality is an itchy skin.

There's a similar reduction of Turnbull in *Les Iks*. The Turnbull of *The Mountain People* brings to his research that set off cultural assumptions about the nature of 'humanity'. He finds these assumptions withering away. He even begins to lose his own 'humanity'. But what he retains to the end is his active intelligence. In a final chapter, he uses this intelligence to turn our responses to the material back on ourselves, to ask us to analyse our own society, to become aware of the Ik qualities in our welfare state. And to become aware of them, not simply in order to throw up our hands and say in horror, 'Well, that's life, and there's nothing to be done' – but in order that we may use *our* intelligence to make a rational effort to change direction.

None of this emerges from Brook's play. Since the central reality of

Les Iks is the Iks themselves, Turnbull is seen, not as an active intelligence, but as a victim. He exists only in relation to the situation he too finds himself *inside.* This is established in one of the first scenes, in which four creatures stare at Turnbull who is in a sleeping bag behind a mosquito net. Presently, he emerges from the bag, takes out a folding table and chair, which he sets up, lights a primus stove, fills a kettle with water from a plastic container, warms the teapot with water from the container, and is on the point of throwing the water from the teapot on the floor, when he glances at the staring creatures and carefully pours the water back into the plastic container.

In such a scene, Brook seems to me to achieve entirely his aim of a 'super-naturalistic' theatre. All Turnbull's actions are totally natural: he boils a real kettle on a real stove. But since they're seen through the eyes of the staring creatures, they take on the quality of a strange, absurd ritual. Our 'normal' actions are judged against a situation in which a drop of water means the perpetuating of a life.

But the actions that are so judged are, in the end, only the superficial, surface actions. Brook has, in this particular scene, found an adequate image to represent the thoughtless waste of the 'civilised' societies. But as the play develops, we're not presented with the kind of analysis of those societies that Turnbull himself sketches out. We're offered instead a picture of Turnbull's personal moral despair. We see him only through his reactions to the creatures who are around him. Our attention is focused, not on our society, but on Turnbull's sensibility.

How painful it must have been for him to have his water delivered daily from the police bore hole! When all around him people were dying because a polluted pool had dried up! How terrible it must have been to realize that your efforts to save one here and there were so futile! No wonder he felt such anger against the universe! And how morally corrupting to find yourself developing Ik-like qualities, in self-defence – hiding away when you eat your provisions, forcing yourself to feel no pity or human sympathy!

Turnbull's book ends with an appeal to us to *choose,* and adds a warning: 'It is difficult to say how long the choice will be open to us before we are irrevocably committed.' He's pessimistic – but he does still recognize the possibility of choice, and therefore of action.

Brook's play ends with a positive statement that all action is impossible. Turnbull's last speech in the play is one which offers his own final solution: to round up the Iks like cattle and disperse them in small groups amongst other tribes far away. 'No need to say,' says an administrator in a final line, 'that your proposition is not acceptable.' It would be impossible to imagine a more direct assertion of the total futility of human action.

In both *The Marat/Sade* and *Les Iks*, then, Brook presents powerful images which deny the usefulness, and even the possibility, of rational action. In doing so, he reflects, as an artist, the despair of a society which accepts that we are caught in a situation that we are completely powerless to change.

There are two paradoxes in the position Brook takes up. The first is that this man, who wants to question everything, and who asks audiences to question their own most cherished values, who believes in approaching experience naked and entirely without either illusion or faith, holds himself with a stubborn tenacity to his own faith in the futility of human action based on intelligence. He does so in the face of the evidence of the texts with which he is working – evidence left by such an intelligence as Shakespeare himself, whom Brook prefers to see as an anonymous, ambiguous figure, existing outside historical time and place. In *The Mountain People*, Turnbull's faith in his own values was questioned by the evidence offered by the Iks. Brook's faith in futility is not in any way questioned by Turnbull's intelligence. This seems to me to represent the other side of the coin from the 'facile optimism' Brook wants to challenge. In place of such optimism he offers an equally facile despair.

And this leads to the second paradox. For, because the despair is facile, the result is that, though Brook is trying to disturb, shock and assault the consciousness of his audiences, the despair joins hands with the optimism and, in the end, only succeeds in bringing an easy comfort. For if all rational action is futile, then the most we can do is to contemplate, with compassion, the sufferings of others. We can, in fact, feel righteous for spending an evening doing this instead of watching those old entertaining movies on telly. Brook himself is so conscious of this paradox that in his production *US* at the Aldwych in 1966 he included a speech castigating people who went to see plays like *US* in order to feel righteous. (The audience, of course, felt even more righteous for having seen through their own self-righteousness).

This paradox was summed up by one of the more irreverent actors in *US*. After eight weeks of 'being' Vietnamese in rehearsal – of being bombed, napalmed, driven from his village, put into a strategic hamlet, tortured – he was asked by Brook how these experiences had affected his attitude to the Vietnam war. 'Henceforward,' he said, with a completely solemn face, 'when I turn on my television set, I shall find the Vietnam war more *enjoyable*.'

Listening to the applause the other night that burst out in the crowded Bouffes du Nord after the last Ik had vomited up in front of the audience his last sack of relief grain, and then dragged his twisted limbs into a hole at the back of the stage, I couldn't help thinking that Brook, the miracle worker, had pulled it off again. He'd made the Iks enjoyable.

New Society 20 February 1975

The Ik

An extract from the English text of The Ik, *including the fleeting glimpse of a missed future in Sudan. The English version was adapted from Colin Turnbull by Jean-Claude Carrière, Colin Higgins and Denis Cannan.*

(TURNBULL *runs the tape back and sets it to play. We hear recorded Ik laughter. He switches off the tape and begins to type.*)

(ATUM *enters and watches* TURNBULL.)

ATUM: Are you going to make tea?

TURNBULL: No.

(ATUM *helps himself to some biscuits.* TURNBULL *knocks them out of his hand.*)

TURNBULL: I can't feed everyone! *(He switches the tape on and off.)* Atum, those other Ik living in the Sudan . . .

ATUM: Yes?

TURNBULL: Is life better there?

ATUM: Yes.

TURNBULL: Why don't you go and live there?

ATUM: Live in Sudan? Impossible.

TURNBULL: Why?

ATUM: Because from there we cannot see Morungole.

(LOMONGIN *enters and joins them. He is whittling wood.*)

LOMONGIN: No. I've never hunted on Morungole. Many people go there to gather fruit or look for honey. There is plenty of honey on Morungole . . . If Atum and I were up there, we would never fight. It is a good place.

TURNBULL: A good place. You mean there is plenty of food?

LOMONGIN: Yes.

TURNBULL: Then why don't you go there?

LOMONGIN: We do go there.

TURNBULL: But if the hunting is good, why not live there?

LOMONGIN: We never hunt there, we just go there.

TURNBULL: Why?

LOMONGIN: I told you, it is a good place.

ATUM: It is the place of god.

(ALL *look for a while at the mountain, then start off.* TURNBULL *calls* ATUM)

TURNBULL: Atum, I want to see what the Ik are like when they have plenty of food. Will you take me to the Sudan?

ATUM: No. It is too far.

TURNBULL: All right. I'll go by myself. And if I get lost, the government will blame you.

(*He takes his rucksack and starts off.*)

ATUM: *Iciebam*, what do you know about our country?

(TURNBULL *stops.*)

ATUM: Come. We go to the Sudan. This way.

(*He points in the opposite direction. He and* TURNBULL *set off. They climb a mountain and reach the top.*)

ATUM: There, that is Sudan.

(*We hear singing, the music of flutes.* ATUM *and* TURNBULL *descend.*)

(LOSIKE *enters with another* IK. *She lights a fire. Other* IK *enter, including* CHILDREN. *They help themselves to food. All eat without greed. They begin to sing softly as the* CHILDREN *fall asleep. One* IK *bathes his hands in the flames of the fire, then makes a slow gesture as though blessing himself and the others.* OTHERS *repeat the gesture.* ATUM *falls asleep. The song dies away. Someone puts out the fire.* ALL *leave, in silence.*)

(*Four* IK *enter, carrying sacks of grain. They open the sacks and begin to eat.* TURNBULL *approaches.*)

TURNBULL: What's in those sacks?

LOMONGIN: Famine relief from the government. We're taking it to the villages, for the old and the dying . . . and the dead.

ATUM: When someone dies, we never tell. So we get their share.

(The IK *are all stuffing themselves with the grain.* ONE *says something. The* OTHERS *laugh.)*

TURNBULL: What's so funny?

LOMONGIN: I said, it's better to carry it in our stomachs. If we carry it in our stomachs, no one can steal it.

(The IK *belch and retch. They put their fingers down their throats to make themselves vomit, then they guzzle more.* TURNBULL *moves among them, watching. Still cramming themselves, they drag the sacks away.)*

*(*TURNBULL *watches as* LOLIM *is chased from his hut by his daughter.* TURNBULL *offers him water.* LOLIM *drinks in silence, then begins to walk away. He is very weak. With a long, whining groan, he shuffles in a circle. Then staggering, stumbling blindly, still groaning, he goes.* TURNBULL *addresses the* DAUGHTER.*)*

TURNBULL: What happened?

DAUGHTER: The old man knew he was going to die. He wanted to die in my house. Of course, I said no. If he died in my house, I would have to give a great feast for a man of his importance. So I said to my father that he must go and die outside. I'm not his daughter any more. But he went on talking about the *abang*. Till I told him that the *abang* do not help us any more. Do you understand?

*(*LOSIKE *returns from the Sudan, carrying her belongings, as when she left.)*

TURNBULL: Losike, why have you come back?

*(*LOSIKE *passes* TURNBULL *without answering. From all sides comes a strange sound, as of insects moving among dead leaves.)*

*(*ATUM *enters and passes* TURNBULL *without looking at him.)*

ATUM: We are moving the village. To be nearer the water at the police post.

(The sound is explained. Sick and aged IK *drag themselves toward their new destination. They make their way across the stage with a crab-like crawl, raising their buttocks with their fists, then swinging forward on their arms, dropping to the ground again a few inches ahead.)*

(LOSIKE appears. She trips and rolls over. She lies on her back, her arms and legs thrashing feebly. The crawling IK around her laugh. TURNBULL goes among them, carrying a cup of water. The IK point at LOSIKE, inviting TURNBULL to enjoy the funny sight of a woman as helpless as an upturned tortoise. TURNBULL helps her to sit up, gives her water. Now she is laughing, too. She laughs at herself. As TURNBULL holds her and puts the water to her lips, she begins to cry. One of the crawling IK stands up. The OTHERS pause.)

NARRATOR: Turnbull left in 1966. In 1971, another anthropologist, Joseph Towles, visited the Ik. He found the population was stable at about one thousand . . . thanks to their unique system of survival. Even when rain came and food was plentiful, each Ik took what he needed for the moment; the rest was left to rot. It had become abnormal to have enough.

(Blackout)

Adapted by Jean-Claude Carrière, Colin Higgins and Denis Cannan
from *The Mountain People* by Colin Turnbull

Notes to the IK language:
Morungole: a sacred mountain, the 'place of God'
abang: the ancestral spirits

'The World that Is': An extract from *The Mountain People* by Colin Turnbull

Colin Turnbull's conclusion suggested that THE IK *furnished us with a grim parody of the state of Western society* in extremis. *The story gives us 'a taste of things to come', for we are all potentially Ik. Although much of Turnbull's moralizing was cut from Brook's version, it directly implied a similar point of view and conclusion.*

If we grant, as the evidence indicates we should, that the Ik were not always as they are, and that they once possessed in full measure those values that we all hold to be basic to humanity, indispensable for both survival and sanity, then what the Ik are telling us is that these qualities are not inherent in humanity at all, they are not a necessary part of human nature. Those values which we cherish so highly and which some use to point to our infinite superiority over other forms of animal life may indeed be basic to human society, but not to humanity, and that means that the Ik clearly show that society itself is not indispensable for man's survival, that man is not the social animal he has always thought himself to be, and that he is perfectly capable of associating for purposes of survival without being social. The Ik have successfully abandoned useless appendages, by which I refer to those 'basic' qualities such as family, co-operative sociality, belief, love, hope and so forth, for the very good reason that in their context these militated against survival. By showing that man can do without these appendages the Ik show that man can do without society in the sense we mostly mean by the word (implying those qualities), for they have replaced human society with a mere survival system that does not take human emotion into account. As yet the system is imperfect, for although survival is assured, it is at a minimal level and there is still competition between the individuals within the system. With our intellectual sophistication and with our advanced technology we should be able to perfect the system and eliminate competition, guaranteeing survival for a given number of years for all, reducing the demands made upon us by a social system with all its necessary structural oppositions and inherent conflicts, abolishing desire and consequently that ever present and vital gap between desire and achievement, treating us, in a word, as individuals with one basic individual right, the right to survive, so that man becomes the perfect vegetable, no longer an animal, human or otherwise.

Such interaction as there is within this system is one of mutual exploitation. That is the relationship between all, old and young, parent and child, brother and sister, husband and wife, friend and friend. That is how it already is with the Ik. They are brought together by self-interest alone, and the system takes care that such association is of a temporary nature and cannot flourish into anything as dysfunctional as affection or trust. Does that sound so very different from our own society? In our own world the very mainstays of a society based on a truly social sense of mutuality are breaking down, indicating that perhaps society itself as we know it has outworn its usefulness, and that by clinging to an outworn system more proper to the neolithic age we are bringing about our own destruction. We have tinkered with society, patching it up to cope with two thousand years of change, but it shows signs of collapse almost everywhere, and the signs are the more violent where the society is more 'advanced'. It is only to the 'backward societies' that this new violence has not yet come. Family, economy, government and religion, the basic categories of social activity and behaviour, despite our tinkering, are no longer structured in a way that makes them compatible with each other or with us, for they are no longer structured in such a way as to create any sense of social unity involving a shared and mutual responsibility between all members of our society. At the best they are structured so as to enable the individual to survive as an individual, with as little demand as possible that any vestigial remains of mutual responsibility should be expressed in mutuality of action. It is the world of the individual, as is the world of the Ik.

What has become of the Western family? The very old and the very young are separated, but we dispose of them in homes for the aged or in day schools and summer camps instead of on the slopes of Meraniang. Marital relations are barely even fodder for comedians, and responsibility for health, education and welfare has been gladly abandoned to the state. That is where we have a technological advantage over the Ik, for they have had to abandon such responsibility to the three-year-olds; it is difficult to say which of us is more advanced in this respect. The individualism that is preached with a curious fanaticism, heightened by our ever-growing emphasis on competitive sports, the more violent the better, and suicidal recreations, is of course at direct variance with our still proclaimed social ideals, but we ignore that, for we are already individuals at heart and society has become a game that we play in our old age, to remind us of our childhood. It is reflected in our cut-throat economics, where almost any kind of exploitation and degradation of others, impoverishment and ruin, is justified in terms of an expanding economy and the consequent confinement of the world's riches in the pockets of the few. The rot is in all of us, for how many of us would be willing to divide our riches among our own family, let alone the poor or needy, beyond of course what we can easily afford – for if we were willing, why have we not done it? Each of us gives according to his conscience, and the amount that is given is a nice measure of today's sociality, just as the amount taken is a good measure of man's individuality.

The great religions which arose as if in an effort to provide some means for uniting the ever expanding and increasingly diverse societies brought about by the agricultural revolution seem on the verge of defeat. They still unite large blocks, but with less and less efficiency, and all are increasingly rent with internal schism. This has nothing to do with their impact on any individual, or perhaps in a way it has, for that is now apparently the growing role of religion, to provide some kind of anesthesia for those unable to face the world as it is. Another, even less laudable (in terms of its own professed beliefs) role played by formal religion is to lend support to the state, even when this is in direct conflict with its own principles. The state itself, resting ever more on both intellectual and physical violence to assert itself, is where the nucleus of the new system is forming, it seems, and the loud-mouthed anti-intellectual blabberings of heads of state and their assistants show as well as anything that we are well along on the Icien road, where man must not only not believe or trust or love or hope, but must not think. The job of government seems to be regarded more and more as simply to *govern*, to conform to the self-creating system, and to enforce conformity on the governed. As yet the word 'democracy' still has some soporific value, lulling the unthinking but nicely filled stomachs into a sense of security, but good government regards those with minds and with the will to express themselves as a nuisance, to be destroyed if they cannot be made to conform. It is worth noting, too, that high places in government are not conspicuously occupied by men with minds, merely by men with certain political (and not necessarily social) abilities.

The sorry state of society in the civilized world today, which contrasts so strongly with the still social society of the 'primitive', is in large measure due to the simple fact that social change has not kept up with technological change, which has not only been almost inconceivably rapid but has been accelerating with even greater rapidity, carrying us with it in an unknown direction, leaving our old form of society behind but, the signs seem to indicate, holding in store for us the future already tasted by the Ik. It is this mad, senseless, unthinking commitment to technological change that we call progress, despite the grim trail of disaster it is wreaking all around us, including overpopulation and pollution, either of which may be sufficient to exterminate the human race in a very short time even without the assistance of other technological benefits such as nuclear warfare. But since we have already become individualized and desocialized we say to ourselves that extermination will not come in our time, which shows about as much sense of family devotion as one might expect from the Ik, and as little sense of social responsibility.

Even supposing we can avert the disaster of nuclear holocaust or that of the almost universal famine that may be expected by the middle of the next century if population keeps expanding and pollution remains unchecked, what will be the cost, if not the same as already paid by the Ik? They too were driven by the need to survive against seemingly invincible odds, and they succeeded, at the cost of their humanity. We are already beginning to pay the same price, but the difference is that we not only still have the choice (though we may not have the will or courage to make it), we also have the intellectual and technological ability to avert an Icien end. Many will say, are already saying, that it is too late – by which they mean it is too late for the change to benefit them. Any change as radical as that likely to be necessary, certainly, is not likely to bring material benefits to the present generation, though for those with a belief in the future, and an interest in it, there will be ample compensation, for only then *will* there be a future. And naturally it is the young – whose future, even as individuals, stretches beyond that of the ruling generation – who are most concerned, and in whose hands, perhaps, society and humanity lie. But it is difficult to predict their feelings, however bold their demand for change may be now, when in a few short years they too begin to think of their old age and personal security. It is also difficult to say how long the choice will be open to us before we are irrevocably committed.

The Ik teach us that our much vaunted human values are not inherent in humanity at all, but are associated only with a particular form of survival called society, and that all, even society itself, are luxuries that can be dispensed with. That does not make them any the less wonderful or desirable, and if man has any greatness it is surely in his ability to maintain these values, clinging to them to an often very bitter end, even shortening an already pitifully short life rather than sacrificing his humanity. But that too involves choice, and the Ik teach us that man can lose the will to make it. That is the point at which there is an end to truth, to goodness and to beauty; an end to the struggle for their achievement, which gives life to the individual while at the same time giving strength and meaning to society. The Ik have relinquished all luxury in the name of individual survival, and the result is that they live on as a people without life, without passion, beyond humanity. We pursue those trivial, idiotic technological encumbrances and imagine *them* to be the luxuries that make life worth living, and all the time we are losing our potential for social rather than individual survival, for hating as well as loving, losing perhaps our last chance to enjoy life with all the passion that is our nature and being.

From *The Mountain People*, by Colin Turnbull

Ubu aux Bouffes: An Account by David Williams

An expanded version of this account by David Williams was originally published in New Theatre Quarterly.

> 'The Holy Theatre deals with the invisible and this invisible contains all the hidden impulses of man. The Rough Theatre deals with men's actions, and because it is down to earth and direct – because it admits wickedness and laughter – the rough and ready seems better than the hollowly holy'
>
> (The Empty Space, p. 80)

For his next project at the Bouffes, Brook turned to the *Ubu* plays of Alfred Jarry. His interest in Jarry was longstanding. A production of *Ubu Roi* had originally been envisaged as part of the RSC's Theatre of Cruelty season in 1964, but had not materialized, although Jarry's works were used as a springboard for improvisations at that time. At the première of *Ubu Roi* in 1896, when Jarry was only 23 years old, the audience was scandalized, and a rather hysterical W. B. Yeats subsequently asked, 'what more is possible? After us, the Savage God.' Ubu had arrived.

This 'virulent protest play' had been intended by its author to offer an exaggerated and distorted reflection of its audience's nature, their true appetites and possibilities. It was deliberately provocative in every way. The figure of Ubu represented a grotesquely caricatured archetype of bourgeois vulgarity, stupidity, and selfishness. The anti-humanism of his merciless greed for power is coupled with a very human cowardice: he manifests the brutal cruelty and cynical sadism of man as beast pursuing the logic of his basest instincts.

Clearly this coincides with that vision of the world represented in the cycle of plays at the Bouffes. Ubu is in many ways an Ik: his conception of reality is one-dimensional. His world, the very antithesis of that in *Conference*, ignores the possibility of any form of transcendent understanding. Rather it is a world of utter materialism and egotism – the world as stomach.

The vision of reality that results is essentially *grotesque* in Meyerhold's sense of the word:

> Grotesque usually implies something hideous and strange, a humorous work which with no apparent logic combines the most

dissimilar elements by ignoring their details and relying on its own originality, borrowing from every source anything which satisfies its joie de vivre and its capricious mocking attitude to life.

As such, Brook recognized in *Ubu* an ideal opportunity for the realization of what he has called 'rough theatre'. This popular and 'poor' theatre is 'usually distinguished by the absence of what is called style' yet 'actually speaks a very sophisticated and stylish language'. Traditionally, it has had a quality of violence and danger, having taken the form in the past of 'bearbaiting, ferocious satire, and grotesque caricature'. Above all, it is by its very nature 'anti-authoritarian, anti-tradition, anti-pomp, anti-pretence. This is the theatre of noise, and the theatre of noise is the theatre of applause'.

Ironically, the threatening life of *Ubu* was quickly snuffed as a result of its absorption by bourgeois society as art, yet today 'it insists on not being subjected to the severe criteria that the word "classic" habitually evokes. The only way to treat a classic with respect is to stage it disrespectfully.'[1] As with so many of Brook's productions, from *A Midsummer Night's Dream* (1970) to *La Tragédie de Carmen* (1981), much of the challenge in approaching *Ubu* lay in finding a way of stripping away 'dead' cultural accretions – of once again baring and liberating the work's vital kernel. How could Ubu be made to live anew, the play as a whole infused with a fresh anarchic danger and its former quality of joyous celebration? Where could a 'sophisticated and stylish language', accessible and appealing to the imaginations of a modern audience, be found?

In his approach, Brook seems to have taken as his example a Czech production of *Ubu Roi* as junk comic-strip, which he had seen a number of years previously on German television. In *The Empty Space*, he records that this performance 'disregarded every one of Jarry's images and indications; it *invented an up-to-the-minute pop-art style of its own*, made out of dustbins, garbage, and ancient iron bedsteads.' Ubu himself was 'no masked Humpty Dumpty, but a recognizable and shifty slob', while Mère Ubu was a 'sleazy, attractive whore'. In this way, 'the audience's belief was caught because it accepted the primitive situation and characters on their own terms'.

This could almost serve as a description of Brook's own production, in which the Gargantuan Ubus were demythified and humanized. In some ways, Andreas Katsulas's Ubu was presented as an ordinary working-class man, immediately recognizable in braces and shirt-sleeves, his crown a woollen hat. Somehow the Ubus became more

[1] Brook in *New York Times*, 4 May 1980.

odious for being more recognizable; they were presented as a living reality, rather than as symbolic puppets.

The first step was a choice of text. Carrière worked together with Brook and the actors to create a composite *Ubu* entitled *Ubu aux Bouffes*, comprising elements from all four of Jarry's *Ubu* plays. The first half of the performance followed *Ubu Roi* until the bear scene, where the action switched to that of *Ubu sur la Butte* (the compressed two-act 'guignol' version of *Ubu Roi*). Included were some of Jarry's original songs, with the music by his collaborator on all of the *Ubu* projects, Claude Terrasse: notably, in the first half, 'La Chanson du Décervelage' from *Ubu Cocu*. The interval came after the Ubus' arrival in Paris, the second half being taken entirely from *Ubu Enchaîné*.

Brook believes that Jarry's writing is created for the actor. It establishes an immediate contact through a certain 'brutal energy emanating from the page'. Appealing to both gut and imagination, the texts demand immediate physical experimentation through improvisation. Artaud may well have been writing about the absence of a Jarry when he bemoaned the loss in his contemporary theatre of 'any true sense of humour, and laughter's physical, anarchic, dissolving power . . . It has broken away from the *profoundly anarchic spirit at the basis of all poetry*.'[2] In this performance, it was above all in the extraordinarily inventive *manipulation of objects* by the actors, discovered through improvisation, that the link with this 'spirit' was once again established.

In antithesis to the proliferation of purely imitative objects in so much naturalistic theatre, those used in *Ubu* were minimal in number, and always simple and recognizable, part of the everyday world – indeed so banal (bricks, sticks, etc.) as to be neutral and taken for granted. Their primary significance is their very insignificance, forming a virtual *tabula rasa* appropriate to the Bouffes space. They are merely a 'heap of broken images', neither blocking nor fixing the imagination, the raw material conducive to transformation. Unmodified and patently themselves, their very presence in the theatrical space, however, invests them with an extraordinary potential, a quality of magic. As in the focus of the carpet space in Africa, they are infused with an animistic dimension, an innate life which can only be released through the clarity and simplicity of the actor's manipulation.

These objects included: two huge empty industrial spools of the sort used for electrical cable, one slightly smaller than the other; a number of

[2] Antonin Artaud, *Collected Works*, Vol. 4 (London, Calder and Boyars, 1974), p. 29.

bricks, some of which were broken; a number of all-purpose sticks and stylized weapons, such as pantomime wooden swords; and a tatty old shag rug, at different times used as Ubu's majestic ermine, a bedspread, and a bear (when, in a scene of great cartoon comedy, it consumed an actor whole, only to regurgitate his hat and a bone).

The *spools* and *bricks* were used to the greatest effect. Initially, laid flat side by side, the spools represented the Ubu's dining table and a stool, thus establishing a location in a non-representative way and suggesting the quantity of food consumed in that location. Subsequently, both spools together were used as throne for Wenceslas and for Ubu the usurper, and as an inaccessibly narrow spiral staircase in an imaginary tower, a temporary refuge for Bougrelas (Alain Maratrat) and for the murdered King Wenceslas's queen (Mireille Maalouf). After their escape by a 'secret staircase' (through Ubu's legs), the fugitives take a route which involves the precarious crossing of a swollen river, communicated by means of absurdly mocking burlesque, Bougrelas jumping from brick to brick with the queen hanging around his neck for dear life. Here there is a direct appeal to the spectator's imaginative complicity in the comic dislocation between the suggested reality (the swirling rapids of a river) and the actual physical reality on stage (a matter of inches from solid ground balancing on a brick). Earlier in the performance, these same bricks had been the unappetizing dishes served to Ubu and the conspirators by Mère Ubu, in the same scene becoming weapons for Ubu to throw at them.

Perhaps the most concentrated and interesting example of the use of objects comes during the extraordinary sequence concerning Ubu's rapacious methods of tax collection from the peasants. The bricks are employed with richly evocative simplicity reminiscent of *Les Iks* to create a complex vision of the peasants' world. Several of the bricks scattered around the space, debris from earlier scenes, are collected together. By upending two bricks and placing another on the top, the actors construct a tiny fireplace, in the centre of which they light a small straw fire. In this most inhospitable of family 'foyers', they fight comically to keep the fire going and to receive warmth from it. Although the use of brick as construction block is naturalistic, essentially they are used as *metonym*; an adjunct is used to suggest a whole through the principle of *pars pro toto* so characteristic of oriental theatre forms.

So, in a direct way, we are shown a concrete image of the misery and oppression of the peasants' existence. When a messenger arrives with news of Ubu's rise to power and impending arrival, he enters the huddle of the 'cramped cabin' by carefully removing the top brick from the fireplace, as if opening a tiny door, and delicately crossing the precious fire; both warmth and refuge are precarious in their world. Once this poignant reality has been established, it is almost immediately invaded by the arrrival of Ubu on his *voiturin à phynances*. Riding in a standing position on top of the bigger stool, he is rolled forward by the others along the central gangway through the audience.

Here the object is used as *metaphor* to create a terrifying picture of a war machine: royal state chariot, bulldozer, and tank. In its total disregard for the fragile humanity just painted for us, the machine ploughs on unstoppably through the peasant dwelling until the devastation is complete; not a brick is left standing.

Although there was inevitably a bitter edge to the comedy, the general tone of the performance was one of playful exuberance and invention, of vaudevillian celebration, its frenetic rhythm reminiscent of silent movies. In this scene, for example, some of the peasants were crushed as the spool ran over them, emerging in its wake flattened into the ground: an image from Keaton, or Tom and Jerry. During a scene of winter snowfall, Ubu tosses a handful of confetti into the air above his head, teeth chattering audibly as it floats down over him. In similar style, the Russian offensive and bombardments of Ubu's army (just two actors, in accordance with Jarry's specification) are conveyed through the dropping of a vast number of silver 'superballs' from the balcony, these 'bombs' bouncing endlessly on the concrete floor and into the audience, to Toshi Tsuchitori's percussive accompaniment.[3]

Like the Czech production Brook had so admired, *Ubu aux Bouffes* established a pop-art style of performance which contributed to Brook's most successful realization of an accessible, immediate and truly popular theatre. The production also marked a rediscovery of the group's sense of fun, so apparent in their improvisations around the world, and

---

[3] This production was the beginning of Brook's collaboration with the remarkable Japanese multi-instrumentalist Toshi Tsuchitori, whose work has become an integral part of the C.I.C.T. His contribution to this production (and subsequently to *L'Os* and *Conférence*) is inestimable. Always visible, like the musicians of oriental theatre, his accompaniment is improvised from the actors' work: he never imposes sound or rhythm on to the action, instead sensitively creating worlds for the actors to explore, gleefully playing *with* them. His work invites an active imaginative response from an audience, as well as being a means of heightening emotional involvement through its sensory, physical aspects. For example, in one scene in *Ubu*, Mère Ubu treads warily through the 'dark' vaults of the Warsaw cathedral crypt. Through sound, Toshi comically suggested slamming doors, the flight of bats, unspecified monstrous insect life, and so on.

both healthy and liberating after the bleakness of *Timon* and *Les Iks*. 'Along with serious, committed and probing work, there must be irresponsibility.'[4]

> From David Williams, '"A Place Marked by Life": Peter Brook at the Bouffes du Nord' *New Theatre Quarterly*, February 1985

[4] Brook, *The Empty Space*, p. 78.

Off the Cuff with Peter Brook and Company
by Eric Shorter

Brook continues to lead his group out of their theatre, most often to the working-class areas of cities where they are performing: like the 'carpet shows' in Africa, the actors arrive unannounced to offer improvisations. Eric Shorter's essay, originally published in Drama, *describes an outing in Paris in 1978.*

No one cries 'Author!' at the end. There is no author to cry for. Nor are there any footlights, or make-up, or lighting. No décor either. Not even a prompter. In fact a prompter would be silly since there is no copy to prompt from. The players have come without a text.

They have come from Paris in the spring to a new town near Versailles to give Algerians lodged in an immigrant workers' hostel, teachers lodged in a mental hospital for teachers, adolescents studying at a college of technology and secondary school children on their afternoon off a taste of their peculiar quality.

New towns in France are like new towns elsewhere: impersonal places contrived in concrete to house all sorts of dislocated human beings who are much warmer-hearted than the architects suppose but whose spirits are apt to languish for want of entertainment beyond the bookshelves or television.

So the news that the troupe of players known as the Centre International de Créations Théâtrales would be dropping in for an hour or two at a handful of institutions in and round about Saint-Quentin-en-Yvelines created at least a ripple of curiosity. Of course, it would have created more stir in Shaftesbury Avenue or St Martin's Lane or along the boulevards of Paris where the troupe can count on its name, or at any rate Brook's, to command a crowded turn-out.

But that is not the point. These are not public performances. They are improvisations. The idea is to divert casual audiences and make them realize, where possible, that spontaneous acting has a theatrical value beyond its importance for the players – that is to say, that artistically it can give as much pleasure to the spectator as a rehearsed text, and that the audience can enjoy a more direct and informal relation with the players than is customary.

In fact, as inadvertent proof of the difference, a roomful of Algerians was watching television in its hostel canteen when Brook in his red Mini and the players in their Mini-bus drew up in the courtyard one evening and began to make ready a classroom.

It was about as untheatrical as any classroom could be: just a long, low-ceilinged, oblong room with windows down one side, crammed with tables and chairs. To make an acting space, the tables were pushed out of the way. Chairs were ranged on either side of the acting area. And even as the furniture was being quickly shifted – the operation being as impromptu as the play to follow – the television set was being deserted as word went round of what was up.

Has there ever been such a scramble to see a play? Still less an improvised play? Spectators stood on chairs and tables. They crouched on the floor. They peered between heads, through legs, over shoulders. They climbed in through a window by the score, and being finally unable to enter the makeshift auditorium they pressed their noses against the windows from outside, watching what must from there have been a mime show but excited by the doings within, by the boisterous, buoyant attention of their luckier compatriots who had quit the box sooner, and by the sheer vitality of the show, the drift of which no one could be sure of. Not even the actors. Least of all perhaps the actors. For it is a rule that Brook's company tries to obey – not to fall back on routine devices or familiar situations while playing off the cuff.

So, what did those Algerians get? Well, first they got a sense of the players having come to them in much the way as the players in *Hamlet* turn up to entertain the Court – with no equivalent to Polonius to advertise their wares.

Their wares are so uncertain. Scene indivisible? That might apply. And as the show got up steam, after a tentative start with the massive Michèle Collison hemmed in by the audience wriggling her hips to the instructions of Malik Bowens as a newly arrived African in Paris, it was hard not to think of Hamlet's rebuke to Polonius: 'He's for a jig or a tale of bawdry, or he sleeps.'

For the tale indeed grew bawdier, though never indecent, as the adventures of this couple in France proceeded they knew not whither; and to each development the hungry audience – hungry for live entertainment as well as women – responded with that kind of vibrant, close and uninhibited attention which could leave no doubt of its captivation.

The Algerians could soon recognize the fears and hopes which this typical couple had brought with them into France – the dreams of riches, the solicitings of the pimps, the demands of landlords and so forth. And from time to time the other members of the company, clustered round the floor, would rise up and join in a given situation. Indeed, the Algerians were so eager to see the performance that they scarcely allowed space for the players to play. Non-pushing playgoers like me had a job to keep a view of things amid the eager throng.

So I may have missed a few plot points during that evening which wound up with nearly an hour's North African singing and dancing. Is that what those Algerians had been waiting for? The chance to dance? The troupe's astonishing drummer Toshi Tsuchitori, who speaks no language anyone knows, but never misses a nuance on these spontaneous occasions where the moods go up and down like a yo-yo, pounded non-stop for more than two hours – more of an asset to the troupe, I suspect, than might appear. Afterwards a spectator roundly declared that he had not laughed before in France; and he had been in France for four years.

Surely, no one slept. It may have been a bawdy tale. There may have been jigging at the end. But Malik Bowens as a bemused black foreigner in Paris had shown not only immense resource and invention in overcoming various obstacles to the couple's survival but also an abidingly human character with whom the audience could identify. And the company proved, to my mind anyhow, that for all the roughness and rudimentary humour it could not have achieved the same instantaneous acceptance if it had been acting from a text.

But of course each audience differs, as at orthodox theatres. Earlier that day it had consisted of about a hundred teachers at a psychotherapeutic hospital for fugitives from the modern classroom. Since some of them were rumoured to be under drug treatment the response was less effusive. But then it wasn't the same play. It never can be.

This time the company sauntered into the room to face an assembly of long, sad faces, seated not in a cluster but in comfortable chairs. The atmosphere was hardly charged with excitement. The players conferred, then sat on their haunches. Brook rose, came forward and addressed the house. He explained by way of prologue that one day after work he had been very tired, and in falling deeply asleep had found himself in converse with God. Out of their conversation which was taking place centuries ago had come the Deity's conclusion that life down here was too easy. What it needed was some stiffening – an injection or two of fear, perhaps? Which led the company into what I suppose during its tour of villages in Africa would have been called the suitcase show. For the others then took up the theme of nobody daring to open it for fear of its contents.

If the links in the narrative sometimes escaped me it may have been because spontaneous acting, plotting, characterization and dialogue drive even the most experienced exponents into tight corners, short cuts, blind alleys – any measure to keep things going.

One's first impression of these performances is of needless challenges; of exercises that matter more to the players than to the audience; of patronizing in the need to sum us up instantaneously and then play something condescendingly deemed suitable; of waste when flashes of inspiration take over and can never be retrieved on principle (the Brook principle being that as soon as an *animation* is registered it is no longer an *animation* and that the quality of work depends on spontaneity); of self-indulgence in the scope for a dominant actor to do his own thing for as long as he likes (though Brook has a tactful way of sometimes intervening); of glibness in never being allowed second thoughts, of complacency in playing to relatively captive audiences who have not paid and therefore do not feel free to criticize; of laziness in not wanting to work up a script when something good occurs; and of an altogether obvious dependence on humour to chivvy things along if they flag.

One thinks of word games, of charades; and during two days spent watching four of these *animations* I recalled my own efforts at Christmas parties – with a shudder. My admiration for the C.I.C.T. immediately rose. At the same time I had lost my critical bearings, for as Brook said on the drive to the next port of call, 'You can't really write a notice of a party, can you?' No? What about New York? Weren't there professionals who 'noticed' parties there?

We seemed at Saint-Quentin-en-Yvelines a long way from New York – a long way from Paris even. And that night, after three shows in a day, the company went to bed exhausted, not knowing what the morrow would bring – except that the Mini-bus would take them to a college of technology. There had however been tentative ruminations in Brook's Mini before they separated for the night. After each *animation* two of the players were deputed to dream up the next; and this time it was the turn of Andreas Katsulas and Mireille Maalouf. So things are not as absolutely spontaneous as all that. Tomorrow's show theme (remembering it was a college of technology) would be about a very mixed marriage.

And just to stir things up what about (suggested Brook) getting Clementine Amouroux to play a French girl whose foreign fiancé speaks only gibberish and whose family to whom he introduces her speaks only gibberish too?

Miss Amouroux had joined the company only three weeks before by successfully auditioning for Isabella in Brook's forthcoming revival at the Bouffes du Nord in Paris of *Measure for Measure*. Her acting experience consisted of two television plays – and whatever she might have picked up with the company.

As she left the Mini-bus she was called over. Vivacious and exhilarated by the evening at the immigrants' hostel, she poked her head in the window of the car and listened to the outline of the role she had been cast for. '*Bon!*' she said coolly without much relish; and as she walked away we saw her spirits sinking.

The deep end. Baptism by fire. She would surely not sleep. Next day she shrugged off proudly my sympathetic inquiries as the college furniture was shifted round and students gathered curiously outside the classroom door before swarming in.

We perched where we could. It was another cluster, not quite as hungry, eager, urgent or intensely responsive as the immigrant workers had been: but still buzzing with interest, peering, puzzled. Meanwhile, the company sat together on the floor as usual. For once, Brook did not join them. He sat on the edge of a table in the wings. Wings? No possibility for anyone of flight – or so I thought as the show began with a meeting in a park between the new young actress and Bruce Myers, a veteran member of the troupe, with a keen Mancunian sense of humour and (as it turned out) a great gift for gibberish. For, as the son of a family from an impenetrably alien country – sometimes resembling Italy, sometimes Africa, mostly and splendidly anonymous – this likeable comedian had to be careful not to let out a recognizable word or phrase, yet to convey his passion and his proposals, chief of which was to return to his family with this shapely embodiment of his masculine dreams.

To assist the changes of mood and emotional temperature, the troupe's Japanese drummer was augmented by a violinist brought from Paris for the day. Together they contributed as much to the atmosphere as the actors; though the burden of sustaining a narrative – knowing how long to make each scene last, when to change direction, how to reach an ending (endings are a noticeable challenge) – remains with the actors.

It is the tension, the uncertainty, the adventure of not knowing what comes next which keeps them on their toes and is communicated to us. They may have roughed out in the small hours the outline for a scenario. The detail, even the drift, of it can never be schemed. One or two preconceived ideas for developing a relationship like that between this young French girl and her foreign admirer may be plotted but in the theatrical event things often go a different way.

And it isn't just up to the central couple. In this instance, the prospective in-laws steered the show, rising to greet them in a gush of curiosity, of overwhelming concern as several generations bore down on the timid newcomer to see if she was fit to join their number. They proved oppressively, excitedly, comically numerous.

No wonder Clementine Amouroux took fright and fled through banks of spectators to seek refuge half-way up a distant classroom wall. I treasure the memory of not only the family's eruption like a tidal wave; but of Mr Myers's efforts to beckon back his petrified fiancée – the violin and the drum being of delicate sentimental assistance.

Would the marriage go forward? Would the family approve? Would the bride be able to bear the host of new relatives? How would the couple manage without a common language? Would one of them attempt to learn the other's? And what about the jealousy of the brothers-in-law? The theme was rich with theatrical possibilities which the company explored wittily and touchingly, reaching a happy end without contrivance or emotional evasion.

To an observer the exercises are no more at first glance than exercises to flex an actor's muscles, not a spectator's. Yet the flexing can give audiences pleasure too. It gave at least one critic enlightenment. It proved the value of a company which performs as an ensemble. It proved that theatres are basically unnecessary. It proved that texts are not crucial to theatrical experience. It proved that all the usual aids and highly valued methods of making the most of dramatic art can be reduced to Pinter's idea of two people at loggerheads. All you need for drama is conflict. And if, after all, it proved nothing that most of us hadn't known already as reflective playgoers, it showed how excitingly simple these theatrical home truths can be made to seem.

Drama No. 129, Summer 1978

The Conference of the Birds: An Account by David Williams

At the beginning of 1979, on receiving an invitation to take part in that summer's Festival d'Avignon, Brook decided to create a performance comprising an adaptation of *L'Os* (*The Bone*), a short story by the Senegalese writer Birago Diop, and a full production of *The Conference of the Birds*.

Diop takes his stories from the oral tradition of his country. A number of them, including *L'Os*, were transcribed by him from the tales of a certain Amadou son of Koumba, a 'griot' from the Dakar district of Senegal. Almost all of them are educative moralities highlighting the foibles of human behaviour. *L'Os* paints a tragicomic picture of ordinary men rooted in a social reality marked by traditional hierarchical structures and social bonds. The central figure Mor Lam (played by Malik Bowens) is omnipotent within the family: he occupies the central scenic space throughout, while his wife Awa cooks and cleans, obeying his orders to the letter. The only threat to the security of his position is in the figure of Moussa (Yoshi Oida), his blood-brother and therefore '*son plus que frère*', with whom he is obliged to share all he has.

On a superficial level, the links with *Les Iks* and *Ubu* are immediately apparent. This is a world of rough comedy, of base appetites, in which hunger is of a purely physical nature. This is made concrete in the physical style of acting and the purely material use of the limited scenic properties (rush mats, sticks, rocks, and pots). Yet the tale transcends this depiction of a market-place social reality to assume a quality of myth: the myth of destructive greed and possessiveness, of the collapse of social structures in the face of an all-pervading egotism. In the tradition of the obsessive monomaniacs of Molière and Balzac, Mor Lam is prepared to pretend to die, to allow himself to be buried alive, rather than share the bone of the title with Moussa. The irony is that in the process he loses both the bone and his wife to him, life continuing afresh with Mor Lam dead and forgotten.

There is a sudden shift away from comedy in the tone of the final moments of the piece, with Mor Lam's recognition of the reality of his predicament only when it is too late. This moment of truth is marked by the sudden appearance of the 'angel of death', who has come to take Mor Lam to the land of the dead. In the Bouffes, this figure burst violently up through a trap next to Mor Lam (at Avignon, and in 1982 at the Almeida in London, he leapt magically over the rush fence at the back of the space to land with a terrifying crash beside Mor Lam prostrate on his mat, a monstrous foot-slapping Kathakali figure).

Over the next two years, *L'Os* was always performed with *Conférence*, a 40-minute curtainraiser counterpointing the 75-minute major work in a structural relationship similar to that of the Noh and the kyōgen. *L'Os* sets the scene in the imperfect material world, the point of departure for the birds' journey in search of fulfilment of their spiritual hunger.

The Conference of the Birds, a twelfth-century Sufi poem by Farid Ud-din 'Attar of Nishapur, is a philosophical and religious fable of almost 5,000 verses allegorizing the human condition and mankind's search for truth within itself. It is a didactic fable challenging the reader to renounce earthly egotism through a recognition of the state of the world, and thereby to transcend socially imposed limitations.

The movement of the journey within *Conférence* is towards a position of renewed unity and self-fulfilment in the heightened understanding gained through an incessant search for the divine. Therein lies the poem's supreme enigma in religious terms: transcendent life and truth can only be found within the self and in relation to a group. The ordeal of the journey away from social reality and into the self is necessary for the individual to recognize that paradoxically it is *within* life that he must work on himself in relation to others. The elements of struggle and search, the thirst for a beyond, a 'something more', the intercultural bird idiom concretizing man's inner aspirations, his desire to go beyond himself into 'flight' – for Brook, all offer the possibility of a true theatre of myth and poetry, of creating a theatrical act as point of *communitas*.

Constantly returned to as source material for free improvisatory work throughout the 1970s (particularly during the group's journeys to Africa and America in 1972 and 1973), *Conférence* has become a symbol of the work for the group, a focal point for the development of a commitment to their own ideals, a challenge to push ever further. At the end of the first decade of the C.I.R.T. work, the poem remained for Brook the only material offering the possibility of realizing his cherished ideal of totality. It was a natural choice for a performance which could be a combination, and in some ways a summation, of the different areas of investigation undertaken so far.

Inevitably the improvised nature of the earlier work on *Conférence* had created only partial and fragmentary impressions of the whole. It was also felt that these earlier versions revealed certain weaknesses in narrative structure, a lack of focus and unifying dynamic. It was hoped that by forging the most vital elements discovered over the years of experimentation within a structured form the company could produce a spectacle of greater order and clarity, a fuller expression of the poem's complexity, capable of being recreated anew on different occasions and in different circumstances. The result was a scripted version by Jean-Claude Carrière, the text and forms of which had been developed and endlessly reworked with Brook and the actors over a concentrated period of six months.

This version is constructed exactly in accordance with the basic impulses of the narrative movement of the original. It begins with the birds' initial enthusiastic acceptance of the Hoopoe's challenge to set out on the journey; proceeds through their fears and excuses resulting from a partial recognition of the awesome uncertainty of confronting the unknown, to which the Hoopoe responds with his didactic anecdotes, to their departure with conviction, the painful crossing of the desert, and their meeting of those lost on the way; the survivors then passing through the Seven Valleys of Initiation into the supreme enigma – their confrontation of the Simorgh, themselves.

However, there is a noticeable change of emphasis. Ninety per cent of Attar's original is taken up with the conference of the poem's title – the birds' debate and the depiction of their frailty and uncertainty *before* their departure on the journey. In the performance version, the emphasis had to be placed on the collective experience of the journey itself, largely in order to increase the dramatic mobility and interest of the whole. Initially located in the recognizable world of squabbles, weakness, and immobility, the world as it is for us, it immediately draws in our attention.

The very fact that throughout the performance *Conférence* remained a story to be related served to unify through shared interest. Various techniques employed show the performance to be a refined form of Brook's ideal of *the actor as storyteller*, an ideal that goes back to a production of *Crime and Punishment* he had seen in a Hamburg garret,

> one of the most striking theatre experiences I have ever had. By sheer necessity, all problems of theatre style vanished; here was the . . . essence of an art that stems from the storyteller looking around his audience and beginning to speak. . . . We were listeners, children hearing a bedside story, yet at the same time

adults, fully aware of all that was going on. . . . We never lost sight
of being crammed together in a crowded room, following a story.[1]

Brook differentiates between the actor (who fully inhabits an imaginary
character, sinking his own personality in an act of identification and
self-transformation) and the performer (a Piaf or Garland who only
becomes fully charged with life as his/her individuality flowers under
the focused spotlight of an audience's attention). He believes one of the
most interesting tendencies in contemporary acting to be in the movement towards an amalgamation of the two in the skilled storyteller, who
retains the actor's capacity for transformability, the profundity of his
emotional and physical study and understanding, while at the same time
rejecting the shallow trappings of the actor as naturalistic impersonator.

The storyteller is still a familiar and popular figure in Asia and Africa;
he acts as a socially cohesive force, uniting the imaginations of a
community in a shared and celebratory experience, and there was more
than a hint of the traditional storyteller in the Bouffes setting for
Conférence. Two huge carpets were laid out on the space (another being
hung on the back wall), establishing a free and open area and a focus for
the action.

At the very beginning of the performance, the actor who is to take the
part of the Hoopoe enters the space unannounced, like a middle-eastern
or oriental fabulist positioning himself in the middle of the carpet,
before quietly beginning a third-person narration directly addressed to
the spectators: '*Un jour, tous les oiseaux du monde, ceux qui sont connus et
ceux qui sont inconnus, se réunirent en une grande conférence*'. He then moves
immediately into the first person as he assumes the role of the Hoopoe,
and throughout the performance, he constantly alternates between the
two.

The multi-transformations necessitated by the mobile identity of
actors as storytellers were inevitably very demanding; they were birds,
narrators, spectators, characters within the episodes, and finally
themselves.

To allow the rapid and powerful shifts of reality in the anecdotal
episodes, the group made much use of masks. Those used were mostly
ancient Balinese masks, although they were not markedly oriental in
appearance. Brook saw them as denser, more essential expressions of a
human truth: poetry and music to the prose of the face.

In practice, these masks were used in many different ways within the
performances of *Conférence* (almost entirely in the illustrative episodes

[1] *The Empty Space*, pp. 89–90.

before the Valleys). Thematically, they were employed for types (warrior king, beautiful princess), to play on the contrast of masked and un-masked, and to convey a change in an individual's state. A young slave spends a night of love with a princess who has drugged his wine: for this idyllic dream reality, he is masked; when the mask is removed after-wards, he returns to the prosaic and material with a bump, traumatized but inwardly transformed by the experience of that contact.

Physically, the masks were manipulated in different ways. For the full assumption or imposition of a role, they were worn normally. To express self-concealment behind a false image, the mask would be held in place visibly, either in contact with the face or a few inches in front of it.

The masks were also used as puppets, extended at the end of an arm wrapped in emblematic material, their movements conveyed through the manipulation of arm or hand. This form was usually marked by a conscious naïvety; when a beggar represented in this way was executed, the wrist was suddenly bent and the mask dropped. As with the bird puppets described below, the physical duality of separation and connec-tion gave the actors a greater intimacy with their material than many traditional puppeteers; at the same time they could look on from a very close position while retaining a certain lucidity and objectivity. Exalted by the contact and fully involved, yet somewhat removed as critical observers, they are distanced without distancing, a concrete image of Brook's ideal relationship between actor and role.

As far as the representation of the birds was concerned, traditional head masks were rejected as being too cumbersome, obstructing the free movement of imaginative response. In performance, it would sometimes be necessary to emphasize the figurative side of the bird idiom (flight), sometimes its manipulation by man (the actor enacting anecdotes within a story concerned with man).

Before they set out, the birds are effectively earthbound, locked within the disharmony of petty squabbles, self-deluding excuses, and selfish materialism. They have neither the courage nor the desire to undertake this voyage of self-discovery and self-transcendence. The individual natures of the birds at this point are characterized by the actors' manipulation of a simple object, their postures and movements.

The diversity of the birds' plumage (at this stage merely decorative, not the potential source of flight) was conveyed by different exotic materials draped around their arms, necks, and shoulders: for example, the dove, the Hoopoe's leading acolyte, was hung with expanses of white silk. The falcon was represented by the actor's holding up two claw-like fingers, hooked forward. This simple posture communicates the bird of prey's aggression, its savagely sharp talons, and its perch on a king's hand – the position of which it is so proud. Andreas Katsulas's owl was expressed by his wrapping his two huge hands around a stick held in front of his neck, as if perched on the branch of a tree; the stick also served as a framing device, pushing the focus of the spectator's attention up to the comic facial expressions used to convey the tired sadness and complacency of his nature.

Others were represented even more caricaturally: for example, Jean-Claude Perrin's parrot held the bamboo bars of his cage in front of his face, while his nervous head movements, twitchy facial tics, and squeaky whine immediately established his character. When freed from his cage by the Hoopoe, he momentarily overcomes his deep-seated fear of the unknown and ventures outside to produce a brief, tentative song of liberation. This potential is quickly stifled when he sees the arrogant and massive peacock and instantly slams himself back inside his cage – holds the bars in front of his face again.

Our first impressions of Katsulas's peacock are of his grand bombastic voice and proud strut. He holds open above his head a beautiful painted fan, both decorative crest and splendid tail feathers. This image of apparent confidence and well-being is quickly revealed to be characteristic of entrancement with the external, ephemeral trappings of beauty. In tradition, the peacock's tail feathers offer him a permanent reminder of his expulsion from Eden, as do his ugly feet (Katsulas's battered sandals). He leaves the space comically trying to cover up this manifestation of his true distorted nature behind the shield of his majestic appearance, his fan. Such scenes are very human moments in which the farce is both penetrating and poignant.

On the other hand, to represent those birds who undertake the journey, the actors used simple and beautiful hand puppets (designed by Sally Jacobs). These consisted of a glove-like head of the bird, responsive to the actor's minutest finger and hand movements, and rich floating silks or laces for the wings. As they flow through the air, they have a quality of serenity and timelessness in sharp contrast with their former plodding physical heaviness. When extended, the wing material possesses a delicate purity of form, a sensuality in the colours of the fluid swathes and a sculptural splendour in movement.

Before the journey, only the Hoopoe had been represented in this way; more evolved than the others, he was the only one able to 'fly'. In this way he was immediately set apart visually, established as leader and guide, and recognized as such by the others. He has already made part of the journey, and possesses proof of the Simorgh's existence, a feather that fell in China. Without the community afforded by the other birds' collaboration, he cannot set out afresh.[2]

It is worth describing the extraordinary moment of transition from the initial representation to the birds in flight. At the moment of their departure (the actors without the hand puppets), the light focuses on the V-formation of the birds (with its suggestion of winged flight and deliberate, collective direction), the Hoopoe taking his position at the leading point. The conscious, determined choice to unite as a group is expressed physically in their formation as a single ordered unit, and vocally in the chorus of improvised sounds that make up a chord of liberation. As a crescendo is reached, they burst out dynamically in different directions through the spectators to commence their journey (vocalization used to convey movement through space).

This is followed by a long pause in darkness and resonant silence, awesome and charged after the explosion of movement and the physical impact of noise. We feel in the air a mixture of excited expectancy and a total lack of reassurance, the sudden solitude imposed by the darkness and silence marking an indeterminate point of junction between material reality and the beyond. Eventually the lights come up slowly to reveal to us the invigorating and liberating sight of the first birds in tranquil flight, supported by the delicate tinklings of the musicians. For the spectator, it is a moment of intense wonder and innocence.

These puppets are finally abandoned when the birds meet a solitary old sage at the end of the desert, who enacts for them the story of the death and rebirth of the phoenix. At one point, he asks them to place their *dépouilles*, both effects and remains, in his black veil, a symbolic act of self-abandonment and annihilation marking the initiatory death of the old self. At this moment, the bird-puppets are seen to be no more than dead objects in reality, and yet thereafter the actor somehow assumes a fuller vitality through the termination of these formerly dynamic extensions of his being: he appears reborn in unity, 'naked' and more fully integrated. The episode is regenerative as the birds move closer to the heart of their search and of understanding. The desert had merely been a verification of their commitment to the journey. They are now in a state of readiness, baring themselves as they are for the true initiation of the Valleys.

One other scene of great power and simplicity using both the mask

[2] Compare Brook's own role in the work of the Centre: 'A director is not free of responsibility – he is totally responsible – but he is not free of the process either, he is part of it' (*The Empty Space*, p. 122).

and puppet forms sticks in the memory. The birds, high above the desert in ethereal, weightless flight see a lone earthbound hermit wandering in the distant void, a figure represented by a tiny Balinese puppet operated by Tapa Sudana. As the birds circle and land, the puppet is replaced by a masked actor (Bruce Myers). An appeal is made to the spectator's imaginative participation: he shares the birds' viewpoint, their changing perspective on the tiny solitary figure. An impression of distance covered is made concrete in this naïve and fairy-tale way, both comical and magical.

In the Seven Valleys which follow the desert, the tone and form of the performance alters drastically, and all masks and puppets are abandoned. The means of representation of the Valleys posed one of the greatest problems for Brook, Carrière, and the actors. They needed to find a precise level of esotericism and simple clarity to match that of Attar's poem, although this part of the journey is necessarily more abstract and complex than earlier scenes, being an expression of the very heart of the process of initiation into the 'supreme mystery'. For the seven remaining actors/birds, each of these valleys contains an enigma to be resolved, accepted, and assimilated – or ignored as distraction from their central concerns.

In performance, some of them remained highly poetic and esoteric, dense juxtapositions of unusual images and sounds of a physical, concrete form to convey the abstract spiritual turmoil of this final section of the journey within the self, a journey which in reality has been immobile. Thus the second valley (Valley of Love) begins when a violinist enters the forward-carpet playing while whirling like a dervish. At the same time, one of the actors beside the carpet knocks a white polo or croquet ball across the space with a mallet; ball and violinist turn at the same speed. Attar's description suggests that this image represents the pain (the blow on the ball) and the solitude (the violinist) of love, as well as its energy and movement which must be used by the birds to carry them beyond.

Some of the other valleys were created with over-literal concreteness. The first valley (Valley of Search) comprised a cloaked individual sifting sand in a painstaking search for something unspecified. But the final valley (Valley of Death) seemed to find the right blend of mystical enigma and market-place accessibility in the use of a type of shadow-play theatre form common in South-East Asia. With only a single candle and pieces of folded material attached to the ends of springy bamboo twigs, the actors succeeded in making real the story of three butterflies in their flight ever closer to the flame. Only one of them reaches full understanding in the direct experience of the heart of the flame, but he is consumed and the light is snuffed.

The final sequence of the performance portrays the arrival of the birds at the gate of the court of the Simorgh. After an initial refusal, the Simorgh's chamberlain brings out a bundle of sticks, one for each of the birds. The circle they form expresses the brilliant solar light of the Simorgh's enlightenment as well as the harmony, balance, and plenitude of their self-realization. To signify the opening of the imaginary hundred curtains covering the entrance to the court of their king, they weave abstract geometrical patterns in the air.

Sub-aquatically slow and precise, are these movements a means of evoking the ineffable, a collective making visible of the invisible? Echoing the work in Africa and America, the sticks seem to be symbols of shared initiation through the experience of a journey towards a re-establishment of unity and innocence. The actors turn to the spectators who are now included in the circle: they receive and reflect the bright light passively and serenely. All pretence now abandoned, the actors face themselves, looking out beyond the spectators; one believes that they *see*. Slowly they advance across the space towards the light to the accompaniment of tiny ceremonial bell sounds.

From David Williams, '"A Place Marked by Life": Peter Brook at the Bouffes du Nord' *New Theatre Quarterly*, February 1985

The Conference of the Birds: Extracts from Attar's Poem

Translated by C. S. Nott from Garcin de Tassy's French version

A man who loved God saw Majnūn sifting the earth of the road and said: 'Majnūn, what are you looking for?' 'I am looking for Laīla,' he said. The man asked: 'Do you hope to find Laīla there?' 'I look for her everywhere,' said Majnūn, 'in the hope of finding her somewhere.'

THE WORLD ACCORDING TO A SUFI
A Sufi woke one night and said to himself: 'It seems to me that the world is like a chest in which we are put and the lid shut down, and we give ourselves up to foolishness. When death lifts the lid, he who has acquired wings, soars away to eternity, but he who has not, stays in the chest a prey to a thousand tribulations. Make sure then that the bird of ambition acquires wings of aspiration, and give to your heart and reason the ecstasy of the soul. Before the lid of the chest is opened become a bird of the Spirit, ready to spread your wings.'

All that you have heard or seen or known is not even the beginning of what you must know, and since the ruined habitation of this world is not your place you must renounce it. Seek the trunk of the tree, and do not worry about whether the branches do or do not exist.

The Conference of the Birds: An Extract from the C.I.C.T. English text

Adapted from Attar by Peter Brook and Jean-Claude Carrière

THE JOURNEY

HOOPOE: One day from high in the sky they saw a little speck, motionless in the desert. As they drew nearer, they saw it was a hermit.

(They fly above the HERMIT. *The* HOOPOE *calls out.)*

HOOPOE: Oho!

HERMIT: Oho!

HOOPOE: Oho!

HERMIT: Oho!

(The BIRDS *settle around him. He is a* HERMIT *with a long beard. The* HOOPOE *asks:)*

HOOPOE: You're still there?

HERMIT: Yes, still here.

HOOPOE: Tell me, have you found the answer?

HERMIT: What answer?

HOOPOE: To your question.

HERMIT: No, I haven't found the answer.

HERON: What's the question?

SPARROW: Yes, what's the question?

HERMIT: You really want to know?

(The BIRDS *make affirmative noises.)*

HERMIT: Very well, listen.

(They fall silent.)

HERMIT: I was, I think, a fairly honest man. I had a wife, children. For some time, I suffered from a gigantic longing for an aubergine. The desire to eat an aubergine never left me, day nor night. At the same time I told myself – something told me that if I ate aubergines, a disaster would occur. I tried to think of other things. About my work, my family, oranges, sheep. But I always ended up with an aubergine. An aubergine.

(He stops for a moment. The BIRDS *are careful not to put questions.)*

HERMIT: In the end, as you can imagine, my desire triumphed. My mother bought me an aubergine. She cooked it very well and I began to eat. But I had hardly eaten half the aubergine when there was a knock at the door. A man came in and put my son's head on the ground. They just cut off the head of my son.

(A deep silence.)

HERMIT: So I decided I would spend the rest of my life trying to find the connection between eating an aubergine and the chopped-off head of my son. I gave up everything, absolutely everything, came here and, since that day, I'm searching for the answer.

HERON: And you've found nothing?

HERMIT: Nothing.

SECOND EXOTIC BIRD: In the meantime, how do you live in the desert?

HERMIT: As you see, I ruminate.

(He stays silent for a moment, combing his long beard with a crudely-made comb. Suddenly the DOVE *begins to laugh. The* HERMIT *looks at her in surprise and asks:)*

HERMIT: Why are you laughing?

DOVE: I'm laughing because I know why.

HERMIT: Why what?

DOVE: Why you haven't found the answer.

HERMIT: And why haven't I found the answer?

DOVE: Because you don't think about your question.

HERMIT: What do you mean? I think of nothing else!

DOVE: You're wrong. You only think about your beard.

(The HERMIT *stops combing his beard and says:)*

HERMIT: You're right. I see that you're right. You're absolutely right.

Listen. One day – I'd only been here a few months, a year perhaps – suddenly on the ground I saw something shining. A shiny stone. I picked it up. Look. Here it is. It's a piece of mica. When I looked at myself in the mica, I saw I had a magnificent beard. So, like a flash, I got a piece of wood and I cut it into a comb.

(He holds up the small stone which serves as a mirror when he combs his beard. As he talks, he gets more and more carried away, furious with himself.)

HERMIT: And you're right! I only think of my beard. Before, it was an aubergine, and tucked away in the desert, it's a beard. My whole life is devoted to my beard.

(He gets up, begins to pull out his beard, throwing the hairs right and left.)

HERMIT: But it's over! You'll see! I'm going to tear you out, vile beard! I rip you off. I give you to the wind. Go beard, gone. Not a hair left! Not one!

(At this moment, the DOVE begins to laugh again. The HERMIT stops, dumbfounded, looks at her and asks:)

HERMIT: Why are you laughing?

DOVE: Why am I laughing? Because even now you're only thinking of your beard!

(All the BIRDS burst out laughing. They leave the HERMIT alone in the desert, in the midst of the debris.)

Adapted from Attar's *The Conference of the Birds*
by Jean-Claude Carrière and Peter Brook

Some Observations on the Theatre of Peter Brook by Kenneth Bernard

Writing in Yale/Theater *in 1980, the playwright Kenneth Bernard cast a critical look at the 'trilogy' presented at La Mama, New York (Ubu, The Ik, Conference of the Birds), discussing its political implications in particular.*

THE POLITICAL NEXUS

It is clear from the productions and from the booklet, 'The Centre', that Brook is on the side of good. He favours social justice, humanity, love, etc., and decries, in particular, man's evil to man, usually the result of vices like greed and intellectual and emotional detachment, which are conspicuously characteristic of the technological, civilized world and appear necessary to success in that world. In this respect, the brutish behaviour of King Ubu is not so much a portrait of the anarchic jungle of self-indulgence that is every man's beast, as it is a preview of the behaviour of modern civilized man. Ubu, flattening his enemies anachronistically as he rides a large cable spool is not so much primal man as he is modern juggernaut, an onslaught of technological man. Where these same characteristics appear among 'primitives', they tend to be the consequences of what had been done to them, i.e. by the civilized world. For example, when the Ik go to an area where they do not suffer the nutritional and cultural deprivation civilization has foisted on them, they succumb quickly to fraternity and song, their natural inclinations, and the impression is one of Edenic bliss uncontaminated by more orthodox notions of man's fundamental moral frailty.

There is here an example of the idea that the ills of the world (all of them) are basically fixable by material application. To be sure, few people wish to argue that starving people should not be fed, but a different point of view holds that a full stomach is only the *beginning* of man's moral and societal problems, not the end. Physical extremities like imminent death obviate much otherwise expressible frailty. Put another way, this idea reflects a broadly Marxist point of view, which sees the human situation in rational rather than metaphysical dimensions. It is strongly utopian, highly commendable, and, incidentally, essentially technological. It is the difference between, say, Brecht on the one hand and Beckett and Ionesco on the other. Brook, at least in *L'Os*,

Ubu, and *The Ik*, has postulated a theatre metaphorically between the abuse of man and the rectification of that abuse.

In the pursuit of this ideal, and as the name of his group indicates, Brook has assembled a multi-ethnic, multi-national group. His aim is to reach down to the fundamentals of theatre that, he believes, will cross all cultural boundaries. To this end he has, for example, eliminated a great deal of verbal articulation in favour of simple statement, sound unattached to specific meaning, language mixtures, and contrived language systems. Brook's use of the poet Ted Hughes's *Orghast* in the 1971 production of the same name was specifically an attempt to create a language expressive of universal emotions, apparently in a way that existing language systems do not. Contemporary English, Brook has stated (Croyden, p. 280), is a 'flat, colourless language that . . . has become debased and meaningless.' Elsewhere (*Theatre Quarterly*, *1972*) he is quoted as saying, 'I do not believe in the word much today, because it has outlived its purpose. Words do not communicate, they do not define.' (Cf. Brook's comment in a *Playback* interview, London, 1973: 'We had no sense of obligation to deliver *The Tempest*. Consequently we were free, we could do a *Tempest* in which nine-tenths of the text was inaudible, incomprehensible . . .') 'The whole of our work,' Brook says, 'has been to purify, to clarify, to simplify.' (Croyden Booklet, unpaged; all subsequent unidentified quotes from this source). But in simplifying, is Brook oversimplifying? To simplify might well be to mutilate or misrepresent. A quest for the universal in universal terms leaves one with limited material. How much can come out of the naked fact of starving, say, or dying? One's response, certainly, is, 'My God, this is terrible. Something should be done about it.' (Not, note, '*I* should do something about it.') Elsewhere he says that he and the Centre are 'deeply committed to one goal – to find out how to make visible on stage what is invisible in human experience.' What in fact he seems often to do, *up to this point*, is to make visible what is already perfectly visible, as when his actors, after gluttonous eating, vomit (repeatedly) on cue. Language, particularly written language, has come to be considered an instrument of deception and oppression, for the subject as well as the object (*vide* the deconstructionist views), a weapon of civilization in justifying and in prosecuting its exploitations and in proclaiming its pieties. In the face of the barbarisms we all know and live with, one can understand without condoning this view. Certainly Shakespeare, Brook's patron saint, would have affirmed the efficacy of language to make visible the invisible, and in turning away from it so strenuously, pruning it, whittling it in the service of greater truth and communication,

Brook appears more than ever cornered in highly 'visible' or realistic theatre.

In simplifying, Brook runs also the risk of some condescension. Is it not roughly equivalent to thinking Third World peoples can best be reached through song and dance, i.e. they have rhythm? I think one must be suspicious of the foot-stomping approval of some of his audience after they have seen the Ik, for example, starve, vomit, die, etc., and then, when fed (the survivors) in idyllic surroundings, resort to song. Similarly, one must be suspicious of any portrayal of the 'primitive' where they *always* have the last laugh over the 'civilized'. Personal encounters between Turnbull and the Ik invariably posit him as the butt, the ignorant, the outwitted, etc. This configuration should be stretched to include at least Idi Amin and Claude Lévi-Strauss.

The pursuit of total communication is a chimera equivalent to thinking poetry, or anything, can be perfectly translated. In art generally, surface coherence at the expense of depth and truth, however awkward, is a mistake. Brook, in legislating that kind of coherence is contradicting himself in that it is the same kind of 'coherence' legislated by scientific rationalism, which he opposes because he feels it obscures and mutilates the very roots of real life and real theatre.

In this pursuit, Brook is similar to groups like the San Francisco Mime, El Teatro Campesino (with which Brook and the company worked in 1973), and the Bread and Puppet Theatre, whose avowed aim is radical social change. Their tendency is to make arguments as broad and simple as classic westerns, with frequent diversions like song, dance, juggling. It is, however, precisely these secondary matters, the frequent *play* atmosphere of the circus, the variety show, etc., that are in fact the real theatre that the audience enjoys. Of course, much of the rationale of agit-prop theatre is the Brechtian notion that social progress demands that the theatre viewer remain in possession of his rational faculties rather than yield to unfathomable emotional involvement, which might have some value individually, subjectively, but not socially or communally. But Brecht himself succeeds as a playwright despite, not because of, his polemic. Again, there is something of a contradiction in Brook (and others). Marxist-Brechtian theatre is predicated on the proper application of the rational faculties; but the essense of the primitive people he projects as saviours is their pre-rationality, their communion with more encompassing and abiding principles of life, their undifferentiated contact with what Brook calls 'the invisible world'.

THE SELF AND OTHERS

Central to the philosophy of agit-prop, Marxist-oriented theatre groups is the belief that the individual ego must be subordinated to group or community needs, an unresolved stumbling block for many who feel committed to the social goals of Marxism. Brook has several things to say about this. 'There are,' he observes, speaking of his decision to undertake a new production of *Conference*, 'very few masterpieces in the world which have gone beyond subjective experience that really touches something that involves a real witness of man's essential experience . . .' In his book, *The Empty Space*, he writes that 'Group creation can be infinitely richer, if the group is rich, than the product of weak individualism . . .' (p. 35) It is perhaps for this reason in part that he feels 'the only way to treat a classic with respect is to stage it disrespect-fully'. This disrespect, however, is more than a desire to ignore the limiting ego that created the work. It is also a new-Lamarckian desire to free one radically and instantly from the constraints of tradition and the past in the service of particular and revolutionary social ends. This may be part of the reason why dead and non-dramatic writers are easier to work with: the material yields itself better to manipulation for specific ends than does material created by a living, and probably intransigent dramatist. But it is only reasonable, I think, to recognize that though we may be receiving something dramatic and powerful we also run the risk of receiving something other than Shakespeare, Chekhov, *Alice in Wonderland*, Greek drama, or Brecht. In *The Empty Space*, Brook also writes that 'today writers seem unable to make ideas and images collide through words with Elizabethan force . . . Is there another language, just as exciting for the author, as the language of words? Is there a language of actions, a language of sounds . . . ?' (pp. 48–9)

Style, the imprint of a specific person, is, of course, the very root of materialistic ego. 'What we have striven for,' Brook says, 'is an absence of style,' of a controlling ego. His supreme example of this absence of style is the writer he admires above all, Shakespeare.

We live in an age in which the director's god-like imprint is foremost, and aside from the fact that this bespeaks no quiescence of ego, there is always the nagging question of whether what has been substituted is superior to what originally existed, whether radical interpretation or version of the director-*auteur* has indeed unlocked the mystery of Handke, Brecht, Shakespeare, Aeschylus. The innovative director runs many risks when he cannot generate a text himself, not the least of which is a form of vampirism or cannibalism. Texts would seem increasingly to exist to be subverted to other ends, if not to ego, then to polemical ends, but the honesty of the professed (or unprofessed) ends is to be questioned, just as the frequent preference for minimally verbal or borrowed theatre is to be related, perhaps, to the inability to articulate text regardless of the communality of the undertaking.

An odd contradiction of the communal enterprise is the frequent substitution of improvisation for text, improvisation being the healthy, natural human and freeing impulse, and text being the superimposition of limitation, mind, tradition, society, etc. The programme note for *The Ik*, for example, speaks of the contribution of the writer as being 'coherent and thought-out; and the physical contribution of actors, disorderly but vigorous and alive.' But while improvisation *is* clearly valid (for writers *and* actors), it just as clearly unleashes the individual ego, a matter probably resolved by the term 'group improvisation'. And there is contradiction again, for Marxist-oriented theatre projects social change that is consequent to disciplined, rational effort – quite the reverse of the id-oriented anarchy that improvisation unleashes. But here we are back again to the romantic view that such impulses, *if true ones*, must contribute to the good of man. Brook, on tour, sometimes would go into a village 'with no starting point and with no sense of what our improvisation would be, and just do whatever happened to occur.' This following of the impulse sometimes led to isolated moments of ecstatic oneness with complete strangers in every sense. And that, says Brook, is 'what I am searching for in the theatre . . . an act of communion . . .'

The subordination of the individual is also reflected in the fact that many undertakings such as The Centre become communal enterprises, requiring total or near total absorption of the individual. After an all night session of *Conference* at the Brooklyn Academy of Music in 1973, Brook, evaluating the experience said, 'This clarity we achieved tonight could never have arisen through theory, but only through the experiences we've gone through together.' And what they do together 'only becomes meaningful when we serve something other than our egos.' Choosing to participate in such a group becomes choosing a philosophy of life that touches every aspect of one's life. One certainly recognizes this aspect in the 'communities', tight or loose, of such diverse groups as the San Francisco Mime Troupe, Meredith Monk's 'The House', Robert Wilson's Spring Street complex, and (still) The Living Theatre of Julian Beck and Judith Malina. This last is close to ideal for Brook, providing 'a complete way of life for every one of its members', who are 'in search of the meaning in their lives . . .' (*Empty*

Space, p. 62). The involvement in the theatre group becomes, sometimes testimonially, a paradigm for a broader world-communal utopian possibility. (I suspect it is also, unrecognized, a form of shelter from the bleakness of the modern world, a holding action.) A major reason for the tour of Africa in 1972 was not success or failure by Western standards (materialistic at best), but, says Brook, to see whether the performance 'created a warm and rich experience, and proved that differences between people of different races with no common language could come together by using the possibilities offered by a renewed use of theatrical form.'

As a brief addendum it is worth noting that while the acting of Brook's group is energetic and often accomplished, it is also notable for mugging *shtick*, quaint turns, bravura moments, usually disruptive of context and flow. To some, this might seem justified as a form of Brechtian alienation. To me, it seemed like actors projecting villainous ego. Only occasionally, in *Ubu*, for example, where the anarchy of the text (the only original theatre text, incidentally) could not easily be suppressed, did the play seem to rise above the actors and director.

THE JOURNEY EAST

The piece the Centre performed in Africa was *The Conference of the Birds*, a Near Eastern *Pilgrim's Progress* about the arduous journey and many sacrifices (including worldliness and the self) of a group of birds in search of God . . . For Brook, there were magical, mystical movements of hearts meeting hearts, 'extravagantly rich and meaningful', where everything was 'completely unified', a total community. This is the equivalent of the message of the God of the birds in *Conference*: God is in each of you. There is also a hint here, as well as in Brook's 1979 film about Gurdjieff, *Meetings with Remarkable Men*, of significant differences between Brook's group and others, like El Teatro Campesino. The latter are primarily social, economic, and political in their ends; they are pragmatic and rational. Brook's group, one finally realizes, is primarily religious and mystical in its ends; its eschatological methodology is intuitive, non-rational. It is a sense of *communitas* based more on 'the search' and *love* than on political and economic justice. It is, for all its proletarian professions, more middle than lower class. It is less programmatic and militant, more mythic and poetic. It is equally optimistic, but gentler and less in touch with evil. Whereas strict agit-prop theatre sees evil as consequence of societal wrongs to be physically and rationally corrected, Brook sees evil essentially as faulty vision to be cured by the proper 'journey' or 'search'. His productions move from recognition of the spectacle of marauding man and his ill deeds, not to programmatic revision or sharing of the pie, but to mystical transcendence, to the proper 'search'. He is close to the 'profile' of The Living Theatre, which, although its ends are declared to be political, sees in the theatrical event 'the climax and centre of their search' (i.e. for the meaning of their lives, cf. *Empty Space*, p. 62) . . . Thus Brook's search or journey is not at all like the picaresque one of ultimate societal integration. It is not political utopianism, nor a search for justice within an existing system, or a search for selfhood, respite, or retreat. It is vastly different from the immobilities of the absurdists and the quests for truth like that of Kafka's protagonist in *The Trial*, who ends in a vacant quarry with a stranger twisting a knife in his heart for a 'crime' of which he is ignorant.

The individual ego in Brook suffers no such rude conclusion, but rather, after tribulation to be sure, absorption into a larger unit; but here it is the One rather than the community. All Brook's groping for absolutes (language, theatre, community) represents a distinctly mystical bent. As he says in his comment on *Conference*, 'We are trying to make a work about theatre and about life. It has to be true in a theatre form, and yet be something beyond theatre.' Thus, at least some of Brook's distrust of language and traditional articulation arises not so much because language has outlived its purpose or even that it has been a primary instrument of a scientific materialistic culture and its attendant evils, but because it is simply inadequate, too rigidly bound by its rational conventions to provide entry to the invisible world that for him is primary and still living in the Third World. And a good deal of his simplifying is not as theatrically and politically programmatic as it sounds, but rather is a Thoreauvian stripping away of inessentials to facilitate epiphanic union with the ineffable.

Thus, but only on reflection, one realizes that the political consciousness that is projected through the programme booklet and through *L'Os*, *Ubu*, and particularly *The Ik* is misleading. The Ik, to be sure, are degraded because of civilization's inroads, but they are not moved to any political action, nor does that possibility really interest Brook, as it would, say, El Teatro Campesino. Their retreat to untainted territory is as temporary and futile as Huck Finn's to the other side of the Mississippi River. Brook is more concerned with inner space. The Ik's major fault, in fact (and that of other Third World peoples), is that even as victims they are still succumbing to the values of civilization (e.g. they eat like pigs when they can, they steal, they are greedy, they are as indifferent to each other's needs as civilization is to theirs); they are abandoning their pre-literate, pre-civilized oceanic oneness with the cosmos, a oneness that Brook explores in *Conference* and will extend, presumably, in his next (major) project, the epic Indian poem, the *Mahabharata*.

Yale/Theater, Fall/Winter 1980

'The Importance of the Group': An Interview with Bruce Myers, by Georges Banu and Martine Millon

One of the central performers with Brook's Centre from its inception to the present day, the English actor reflects on the role of training and improvisation, and the importance of the African journey for subsequent work.

G.B.: In Brook's work, exercises aren't necessarily directed towards the stage, but more often towards improvisation: it obviously has a central role, as much during the elaboration of a production in rehearsal as in the street work you've often undertaken: in the States, in South America, in Italy, here in Paris etc . . .

B.M.: The preparatory work helps the inner dynamic of the group, they come to know each other in this way. You can't improvise any other way. You have to be like a good jazz orchestra, knowing when to leave room for a solo, when to impinge, withdraw or support. The most difficult thing of all is to find a shared theme that is then taken up and developed by several people. We have tried to find root principles for improvisation. When you're alone, it is easier; with two, the relationship becomes stimulating; with three, it already seems fairly difficult to control. When there are even more, the group as a whole must split into a number of smaller groups who can sustain interrelationships throughout the improvisation. The first lesson to learn in improvisation is knowing how to listen, to remain open to what's going on. Without truly listening, you can't work as a group, you never create anything homogeneous, shared. An audience immediately senses the degree and quality of homogeneity within a group. That's what allows an event to be shared. Listening is the first step in this process: it's proof that one wants to be together with others. It is terribly rare to want to perform uniquely in order to share, with no ulterior motives. That is what we were looking for in the improvisation work.

When we went to work with Luis Valdez in California, we had to improvise short fast sketches to agricultural workers, despite the presence of heavies from an intimidating union. We improvised well because it was necessary and because it was dangerous. Improvisation sweeps away an actor's habits, his certainties. It's all very well declaiming a

314

Racine text, but on your own with no safety net are you able to sustain contact for five minutes with people you don't know? At that point the greatest actor in the world would find himself in difficulty.

G.B.: In *Conference*, you had your first real performance experience with masks. What effect did that have on you?

B.M.: Masks helped me, because they immediately gave me the essence of the characters to be performed, their very presence. It's located immediately. Subsequently I felt very free with the masks, which I discovered demand an immense precision of movement. There's one kind of precision for the mask while another part of the body is performing something else. So the mask serves as a limitation, a framework, without ever really becoming too restrictive. When you perform with a mask, nothing can be blurred or vague, everything must be visible, clear, clean. The position of the head is important, it makes the mask and its values more visible. I think the mask gave me a sense of the value of having a precise form as a performance base. Masks focus perception. With a mask you can even play gods: and *Conference* was concerned mainly with mythical characters. Representing them was facilitated by the use of masks and puppets.

G.B.: What is the relationship between your improvisatory work and the writing of a text?

B.M.: Peter Brook prepares the text with two or three collaborators: by the time rehearsals begin, it's always ready. Given that the period of improvisations usually lasts a long time, we have to have a text as a reference point, a springboard from which we can improvise. In the case of *Conference*, once the text was ready we re-read Attar's work and suggested the inclusion of those stories that touched us the most deeply.

The first reading is very important: it's also the first 'listening'. On that day the atmosphere is always special, very concentrated. Sometimes certain individuals are able to find their character from that moment. We read through for almost two weeks: reading at a steady rhythm, with no pauses, with great calm.

Then we move on to improvisations around the central themes of the piece. That forces us to really discover the text. We talk very little: on the other hand we try out physically many of the possible responses. Most important are the themes behind and beneath, the fact that they are clearly focused. The blocking of a performance takes place at a rather late stage: Brook concerns himself with this area of work at a much later stage than other directors.

The basic structure Brook suggests is a framework, within which great flexibility is permitted to the individual actor. It's all based on the interplay between freedom and precision: in order to be free you must attain a fairly rigorous degree of discipline. You have to pay the price for this freedom. Theatre is the great improvisation which enables you to be free. But there are also smaller improvisations . . .

M.M.: In *Measure for Measure*, you played Angelo: how did you approach the role?

B.M.: The only way I found of approaching the role of Angelo was to think of Judaism or Islam. Judaism is an extremely rigid religion: it contains 379 interdictions! Angelo lives a very powerful experience, in some ways similar to what happened to Christ's disciples. Isabelle's pardon is like a conversion for him. Quite suddenly he understands, and his whole life is for ever changed. He is touched by grace.

Psychology is of no help to the actor for Angelo's character. Of course you could make him an obsessive neurotic, but that is less interesting: a schizophrenic concerns us less than someone close to us. Angelo is a man of duty, totally sincere: he follows God's law, which perhaps he does not understand very clearly; anyway, he observes resolutely what he believes to be divine law. He is not a politician like the Duke, he goes straight forward. He's a man of duty ready to kill to apply the law. As a story, *Measure for Measure* would be entirely plausible in modern-day Iran.

M.M.: You have said that for improvisations on Mexican street corners, work on kyogen showed itself to be more useful than delivering a Shakespearian text.

B.M.: Yes, an apparent contradiction. But the very fact of trying to do Japanese theatre enables a Westerner to discover that he also possesses that possibility within him: you discover something Japanese or Indian within yourself. Your body becomes more flexible in spite of its limitations, and it can communicate true things. When you learn the movements of a Japanese archer, you assimilate something of the Oriental mentality, a particular kind of dignity. Similarly when you imitate the Western movements of piety – getting down on your knees, lowering your head – at the same time you experience something of that piety. By practising Oriental gestures, a fairly sensitive body relocates certain Oriental sensations. Of course it's a slightly contrived approach, but there is something true in a search of this kind. It's extremely difficult to do. In Africa, I was very ill, very distressed.

M.M.: Were you afraid of abandoning those techniques on which you had based your prior work?

B.M.: I did not know that I was basing my work on useless things, and it was there that I discovered that. I began to recognize that many elements of my work stemmed from a desire to conform to an audience's aprioristic aesthetic criteria: do your job as an actor well, and you'll be rewarded. But in Africa the only thing that counted was simply but truly telling a story. If we performed here what we did there, it might well look badly performed: but in those conditions, it was true. It was never technique that was applauded: for example the beautiful delivery of a text would never have worked.

I have never felt more than in Africa the possibility of expressing myself with great force and at the same time with precision. People were so open . . . Of course there were failures, some of them very painful, but we knew that every failure was a result of our not being sufficiently open and available. Only when anything can happen will an improvisation work well. Which is not at all to say that there is no starting point, no preparation. All theatre is based on the need to tell a story, as if you were in a Middle Eastern market-place.

M.M.: How does Brook work with the actors?

B.M.: Brook tries to encourage each one of us to find our own truth. He very rarely intervenes in my work, allowing me to explore. He does interrupt if it goes off in an unexpected and false direction. It's as in Shakespeare, in which the characters must learn to see clearly, to get to know themselves. When you are very open, available and free, you will necessarily be touched by grace, even if the character is evil, narcissistic, violent.

With Brook, everything is focused around the story you are telling. He demands that we never forget it, that we sense the presence of the author, that we pay homage to him. Attar is being celebrated when we perform *Conference*. At the same time you must go beyond that, you must share and enlighten while encapsulating all facets, odd or otherwise. When I performed Angelo, I think I was highly prepared to show his dark, problematic side, and much less so his illuminating aspect.

G.B.: What are your principle conclusions from working with the Centre?

B.M.: First of all, the importance of the group, without which nothing can evolve. Establishing communication. Trying what you don't know how to do. Not being scared. Listening very clearly. Being flexible. Knowing how to share. Being healthy.

June 1983, Paris
Translation by David Williams,
Les Voies de la Création Théâtrale XIII.

V

New Horizons in the Eighties: From Chamber Opera to Epic Storytelling

---

The Cherry Orchard, March 1981

The Tragedy of Carmen, November 1981

The Mahabharata, July 1985

The Cherry Orchard

Over the next few years, the Centre members dispersed to pursue their own work around the world, while Brook staged a number of productions in which the experiences shared and ideas developed within the Centre were conveyed to and further evolved by different groups. First there was a crisp and minutely observed new version of Chekhov's bitter-sweet masterpiece *The Cherry Orchard*, with Brook's wife Natasha Parry as Ranevskaya. Performances of an immense physicality and energy fully animated the text's rhythmic montage of subtle emotional changes to present us with an image of the movement of life itself: for Brook, Chekhov is 'the dramatist of life's movement'.

The text was entirely reappraised: Brook and Carrière both reread a number of existing versions in French and English, and returned to Chekhov's original, studying his correspondence with Stanislavski. (Although Brook reads Russian to a fair degree, he was further aided in his research by his wife's Russian-born mother, Lucia Lavrova). The aim was for absolute fidelity to Chekhov's concerns: Brook wanted to refocus every element, deeming existing versions to be blurred, vague approximations. Even Chekhov's punctuation was felt to be of primary importance, 'as primordial as the pauses in Beckett, a series of coded messages' reflecting the rhythm and tensions of the play.

The distinction Brook makes between naturalism and what is natural was made concrete in a marvellous production: it succeeded in unearthing the human comedy, Chekhov's dispassionate relish for recording an *impression* of the minutiae of life passing, with the simplest of means. Minimal design: the Bouffes itself becoming Ranevskaya's house, a space we share, unlike conventional proscenium stagings of Chekhov: only a few carpets and cushions, a screen, the bare scarred walls – silent witnesses to the passage of time. No attempt was made to represent the orchard itself, an indefinite light source (like the Simorgh in *Conference*). Nothing blocked the actors' work: all was intimacy, poetry, immediacy, fluidity, energy. And no melancholic Slav pauses. Movement was feverish, incessant: the characters' boredom, frustration and inner suffering infused them with a desperate vitality, a dance of death in some ante-Purgatory. We shall meet the apocalypse dancing.

Two images struck me like hammerblows. Charlotta, the sad entertainer, cradles a small screaming child in her arms as she stands at a gaping hole high in the left side wall: then tosses it to the ground, with a blend of bitterness and frivolity, the ventriloquist's illusion shattered as a pillow lands with a dull thud: a dead child, like Ranevskaya's, a lost possibility – but also a game.

After buying the orchard at auction, Lopakhin celebrates his acquisition: clumsily tripping as he surveys his property alone (he is drunk), he careers into a screen mid-stage. As it flattens with a crack, we see the family of Ranevskaya, grouped in silence behind, as horror-struck as he to be revealed. An old and a new order: one unable to take true action, transfixed and skulking while the world moves on around them, the other destructive and insensitive.

The performers' use of the Bouffes space was invigorating, the audience fully integrated and implicated in the drama. The Jewish orchestra in the third act is invisible behind the ground-floor spectators: the action goes on onstage, the performers using passages through to this other imagined place incessantly. At one point in the fourth act, Ania is on the third balcony, an attic, Varya on the first, others below: every level comes alive. The distant sounds of a cord snapping and of axe-blows in the orchard resonate throughout the building, the very foundations vibrating. At the end, when the last door has been slammed, we are left alone with Firs, prisoners of a reality left behind: bare concrete floor (the decorative warmth and resonance of the carpets now gone), disintegrating walls. The shadow of faded beauty, stripped, elemental, the movement that filled it with life now a memory . . .

A Note on Chekhov by J. B. Priestley

An extract from J. B. Priestley's Anton Chekhov *included in the C.I.C.T. text for Peter Brook's* The Cherry Orchard

More than once, thinking about Chekhov, I have felt that he might have been a model for a new kind of man that our century badly needed (and – alas – has failed to produce). Consider what was combined in him. His training and outlook were scientific; he took his medicine very seriously, and to the last described himself as a doctor. But he was no theorist, no dogmatist, of science, and was entirely lacking in that arrogance which so often invades lecture rooms and laboratories. What he did . . . was essentially practical, immediately helpful to people he wanted to see in cleaner and brighter surroundings, people who might soon be healthier and happier. Unlike most Russian intellectuals, he refused to accept any ideologies. He was suspicious of systems dealing largely in elaborate abstractions: he was at once pragmatic and sceptical. Russian drawing rooms were full of people who were neither, who were unpractical and over-credulous. It was the same with religion and faith; so he could write, 'Between "There is a God" and "There is no God" lies a great expanse which the sincere sage traverses with much difficulty. The Russian knows only one of these two extremes, for the middle ground between them does not interest him. Hence, he usually knows nothing or very little.'

Yet this same Dr A. P. Chekhov, so practical, so sensible, so clear-sighted, so deeply convinced that science could rescue men from ignorance, sloth, brutality and suffering, was also Anton Chekhov the writer. Doctors have turned to writing both before and after his time, but not to writing like his. Whatever else Chekhov may have had, nobody able to read can doubt his extreme literary sensibility. Other writers may have been as acutely observant as he was, others may have known his wealth of social experience, others again may have shared his broad compassion, his tenderness with all genuine suffering; but where else is all this combined with so exquisite a sense, amounting to genius, of what must be said and what can be left out, of a setting, an atmosphere, a situation, a character, all presented in the fewest possible strokes? We have then at one end of this man's personality the approach and methods of science and at the other end the most delicate antennae in Russian literature. He is lancing (for nothing) peasants' boils in the morning, planning a garden, a school, a library, in the afternoon, and writing a little masterpiece at night. And all done without dogmatism and theorizing and bitterly-held ideology; all done with delicacy and gentle humour and compassion. So I say again that here was the model for a new kind of man, but the mould was broken before our blind mad century was five years old. There has only been one Anton Chekhov.

From the Anecdotal to the Essential: An Interview with Maurice Bénichou

Assistant Director/Yasha in Peter Brook's 1981 production of The Cherry Orchard *and a central performer since the mid-Seventies – the Hoopoe in* Conference, *Krishna in* Mahabharata.

Q.: First of all, can you describe this very particular space, the Bouffes du Nord?

M.B.: When Peter Brook found this theatre in 1974, it reflected his working principles exactly. There is no stage, no curtain, so the actors are very close to the audience, which enables a more direct, natural and modern kind of performance. The actor can speak loudly or softly, and if he is clear in his thought, his voice will convey his inner relationship to his material like a violin. It's wonderful. But it is not a tiny pocket theatre: you cannot work constantly at a very low register, the effect would be impoverishing and banal. You are obliged to find a certain fluid vitality in adapting to this space, which changes all the time.

Q.: Although you never represent the orchard, as a spectator one seems to see it. How is that possible?

M.B.: The spectator's imagination creates it through the actors' mediation. The performers experience the images of the cherry orchard so strongly that they manage to convey them to the audience. Thirty real trees on stage would not be nearly as evocative. You can't illustrate a feeling. The orchard alludes to a happy enchanting time, a reality which cannot be reduced to a summary anecdotal level. It is more a question of a parable showing us people going towards their destiny, towards death.

Q.: Don't you think the play also refers to a precise historical moment?

M.B.: Our aim is not to reconstitute Russia in 1904. Of course the Revolution was not far off, and Chekhov sensed it. So for example at a certain moment in the play, we hear an odd unexplained sound, perhaps signalling that something dramatic is coming to a head. But it is quite sufficient to know that the period preceding the Revolution and the period after it were different. That being said, many people found our production very 'Russian'.

Although we referred very little to a precise historical reality and the

Russian aspect of the play, nevertheless we respected the text itself to the letter . . . Perhaps that's what gives the spectator the impression that we stick resolutely and authentically to the play's specific climate.

It's a misleading climate. These people do nothing, talk a great deal but rarely make decisions: but in fact they are very vital and active. They fill the long Russian winter nights, organizing gatherings, parties, entertainments, both to animate their lives and to defuse or distract their sense of suffering.

Q.: Did you consult historical works?

M.B.: We were chiefly interested in Chekhov, in his stories and sketches. And we came to recognize that our received image of him and his work is false. He was neither maudlin nor excessively sentimental. On the contrary, he was very caustic and tough towards the people he described, whose lives he observed in infinite detail.

The characters in *The Cherry Orchard* resemble us. They have a history, they are simultaneously moving and ridiculous, sometimes even grotesque. So they are not heroic in the traditional sense of the word, but human beings: complex, ever changing, with facets that charm and attract and others that irritate. What they love above all is life, a love which means they do not want to allow themselves to be destroyed. So beneath every character, behind every reply, we discern a total commitment, which transforms the dialogue into a sort of duel, a sword fight, even if it is most usually implemented with great delicacy. In other words, one might say that Chekhov does not describe reality's anecdotal aspect, he reveals its essential dimensions.

Q.: Chekhov insisted on describing *The Cherry Orchard* as a 'comic' play, and there is a great deal of humour in your production. Can you clarify what you understood by this term?

M.B.: It's not a vulgar 'boulevard' comedy, but the true comedy of existence. Here is a farce that is both ferocious, biting, and at the same time tender. If you observe life from the outside, you recognize that there is something comic about it: even death and funerals can become laughable. The stories and plays of Chekhov were written with that sort of distance, with a kind of dispassionate passion. This tormented woman moves us profoundly, but Chekhov never allows our emotions to become too strong, dominating the audience. He allows emotional involvement to develop to a certain degree, then checks or breaks it, for it's too uncomfortable. One cannot live solely with great sentiments.

These moments of rupture stem from the play's rhythm: no sequence develops to completion and resolution. Chekhov leads us off in one direction, then suddenly modifies it, by for example bringing on another character who knocks the situation off balance, turns it around. In this sense, he is one of the seminal inventors of modern theatre. He lures us constantly from comic event to tragic event, following a dynamic contrapuntal rhythm which never comes to a halt.

It is a comic play: neither sentimental nor tragic, but pathetic. Audiences do not cry because what they see is sad but because it is recognizably living. Nobody could bear to listen to people complaining for two and a quarter hours. Not so much because that would be irritating, but because that does not exist in life: and therefore it would not touch or move us. These characters are childish, excessive: when disasters occur, we cry with them; then we forget them, just as they do.

Q.: Can you give an example of this rhythmic structuring?

M.B.: Take the arrival at the house. Everyone is happy, congratulating themselves, talking, joking, laughing. Then the tutor of the dead child appears. A leaden silence embraces all: suddenly emotion and tears replace the carefree frivolity a few moments before. Then all of a sudden Ranevskaya looks at Trofimov, and asks him why he has become so old and ugly. It's over, the pain is dissipated. It's ridiculous for her to continue crying in front of everyone else, so Chekhov finds her an escape route. They move on to other things. A trace lingers on in her heart, and in the spectator's imagination: we now know she retains a deep scar inside her. And we have learnt this much as if by chance: nothing is prepared – which is what gives theatre that illusion of the unpredictability and movement that dominates reality.

Q.: Moving on to your design, was it a choice or a technical necessity?

M.B.: Given the specific form and nature of the Bouffes space, we could not construct a different set for each act. In any case, that is not how we conceive of production: we believe set changes break the rhythm and atmosphere within which the spectators are gradually immersed; they threaten to emphasize the anecdotal to the detriment of the essential. Our starting point is an empty space, which is transformed in the course of the play by means of a small number of items of furniture or objects suggesting the different locations in which the action occurs. Today one can no longer stage plays in a naturalistic way; cinema has filled that function.

We chose the carpets primarily for the beauty of their material and colour, but also for the signs they convey effortlessly. So in the first act, they represent the interior of a wealthy house, whereas in the second act, which takes place outside, they encourage us to imagine the irridescent colours of the countryside, the changes in light. The screens we used served to break up and mobilize space.

As far as the other objects are concerned, it was quite simple. We use those objects and furnishings which are indispensable to the story: the bookcase/wardrobe that represents the house's past and the childhood of those that live there – Gayev delivers a memorable speech 'to' it; cups, when people drink coffee; cards for Charlotta's tricks; luggage at the moment of departure. We were obliged to have some realistic objects.

We couldn't put a real billiard table on stage: it would be too cumbersome and constricting. Through simple use of a billiard cue, brought into the space, spectators are able to imagine that there is a full billiard room somewhere out of sight where people are actually playing. In the play, the game itself has an important significance and resonance. In some way it reflects a society and its decline. Indeed, in the third act, the servants go into the billiard room without any misgivings, doing whatever they want, even breaking a cue. For Gayev, who is obsessed with billliards, it's like someone ruining his prize toy. All this takes place towards the end of the play, just before the house is sold.

Q.: Why did you choose to have the characters sitting on the ground?

M.B.: There was no fixed principle. In any naturalistic setting, there are items of furniture and you use them. We started to rehearse using chairs and tables, because it helped the actors. Then we realized we were consistently reproducing a fixed vocabulary of positions. So we removed these objects gradually, replacing them with cushions which in the end were also removed, to give the actors a greater freedom of movement. The process is one of stripping away superfluities and obstacles, and in the end in this instance it became a necessity.

Movement comes from an inner feeling, the end result of extensive work on the body (physical exercises, exercises to explore and stimulate relationships with others, improvisations): this work fed and sustained the actors, took them to a point at which they were able to move and react through the text in complete freedom. It is interesting to remove seats, for example, to leave an open suggestion: particularly in Act I. In Act II, the problem does not arise since they are outside in the country, therefore sitting on the grass. In Act III, for the party, there are a few seats, perhaps hinting at the presence of people who are not everyday guests. Finally, in the last act, the carpets are rolled back, the floor is bare, cold: there's only the armchair in which Firs dies.

So the decision to strip away, to essentialize, is born from practical concerns on the whole: if this process works in performance, the spectator will only need the actor's craft to stimulate his imagination.

Q.: How did you arrive at the costume designs?

M.B.: The costumes are the fruit of true research. They were elaborated by Chloé Obolensky, a specialist who had written a book about Russia at this period, a work heavily documented with photographs. That was why Peter Brook asked for her collaboration on this production. The form and design of the costumes – the refinement of Ranevskaya's dresses, her parasol etc. – do in fact reflect the reality of that particular period, but the aim was never to fully reconstitute it as such.

Q.: Did you in any way take other productions of *The Cherry Orchard* into account?

M.B.: We never do that. It's very dangerous, particularly when they have been of a high quality. We only consulted Chekhov's and Stanislavski's notes, of which there are a great number. We wanted to evoke a time that has disappeared: most contemporaries are dead today. All that is left is a text, some words. We tried to present it in the most vital way possible, transcending what is anecdotal to discover and expose what is universal.

Q.: What aspect of your production seems most important to you?

M.B.: Its profound unity, which is the direct result of our conception of theatre work. It must be a privileged meeting between a theatre space, a play, a director, some actors – a meeting which can create strong impressions in the hearts and minds of spectators.

Maurice Bénichou interviewed by Josette Casalino-Vasari and Catherine Vandel-Isaakidis: translated from the French by David Williams. (From Anton Tchekhov, *La Cerisaie*, Hatier, Paris, 1985)

The Cherry Orchard: A Review by Mel Gussow

Mel Gussow, New York Times *theatre critic, applauded Brook's first ever production of* The Cherry Orchard *as a faithful realization of Chekhov's vision.*

It was different from any other *Cherry Orchard* that I have seen, beginning with the starkness and simplicity of the setting. In the centre of the stage was a large carpet, and on it were placed several cushions and a few straight-backed chairs. Natasha Parry, playing the elegant Mme Ranevskaya, returning to her country estate, swept on stage and grandly sat in one of those hard chairs. In the classic Brook sense, this was 'a free carpet show', Chekhov stripped of ornamentation and affectation; there was not even a semblance of a tree in sight. The actors were thrown back on the words, as adapted by Jean-Claude Carrière, and on their own resources. In lieu of scenery, the costumes were elaborate; each summarized its character. The few remaining properties assumed even greater metaphorical significance – the bouquet of keys that Varya, Ranevskaya's adopted daughter, wore at her waist became the badge of her office as supervisor of the family estate. When she flung them at the estate's new owner, the outsider, Lopakhin, it was as if she were challenging him to a duel.

The production was not a reinterpretation in the manner of Andrei Serban's version at Lincoln Center, but a return to Chekhov's own vision. The evening was comic without being farcical, and it was immensely human – and an authentic ensemble piece. Other productions have centred on the conflict between Ranevskaya and Lopakhin, treated as a representative of the aggressive working man on the move. Without overlooking Ranevskaya's commanding presence – even in this version, she was always surrounded by her entourage – Miss Parry emphasized her charm, femininity and fragility. This was a glamorous woman who needed to be taken care of. In his essay on Chekhov, Vladimir Nabokov describes the Chekhovian intellectual, but he could have been speaking about Miss Parry's Ranevskaya as someone 'who combined the deepest human decency of which man is capable with an almost ridiculous inability to put his ideals and principles into action.' Gracefully, Miss Parry captured her character's helplessness and her generosity of spirit. Niels Arestrup's Lopakhin was not the boorish rustic we often find in productions of *The Cherry Orchard*, but a man of considerable sensitivity. When Trofimov tells him that he has the hands and the soul of an artist, the remark should not seem humorous or gratuitous. Lopakhin has suppressed the lyrical side of himself, but the instinct is there. In Mr Arestrup's portrayal, we saw a man lacking in table manners but not in taste or in sympathy. Instead of wondering, as we sometimes do, why Varya wants to marry such an oaf, we wondered why he wanted to marry her, a pale reflection of Ranevskaya. Mme Ranevskaya's brother, Gaev, shooting billiard balls into imaginary side pockets, has been portrayed as a doddering old simpleton. In a performance of remarkable tenderness, Michel Piccoli restored him to his position as an aging innocent and seraphic wastral, frittering away his life and his sister's resources. He is simply unable to function in a real world; even if he had the money, he would never be able to buy the estate. When the estate is lost, he offers his sister immediate consolation, trying to soothe her because he knows that her heart is shattering.

Even the minor characters achieved an inner importance – the maid Dunyasha, flirting with the idea of freedom, and Yasha, the big-city servant with illusions of position, already boasting a cigar and a bowler hat. In the final act – the play was staged without intermission – the carpet was thrown back and the stage was emptied of its few accoutrements. The house was ready for abandonment, and for formal old Firs, the most dignified member of the family. Exquisitely personified by Robert Murzeau, he delivered his final lines not as the last words of a man about to be entombed, but almost in a whisper, a quiet verbalization of the offstage cry of the falling trees. As an era ends, Firs remains an afterthought. Paradoxically, this revival of a well-known classic became, in Mr Brook's hands, one of the most original events of the theatre season.

Several days after seeing *The Cherry Orchard*, I visited Mr Brook in his Paris apartment. That apartment, which also serves as studio and rehearsal space, was almost as bare of furnishings as the stage at the Bouffes du Nord. In fact, his living room looked like the setting for his *Cherry Orchard*. We both sat on mattresses on the floor and took part in a free carpet conversation. He began, 'The reason *The Cherry Orchard* touches people in extraordinary ways is because, as in any great work, behind it is a myth. This is a poem about life and death and transition and change. Chekhov was writing it when he was dying. Knowing that he had a short time left, he felt a theme emerging: something loved has to be relinquished, disappointment has to be accepted. And he wrote it in a language that he forged for himself; it was not the language of Shakespeare or of Pushkin.' Mr Brook compared

Chekhov, in his distillation of words and images, to such modernists as Beckett and Pinter. 'While playing the specifics,' he said, 'we also try to play the myth – the secret play.'

One of his first problems was the choice of cast, whether to use the ensemble-trained performers in his international company or the Shakespeare-trained members of the R.S.C. He decided to take a third course, to put together a new company, made up primarily of actors who had worked on the French stage. 'The very basis of the international group is that anyone can play anything. Blacks play whites and young play old. But there are degrees of obligation, correspondence and physique in Chekhov. Every actor has a different background, but they have several things in common: a degree of aptness physically and a level of competence with Chekhov. They are experienced professionals who have not lost their innocence, their knowledge of what first brought them into the theatre. But I could not advertise: open call for innocent actors.'

Largely he had to go on instinct and recommendations. Two people came from his international company, his wife, Natasha Parry, who is equally adept at playing classics, and Maurice Bénichou, who also acted as assistant director. Some actors declined his offer because they felt a lack of identification with the material; there is no great French tradition of playing Chekhov. Others declined because they felt the roles were too small. However, Mr Piccoli, a major international film star, was one who was not at all disturbed at playing what might be considered a subordinate character. From the beginning, the director was clear that the roles were equal. 'The audience has no way of telling who has the biggest part. It's like a family on Christmas day. After the day is over, one can ask, who spoke most and who spoke least?' One of the most difficult roles to cast was that of Firs. They could not find any aged French actor with experience playing Chekhov. Finally, Mr Brook's assistant asked, 'Where is Robert Murzeau?' For years, Mr Murzeau had been a popular stage actor in comedy roles, 'almost the Sam Levene of the French stage.' He was found living in retirement in the country. When he was asked to play Firs, he said gratefully, 'The reason I went into the theatre was to play Shakespeare and other classics. I've wanted to do Chekhov for nearly 60 years.'

Rehearsals began in Mr Brook's apartment with a lavish Russian dinner, prepared with the advice of the director's mother-in-law, who is Russian. It was a chance for the disparate actors to meet and to begin their immersion in Chekhov. Rehearsals continued for 10 weeks. 'For everyone to share the totality of the material, we would do improvisations, have discussions of the play and read Chekhov stories. They would argue and attack one another. Gradually the cast assumed the play. To do a naturalistic play you have to respect the specifics of the period, place and social conditions, the demands of scenic language, which is like photographs of everyday life. But this is not a behavioral study. Meyerhold called it a symphony, a dance.' Mr Brook approached it as a 'theatrical movement purely played.' 'From the start, I wanted to avoid sentimentality, a false Chekhovian manner that is not in the text. This is not gloomy, romantic, long and slow. It's a comic play about real life.'

Two-thirds of the way into rehearsal, the director suddenly uprooted the actors from their studio sanctuary and had them perform the play without scenery or props in a school basement for an audience of 100 teenagers. 'The actors had a fascination, panic and skepticism. There was no way out! It was a tiny space. They sat among the kids on the ground and on low benches. It was a free carpet show. There was nothing to give it cultural distance. They realized that it was a play of energies and dynamism.' When they returned to rehearsals, they were not allowed the comfort of props or scenery. Explaining the technique, Mr Brook said, 'One must give food to the imagination – and work to the imagination.' He was speaking about the audience as well as the actors.

New York Times, 9 August 1981

The Tragedy of Carmen

'Grand opera, of course, is the Deadly Theatre carried to absurdity. Opera is a nightmare of vast feuds over tiny details: of surrealist anecdotes that all turn round the same assertion: nothing needs to change. Everything in opera must change, but in opera change is blocked'.

After *The Cherry Orchard*, Brook returned to opera for the first time in thirty years, directing a revolutionary and compelling new version of *Carmen* which has sold out wherever it has played in the world to date (Paris, New York, Japan). Almost 200,000 people have seen it live (some sort of record in opera?) The production flouted every convention one cares to name, and there were a few predictable cries of vandalism. But it brought a radical new life – and audience – to opera, the genre of pompous élitist immutability *par excellence*: in Brook's experience, 'a prehistoric monster'.

'Opera properly done should be seen as more natural even than film, because it strikes at the heart. Because of the deadening influence of the snobbery of culture, all the formal aspects of opera, including virtuosity, have gradually replaced the direct appeal to the heart . . . Our object in any form of theatre is to make it something totally accessible, not in the sense of popularising, but of making it meaningful to whoever watches it'.

(Brook in *The Sunday Times*)

In order to make this *Carmen* 'meaningful', Brook chose to reappraise the working conditions of opera at every level. For ten weeks he led his performers in strenuous daily movement sessions. He wanted to free the singers from gestural and vocal clichés by establishing an organic relationship between voice and movement, one of the cornerstones of his work with the Centre. Brook was trying to stimulate a development of 'the properly integrated person out of whom can come body language, sung language, spoken language, depending on the expressive needs of the moment'. He wanted these performers to be able to find 'a highly

334

charged body that is not asleep the way our bodies are most of the time, but by being awake is inventive and creative at every moment . . .' And indeed in Brook's re-embodied *Carmen*, performers sang with their whole body. The nature of the tragedy and its rhythm made song seem the most natural form of expression – crystalline, transparent, a dense and universal poetry of the soul whose emotional essence (love, hate, joy, sadness, desire, shame) communicates instantly. Here was the uninsulated language of passion.

Brook and Carrière returned to three textual sources: Prosper Merimée's short novella, a savage folk-tale with its origins in an oral tradition, Bizet's score and Meilhac and Halévy's libretto. By excising all that was felt to be superfluous, all prettification, they compressed and focused the material to leave a simple narrative line which works dramatically with great intensity and without melodrama. In this way, the performance was cut from its original three hours to just eighty minutes. In terms of the music, composer Marius Constant's sinewy score made the melody immediate and active. This process of clarification, which Brook compares to the restoration of an old master, heightened the tale's impact and eloquence.

Brook set the dramatic line above the musical line at every level. No choruses, no star system. Each performance involved only four singers and three actors; and to enable the work to be performed nightly like a play, three casts were prepared in parallel. Ten singers from a company of thirteen alternated performances: 3 Carmens (one French, one Israeli, one Czech), 3 Don Josés, 2 Micaëlas, 2 Escamillos – all clearly individualized. Each separate permutation established its own unique dramatic and musical relationship. Brook also abandoned the traditional orchestra pit: a barrier separating audience from performers, and a spatial reflection of opera's innate power hierarchy (conductor – singer – hidden musician). The orchestra itself, reduced in size to a fourteen-piece chamber ensemble (was this the first 'chamber opera'?) was split into two parts placed in full visibility, and full stereo, behind the singers. Instead of the singers taking their lead from a conductor, here the orchestra accompanied and supported them. Attention and responsibility were therefore refocused back on to the performers – their youth, physical energy, presence and creative powers. They were also able to sing *mezzo voce* with comfort, communicating more intimately and directly as if the arias were lieder.

A number of arias were sung *a cappella* or accompanied by solo piano, with the performers inches from the audience in the most intimate of relationships. The toreador Escamillo's entrance to the bullring was performed against an ironic backing of highly amplified taped music, the stage orchestra visibly pantomiming their instruments. At Lillas Pastia's inn, a violinist steps forward to accompany Carmen's dance, her castanettes fragments of a plate she has shattered. The interrelationship of singer and instrumentalist was organic, fluid: in some ways reminiscent of popular Indian dance or of Middle Eastern epic theatre.

Searching for Carmen by Jean-Claude Carrière

Carrière's preface to the C.I.C.T. text of Carmen, *the libretto of which he adapted.*

At the period in which Mérimée situates his *Carmen*, in 1832, in the eyes of the rest of Europe Spain was still a savage country. Goya had died four years beforehand. The French retained vivid memories of the terrible guerrilla conflict (that was when the word came into our vocabulary) in opposition to Napoleon's invasion. The Sierra Morena bandits were a reality. Right up until 1850 or 1860, a specific literary genre, 'the Journey to Spain', attracted such writers as Théophile Gautier and Gustave Doré. They wrote of a dark and beautiful country, both dangerous and hospitable, the heart of which remained undiscovered. What little we knew of the customs seemed strange, alien, almost African.

In 1852, just after the century's mid-point, Louis-Napoléon Bonaparte was installed on the French throne under the name of Napoléon III. He married a young lady from a well-known Spanish family, Eugenia de Montijo: it was in the wake of this princess that Spanish folklore, unknown until then, began to permeate into France and the rest of the world. Of course, court protocol demanded that it be consumed in a sugared, softened, emasculated form, while travellers continued to declare themselves stunned by the sensual violence of Spanish dance.

In other words, the image of Spain swung brutally from one extreme to the other: from Goya's dark and monstrous visions, the fruit of 'the sleep of reason', a truly dynamic Spanish current, fusing blood, faith, madness and sex (it recurs much later in Buñuel's films, *Las Hurdes* and *Viridiana*), to the miserably limp and hollow imported imitations whirling and stamping their feet in the *café-concerts*.

Even today, classical and contemporary Spanish culture remains almost entirely unknown in France, with the exception of two or three painters and a film-maker. Of course it's simpler and more palatable to stick to the clichéd folkloric surface. But it could also be suggested that a fundamental difference exists between France and Spain. Rational on this side of the Pyrenees, irrational on the other. The place of reason in the two cultures – the respect it inspires, the confidence it instils – is not

337

at all the same. Indeed, much stronger links exist between Spain and Russia than between Spain and France. André Malraux even wrote, in a preface to a work by Jose Bergamin: 'If a masterpiece proclaims that supreme truth is inseparable from the irrational, it's either Spanish or Russian.'

Despite Bizet's efforts to avoid all hackneyed folklore (there's not a single guitar note in the score), *Carmen*, which became a comic opera in 1875, didn't entirely escape boleros and castanets. It might even be suggested that this work has acted as a kind of standard-bearer for the completely denatured Spanish culture, diminished to a mediocre folkloric spectacle, that has become known around the world. *Carmen* opened the door to gazpacho, fixed bullfights, skyscraper holidays in Andalusia.

Everyone is more or less agreed on this point. Difficulties arise as soon as one tries to go a little further, reading the novella for example. Mérimée presents himself as a sort of scientist, an archaeologist: never mentioning a word of the clichéd folklore which does not yet exist, he tells a particular story; he claims it is close to reality, insisting on the gipsy aspect. Today he touches us through a certain elaborately detailed dryness and coolness, a long way from romanticism.

I have made several attempts to work out how Meilhac, Halévy and Bizet worked. They were confronted with a precise problem: how to present *Carmen* to an audience of their time. They were profoundly aware of the fact that they would never be able to portray on an official public stage a thief-cum-prostitute-cum-witch: the dark criminal (or at least the instigator of crimes) as she appears in the novella. Nevertheless, groping tentatively forward in a minefield of taboos, they managed to create a character who seemed wholly scandalous to audiences in 1875. A scandal which, like most others, is incomprehensible to us today, as a result of the total eclipse of that era's moral restrictions and constraints.

To make the transition from Mérimée's dispassionate and almost indifferent concern for detail to the sentimental and decorative simplifications of the lyrical work, they found certain ingenious solutions: for example, the creation of Micaëla, an indispensable character dramatically, the sole representative of Don Jose's village past, his roots, his attachment to his mother. Similarly the development of the character of Escamillo (a simple picador in Mérimée, just one amongst many others) is useful from all points of view. He embodies all the men Carmen could have known. But Escamillo's development is pushed too far, and in the end to absurd lengths. His appearance in the mountains in the third act, bang in the middle of the smugglers' camp, has always seemed unrealistic.

Somewhere along the line, Meilhac and Halévy also diminished the character of Don Jose. In the novella, he appears much stronger and more dangerous: a true bandit. During a ball game in his Basque village, he became involved in a fight with another player whom he had seriously injured. For this very reason he left home and enlisted in the dragoons, long before meeting Carmen.

Later on he finds himself face to face with Garcia, Carmen's 'husband', a formidable character. Yet Don Jose provokes him into a duel and kills him. Another episode missing from the lyrical work.

Although Carmen herself has inevitably lost a significant part of her youthful sensuality and her total absence of scruples, nevertheless I believe she owes her dimension as great tragic heroine to the opera. With great clarity Bizet established the fundamental contradiction in her character – uniquely through the card aria, one of the most beautiful moments in the work. On one hand, Carmen submits entirely, almost blindly, to destiny, which she knows to be implacable. Things happen just as they are written: you cannot change one letter. On the other hand, she constantly affirms her freedom, savagely defending it, even at the cost of her life. 'She was born free and free she will die', she sings. And therefore we owe these two classically contradictory affirmations – fatality/liberty – to the lyrical work.

Any 'adaptation' presupposes that the conditions surrounding the genesis of a work have changed, that they never stop changing. They had already evolved between Mérimée and the lyrical work, and more than a century has passed since then. How can we fail to take that into account?

Preface to the C.I.C.T. text, translated by David Williams.

The Tragedy of Carmen: A Rehearsal Log
by Michel Rostain

Michel Rostain, a young French director who acted as Brook's assistant on
Carmen, *made a daily record of his impression during the ten-week rehearsal
period. The full version of his log was originally published in French in* Les
Voies de la Création Théâtrale, *Vol. XIII.*

Tuesday, 1 September 1981

First meeting at the Bouffes du Nord. The whole team is there (except
for two singers who will join us in a few days): three English, one Swede,
one American, one Israeli and four French. Three actors from Brook's
group are also there, as well as design, lighting, and stage management
people, and of course our pianist.

Before anything – rehearsal, discussion, performance – a collective
warm-up in which everyone participates. An hour devoted to limbering
and mobilizing the body: Maurice Bénichou directs this work. Not only
a time to warm up: also a time for concentration and initial contact. It's
never really gymnastic, more a tuning of an instrument, a training which
is never forced: maintenance work. We do it gathered in a *circle*. Then
without any break, we move on to games and collective exercises. First,
we had to bring the circle to life, to make each individual sensitive and
attentive to its existence. The creation of collective rhythms. Everything
rests on listening, on the vitality of responses. Gestures are passed from
one to another around the circle. A gesture arrives from the left, I
transmit it to the right. Then another one. Rhythms, sounds are added:
then more and more are circulated in both directions. Sometimes
actions telescope. It grinds to a halt. We are rather clumsy at maintaining
the life of the circle: openness to what's coming from right and left is not
very great. Interruptions. Someone asks questions. A rule is proposed:
do first, try the exercise, discussion afterwards. The aim is really to find
the right rhythm for this circle, not to break contact and the quality of
listening while the rhythm is being elaborated.

While we have something to eat together in the theatre, Peter uses the
time to give us a few ideas about the *Carmen* we're preparing. Brief
glimpses which suggest very little dramaturgical predefinition: more like
suggestions for reference points. For example Peter talks about gypsies,
Spain. For this performance, we must be quite obviously gypsies, while

340

avoiding any kind of folkloric romanticism. We will need to work on the Basque peasants of the last century, while remaining very much of today. In this way Brook's *Cherry Orchard* was profoundly Russian without any folkloric impositions, simultaneously dated and contemporary.

From Bizet's opera, Peter continues, we will only retain one aspect: that which concerns the major characters, the essential drama. We will eliminate the conventional comic opera framework which has been superimposed on this essential kernel. So there will be Carmen and Don José, Escamillo and Micaëla. As far as the latter pair are concerned, we will have to uncover their real force. The score does not condemn Micaëla to being limp, nor Escamillo to being a rather second-rate, comic matador. That's merely tradition. We can find other things within them and the music, by paying particular attention to what Carmen can make a lover feel; to the extent to which Micaëla, and Don José, have their roots in the land; to the cultural and social traditions of Basque peasants and gypsies.

The day comes to an end with a reading of Mérimée's novella. Throughout the rehearsals, we will return again and again to Mérimée's text: its concision and rigour are invaluable, free from the muffling insulations of operatic traditions. Each person reads a page or two of the text, in either French or English, before passing it on.

Thursday, 3 September

The designer Chloé Obolensky has brought a mass of photographic material: gypsies, groups of Spanish dancers, peasants. One photo shows a group of flamenco dancers, musicians and spectators. Each of us chooses a character in this photo. After studying it closely, they adopt the pose of the chosen character. Exactly the same gesture, the same attitude. It's much more difficult than it first appears to be. The onlookers correct attitudes without recourse to psychological commentaries on situation or intentions, uniquely concerning themselves with the body itself: altering the position of an arm, finding the tension in a movement, etc. Then we work on the seconds immediately preceding this photograph, and on those that follow. Where does the instantaneous gesture come from? Where does it go? The exercise ultimately recomposes a whole section of the original photo.

In the afternoon, we return to the score. Marius insists that both text and music be taken flat, at face value: initially we can only work from the notes, rhythms and pronunciation, without allowing ourselves to be in any way influenced by traditions of interpretation. None of these traditions are imposed. Marius suggests an experiment: instead of singing the toreador's aria in the sparkling grand fashion in which it is usually presented onstage, try to find its '*lied*' side. A scene is improvised. Escamillo sings something very contained to Carmen, a sensual, tender and full melody. They make love.

Friday, 4 September

When we do exercises in which gestures and sounds are mixed, it is still rare for one not to illustrate the other, as if they were interdependent. As soon as the action slows down, immediately tempi slow, sounds become '*piano*', etc. In this way activity is subjected to musical rhythm, sounds are adapted 'psychologically' to the gesture, and so on.

Today's rehearsal culminates in a musical reading of the whole of *The Tragedy of Carmen*, but this time, instead of all being seated on chairs around the piano, the singers take to the playing space. They all sing together, so we have three Carmens, three Don Josés, etc. It has an improvized feel – Peter's only instruction beforehand, 'Don't perform'. The singers need to feel the others, be aware of their presence: no need to *do* anything. One thing strikes me as I watch: at certain moments, two Don Josés, for example, make the same gesture at the same time, on the same phrase, without conniving or even seeing each other. Two identical gestures, as if the music lured them out. Of course in general, simply two gestures communicated and demanded by lyrical doxa, as if the common language of tradition was suddenly reawakened in their bodies before they had even worked on the role. Superimposed conventional expressions, 'theatre' of the emotion, far from anything true or natural. That's what we will have to tackle head on.

After this run-through, Peter insists there shall be no illustration. At this stage in the rehearsal process, it's not the time for grand gestures. We have to begin with the search for a state, for points of contact: so instead it's towards small gestures we must turn our attentions. During the discussion, some of the singers evoke what has already been taught to them, those grand gestures which would be so necessary on lyrical stages. As if from time to time emphasis must replace truth. Production styles and conditions in the lyrical theatre tradition very rarely allow access to a truth: so compensation is found by adding in these grand gestures.

Wednesday, 9 September

Peter makes a remark on the issue of natural gestures/stereotyped gestures. They can each be as false as the other. The real debate is not between gestural schools; it's located within the actor, at the level of truth in action. Hélène claims it is possible for her to play Carmen and her emotions without being moved in the slightest. Precisely, replies Peter, there are several Hélènes, the important thing to remember is that there's only one who speaks the truth. Peter pursues the discussion of gesture, giving as an example the conversation at some distance through barbed wire between a political detainee in Chile and one of his friends, who is free: by means of a single arm gesture, tirelessly taken up by one then the other, a simple movement varied in the speed of its execution and in its inner tempo, the two friends were able to establish and sustain a very lengthy contact with each other: a true dialogue, without words or mime, without any 'theatrical performance'. A true communication.

Tuesday, 15 September

A fantastic exercise: a singer turns his/her back on another and tries to recreate the gesture accompanying the other's singing, without having seen it. You hear the sound, you see nothing, and yet something really can be communicated. Sometimes it really works. Magical.

Friday, 18 September

More work on fights: we often come back to this. In the course of these fights, Peter says, there are moments when one feels it is 'right', that a blow has been delivered and parried convincingly. Yet our situation is necessarily artificial: punches don't land, nobody gets hurt. There has to be artificiality in the search for theatrical truth. Peter goes on: 'What is anger? How do you play anger, fear, joy, etc.? Do you draw on an album of images, taking out a cliché for anger, fear or joy? Do you take the "characteristic" sounds of joy from your personal library of recorded sounds? At every moment, in every situation, anger is radically different. Each feeling is absolutely unique and singular. That's what truth is.'

The Escamillo/Carmen duo ('*Si tu m'aimes. . .*'): we work first on the dialogue, spoken in a low voice without any external performance. Then we discuss this scene at length, which is rare. The proximity and similarity of the situations of Carmen and Escamillo are emphasized: both of them close to death, and aware of it. Do they really love each other? Opinions differ. This needs exploration, but on stage, in improvisation. We also talk about Carmen's relationship to destiny: a sense of her destiny which does not prevent her from living, loving, feeling joyous, at the same time an intimate certainty that colours every moment of her life. Peter evokes the destiny of certain races, the Jews and the gypsies: he also refers us to *The Diary of Anne Frank*, her illuminating or funny observations alongside a sense of tragedy which is omnipresent, like a red line on every page, colouring a whole life.

We approach the final scene: Don José's arrival, his dialogue with Carmen. At this first stage in the work they don't move, they speak to each other without singing. As soon as we move into song, all the inner qualities of the dialogue evaporate, performances become limited to attractions and rejections. It's always as if song paralyses improvization. One of the improvizations is set up like an over-dub recording: two actors take on the parts of Don José and Carmen, two singers sing while watching them. And immediately all sorts of new openings become apparent: the violence, the sense of abandonment, the corrida which takes place nearby, doubt, the destiny painted by the cards, the certainty of being right, madness, etc. The actors' theatrical experience is much greater than the singers'. Improvising without having to sing undoubtedly helps enormously, but by means of this 'over-dub' technique, areas of truth and naturalness emerge with a strength and clarity unknown until now.

Tuesday, 22 September

After the warm-up this morning, each of us is given a text of a few lines written in some imaginary language: about thirty words, all we have at our disposal to communicate with each other. Some try to set up exchanges, to say something in this language which is unknown but common to all of us. It is not a 'surrealistic' exercise, based on the contrast between what one wants to say and the material one can use; neither is it a question of pretending to speak fluently in some gibberish language. No, it's about really communicating, conveying something to the person you are speaking to. And yet it is not a normal situation. But between these two poles – gratuitous playing and normal language – there is room for something true, which occurs at certain moments. Then it is swept away in a second: end of exchange, return of some kind of 'theatre', stereotyped gestures try to hang on to meaning. Then something else jells, another knot is tied, phrases are circulated, not a gibberish conversation in gibberish. Sonorities convey a certain physicality, a human consistency. Then it all collapses again . . .

Friday, 25 September

A private showing for us in a local cinema of a Turkish film that I see again with intense emotion: Yilmaz Guney's *The Herd*. The idea of showing it came through the character of Micaëla: research into the corporeal behaviour of a peasant woman moulded by living traditions. After the film, we gather for a picnic in the theatre, in the playing space. The actors discuss their experiences of improvisation, pointing out that they never try to fix themselves on to an emotion: quite the opposite. To give us an example, Peter grabs a knife suddenly and threatens Maurice. Depending on Maurice's response (defensive, aggressive, mocking, etc.), Peter's gesture will need to live in a different way.

The gypsy wedding improvisations remain very blurred and un-decided. On the other hand the work on Garcia's arrival develops an interesting twist when, after several messy attempts, the protagonists improvise and communicate with each in their mother tongue, or in an invented language. Eva speaks Czech, Julian English, Alain something else, and suddenly it works, despite the fact that the attempts in French had been dull and lifeless. In particular, the fabric of a truly intimate relationship between Carmen and Garcia is being woven: a gypsy relationship from which Don José is excluded. We decide that when we return to work on this scene again, Garcia and Carmen will speak the gypsy language together if possible.

Monday, 28 September

Beginning of a new phase in the work. Up until now, we have tried to create a freedom for the body, in particular in relation to the voice and music. Imaginations have opened out, gestures are more spontaneous, relationships with others are truer. Peter now insists on a new aspect to the work: inner research into the body and the behaviour of each of the characters. It's no good having a general idea of a character: one must free its life at every moment. Peter throws in an improvisation suggestion for Carmen: each of the three performers have to tell the fortune of someone there in the group. All sorts of problems bearing on the subject of the improvisation come to light (stopping a passer-by, telling him the future, getting him to pay, squeezing as much money as possible from him, etc.): but they also bear on conceptions of the character – her inner freedom, her humour, her vision of destiny etc. Does Carmen believe in divination?

This relentless work on the details of characters and situations makes me reflect on the immutability of opera, its 'fixedness'. Of course this has nothing to do with the degree of movement filling the stage: in truth, it's the nature of performance in that kind of theatre: a sort of wafty vague ballet, an atmosphere set up around a particular piece of music or a situation. Above all it is the absence of inner life in each body, the absence of true relationships between the bodies.

Monday, 5 October

The red earth has almost entirely taken over the stage. A month before performances start, it's there, with no apparent technical impositions or constraints, although it brings with it certain complications: dust, traces of earth almost everywhere in the theatre. But clearly the presence of this earth changes the workspace, feeding it in a new way. It bleeds into every level of performance, becoming a rich element with which to improvize. The pebbles Carmen gathers and toys with, the handful of earth she tosses into Zuniga's eyes, sand on which she traces mysterious words and symbols. We never discussed it, it was simply done. I am struck, sometimes confused, by how little we talk: to be more precise, in fact we do talk a great deal at certain times – but almost never *before* something. As little as possible before an improvisation, an exercise or scene: and it's the same thing on the organizational level of the work. Of course this demands a great deal of concentration at every moment, where we are in the work at this precise instant. Above all, the fact of approaching each scene in this way, with no prior discussion or justification, enables a natural life to emerge as the essential point of reference.

Today we go back to the toreador scene again. Three or four improvisations during which Peter intervenes much more than usual, directly outlining specific elements, feeding individual understanding. (I seem to be contradicting what I wrote a few lines above, but today's an exception proving the rule). The two baritones are asked to alternate in the role of Escamillo. For the moment their ways of living this scene are diametrically opposed, to such an extent that it is impossible to construct the scene around common elements. One of them makes Escamillo a very introverted person: the other presents him as someone overflowing with vitality. Peter makes no attempt to force the two versions to come together, and for the moment we are left with two distinct *mise-en-scène* for the aria.

Saturday, 17 October

To tie the last scene together – the duo followed by Carmen's death – Peter asked the singers to improvise freely, to search, to commit themselves fully: for the moment without referring to the outline scenario we use for all the other scenes. At the end of this run-through, during the discussion Hélène suggests that Carmen starts to yell mournfully at the sight of Escamillo's corpse. Typical response from Peter: 'Perhaps. But that sort of thing cannot be discussed in this way. Try it in the space.' At such moments, I'm flabbergasted, dumb-struck:

the idea seems very cumbersome to me. It doesn't matter to Peter: perhaps he likes the idea, perhaps he hates it, perhaps in reality he refuses to make up his mind aprioristically. He entrusts the task of deciding to the life of a performance when it is put into practice onstage: not to discussed ideas, in a vacuum. Of course I am bound to schematize and idealize. For two years in one way or another this performance has been in preparation, and all sorts of ideas must have fallen by the wayside by this stage. But in rehearsal the enormous confidence placed in the vital invention of bodies is a fundamental building block. All the exercises, the working rhythms, the ways of approaching each step in the work, of improvising, of 'fixing a scene', then of reinventing and reanimating within this framework: every aspect concentrates and crystallizes around the search for invention and life. Placing the actor in a position where he is responsible for bringing, inventing, feeding life at every moment. Are we witnesses to the abolition of the director? First of all there is this fantastic creative demand made on the actors and singers. But behind this demand, there is someone called the 'director': with all that he brings in his own right: a working direction, a research style, theatrical techniques.

Wednesday, 21 October

We have run through the first four or five scenes. Peter's only instruction was to be as free as possible in relation to the *mise-en-scène* fixed to date, provided that true relationships are established at every moment. At times, it fell apart: at others, astonishing material was thrown up: brand new inventions, brought to bear in the course of a scene or a song. And that's something new: the singers in turn are seen to be fully capable of improvising. Immediately after this half run-through, we noted down and fixed the new elements of the improvisations.

Week of 27 to 30 October

Peter seems to be leading the singers in real interpretation classes. How to avoid getting stuck in a mechanical Habanera, how to make the Bohemian song into an authentic song, how to find a true phrasing for Micaëla: all part of the *mise-en-scène* work. For example, in order to find a quality of rejoicing in the Bohemian song, with no other end than the joy of singing (and with no particular attention paid to the words), we all gather around Carmen, calling for her to sing. We clap, whistle, stroke her, dance – until the song finds its own movement, vibrant, leaping into the air and taking flight in the singular joy of singing. The Habanera is very long, some people find it difficult to find a bonding coherent line:

Peter takes each couplet in turn, outlining its shape and thrust, the progression of movement; he calls for different vocal qualities – tenderness, excitement, orgasm, profane earthy love, passion . . . Black magic, sorcery, forces of the earth . . .

A circle exercise. Take the phrase '*Je cherche quelqu'un qui me reconnaisse*'. A single word is given to each person around the circle: the first one says '*je*', the next one '*cherche*', and so on, the aim of the exercise being to pass the words around the circle in sequence as a real phrase delivered quite naturally. Of course the difficulty is in not allowing the utterance to become mechanical: you must respond to impulses and nuances, pass them on. A single phrase is made up of all sorts of subtle inflections: ideally it should be the same for a whole dialogue, even for a scene and indeed the performance in its entirety. Openness to and respect for the linking of words (phrases, gestures, situations, etc.) demands a high degree of attention to the natural life of words and their evolution.

From Thursday, 5 November to Saturday, 7 November

On the Thursday, an extraordinary audience: we come into contact with our neighbours, people we have been bumping into in the local area for the last two months. An audience which laughs freely, has a good time, not at all stuffy. They applaud at the end of every aria. Zuniga causes a stir on each of his appearances.

Before Saturday's public run, we all meet in the dressing-rooms to evaluate where we are. Peter details the coming days' work: it will deal particularly with the performance's dynamic. There's a problem with the through-line of actions: sometimes the impetus is interrupted, or slackens a notch. We must arrive at the point when there is never a diminishment of energy and direction within an aria or between two scenes.

The performance should be approached as a wave that rises and rises, never falling off. The wave comprises both comic and tender moments, it moves forward incessantly. This dynamic focus must be found, as in a symphony. Usually the orchestra leader directs this progress: everyone is responsible for it here.

Peter goes on: 'I don't like ideological messages. There's something useless about them. But we can convey something to the audience. We are a small group of human beings. If our way of living and working is infused with a certain quality, this quality will be perceived by the audience, who will leave the theatre subliminally coloured by the working experience we have lived together. Perhaps that is the small contribution we can make, the only thing we have to convey to other human beings.'

From Tuesday, 10 November, to Saturday, 14 November

Every evening this week, a preview with a paying audience: during the day, we continue to rehearse. Exercises and meetings enable Peter to clarify further elements. The relationships with the characters: 'One part of you is Don José, another part is Laurence. And this other part must also be mobilized and present.' The relationship between singing and life: 'Our thoughts move much more quickly than what we sing. If you only perform the words that are sung, something false comes into the performance. In the same way, if the body only obeys and responds to the apparent music, the work is false: turn down the sound during an opera broadcast on television, and it becomes grotesque. It leads to an odd sort of ballet, dull and artificial. One must get to the point at which the body lives with its impulses, with our thoughts, at their natural speed.'

Certain things in the production are still changing: sometimes mere details, sometimes more than that. Peter tells me: 'As you see, I am now able to work on a mass of details, we don't get bogged down in them. A month ago, it would have been impossible. Generally, a considerable amount of time is lost in devoting oneself to these details too soon. In the same way, I am able to change many things at the last moment: given the kind of work we have already done, it doesn't pose any substantial problems. In the past I have changed a whole *mise-en-scène* at the last moment. The actors were terrified that they wouldn't remember: but in fact there were no difficulties.'

Translated by David Williams, December 1986,
Les Voies de la Création Théâtrale XIII.

The Tragedy of Carmen: A Review
by Frank Rich

Frank Rich, critic on the New York Times, *applauded Brook's* Carmen *as a magical modernist tragedy, a hybrid fusion of opera and theatre.*

For his *Tragédie de Carmen*, Peter Brook has transformed the Vivian Beaumont's stage into a bullring carpeted with gravel and earth. It's an arena buffeted on every side by fate, and its round shape is echoed in every step of this production's relentless thrust.

When we first meet the gypsy temptress Carmen, she tosses tarot cards into a small circle of rope placed on the dirt. When we last see her 80 minutes later, she and her outcast soldier lover, Don José, make one final walk around the ring before meeting up with the destiny those cards have dealt. Many other circles come in between – drawn in sand and outlined in rope – but the largest of them all is not seen, only felt: it's the noose that Mr Brook, through the astonishing power of his art, steadily tightens around the audience's throats.

The impact of this *Carmen* is so strong that even the evening's inevitable climax makes us gasp. The gasp is not motivated by surprise: as Mr Brook's *Carmen* is an adaptation of Georges Bizet's opera, we know that José will ultimately rip a knife into the heroine's heart. We gasp because Mr Brook has forced us to feel the fated denouement as if it were new again. In a world rife with aesthetic overkill, this director has found the one way to put savagery back into tragedy: complete and utter simplicity.

Yet the evening is not just an emotional purging. There are other wonders of lighter effect – slapstick comedy played at silent-movie pace and gravely beautiful romantic tableaux cast in a Goyaesque glow. Magic is everywhere, and to appreciate it a theatregoer need only bring an open mind. You'll get the most from this *Carmen* if you focus on what it contains rather than what it leaves out.

What's been left out is much of the letter and some of the spirit of what may be the world's most popular piece of musical theatre. Mr Brook and his collaborators, the screenwriter Jean-Claude Carrière and the composer Marius Constant, have demolished their source: they've removed roughly half of Bizet's score and retained only four singing roles from the original Meilhac-Halévy libretto; they've stripped away the traditional settings; they've cut the orchestra down to 14 pieces and shoved the surviving musicians into the wings.

And what, you ask, remains? Not Bizet's *Carmen*, that's for sure. This version is no substitute for the glorious original and can't be taken as such. Nor have we regained the whole of Prosper Mérimée's *Carmen*, the novella that inspired Bizet and to which the current collaborators have returned for some of their revisions. But neither do we have a pop *Carmen*, reduced to its greatest hits. If that were the creators cynical intention, they wouldn't have excised one of the biggest hits, the Act II quintet, or reduced another, the 'Cigarette Song', to an incidental musical joke. Even the music that remains has been re-arranged and radically reordered. The overture turns up 15 minutes before the end, in the sacrilegious form of a recording.

No, *La Tragédie de Carmen* must instead be seen as a new, pointedly retitled work that bends Bizet's score and themes, like found objects in a collage, to reflect the concerns of its creators. It's a modernist tragedy that opens with a Beckett image – Carmen emerges from what might be a dung heap – and continues to pile up sparsely populated stage pictures that ache with desolation and loneliness. The setting can hardly even pass for Spain any more. The bullring is backed by a grey wall of wood that is nothing if not the void that Mr Brook has been exploring at least as far back as his *Endgame* inspired *King Lear* of two decades ago.

One can also hear the voice of Mr Carrière, the scenarist of Luis Buñuel's late films, including *Belle de Jour*. The production's few props, mainly knives and cigars, are phallic. The action is charged with dirty, roughhouse sex and violence – twin passions that are interwoven with incendiary force. The once angelic Micaëla is now in full-fledged pursuit of José's affections; she and Carmen tumble into the dirt in a catfight. José's obsessive jealousy drives him to commit two murders unknown to the original opera. Escamillo, the matador, is now a preening whore-house roué who delivers his 'Toreador Song' as a narcissistic sexual proposition.

Heated up and stripped of its social context, *Carmen* is no longer a conflict between Carmen's liberated gypsy passions and José's im-prisoning bourgeois values. Carmen and José are now equal partners in a raw, brutal tale of mutual self-destruction that's fuelled by both lust and existential bloodlust – and is as deadly for others as it is for themselves. The writing and staging are pitched accordingly, from the repeated emphasis on Bizet's death-intoned card aria (the first music we hear) to the hallucinatory telescoping of the story. This *Carmen* is indeed written like a Buñuel screenplay: fragments of the original libretto, sprinkled with new dialogue, have been reassembled to achieve the associative shape and force of an archetypal nightmare.

Mr Brook's direction achieves its own dreamlike intensity through stark, fluent, exquisitely composed movement. His staging is of a piece with the other so-called 'magic carpet' shows he's done with his Paris-based International Centre of Theatre Research. In the past, however, Mr Brook has at times tried to realize his goal of creating ritualistic, truly international theatre by inventing sounds and language. How much better the director's strategy works when the universal language isn't gimmicky, nonsensical bird chatter but Bizet's sumptuous music and the French words wedded to it.

That music is effectively sung by performers who share several crucial virtues: they can act, they are sexy and they are young. Liberated from the conductor, the proscenium arch and any vestige of nineteenth-century pageantry, they achieve direct contact with one another and the audience, as well as balletic freedom of movement . . .

The only problem with Mr Brook's *Carmen*, as with his landmark *Midsummer Night's Dream*, is that its lessons will undoubtedly be misapplied by faddist imitators for years to come. Other directors should not regard the production's radical surgery on a sacred text as either an end in itself or a manifesto calling for the demolition of all operas (or all 'Carmen's) . . .

What one sees and hears can be mesmerizing. In one haunting interlude, Carmen and José find their brief and only peace by pledging their troths in a secluded gypsy campsite bathed in the flickering, rust-coloured twilight of ritual bonfires. Later, when Escamillo makes his final entrance in full matador regalia, the evening's only bright costume is chillingly mocked by the premonitorily embalmed expression on the toreador's face.

But most memorable of all is that final image of Carmen and José – dressed in black, drained of blood, kneeling in the dirt to meet their fate while a mournful, kettle-drum echo of Carmen's first song, the 'Habanera', plays in the distance. Though only 80 minutes have passed in Mr Brook's bullring, we none the less feel we've shared the whole, cruel arc of the lovers' journey – a full circle that has led inexorably from dust to dust.

From the *New York Times*, 18 November 1983

The Mahabharata
(July 1985, Festival d'Avignon)

'In the theatre, the tendency for centuries has been to put the actor at a remote distance, on a platform, framed, decorated, lit, painted, in high shoes – so as to help persuade the ignorant that he is holy, that his art is sacred. Did this express reverence? Or was there behind it a fear that something would be exposed if the light were too bright, the meetings too near? Today, we have exposed the sham. But we are rediscovering that a holy theatre is still what we need. So where should we look for it? In the clouds or on the ground?'

(*The Empty Space*, pp. 71–2)

Peter Brook's 'Great Poem of the World' by David Williams

Extracts from an article commissioned by The National Times, *Australia, in which David Williams applauded 'the theatrical event of the decade', Brook's production of* The Mahabharata.

For over five years most of Peter Brook's energy has been devoted to the realization of an adaptation for theatre of the world's longest narrative poem, the ancient Sanskrit epic *The Mahabharata*. At eighteen volumes and almost one hundred thousand verses in its full form, it is almost eight times the length of *The Odyssey* and *The Iliad* combined, and fifteen times the length of the Bible. Along with the other Sanskrit epic *The Ramayana*, it forms the core of Hindu culture in India and throughout South East Asia, where it has become the common source for most of the dramatic material of dance drama, story-tellers, popular folk players, puppet shows, films and even strip cartoons. It is considered by scholars

353

and public alike as the greatest work of imagination that Asia has produced.

Brook's version was premièred at the 1985 Avignon Festival in France as a twelve-hour cycle of three plays (*The Game of Dice*, *Exile in the Forest*, and *The War*) with a limpid, restrained and timeless French text by Jean-Claude Carrière. It was performed in a remote amphi-theatrical quarry on the banks of the Rhône south of Avignon, the towering cliff face texturally reminiscent of the scarred and pitted back wall of Les Bouffes du Nord, Brook's Parisian base.

Why *The Mahabharata*? As a vision of a society in discord coming to the brink of auto-destruction, Brook believes that this 'great poem of the world' (the meaning of the Sanskrit title) offers us the closest mytho-logical reflection of our own times. It tells the story of two warring families, the evil Kauravas and their exiled cousins the Pandavas, from their mythical and magical origins to their apocalyptic mutual destruc-tion during an eighteen-day battle on the plains of Kurukshetra.

In the tradition of heroic romance, the central narrative in the original is loaded with countless loosely-related episodes. Brook and Carrière have distilled and refined the material to bare the gleaming spine of the narrative. In the same way as the work of Shakespeare or Attar, Sufi author of the twelfth-century *Conference of the Birds*, Brook considers *The Mahabharata* to be 'anonymous', an expression of what is essential in human experience rather than the product of an individual ego; it belongs to the world, not only to India. Brook even suggests that this poem is 'richer in dramatic material than *Conference* and more universal than Shakespeare's complete works'.

This *Mahabharata* presents us with a dense narrative of immense moral complexity and metaphysical ambiguity, exploring the most profound and primordial of human themes: self-discovery, the forces of moral and personal determination and predestination, man in society and man's destruction of that society. While resolutely refusing any easy answers – politically, psychologically, morally – it constantly gives flesh to a positive attitude in the face of a contradictory plurality of experi-ences, within which personal and universal are indissolubly intertwined.

In performance, parallels with the Western literary tradition (par-ticularly Shakespeare and Homer) abound. However, all is left open, suggested. So, for example, the tragic figure of Dhritarashtra, an old king blind from birth who can only ever hear second-hand reports of the actions of others, comes to life in an astonishing performance by the facially ravaged Ryszard Cieslak. He saws and spits his way through the text, disinterring echoes of Lear, Gloucester and Oedipus.

In some ways a full reflection and realization of all Brook's Paris-based research work since 1970, *The Mahabharata* is the most spectacularly conceived of productions, reflecting elements from a variety of popular theatre traditions, as well as Asian dance and martial art forms. Unlocated historically and geographically like all Brook's work (although Indian culture is visible in many more ways here than, for example, Persia was in *Conference*), the performance is marked by a consciously naïve mixture of styles, traditions, races and accents. Everywhere we recognize evidence of the journeys to Africa, the Middle East, Asia and even Australia. The only determinant in this hotch-potch of conventions, some borrowed directly – the Kathakali curtain – others invented and erased in an instant, is that what works, works: the ultimate theatrical sanction in a style of theatre characterized in truth by an absence of imposed unity of style.

The performance is essentially the telling of a story by a group of mixed nationality to an assembled ring of spectators. Indeed, the entirety of the performance is enacted for the entertainment and edification of an unnamed young boy, almost continuously onstage. We watch the tale of his ancestors unfold through his eyes, for he is our representative. The performance begins with an actor/fabulist quietly delivering a third-person narration directly addressed to the boy and the spectators. The poem he has composed in his mind, with its aim of 'writing *dharma* into the hearts of men', is also dictated to an amanuensis, the elephant-god Ganesha.

Above all, *The Mahabharata* seems to represent the ultimate refinement of Brook's ascetic use of minimal scenic means to maximum effect. As is usual in his work, décor is deliberately limited throughout. A deliberate quality of naïvety at all levels of performance – immediacy of text, clarity and directness of forms, the coexistence of elements from different popular theatre traditions – is perhaps most apparent in the childlike simplicity and legibility of Chloé Obolensky's costumes, materials and objects.

The white robes of the saintly Bhishma alone remain pure and unmarked by the battle, although he has fought at the very epicentre of the carnage. When Karna is made king, a new swathe of elegant silk is simply placed around his neck. Similarly, when Yudhishthira wagers the Pandava kingdoms, properties and his own family in the game of dice, it is the saffron and white scarves of his brothers and himself that are snatched and lost to the Kauravas. The death of a young king is signalled by dipping the corner of a vivid scarlet cover into the waters of a river. Some costuming is satirical, even darkly comical. The flapping black capes of the Kauravas preparing for battle – suspended at different heights across the back wall – suggest huge clumsy crows.

Virtually the only objects used throughout, apart from an arsenal of gruesome weaponry, are sticks and bamboo screens; they serve as bows, arrows, war machines, shields, tents, shelters, beds, even 'invisible force fields'. Space too is non-specific, virtual, mobile – as open, free and inviting as the Elizabethan theatre's *tabula rasa*. Swathes of Indian material are laid on the bare earth to establish a constantly redefined location; we jump in time and space in the twinkle of an eye, both dimensions condensed or distended effortlessly. And all four elements are omnipresent, active and protean in this most elemental of stories.

The beaten red *earth* of the egg-shaped playing space – Mother Earth, source and end of all, and the storyteller's milieu in an Indian village. The free-flowing *water* of a river beside the back wall – life, movement and fertility in Ganga, the river goddess ancestor of the protagonists and of Hindus to this day. The enclosed water of a pool – fixed, sterile, a reflective surface to mirror the action, a place for refreshment and ritual ablution, a place to die. Candle *flame* as illumination, invocation, purification and creativity, and ball of flame as weapon, injurious to humanity. The *air* that we share with the actors and, in Avignon, with the open sky above us.

The central chariot confrontation between Arjuna and Karna is a masterpiece of understatement and economy. Their charioteers roll a single wooden cartwheel (the wheel of fortune and 'dharma') before them at high speed, crack whips, mime horses. Eventually the elements conjoin to affect the course of events; suddenly, inexplicably, mud entraps Karna's wheel, holding it fast, rendering him impotent and defenceless. The earth cries out to stop the carnage.

The performance in general is marked by an exacting sense of the visually exciting. A scarlet-faced figure of death, a Kathakali/martial-art hybrid, dances around the thrusts of an opponent in slow-motion, then floats off into darkness with tiny steps, his propulsion apparently generated by the hissing blades of a spring sword he whirls around his head. Arjuna's unwitting confrontation with Shiva is both disturbing and comic (the division between the two is often blurred in Brook's work). The young warrior's arrows are no match for the deity's own prodigious and elemental powers – he manipulates two tiny yellow flags whose movement through the air shatters the silence like the muffled echo of a distant thunderclap. During the frenzied, stylized battle scenes of *The War*, while actors openly toss handfuls of ochre powder into the air (the dust and smoke of battle) a percussive score improvised by musicians visible to one side underlines the starkly disciplined ensemble manoeuvres and sudden freezes. Our perspective is multi-directional, continually evolving, as in a film.

A number of pyrotechnic images etch themselves into the memory. A small blue tongue of fire snakes its way through the sand in the wake of a celestial nymph, like a comet's tail. A magic circle of flame entraps a group of warriors, forcing them to observe a vision they had invoked (but no longer wish to see) by creating the circle around the pool. In the next scene, charred sand rings the pool in black, like kohl around a glistening eye; it has become a poisoned lake. A torchlit battle/ballet, conducted in growing darkness, culminates in a terrible white explosion, a magnesium flare of positively nuclear dimensions at the foot of the cliff, as the 'ultimate weapon' is finally unleashed. A pall of acrid smoke engulfs stage and spectators.

It is also a work brimming with disarmingly simple images of violence. The giant Bhima tears open his enemy's stomach grotesquely, driving his bared teeth into the abdomen; he re-emerges triumphantly bloodied with a lacerated elastic red ribbon clenched taut between his teeth. On hearing of the death of his beloved son, the master warrior Drona (Yoshi Oida) abandons the battle to acquiesce passively to death with the silent dignity of a samurai facing 'seppuku'. Subaquatically, slowly, he lifts a massive earthenware water carrier as if to wash the dust and sweat from his lips for the last time. Instead he empties its contents over his head, for it is full of blood; steeped in gore, death is a merciful release.

Finally Brook has reached a culmination of his synthesis of theatre and film techniques in *The Mahabharata*. Like cinematographers, Brook and his actors concentrate our focus of attention on a single individual, a group, a simple telling detail (the close-up), then rapidly expand it outwards to take in the whole (wide/deep focus).

In one scene, Arjuna (Vittorio Mezzogiorno) prepares himself to shoot blindfolded at a target, like a Zen master. The lights dim to a virtual blackout – his blindfold – as he kneels inches from the spectators, taking aim towards the invisible back wall, quietly explaining his actions to us. The moments of immobility and silence as he clears his mind are charged, focused, meditative. At the sudden and mysterious whipping sound of an arrow discharged, full lights shoot up to reveal the entire court assembled in all its pomp and glory: an explosion of sound, colour and light. To cheers and congratulations, Arjuna watches as a bird-kite floats down towards him from an unspecified source at a great height, an

arrow lodged in one of its wings; he catches it before it hits the ground.
The movement from the privacy and intimacy of intense concentration
to grand public spectacle, from 'blindness' to sumptuous sight, is
remarkable for we have shared Arjuna's own perspective, his personal
journey.

A final example occurs in the death scene of the 'immortal' warrior
Bhishma on which the outcome of the battle, and by inference the
predicament of the universe as a whole, hinges. The scene is built
entirely around the cinematic technique of slow-motion. As Arjuna
kneels in silence, draws back the imaginary string of his illustrious bow
Gandiva and takes aim, all freeze. Krishna, smiling agent of Arjuna's
resolve and of 'dharma', plucks the bamboo arrow from the bow and
carries it slowly twisting through the air towards Bhishma's heart a few
paces away.

The suspense in the extension of the instant between life and death is
concentrated by the silent immobility of those present and the unearthly
enigmatic smile of Krishna, victim of his own prescience. A fragment of
extemporal 'holiness' in the dislocation from habitual time of a 'moment
of truth', like the deceleration of real time at the moment of a matador's
delivery of the *coup de grâce*. As the arrow strikes home – with child-like
gravity, Krishna plants it in Bhishma's clothing seconds later – the
onlookers erupt in a frenzy of cries and movement, Bhishma collapses
mortally wounded, and the baleful drone of the *nagaswaram* (an
anguished cousin of the Western oboe) sings out like the cry of a
wounded elephant. Linear sequential time returns, the narrative is
pursued relentlessly, renewed.

Conference ended with the birds at the threshold of Paradise; the final
image of *The Mahabharata* presents us with a vision of Paradise as a
gentle place of music, food, conversation and harmony. The blind can
see, the wounded and slaughtered are restored, all animosity is forgotten. The players quietly and without pretence celebrate their collective
bringing into life of a resplendent '*teatrum mundi*'. In Avignon the sense
of rebirth was heightened by synchronizing the performance's end with
the first light of dawn colouring the stone of the quarry: a new day for a
new world.

Brook gives us new eyes.

March 1986

The Mahabharata: An Introduction, by Jean-Claude Carrière

Jean-Claude Carrière's preface to the C.I.C.T. text of Le Mahabharata

The *Mahabharata* is one of the world's greatest books. It is certainly the longest poem ever written. The Sanskrit original comprises more than one hundred thousand verses. It is about fifteen times longer than the Bible.

The first versions, collections of ancient stories, go back as far as the fifth or sixth century BC. The process of composition continued for seven or eight hundred years, until a more or less definitive form was found in only the third or fourth century AD. Throughout this process, numerous additions were made to the original narrative, and even into the twentieth century, all sorts of variants have continued to appear, the fruit of different provinces, traditions, interpretations and schools of writing.

The *Mahabharata*, simply called 'The Epic' in Indian tradition, is the major source of a very rich literary tradition in Sanskrit. This one poem is the origin of a multitude of beliefs, legends, philosophical reflections, lessons, characters – all still forming part of modern Indian life.

It was totally unknown in Europe until the eighteenth century. A first edition of the *Bhagavadgita* on its own was published in London in 1785, in a translation by Charles Wilkins, and in Paris in 1787, translated from the English into French by Monsieur Parraud.

In the nineteenth century, a French orientalist by the name of Hippolyte Fauche undertook the colossal task of translating the entire work into French, with only two hundred subscribers to back him. After many years of effort, he died. His work was taken up by Doctor L. Ballin, who also died before reaching the end. This translation, although sometimes very beautiful, is often imprecise or even incomprehensible. In any case it is unfinished. And no full text of the world's greatest poem exists in French to this day.

Peter Brook has described our astonishment at those first stories from *The Mahabharata* that Philippe Lavastine told us one evening in 1975. For five years, our meetings with Philippe Lavastine became increasingly regular, until we had heard the poem without reading it. I took notes and, in 1976, started to put together a rough draft for a possible play.

Subsequently, with the advice and encouragement of various others (particularly Madeleine Biardeau, the author of several works on Hinduism), we embarked on an actual reading of the text. First of all separately: Peter Brook read it in English, I read it in French. We then read it at length together, comparing translations, with the watchful collaboration of Marie-Hélène Estienne. After this period of detailed study, which went on for more than two years, several journeys to India allowed us to gather all sorts of impressions and images: from dance, cinema, puppet shows, theatre, popular festivals.

Although as far as we know no full adaptation of *The Mahabharata* exists (the film director Satyajit Ray worked on one over a long period of time, but eventually had to abandon it for lack of funds), numerous episodes from the poem remain fully alive in India and Indonesia today. They appear in countless forms – they are the staple material of hundreds of strip cartoons, which can be found everywhere.

This kind of research was simultaneous with the discovery of a small number of revelatory texts. Some short plays by Rabindranath Tagore, freely adapted from the poem, a brilliant essay by Irawati Karve entitled *Yuganta*, and the long series *Krishnavarata* (the 'descent' of Krishna) compiled by K. M. Munshi, all provided us with invaluable keys which enabled us to develop the characters in a more subtle, profound and, in some sense, realistic way.

The Indians to whom we spoke about our project, once they had overcome their initial amazement, quickly turned out to be more than amenable. The idea that the great Indian epic poem was going to be performed for the first time in the West intrigued and interested them. We received the advice of professors and the blessings of saints. In Calcutta we were welcomed by an enthusiastic man who was in the process of finishing a complete translation of *The Mahabharata* into English verse (he calls it a 'transcreation'). This man, Professor P. Lal, encouraged us enormously. He is convinced that the great Indian poem can appeal to the rest of the world in other forms.

Maha in Sanskrit means 'great' or 'total'; *Maha-radjah* is a great king. *Bharata* is first of all the name of a legendary character, then that of a family or a clan. The title could be understood as 'The Great Story of the Bharatas'. However, in addition, *Bharata* by inference means 'Hindu', and, in more general terms, 'man'. We are dealing with 'The Great Story of Humanity'.

In fact this 'great poem of the world' tells of the long and violent animosity that separated two groups of cousins, the Pandavas, five brothers, and the one hundred Kauravas. This family quarrel, which explodes and develops to encompass the empire of the world, culminates in an immense struggle which puts at risk the fate of the whole universe.

Most specialists admit that the events described in *The Mahabharata* have their origins in history. Indian tradition locates the great battle of Kurukshetra in the year 3200 BC. Certain historians have tried to see in the epic poem a more or less faithful reflection of the wars between Dravidians and Aryans, which took place in the second millennium BC. Others dispute this interpretation, insisting instead on the mythical aspects of the poem. Others underline the importance of the books of teaching (political, social, moral, religious) and tend to see *The Mahabharata* as a lengthy treatise of royal initiation.

Commentators also point out that the pages that sing the praises of brahmins (and there are many of them) seem to have been added at a relatively late date.

Interesting as they are, we did not spend much time on these various commentaries. In our eyes, this immense poem, which unleashes a flowing river of inexhaustible richness, defies all analysis – structural, thematic, historical or psychological. Doors which open endlessly lead on to other doors. You cannot grasp *The Mahabharata* in the palm of your hand. Multiple ramifications, sometimes apparently contradictory, follow on from one another and become entangled without our ever losing sight of the central action, which comes in the form of a threat: we live in a time of destruction. Everything points directly at it. But can this destruction be avoided?

The actual writing started in the autumn of 1982. It continued throughout 1983 and 1984, when the actors' research and work connected with the music began.

At the beginning of rehearsals, in September 1984, the play was written, but not in a rigid or definitive way; countless modifications were made throughout the nine-month work period. For quite some time, it was difficult to say what length we were aiming for, how many hours of performance, even how many shows would be necessary.

It became clear fairly quickly that we would have to remove the majority of secondary stories, some of which are very beautiful. The narrators of *The Mahabharata* like to bring the great river to a halt for a moment, as if they find themselves in some peaceful and protected bend in its course, in order to tell another story, which illustrates or comments upon the central one. Some of these stories can take up as much as fifty pages: the rivalry between Drona and Drupada, the love of Nala and Damayanti. Others are shorter: the artful bravery of Savitri who snatches her husband from death. Some, like the love of Arjuna and the daughter of the king of the snakes, scarcely fill a page.

On a number of occasions we tried to begin directly within the conflict, the drama. And every time it seemed to us that the family's fabulous origins – the adventures and vows of distant mythical ancestors – were indispensable, even if that necessitated forty minutes in performance before the appearance of the principle characters. Similarly, it became clear that the author-storyteller Vyasa was also necessary, even if the characters that he has created (he is both their author and their father) sometimes break free from him, even if Ganesha and later Krishna contest the reality of his invention. So there was already a clear line: from a mythical reality (under the direction of a storyteller, presenting demi-gods onstage) to increasingly human characters, who bring with them theatre.

There are sixteen main characters in *The Mahabharata*. Each of these characters is clearly drawn and often complex; they all have a particular story which is instrumental, directly or indirectly, in the central action. We have only left out one of them, Vidura, half-brother of Pandu and Dhritarashtra; his mother was a servant and as a result he was unable to exercise royal power. Vidura is a wise and moderate man who gives excellent advice; his actions are minimal. All of his interventions – almost always verbal – have been easily assimilated by other characters: Bhishma, Yudhishthira or Vyasa himself.

Krishna posed a particular problem. Today it is almost impossible to separate Krishna from the immense body of legend that built up around him until the Middle Ages. In *The Mahabharata*, or at least in the parts that are generally felt to be the oldest in the poem, there are as yet no clear indications to suggest that he is one of the 'avatars' (the terrestrial incarnations) of Vishnu. He is a man very much like others – he grows old, he becomes tired, at times he is 'surprised' by events, even 'alarmed'. Violently bloody and mysterious forces destroy his town. And he dies, killed by a hunter in a forest. A sudden death, only briefly touched upon.

Certain commentators, such as Norbert Claes in *Conscience and Consciousness*, have maintained that, in the original *Mahabharata*, Krishna is only Vasudeva: in other words, the best, the highest of men, a paradigmatic person who can only exist once in the same epoch – but not God.

And yet the poem describes certain of his miraculous powers. Krishna lengthens Draupadi's dress indefinitely. Through an illusion, he makes his enemies believe that the sun has set early. He possesses an irresistible weapon, a disc, which he uses to decapitate Sisupala. And above all, just before the battle, he gives to his friend Arjuna the *Bhagavadgita*, a famous text in which he expresses himself as the divinity and reveals his 'universal form'.

Man or god? Obviously it is not up to us to decide. All historical or theological truth (which is by definition debatable) is out of bounds for us; we can only aim at a certain dramatic truth. That's why we have chosen to retain both of the faces of Krishna which are in the original work, and to show their opposition, the continual interplay that animates them.

In order to adapt *The Mahabharata*, to transform an immense epic poem into a play (or rather three plays), it was necessary to invent new scenes, while at the same time respecting the flow and meaning of the story (about half of the scenes in our version do not exist in the original) – in this way confronting characters who never meet in the poem, and allowing them to plumb their own depths, to go to the very ends of themselves – without, as much as is possible, the intervention of our own conceptions, our authoritarian judgements, our twentieth-century analyses. All these characters closely examine the rectitude of their own actions, their 'dharma', they all confront their idea of destiny.

It was also necessary (particularly in the second play, which covers the long years of exile) to find a space and a time which would allow a rapid and fluid concentration of action, without either compromising energy or stifling mystery.

As far as the actual writing is concerned, all archaic or archaistic language soon seemed unacceptable, for it would have inevitably evoked cumbersome images of the Middle Ages and of our old tragedies. On the other hand, all familiar, modern, 'slangy' language was of course impossible. We also had to reject all those stilted and time-worn words of French classicism and neo-classicism ('tormented', 'afflicted', 'wrath'). All that's left is a restrained, simple and precise vocabulary, and the possibility of juxtaposing or opposing words that do not usually coexist side by side.

The detailed choice of language posed a problem that we would have to confront again in the production, the music, the costumes, the colours, the properties – 'India's part', you could call it. It was necessary to write in French without writing a French play, to open our language up to certain rhythms, certain images from the East, while trying not to fall into the other trap: the exact opposite, a shortsighted and picturesque use of local colour.

While we have retained the characters' names, we have chosen to eliminate most Sanskrit words by finding equivalents. With two significant exceptions: the word 'kshatrya' which in ancient India designated a precise social category – it can be translated neither by the word 'noble', nor 'warrior', nor even 'knight' (barring an enforced assimilation which would resemble a king of linguistic colonization). The same goes for the word 'dharma', which refers to a central notion in the poem. 'Duty', 'justice', 'truth' are all unsatisfactory. 'Dharma' is the law regulating world order. It is also the secret and personal order that all people carry within themselves, which they must obey, individual 'dharma' in some way constituting a guarantee of cosmic order – if it is respected.

Indian tradition tells us; 'Everything in *The Mahabharata* is elsewhere. What is not in *The Mahabharata* is nowhere.'

Originally published as an introduction to the C.I.C.T. text of *The Mahabharata*, Paris, 1985; translation by David Williams

The Language of Stories

Extracts from Georges Banu's interview with Peter Brook

I think that today people are just beginning to recognize, in a clear and simple way, the quantity of languages that exist. Particularly in theatre, where it has become a cliché to say that other aspects of experience, and not only words, form a language: the language of the body, and so on. And it tends to be forgotten that a story itself is a language. We tend to take a story as an end in itself, something simply to be told and heard, without realizing that the very principle of myth is in the telling of the story and the full experience of its charm (in other words, quite simply following the plot, wondering who these people are, what they are going to do, what's going to happen). At the same time we receive impressions which taken together express something which couldn't be expressed in such a profound way uniquely through spoken or written language.

In the theatre a clear example can be seen in the indefinably potent fascination that the early work of Robert Wilson provoked. His work allowed us to see that a continuous flow of images is a language. And in our century there have been many experiments in cinema and theatre in which, by removing the narrative element, people have endeavoured to communicate by means of a flow of images with no clear anecdotal thread linking them.

In some ways, the *Mahabharata* is a culmination of a whole series of experiments that I have made – like all experiments, a way of returning to a source. We have come back to the fact that the best way of making the contents of the *Mhb* available is to follow the story. In the *Mhb* itself, we are often told something which seems rather strange to us: if you listen to this story, you will be somehow different by the end; the very fact of listening to the story will make you virtuous, etc. It is in this sense that a true story contains within it an 'action'; and in the *Mhb* this action goes beyond any analysis of contents. It's very difficult for the Western mind to accept this idea of a mythical language. We accept it to a certain point, but ultimately at another level we think it is about this or that. In fact it's exactly the opposite. The 'this' and 'that' are approximations which become more precise when the apparent precision of analysis gives way to the precision of the image, the flow of the story as it unfolds.

365

A traveller involved in theatre

I have spent all my life travelling. When I began to work, I felt more like a traveller involved in theatre than a director who travelled to relax or better himself. I think that there has been an entirely natural movement in these journeys. I have spent a lot of time in Europe, Africa, the United States, South America, and my exploration of the East has happened progressively through the Middle East, Afghanistan and into India. Today I would very much like to go further. I have not yet been to south-east Asia, China or Japan, but these are perspectives for the future.

Rooted in the earth of India

If you want to compare the *Mahabharata* with *Conference of the Birds*, I would suggest that *Conference* as a story takes place on an imaginary level. The birds talk to each other, and their language is no more Persian than it is French. So it is situated in a fictional, vaguely Oriental universe, to free it from any specific and familiar location. Also there is no realistic context in this story. And we used masks for the simple reason that it takes place in the imagination.

The *Mhb* is much meatier. It exists continually on two levels: that of *Conference*, the level of the imaginary, and that of *The Ik*, the level of what's grounded and rooted. Both are there. And as usual we're not trying to show, but to suggest. We are telling a story which, on the one hand, is universal, but, on the other, would never have existed without India. To tell this story, we had to avoid allowing the suggestion of India to be so strong as to inhibit human identification to too great an extent, while at the same time telling it as a story with its roots in the earth of India. If it were to be placed uniquely in the realm of the imaginary, it would both betray and diminish its vitality to some degree. Ganga, the first person to come onstage, is the goddess of a particular river which is central in the thought of all Indians. At the same time, for us, she is an actress making abstract theatre, in as much as she gives the impression of being a goddess who comes from the water, when she is in fact firmly on the ground, with her feet in the water of a stage stream.

Casting an epic

When we were bringing together the group of performers, as usual we did not set out with any schematic ideas in mind. We didn't cast in the spirit of UNESCO, saying that one country will represent such and such a thing. We worked by searching and 'sifting' (as it says in *Conference*). On this level, Marie-Hélène Estienne undertook an enormous amount of work, looking everywhere for actors; that took a lot of time. We held numerous auditions, we saw hundreds of people; we travelled a lot. We even went as far as Dakar to meet Senegalese actors. We also watched film rushes here in Paris to see African actors from other countries . . .

The necessity of having actors capable of speaking French reasonably well imposed certain practical limitations. In addition, we respected our usual criterion: openness in the actor. He must be open internally to the subject matter, and externally to the collective work. As with *The Cherry Orchard* (but not at all like when we established the first group at the Centre, in 1970), here there were jobs to be filled: roles. For example, we looked everywhere for a Bhima, because it's quite rare to find a giant who acts well. We hesitated between several actors before discovering the one who now plays him. Initially we didn't imagine that Bhima would be an African, but we eventually found him in Dakar. And now, after extensive work on this role, Mamadou Dioume can see that all he has within him can serve the part – not only his external qualities, but what's deepest inside him, what comes from his roots.

As far as the Pandavas are concerned, it is made clear from the start that they do not share the same father. Here is a family that does not need to comprise a family in the same way as in *The Cherry Orchard*, for example. On the contrary, since they have different fathers, it's quite plausible that they should be very different from the point of view of race, culture and origin. That widened the horizon from the outset. From there, we tried to make of them a group, a coherent unit. We eventually discovered a certain natural logic: there is something which corresponds with each actor in relation to who he is and what his culture represents. From the very beginning, therefore, we wanted quite different kinds of people. And the fundamental meaning of the Pandavas echoes that of a Brothers Grimm story, *The Five Servants*, that we performed for children here in Paris. These five men have to live and work together because each one complements the others.

Design: finding what's right, what's fresh

Chloé Obolensky and I worked together for many months while we looked for a scenic base for the performance, how to stage it. As always, something which seems very simple is in fact the result of all sorts of abandoned projects: simple solutions never present themselves at the outset. We thought we would need several platforms to designate different areas, we thought about surrounding the performance space with water, and so on. Through a process of elimination we gradually arrived at something which retained the idea of an arena, but meant suppressing certain small anecdotal details in the Bouffes that we have used a great deal in the past: the doors, the lateral windows. When I work, two things are always present in my mind: find what is right for the piece, and find what is fresh. In fact we had exhausted certain of the Bouffes' possibilities – and it must never be allowed to become a museum. In addition to blocking the lateral openings, we wanted to give the crumbling beauty of the Bouffes (which, although this is the theatre's real beauty, had started to get rather sordid and dirty) a new, luminous quality, and this has meant some repainting. In some ways, given the reality of the Bouffes, we have had to reimagine it. And a scenographic base has been found in the elements themselves – water, fire, earth.

The fact of playing with and implicating the audience (by the actor's penetrating the auditorium, for example) is an effect, and like everything else it wears itself out. It becomes something we've seen before, it loses its freshness. Beyond that there's also something else: in plays like *The Cherry Orchard* or *Carmen*, the image is sufficiently close to us today for the audience to be able to really believe that it shares this same world. It takes the tiniest provocation of the imagination for us to think we are in the same house as Ranevskaya. And of course that serves to heighten the play's proximity. But in the *Mhb*, the war, for example, has to be treated on two levels constantly. First of all, when necessary, one can play on the great proximity that close-up affords. At the same time, one must remember that this battle is in our world, but not all the time. Showing this war is not the same thing as showing a war from a contemporary or nineteenth-century work. If I had to stage *War and Peace*, I wouldn't adopt the same solution as far as the relationship between audience and war is concerned.

Music: the taste of India

At first I spent a lot of time searching around, because I felt that a nine-hour performance would need an unusually varied kind of music. I even wondered whether we needed a composer on this occasion. I looked everywhere, but apart from Richard Peaslee, I have never found a musician to parallel Jean-Claude Carrière in the writing area: in other words, someone who is a great specialist in his field and at the same time totally committed to what we are doing. (It's true, we did have just such a relationship with Marius Constant for *Carmen*, but oriental music is not his field at all). I saw Middle Eastern and Indian composers, but on every occasion either the composer was completely locked within the Western tradition of scoring, or else he had nothing to suggest beyond what comes naturally in improvised music.

In the end, the richness of the music in this performance comes from the work of Toshi Tsuchitori, who carried out an enormous amount of preparation. He lived in India for two years, travelling on foot from one place to another, listening to all sorts of music. We have ended up looking for a form of music which is neither entirely Indian nor non-Indian, music which has a 'taste' of India. There was a lot of collective work to arrive at a certain tonal colour, which in fact is a direct result of the musicians' own avid research. For example, Kim Menzer spent three months in India learning to play the 'nagaswaram'; he is now the only musician in Europe able to produce this sound. Kim is a wonderful player of wind instruments, but it took him three months to be able to produce the first sound from the nagaswaram.

A number of Indians worked with our musicians to help them find a point of access into the style. They also listened to tapes and records, and travelled to India with all of us. They were in exactly the same situation as the international group, in as much as they were both trying to reflect India through their own understanding and experience, to colour it with their own culture. That's why the music is neither Indian nor non-Indian. Above all, it's theatrical, for it has to respond to the needs of the performance. It serves the same material, the *Mhb*. So the contents of this poem link the performances of racially mixed actors, the music of racially mixed musicians and the work of technicians. Through collaboration, theatrical aim and necessity gradually become clear at every moment, and we are able to find what sustains them . . .

Storytelling: the troubadour and the child

By looking closely at Indian theatre (and we have had to remain open to Indian ways of telling the story), it became immediately apparent that we would have to completely eliminate classical Indian art at every level: in the style of acting, dance, song and music. Because it is an art only accessible to those Indians who have devoted themselves to it for several generations. On the other hand, we saw that there was another style of theatre in India, another way, just as Indian, of telling the *Mhb* story: it exists everywhere, for it's popular. This popular style is exactly like our own, what we call a 'carpet show' in our terminology. It's like *Ubu* – the same way of playing, the same atmosphere. And we believed that in order for the *Mhb* to be simultaneously very close to our audience and at a certain distance from it, we would have to begin from a 'low' point as opposed to a 'high' one. In other words, we would have to find a starting point at a level of very natural contact.

As far as Vyasa is concerned, we could have plumped for a realistic relationship to the story by presenting him as an impressive old guru, a yogi of at least 70 who would tell us the story. But I don't know any actor capable of doing that, and we would have been obliged to remain permanently at that level. The other possibility was to do something which comes from our own work: to introduce a storyteller who is on our side, a Frenchman close to the French audience. Along with Ganesha (Maurice Bénichou is French as well), he establishes a direct contact with the spectators from the very beginning of the performance. Early on in rehearsals, we even started the play with these two, not as characters, but as people talking with the audience. Although that has since been modified, the initial idea was for them to speak directly with the audience. We subsequently found it was more touching to see Vyasa addressing the spectators accompanied by a child. People arrive for something rather solemn and grandiose, and on the contrary at the very beginning they find a very human, very simple atmosphere. But then the actor performing Vyasa gradually becomes something else. In the middle of the play, he becomes a character in it.

The child is there to receive, and to give us what's in the *Mhb* itself. It is a story 'told to' someone. In the original *Mhb*, in fact the story is told to a young king who is in the process of sacrificing all the snakes in the world. This massacre is interrupted when he is told the story of his ancestors so that he will understand what lies before in the future. The whole of the *Mhb* is told so that a young man can prepare for life. We didn't want to follow this literally. In a certain kind of academic theatre, you would have a young king as in the original story. But if you start with a young king, everything is at such a distance that you won't be able to identify with it, or be touched by it. But a child touches us directly. And it is clear that this child's role is to listen to the story. We watch as he listens and asks questions. We sense that for the child in all of us there is a lesson of great immediacy to be learnt in these fabulous adventures from another era.

A positive attitude

Today it's impossible to pretend that we are not in an age when the destruction of the world exists incessantly around us. It's not up to me to suddenly point out to people that the world is in danger, it's all too obvious. But like everyone else I am conditioned by our century. This is why the *Mhb* is something to be heard today. When you read in the paper about what's happening in Beirut, you see in a very shocking way what you already know, but nothing helps you to understand what you can do, how to feel and be if confronted with that. Today nobody can do a thing to stop or influence the course of events. It's an illusion to think that marches, speeches, books, art can change an immense movement that's sweeping the world. You can struggle on and fight, but it must be freed from the illusory belief that it will in any way block this relentless mechanism.

In the *Mhb*, there is a constant appeal to a positive attitude. The *Mhb* tells a story which is as dark, tragic and terrible as our own story today. But tradition allows us to see on every page, in every word, that the attitude when confronted with that situation was not negative, not Spenglerian. There is no pessimistic despair, nihilism, empty protest. It is something else. A way of living in this world in a catastrophic predicament without ever losing contact with what enables man to live and fight on in a positive way. But what does 'positive' mean? It's a word that takes us back to our starting point, and in a very concrete way that points us to the epicentre of the *Bhagavadgita*: should you reject and withdraw from confrontation, should you act, or what? That question 'or what?' is on everyone's lips today, and although the *Mhb* provides no answer, it gives us immense food for thought.

From *Alternatives Théâtrales* 1985:
translation by David Williams

The Bridge of Sand: An Interview with Jean-Claude Carrière

Edited extracts from Georges Banu's interview with Jean-Claude Carrière

The writer's work

Working in the conditions that exist with this group in Paris – able to write with twenty-five people, refining and reworking as and when necessary – is the greatest luxury imaginable for a theatre writer. We are convinced that both Shakespeare and Molière wrote in this same way. Although I put together some rough drafts at the very beginning, I didn't really start to write the play until after our first trips to India. And once rehearsals were under way, I made countless modifications. At first Peter and I would work on the text together, then we invited the actors' participation in this process. They were immediately intrigued by our proposition and, particularly after the group journey to India, they started to defend their characters to me: not the parts, the characters. There was then a lot of work with the public. Their reactions are fascinating because one gets to see what interests them, what's missing. Sometimes a single phrase is sufficient to alter the shape and tone of a whole scene.

In rehearsal, we begin by looking at a scene with the actors. Once, and then a second time. Often we are not happy, so we ask: is it because of the scene itself (in which case it has to be rewritten), or is it because of the actors' work? And there's no absolute answer. Sometimes it's one, sometimes the other. The penultimate part of the writing process is carried out collectively. But for the last part I'm as alone as I was at the beginning, because at a certain point you must decide to work on your own, as a writer. However, the passage through collective writing is indispensable, and I consider it to be a supreme luxury.

The path of dharma

One of the most profound themes in the *Mhb*, and certainly the one that touches me most deeply, is that of the destruction of 'dharma'. At the very beginning, Vyasa says: 'I wrote this poem to inscribe dharma in the hearts of men'. He tosses out this invocation knowing full well that the human species has already entered an age of inevitable destruction: 'Kaliyuga', the age of Kali. It's not something that people can change;

it's their destiny. This period of time lasts several thousands of years, it began with the *Mhb* and we are now bang in the middle of it. You cannot alter it, but within the cycle of destruction and decay, something can be saved.

That's Krishna's precise role in the poem, his mission if you like; if you allow the destroyers to go on destroying, they will indeed destroy everything. On the other hand, if one arrives at a point of crystallization within oneself with regard to dharma – the very task for which we were born – it is possible to save something, to alleviate some of the destruction.

Indian thought is very complicated, it refuses any utopia as far as human beings are concerned. It does not tell you where happiness is, how to reach it. It's very difficult to follow the path of dharma. It's not enough to entrust oneself to God, as in Christianity. Indian thought makes no naïve concessions to human nature. It has no illusions concerning our deepest desires and motives, our '*coeur profond*'. So the task in hand is very hard. It's extremely difficult to save anything given man's motives and desires and the fact that we are living in an era of cosmic destruction. That's why the descent of a god, with his incredible powers, is needed. Krishna shows us that in order to save dharma, in fact you must not respect it – but if you make that into a general rule for everyone, then you're lost. For this reason Krishna's role is essential, in some way he must remain ambiguous and esoteric and die in the end. Gandhari curses him for having resorted to tricks and lies, but something will have been saved. The battle for dharma has to begin again every day; that is the poem's fundamental meaning. The *Mhb* is an astonishingly proud poem, but it's entirely without vanity. It represents a whole world, but it offers no solutions.

The bridge of sand

I'm very fond of one story we left out. A very fervent young man decides that he is going to receive knowledge directly from the gods. So he undertakes extraordinary penances, for the gods can refuse nothing to such a person. He goes up into the Himalayas and decides to remain on one big toe for however long it takes. The gods are thoroughly fed up with him. They tell him that this is not how to obtain knowledge; instead he should work, learn and search for masters. But he will hear nothing of it and continues his penances.

One day, although he is absorbed in the strictest of ascetic austerities, he sees an old man carrying an enormous sack of sand on his back passing by. The old man puts the sack of sand down on a nearby river bank, and drops a fistful of sand in at the water's edge. The strong current immediately sweeps it away. A second handful disappears just as quickly as the first. Although he's deep in meditation, the young man notices this strange activity, and after a time asks the old man: 'What are you doing?' 'What do you mean, what am I doing?' 'Well, what are you doing?' And the old man replies: 'I'm building a bridge.' 'You're building a bridge of sand in the great river? That's totally absurd. Can't you see that the current sweeps away the sand you put in the water every time?' 'Well, it's no more absurd than what you're doing,' replied the old man, who immediately reveals himself to be a god.

In our work on the *Mhb*, this image of the bridge of sand has haunted us.

From *Alternatives Théâtrales*, 1985: translation by David Williams

An Interview with Vittorio Mezzogiorno (Arjuna) by Martine Millon

Vittorio Mezzogiorno is best known as a film actor, taking major roles in Rosi's The Three Brothers *(*I tre fratelli*) Beineix's* The Moon in the Gutter, *and Chéreau's* L'homme blessé: *although he started his career as a stage actor in Italy with Eduardo de Filippo.* The Mahabharata *marked his return to the theatre.*

Brook wants everything to come from the actor, he must find it himself. He doesn't want to impose anything on him, and particularly not a culture that doesn't belong to him. The actors incorporated and assimilated impressions of the Indian world: we had to find whatever resonances it created within our own cultures, our own temperaments and sensations.

I was most struck by the fact that from the very beginning we never rehearsed in the true sense of the word, with its suggestion of repetition: everything was improvized, either starting from the text, from situations related to the text or from pure improvizations. The aim of all of this work was to awaken and stimulate a sensitivity in the body. The intensive physical work on the body was very important: seven months of extremely hard work. Sometimes I didn't understand what was going on. When I first arrived, I was very closed in on myself: I arrived after the work had already started, which didn't help. And then I felt a certain amount of fear. I didn't know anyone, all these different nationalities, so I tended to shut myself off even more, retiring to my corner until things became slightly more understandable.

This body training was not something empty, the acquisition of a particular style or fixed gestural vocabulary: you had to infuse every gesture and movement with your own life and meaning, you must commit all you have. Sometimes we did very light spontaneous things that the actors invented without thinking, like children playing. So for example, over a period of months there were long archery training sessions, very hard and serious sessions: but when we came to rehearse the relevant scenes, we only had small bamboo sticks in our hands – and that's how I found the gesture that is retained in performance. I would never have imagined that after all that work on archery all that would be left in performance would be this simple gesture of a child playing. That really stunned me in some ways: I was knocked out because I think it

375

sums up the characteristics of the working process as a whole. That spontaneous gesture would not have been the same without all of the preparatory work with a real bow.

Brook has an extraordinary way of existing and of allowing us to exist. We created everything on our own, but he controlled every aspect in a concealed way, like a puppeteer. Initially I was very ill at ease: where was the director? With nobody there to tell me what to do, I was lost. He didn't even say, 'Here we work in such and such a way.' Nothing. So in the early stages I felt very distressed and uncomfortable: then after a certain point my survival instinct forced me to understand that what was being asked of me was to free things from within myself, to give, to be myself. So what started as discomfort became freedom. I understood that the actors were not supposed to execute certain prescribed things so much as to participate with their whole being in the creation of something. The actor's performance comes from what he is in himself.

Working on my character has been a unique adventure. For a very long time I felt trapped in the dark. As a character, there's something horrifying about Arjuna. An ordinary character with faults and weaknesses has a particular psychological make-up, chinks through which you can penetrate him: but with a character such as this one, how do you find a way in? He has everything, he's perfect from birth. Yet the worst thing that could happen would be to fix the character on a heroic level: and that is exactly what I did at first. Having not been involved in that much theatre, I suddenly found myself confronted with a character who is a hero, a demigod, a mythical figure, similar to those in the German epic sagas or to Achilles ... Which is not to say that I drew any inspiration from these figures: with such an enormously complex body of work I would have no idea where to start ...

Groping tentatively forward in the dark, I gradually began to understand (and I am still coming to grips with it) what is at the heart of Brook's work: that I have to bring the character ever closer to me, bit by bit, as opposed to my trying to go towards something monumental. Such as I am, I cannot be a hero, but if I see the character as a human being, I can begin to work in a calmer way. One day when I was very lost, Brook said, not directly to me, 'To think of playing a god is madness.' That sentence struck me so forcibly that I started to work in the opposite direction: trying to live with true feelings and situations, forcing myself to make myself available, to open myself to a character such as Arjuna.

And now in performance he has something of the energy of a human being in direct conflict, totally committed to the situation he finds himself in. It's difficult to tell whether he has a heroic quality: unlike in cinema when I am able to see my work, here I have no real perspective on what I'm doing. But perhaps that long period of work on ourselves, the really hard physical work, has helped us to become in some way *better*: it may sound kind of facile, even a little stupid, but I can't think of any other way of putting it.

In the third part, *The War*, although Arjuna does not die in battle, he becomes increasingly besmirched with mud and blood from his wounds. He never stops changing, evolving in the course of the story: he moves on incessantly. At the beginning, he lives life as a game, naïvely: being a warrior hero is a sort of sport to him. He is rich, a legitimate member of a royal family: he has it all. In the second part, he realizes that it is not sufficient to possess all these qualities, he has to work. So he sets out on an initiatory journey through life, embracing experience. In the third part, he confronts his true self. His lengthy refusal to do so is very human. We all have a latent reality within ourselves which waits to be uncovered and embraced: one can either commit oneself to confronting it (which is very difficult) or one can skirt it, pass it by. Similarly, I am gradually getting closer to Arjuna, but it is a long struggle.

May 1985
From *Alternatives Théâtrales*
1985: translation by David Williams

An interview with Andrzej Seweryn (Duryodhana) by Martine Millon

Seweryn has acted in almost 40 films in his native Poland, starring in a number of films by Wajda, including The Man of Marble, The Man of Iron *and* Danton. *For the first 11 years of his career he worked as a stage actor at the Athenao in Warsaw. Since 1980, he has featured in productions in France by directors such as Wajda, Claude Régy, Patrice Chéreau, and Andrei Serban.* The Mahabharata *is his first collaboration with Brook.*

The first difference in Brook's approach I noted was the fact of working for ten months before the première, a period of very intensive and specific work on the body: Brook wants to awaken everything that is within us, every finger, every cell. There was also a great deal of work on the voice and breathing, as well as exercises to learn how to enter a rhythm almost unconsciously. Many of these elements remind me of my early years at theatre school in Warsaw, but here it is a thousand times more precise: and as a result better understood by me than at that time. Brook makes much greater demands, he directs with infinite precision.

During the trip to India, we only truly worked on one or two occasions. We gathered together and were given specific tasks to fulfil. One occasion was at a temple in the forest. Peter asked us all to go out into the woods, and to come back with something. Some gathered leaves, others dry branches, flowers: I brought back a handful of earth. We put all this material in one corner, then began to work on an exercise with our eyes closed. As I was doing it, I suddenly became aware of a strange presence: opening one eye, I saw an Indian woman approach the little altar we had built; she knelt in front of it, prayed and left. For me that was one of the most remarkable moments of the whole journey. It had proved to us quite simply that God is everywhere. Incidentally, on one of our last days in India, Peter suggested that we shouldn't tell others about the trip and our experiences: not because it is secret, but because it's difficult to recount, and it's right that something shared by us should remain between us. As a collective experience, the journey helped cement the group: we finally became a unit after five months of work.

Georges Dumézil in his work on Hindu myth always refers to Duryodhana, the character I play, as 'bad' in inverted commas, as opposed to the 'good' Pandavas. But we were primarily interested in understanding his motivation, we wanted to discover his humanity. It is a European tendency to be intrigued by evil, goodness interests us less: I'm merely using that impulse to make of him someone we can understand. Sanskrit possesses no word for 'evil'. He is a poor victim of his fate: he fulfils his karma. The destruction of the world is never his aim: he believes he is defending his kingdom, he is an idealist. He loves those on his side. He *becomes* a destructive force, an agent of annihilation, but he had been a very good king, his mother pays homage to him at his death: 'I have seen the earth governed by you'. His problem was that he saw no need for the gods: it becomes very clear in the scene with Krishna and Arjuna when he says he does not need Krishna, only his armies. He is a representative of a world without God: he is convinced he will succeed in realizing what he wants to do on his own.

He is a solitary character, always set against everything: his father, his mother, Bhishma, Drona. He says, 'You all hate me.' But he excludes himself from many things, from an open vision of the cosmos. However, he goes to the very end of himself, he is at least consistent.

M.M.: *One of the difficulties of interpretation must be to make him human without working psychologically, in a Stanislavskian way.*
What do you mean by psychology? What is the Stanislavski system? There is a great deal of confusion in language in this area. I come from a Polish school where one is steeped in Stanislavki's method: I am the product of that school and approach. If I'm playing a human being and not a chair, how do I bring it to life without psychology? It seems that in France, psychology chiefly means slow . . .

M.M.: *It also means attenuated, in half-tints, on a small scale. But in this production performances are grand, on an epic scale: sketched with broad strokes. All is energy and clarity . . .*
But that is exactly it, to my mind. Without psychology, you can never achieve this kind of clarity. In order for there to be life in each hundredth of a second, as Peter would say, you must know what life is. Perhaps we should call it life as opposed to psychology.

You start with enormous complexity and end up with simplicity, thanks to what I would call 'psychology' and what Peter would call 'detail'. Initially our aim was to free the body of its own inner obstacles – and a similar process with the voice and pronunciation. It is a very difficult state to attain: sometimes for a minute or two in performance, it flows without blockages, unimpeded – the state that Peter refers to as 'transparent'.

There are two sorts of improvisation: what I call pure improvisation, and those starting from the text or situations in it. Pure improvisations have opened me up enormously, they oblige me to forget one of my tendencies which is to think too much about form. I felt completely free, I did things that surprised me. Ensemble work is another crucial element. I found my place, my role in the work very quickly: after a month and a half, I knew where I was. I think it was the others who largely helped me on this level, they began to locate me, my areas of sensitivity and insensitivity. This infused me with a feeling of security I really needed. Until that point I had been scared, of what I don't really know: perhaps of not being rich enough to be a true partner.

What you learn here is that it is not only a job, a craft: you also come to recognize what is human, and what it is to be human. I hope we become – I almost said 'better' – more demanding of ourselves, more disciplined, more open, more respectful of others. The theatre becomes a way of life. I would love to go on living with this group. We see each other fourteen hours a day at work, but I would like to live with them outside the theatre as well. I'd also like to see them again as they were during the trip to India. In that way I would get to know different, new facets, and that would nourish our work.

25 May 1985
From *Alternatives Théâtrales*
1985: translation by David Williams

An Interview with Yoshi Oida (Drona/Kichaka) by Martine Millon

Oida, a Japanese actor, is one of the core members of the Centre, having collaborated with Brook for almost twenty years. In Japan, he trained as a Noh actor, subsequently becoming involved with Kabuki and modern experimental theatre.

I have been working with Peter Brook since *The Tempest* in 1968. That's when he first had the idea of working with different nationalities. He found the experiment interesting, and that's how the C.I.C.T. was born.

For the *Mahabharata*, because of the nature of the mythology he wanted to represent, Peter did not aim to create a unified style of performance. The African and the Japanese each tell the story in their own way, although the demands of a general balance forbid me to remain too Japanese. For me, the *Mhb* is easier than some other texts – Shakespeare, for example: as an Oriental, I have certain affinities with the culture that produced it.

Of course the tale itself is full of clearly differentiated archetypes, popular, recognisable. But the mixture of Westerners, Orientals and Africans also has the effect of obliging the spiritual heart of the work to pass as much through the body as through words. Westerners use the body less than Orientals or Africans, but they can construct whole philosophical worlds by means of words. In performance, both possibilities are present and active.

Conference was more difficult for the actors to perform than the *Mhb*; apart from the Hoopoe, roles were not substantially characterized. As a performance, its spirit was more mystical and religious than the *Mhb* which goes beyond a purely religious point of view. There's room for everyone to interpret it in their own way. *Conference* was a difficult, even severe text; the *Mhb* is more accessible, more like a children's show.

During training, we studied various martial arts, notably kung fu, in order to locate the spirit of combat. We practised vocal exercises with the musicians under Toshi Tsuchitori's direction: Aboriginal and American Indian chants and cries, and elaborate rhythm exercises to learn how to mobilise each part of the body spontaneously and in a unified way.

When we came to the text, initially some scenes were approached in the individual mother tongues to free certain actors from the difficulties of the French language. In this instance, I don't think it's really valid to talk about improvisation, at least not pure improvisation. Contrary to *The Iks*, here there was a precise text. In one way, of course, even during performance there is some improvisation: the work is never completely fixed and Peter has always wanted us to retain some of the freedom of improvisation. If true improvisation remains a goal, then the preparatory work should be seen rather as an apprenticeship. Once body, voice and spirit are freed, once one has found one's character, only then can improvisation begin.

During our two-week journey to India, we saw a performance of Kathakali. I found much personal inspiration for the character of Kichaka in Kathakali. But above all this journey was a way of gaining impressions and personal sensations to lead us on our own individual inner paths. For example, one day from a boat on the Ganges I saw some dead bodies being cremated; it made a huge impression on me. Peter wanted to avoid any kind of intellectual or erudite explanations of what we saw. He felt that that kind of knowledge wouldn't help us as actors in this performance at all.

In the *Mhb*, the ironic, even cynical attitude of Drona, the martial arts master, owes something to Zen Buddhist teaching, but I think originally it's more of a Chinese attitude: certainly not a very Indian characteristic. In response to his disciple's question 'What is God?' the Chinese priest says, 'God is shit.' In my performance, Drona behaves as a cynic. Irony allows us to communicate a more complex indirect truth, a truth difficult to convey using only logic: the kind of truth each individual can interpret differently. I once tried playing Drona as someone very serious, devoid of irony. When I asked Peter which interpretation he preferred, he told me, 'If you play the character with irony, there'll be more room to act than if he's serious.' Having known me for fifteen years, Peter has been able to encourage me to play Drona as a multi-faceted character.

As far as Kichaka is concerned, I've treated him as a farcical character, a lecherous old man: the whole episode is dealt with in a comic spirit, with certain allusions to Kathakali. Right now I'd like to approach him in a more serious way, as a young general possessing real power. Perhaps I'll try just such an interpretation when we return to work on this episode.

Drona's death is tragic, violent and beautiful: the death of a Samurai. It was Peter who found the gesture of me pouring blood over my own head. At the age of forty, I began to think about death. The attitude I take in this performance reflects what I understand by death, the relationship between body and spirit at that precise moment. I take up a meditation position, I await death without feeling any fear. I try to go beyond the body, to separate body and spirit. If my body must die, I will let it die. At that moment when he sits in the yoga position, Drona abandons his body, he throws it away, then struggles to keep his spirit alive: and at that moment someone physically kills his body. If one day I find myself in the middle of a desert, with nothing to eat, I think that's how I could die.

In an Indian comic strip version of the *Mhb*, Drona can be seen adopting this yoga position at his death. When you get to a certain age, and you have a certain experience and wisdom, you know how to detach yourself from your body while keeping your spirit alive. I understand Drona as a character fairly well, his behaviour when confronted with death ties in with my own conception. And yet it's rather a mysterious death: why does he decide to die? Before learning of the death of his son, he says, 'My death is near.' At the same time, in my interpretation, Drona tempers his feelings with irony. His death seems tragic, but perhaps that's not the case in his eyes. In a sense he's happy. Going beyond the body is a catharsis. It produces great joy.

Paris, 14th May 1985
Alternatives Théâtrales
1985: translation by David Williams

The Mahabharata: A Review
by Margaret Croyden

Margaret Croyden, theatre critic on the New York Times, *describes the Avignon première of* Le Mahabharata *in 1985.*

Imagine staging a nine-hour production based on an ancient Hindu poem combining strains of the War of the Roses and Götterdämmerung into the cosmic grandeur of an Indian epic. Stir in a clash of two great dynasties in the hands of the gods, opposing armies locked in battle and the moral struggle of ideal heroes representing divine forces arrayed against demonic ones. All this, set against a background of primordial forests and sumptuous palaces, is encompassed in the monumental saga, *The Mahabharata* – a theatrical challenge that would intimidate most directors.

Mr Brook, is no stranger to challenges, but for the sixty-year-old director, his production of the Indian epic represents a culmination of a lifelong search for theatrical expression of mankind's greatest dramas and deepest dilemmas.

In Avignon, Mr Brook's 'theatre' was an open limestone quarry outside the city where spectators sat on scaffolding facing massive boulders, rose-tinted cliffs 100 feet high and a vast playing space filled with tons of luminous yellow sand. A canal of real water constructed by the technical director, Jean-Guy Lecat, flowed across the back of the space; a small pond reflecting the action was down front.

At one side was an altarlike arrangement of low burning flames and Indian garlands; at the other, the percussion, string and wind instruments for the musicians who each night improvised the music and became an integral part of the action. When it grew dark, the lighting transformed the rocks, water, sand and cliffs to gold-yellow, deep beige and slate blue, so that the terrain appeared as a unifying image in a dream expressing the enigmatic, primitive beauty of the elements.

The musicians took their place. A character in a beige Indian cotton robe – his red hair and shaggy beard standing out against the stones – entered, accompanied by a young boy, also in beige cotton. The character was Vyasa, symbolic poet of *The Mahabharata*. He told the boy that he was writing a story about the history of his ancestors, their vast wars and, by inference, the story of mankind. The tale, said Vyasa, was the great poem of the world. The great God Krishna appeared wearing an elephant's head, traditionally used at the beginning of a stage performance in India, and offered his services as a scribe. Krishna wrote in a large book and thus *The Mahabharata*, the awesome story of the great Bharata clan, emerged. Under the power of Krishna, the Bharata would re-enact their tragic destiny.

Part I introduces the main characters, their mythic origins, their characteristics and aims, the role of the Gods, especially Krishna, and the growing discord between the Pandavas and the Kauravas, two branches of the Bharata clan. In a game of dice, which the Pandava leader loses to his cousins, the Pandavas forfeit all their property and worldly possessions and are exiled to a forest. In Part II they live there in a primordial existence while procuring arms for the inevitable battle to come.

In Part III the devastating war is unleashed that threatens the entire universe – a war foreordained and controlled by the God Krishna. After a gruesome massacre, Pandava regains his rights and is later reconciled with his enemies in heaven. Vyasa, the story teller, warns ambiguously that *this* – meaning heaven, or earth, or the entire play – is 'the last illusion'. According to Hinduism, life is God's dream and, as rendered by God, is but an illusion. The characters, dressed in pure white, drop their personae, eat delicacies and exit. God's game is over.

Embedded in the text are eternal philosophical questions examining the paradox of the human condition: Why do men lust for power? What are the causes of jealousy and hate, of the destructive forces of mankind? What is the mystery behind man's motivations and his relationship to destiny and choice? Will mankind survive? Does man have a choice? What is God's game?

Since the epic takes place in the Indian era of Kaliyuga, the time of destruction, where demonic forces are in the ascendancy and threaten the cosmos itself, a modern analogy is obvious. Does Mr Brook posit such a connection? 'Of course, the basic themes are contemporary,' he says. 'One of them is how to find one's way in an age of destruction.' Through *The Mahabharata* runs the story of a noble king, the leader of the Pandavas, searching for the right way – his dharma, the Hindu concept of moral law – and the trials he must suffer to find it.

'This kind of search is for every man, king or not,' said Mr Brook. 'Every man is potentially king of himself, if he manages to get himself together. His country is himself. In that way, everyone can put himself firmly into the story,' which is essentially a quest for morality.

'What is brought out in *The Mahabharata*,' Mr Brook continued, 'is that there is a certain world harmony, a cosmic harmony, that can either be helped or destroyed by individuals. And so one must try to discover what his place is in the cosmic scheme and how he can help to preserve the cosmic harmony rather than destroy it, knowing that the cosmic harmony is always in danger, and that the world goes through periods of lesser or greater danger. We too, are living in a time when every value one can think of is in danger. What is the role of the individual? Must one act, or withdraw from the game?'

Mr Brook attempted to convey the essence of *The Mahabharata* through the strength of his aesthetic vision rather than through philosophy. In bringing to life this huge humanistic work he encompassed all his past efforts to create new dimensions in the theater. Eschewing minimalism, he treated *The Mahabharata* with unabashed grandeur and daring theatrics. He evoked every theatrical mode at his command and used all the aspects of his years of travel and research in Asia and Africa – ritual theater, Oriental storytelling, Indian classical theater, magic and clowning, the broad scope of epic staging, the tone and timbre of Shakespearean tragedy and the savagery of the theatre of cruelty. A unique feature is the classical acting by a cast of international actors in accented French whose expressive faces and varied styles and physiques give the production a generic quality . . .

'*The Mahabharata* comes out of Vedic times,' Mr Brook explained, 'and what was interesting about India is that you have a highly developed civilization artistically, and at the same time you have a civilization very close to nature, and although Indians have created great works of art, this was in no way an indoor civilization, like the Renaissance. Their work had constantly to do with images from the natural elements.' He could not stage such a work with 'a couple of chairs and everyday costumes,' he said, adding: 'The epic contains the most luxuriant poetic writing, and the energy of the imagery in the writing is the only way of telling the story. I had to find the appropriate form, the necessary language to tell such a story.'

The ruling images in the production are fire, water and earth. Fires of all sizes and shapes are ablaze. Some are used for religious ritual or ceremonial scenes; some burn through the night to evoke the divine forces; in one dazzling scene, a trail of fire ignites the waters, calling forth the hated enemies. The water, a constant factor, is used by the characters to drink from, to wash in, to wade in, and to fight in unto the death. Dominating everything is the sand-covered ground. It lies before us like the benign universe, its golden colours changing with the night, enveloping all the action, reminding us of its mysterious essence.

In the spectacular war episode, hundreds of arrows are hurled through the air in choreographed motion; flags fly down from the mountain tops; armies are poised high on the rocks, their primitive weapons ready for the kill. Warriors are choked, knifed, strangled, disemboweled and decapitated. Characters fight with knives, axes, poles, arrows, clubs and tree trunks. They scream and grunt and howl, they sink into the water, covered with filth, their mud-streaked faces unrecognizable. Finally, in a *coup de théâtre*, the divine secret weapon blows off half the mountain. The end of the world is before us.

The horror is counterpoised by lyrical moments. In an exquisite court scene, we see princesses dressed in scarlet, rich maroon and vibrant yellows. Lying on elevated couches, they listen to sweet music and watch a delicate hand-held miniature puppet show, while lotus flowers float on tiny sparks of fire in the pond. In another scene, the melancholy Krishna plays the flute on a hilltop and the proud god Shiva shows off his powers in an amusing dance.

Then there is the sensuality of the princess married to the Pandavas: her long black hair against her corn-yellow garment recalls Indian miniature painting. Other lovely young women pass by – the river goddess, Ganga, dressed in her finery, walks through the waters after giving birth to one of the heroes, and a jewelry-bedecked princess, on her way to marry the blind King, is carried on an elephant's back created by the bodies of the actors. And throughout there is the innocence of the young boy listening to the storyteller, watching, questioning, searching.

At the end of the performance, many in the audience – like the boy – were full of wonderment and awe at what they had seen. For them, Mr Brook's theatrical magic had worked, evoking the possibilities of live theatre with grand themes in the hands of a master magician.

New York Times, 25 August 1985

Images of Tenderness, Triumph and Death:
A Review by Irving Wardle

Irving Wardle reviewed The Mahabharata *at the Avignon Festival for* The Times.

As with *Orghast* at the Shiraz Festival in the early seventies, Brook's spectators undergo a pilgrimage – a long walk up a dusty hillside – before being rewarded with a location hardly less magnificent than Persepolis: an amphitheatre facing a blasted cliff-side, with a lofty upper pathway for the actors, and a desert floor divided by a canal. Surrounded by the most sophisticated of lighting rigs, the show is rooted in the basic elements of the universe – water, stone, and fire.

What Brook and his adapter, Jean-Claude Carrière, have drawn from this immense narrative is the story of the struggle between the five Pandava brothers and their cousins, the Kauravas, for power over the country. As that country constitutes the entire known world, and as the title embraces both sides within the family of man, there is no missing its application to the modern world.

The seeds of discord are sown in the first play, *The Game of Dice*, and ripen in the second (*Exile in the Forest*) where the world is split into two opposing camps. As the work advances towards a conflict of total devastation (*The War*), it jumps the centuries from swords and clubs to a blinding magnesium flare that erupts in the rock face as the ultimate weapon.

Brook, however, is not an artist who ever allows himself to be driven into a corner: nor is he the man to regurgitate an Asian masterpiece as a Western editorial. His purpose is more modest and vastly more ambitious than that. In line with all his public work since he set up the International Centre of Theatre Research, he seeks out the blackest evidence in human history as a means of exalting the human race.

There is no guilt or sin in *The Mahabharata*: the enemies never cancel their family ties; they happen to inhabit an age of desolation, sorrowfully attended by the demi-god Krishna who nourishes hopes of regeneration. But the work does not deal in uplifting messages. If it has a motto, it comes from the poet Vyasa: 'One should always listen to stories. It's enjoyable, and sometimes it makes things better.'

Essentially the whole cycle – with its multiple settings, sixteen principal characters, its musical and visual splendours – consists of one man telling a story. Vyasa (Alain Maratrat) begins by dictating his great poem to a scribe (Maurice Bénichou), and whatever his later transformations, he retains his identity as a storyteller, just as the company are ready to change from dramatic characters into a circle of listeners.

Carrière's text consists of a main narrative carried along by a sequence of stories, like threaded pearls. Some of them, like the fatal dice game in which the ruling Pandava brother loses his kingdom, are central to the dramatic conflict. Others are peripheral, preparing the way for plot developments many hours ahead. But each is spell-binding in itself.

Within a framework as determinist as *The Wars of the Roses*, the production also enables you to live in the moment with no thought of any final climax. A single note on the sitar tingles and shifts through a spectrum of harmonies, and time stands still. By such means, Asian and European expectations are reconciled: and the repeated withdrawal from linear drama into fairy-tale also establishes the Hindu perspective on earthly existence as a mortal illusion. Thought alone is real. And in one exchange between Vyasa and Krishna you are left to decide whether the god has invented the poet or the poet invented the god.

Of the main characters, there is Karna (Bruce Myers), a child of the sun: there is a fisher king, and a rejected princess who goes beyond death to avenge her humiliation. There is a blind king whose wife unites herself to him by blindfolding herself for life.

As such examples suggest, the text is full of echoes from other cultures. And, true to their policy, Brook's company assert the universal quality of the material by removing it from any specifically Indian context.

Played in clear, simple French, the performance is a melting-pot of national differences. Among the musicians, percussion combines with the barbaric blare of the nagaswaram (a harshly funereal quarter-tone trumpet) and the homely sound of trombones. Boots and trousers mingle with robes and skirted battle costume. And the accents of the cast vary between German, Greek, Polish, Japanese, and declamatory Parisian French.

Again and again, dramatic point is reinforced by nationality. Bhima, the strongest of the Pandavas, is played by the African giant Mamadou Dioume, characteristically seen leaping on an adversary and tearing out his entrails. Yoshi Oida, as a lecherous general attempting a seduction, goes into a full-blooded *kyogen* routine, including a throttled Japanese love song, before ill-advisedly climbing into the sack with the dreaded Bhima.

Some of the company, like Oida, are long-term members of the troupe. But there is no company hierarchy. They create and grow into the roles, and when necessary they draw on a shared repertory of extraordinary skills.

A court banquet materializes on the sand, complete with a royal entertainer who puts on an elaborate puppet show, until one of the chirruping marionettes escapes and the puppeteer chases frantically round the spectators to recapture it.

Enter the Pandavas in disguise, seeking employment as servants: one as a cook, one as a dice-player, and one – the invincible warrior Arjuna (Vittorio Mezzogiorno) – transformed into a bewitching bisexual temple dancer.

Brook the magician surpasses himself in this production. For his ceremonies, trails of fire race across the sand and ignite the waters. For his battles, you can trace the flight of the mimed arrows, and visualize the horses from the sight of chariot drivers whipping a single heavy wheel over the desert. As before in his work, the immediate impact produces amazement and pleasure: the long-term effect is the imprint of images of tenderness, triumph and death that lodge in the memory for ever.

The Times, 13 July 1985

Bibliography

ADAIR, Gilbert, 'A Meeting with Peter Brook', *Sight and Sound*, vol. 49, no. 1, Winter 1979–80.

ALBERA, Philippe, 'Attentat à l'Opéra' (interview with Peter Brook), *Révolution*, no. 136, 1982.

ANSORGE, Peter, interview with Peter Brook, *Plays and Players*, vol. 18, no. 1, October 1970.

— review of *A Midsummer Night's Dream* (Aldwych), *Plays and Players*, vol. 18, no. 10, August 1971.

ASLAN, Odette, 'Les Paravents de Jean Genet', in *Les Voies de la Création Théâtrale*, vol. III, Paris, Editions du CNRS, 1972.

ATTAR, Farid Ud-din, *The Conference of the Birds* (translated from de Tassy's French version of *Mantiq Uttair*), London, Routledge and Kegan Paul, 1978.

— *La Conférence des Oiseaux*, adaptation by Jean-Claude Carrière, Paris, C.I.C.T., 1979.

— *The Conference of the Birds*, adaptation by Jean-Claude Carrière and Peter Brook, The Dramatic Publishing Co., Connecticut, 1982.

AVIGAL, Shoshana and RIMMON-KENAN, Shlomith, 'What do Brook's bricks mean? Towards a theory of the "mobility" of objects in theatrical discourse', *Poetics Today*, vol. 2, no. 3, Spring 1981.

BABLET, Denis, 'Rencontre avec Peter Brook', *Travail Théâtral* no. 10, October/January 1973.

BANU, Georges, 'Peter Brook, ou l'écume du théâtre', *Travail Théâtral*, nos. 18–19, January/June 1975.

— 'La Tragédie de Carmen', in *L'Annuel du Théâtre* (saison 1981–2), Paris, L'Aire, 1982.

— 'L'Os et La Conférence des Oiseaux', and an interview with Jean-Claude Carrière, in *Les Voies de la Création Théâtrale*, vol. 10, Paris, Editions du CNRS, 1982.

— 'Le cercle et le fleuve: notes sur Peter Brook et Jerzy Grotowski', *Le Scarabée International*, no. 2, 1982.

— *Brook: Les Voies de la Création Théâtrale*, vol. XIII, Paris, Editions du CNRS, 1985 (entire volume).

— *Le Mahabharata*, *Alternatives Théâtrales*, no. 24, July 1985: entire issue.

BANU, Georges and MARIENSTRAS, Richard, '*Timon d'Athènes* de Shakespeare, et sa mise en scène par Peter Brook', in *Les Voies de la Création Théâtrale*, vol. V, Paris, Editions du CNRS, 1977.

BARBER, John, 'Magic touch of fairyland' (review of *A Midsummer Night's Dream*), *Daily Telegraph*, 14.9.1970.
— 'Real food for thought' (review of *The Ik*), *Daily Telegraph*, 20.1.1975.
— 'Down to the bare boards' (interview with Peter Brook), *Daily Telegraph*, 10.12.1977.
BARNARD, Roger, review of *US*, *Peace News*, 21.10.1966.
BARNES, Clive, review of *Oedipus*, *New York Times*, 31.7.1968.
— review of *A Midsummer Night's Dream*, *New York Times*, 28.8.1970.
BEEMAN, William O., review of *La Tragédie de Carmen*, *Performing Arts Journal*, no. 22, vol. 8, no. 1, 1984.
BERNARD, Kenneth, 'Some observations on the theatre of Peter Brook', *Theater* (Yale School of Drama Publication), Fall/Winter 1980.
BILLINGTON, Michael, 'RSC in *US*', *Plays and Players*, vol. 14, December 1966.
— 'From Artaud to Brook, and back again', *Guardian*, 6.1.1976.
— 'Written on the Wind: the dramatic art of Peter Brook' (from BBC Radio 4's *Kaleidoscope*), *The Listener*, 21 and 28.12.1978.
— 'A Fire Snake in the Sand' (account of *Le Mahabharata*), *Théâtre en Europe*, no. 8, October 1985.
BISHOP OF WOOLWICH, 'The Aldwych Liturgy' (review of *US*), *Guardian*, November 1966.
BROOK, Peter:
— 'Oh for Empty Seats', *Encore*, no. 32, January 1959.
— 'From Zero to the Infinite', *Encore*, November 1960.
— 'The Cuban enterprise', *Sight and Sound*, Spring 1961.
— 'Search for a Hunger', *Encore*, no. 32, July/August, 1961.
— 'Happy Days and Marienbad', *Encore*, January 1962.
— 'Filming a Masterpiece' (*re Lord of the Flies*), *Observer*, 26.7.1964.
— 'The Road to *Marat/Sade*', *New York Herald Tribune*, 26.12.1964.
— Introduction to Peter Weiss's *Marat/Sade* (English text), London, John Calder, 1965.
— 'False Gods', *Flourish*, Winter 1965.
— 'Finding Shakespeare on film', *The Drama Review*, vol. 11. no. 1, Fall 1966.
— 'Is MacBird pro-American?', *New York Times*, 19.3.1967.
— Preface in *Towards a Poor Theatre* by Jerzy Grotowski, Teatrets Vorlag, 1968.
— *The Empty Space*, Penguin 1968.
— '*Tell me Lies* in America', *The Times*, 17.2.1968.
— 'La merde et le ciel' in *Le Théâtre Baroque 1*, (Cahiers dirigés par Fernando Arrabal), Paris, Christian Bourgois, 1968.
— 'Eighth World Theatre Day: International Message', *Le Théâtre en Pologne*, vol. 6. no. 3, 1969.
— 'Les lieux du spectacle', *Architecture d'Aujourd'hui*, no. 152, October/November, 1970.
— 'Le Théâtre sans Fard', *La Nouvelle Critique*, no. 33, April 1970 (from an ORTF interview in the series 'Un certain regard').

BROOK, Peter:
— *In a Sense* (re Orghast), Paris, C.I.R.T.
— Preface in *Voice and the Actor* by Cicely Berry, London, Harrap, 1973.
— Brook at the Brooklyn Academy of Music (workshop sessions recorded and transcribed by Sally Gardner), September/October 1973: unpublished.
— Preface in *Le Marathon* by Claude Confortès, Le Manteau d'Arlequin, Paris, Gallimard, 1973.
— 'Lettre à une Etudiante Anglaise' in *Timon d'Athènes*, Paris, C.I.C.T., 1974.
— 'The Complete Truth is Global', *New York Times*, 20.1.1974.
— 'The Three Cultures of Modern Man', *Cultures*, The UNESCO Press, vol. 3, no. 4, 1976.
— Preface in *King Lear: The Space of Tragedy* by Grigori Kozintsev, London, Heinemann, 1978.
— 'Théâtre Populaire, Théâtre Immédiat', *Le Monde*, 24.11.1977.
— 'L'Espace Théâtral' in *L'Espace Théâtral: 4ème Colloque*, Teatro de Naciones, Caracas 1978.
— 'Pour des Espaces Indéfinis' in *Techniques et Architecture*, ('Ruptures dans l'Architecture du Spectacle' special edition), no. 310, 1978.
— Untitled essay in *Le Fait Culturel* by Gérard Montassier, Paris, Fayard, 1980.
— 'The Living Theatre of the Outback', *Sunday Times*, 17.8.1980.
— 'Espaces pour un théâtre', *Le Scarabée International*, no. 2, Summer 1982.
— 'Message pour Santarcangelo': conference devoted to Peter Brook and Jerzy Grotowski, Santarcangelo di Romagna, 9–11.6.1983: transcription reprinted in *Les Voies de La Création Théâtrale* XIII, 1985.
BROOK, Peter and MAROWITZ, Charles, 'A Theatre of Nerve-ends', *Sunday Times*, 12.1.1964.
BROOK, Peter and REEVES, Geoffrey, 'Shakespeare on Three Screens', *Sight and Sound*, vol. 34, no. 2, Spring 1965.
BRYDEN, Ronald, 'Oedipus Newly Born', *Observer*, 24.3.1968.
— 'Stripping down the *Dream*', *Observer*, 13.12.1970.
CANNAN, Denis and HIGGINS, Colin, *Les Iks*, (adaptation of Colin Turnbull's *The Mountain People*, translated into French by Jean-Claude Carrière), Paris, C.I.C.T. 1975. English version, *The Ik*, subsequently published, with an introduction by Colin Turnbull, by The Dramatic Publishing Co., Connecticut 1982.
CHARLOT, Daniel, *Mission avec le C.I.R.T · Peter Brook, 1972–3* (UNESCO report, unpublished).
CHEKHOV, Anton, *La Cerisaie* (French version by Peter Brook, Jean-Claude Carrière and Lusia Lavrova), Paris, C.I.C.T. 1981.
— *La Cerisaie* (Collection 'Théâtre et Mise en Scène', compiled by Christine Geray), Hatier, Paris 1985: with an interview with Maurice Bénichou, co-director of Peter Brook's C.I.C.T. *La Cerisaie*.
CONSTANT, Marius, BROOK, Peter and CARRIERE, Jean-Claude (adapters), *La Tragédie de Carmen* (from Bizet, Merimée, Meilhac and Halévy), Paris, C.I.C.T. 1981.
COOK, Judith, *Director's Theatre*, London, Harrap 1974.

COVENEY, Michael, review of *Ubu, Plays and Players*, vol. 25, no. 8, May 1978.

COX, Frank, interview with Peter Brook, *Plays and Players*, vol. 15, no. 7, April 1968: *re Oedipus*.

CROYDEN, Margaret, 'Exploration of the Ugly' (interview with Colin Blakely *re Oedipus*), *The Drama Review*, vol. 13, no. 3, Spring 1969.

— 'Peter Brook's *Tempest*', *The Drama Review*, ibid.

— 'A Hidden Dream of Sex and Love', *New York Times*, 17.1.1971.

— 'Peter Brook learns to speak Orghast', *New York Times*, 3.10.1971.

— 'Peter Brook's "Birds" fly to Africa', *New York Times*, 21.1.1973.

— *Lunatics, Lovers and Poets: The Contemporary Experimental Theatre*, New York, Delta 1975.

— 'Filming the Saga of a Sage with Peter Brook', *New York Times*, 26.2.1978.

— 'Getting in touch with Gurdjieff', *New York Times*, 29.7.1979.

— 'Peter Brook's search for Essentials', *New York Times*, 4.5.1980.

— 'Comedy, Tragedy and Mystical Fantasy: Peter Brook's New Trilogy', *New York Times*, 25.5.1980.

— *The Centre: A Narrative*, Paris C.I.C.T. 1980.

— 'Peter Brook transforms an Indian Epic', *New York Times*, 25.8.1985.

CUSHMAN, Robert, review of *The Ik*, *Observer*, 18.1.1976.

DAWSON, Helen, 'Brook goes backwards' (*re Oedipus* rehearsals), *Observer*, 21.1.1968.

— 'Doubling up for a Triumph' (review of *A Midsummer Night's Dream*), *Observer*, 30.8.1970.

ERTEL, Evelyne, 'De Briques . . . et de Broc' (*re Ubu*), *Travail Théâtral*, no. 30, January/March 1978.

ESSLIN, Martin, 'The Theatre of Cruelty', *New York Times*, 6.3.1966.

— 'Are we to blame for *US*?', *New York Times*, 6.10.1966.

— review of *Oedipus*, *New York Times*, 31.3.1968.

— 'Oedipus Complex', *Plays and Players*, vol. 15, no. 8, May 1968.

FINDLATER, Richard, 'Myth and magic among the Persians', *Observer*, 12.9.1971.

GIBSON, Michael, 'Brook's Africa' (interview with Peter Brook), *The Drama Review*, vol. 17, no. 3, September 1973.

GILLIATT, Penelope, 'Thug in the Cradle' (review of *Lord of the Flies*), *Observer*, 2.8.1964.

GREER, Herb, 'Credo Quia Contra-Courant Est' (interview with Peter Brook), *Transatlantic Review*, no. 57, October 1976.

GURDJIEFF, G. I., *Meetings with Remarkable Men*, London, Picador, 1981.

HAYMAN, Ronald, 'Life and Joy' (interview with Peter Brook), *The Times*, 29.8.1970.

— *Theatre and Anti-Theatre*, London, Secker and Warburg, 1979.

HEILPERN, John, 'Session based on Voice' (unpublished article commissioned by *The Observer*), Paris, C.I.R.T., 1972.

— 'Peter Brook: the Grand Inquisitor', *Observer*, 18.1.1976.

— *Conference of the Birds: The Story of Peter Brook in Africa*, Faber and Faber, 1979.

HENTOFF, Nat, 'Brook: Yes, let's be emotional about Vietnam' (interview with Peter Brook), *New York Times*, 25.2.1968.

HIGGINS, John, review of Royal Shakespeare Company's *Antony and Cleopatra*, *The Times*, 18.10.1978.

HOUSTON, Penelope and MILNE, Tom, 'Interview with Peter Brook', *Sight and Sound*, vol. 32, no. 3, Summer 1963.

HUGHES, David, 'Peter Brook: A Revolution at the Opera', *Sunday Times*, 15.11.1981.

HUGHES, Ted, *Oedipus* (adaptation of David Anthony Turner's translation of Seneca), London, Faber and Faber, 1969.

— '*Orghast*: talking without words', *Vogue*, December 1971.

HUNT, Albert, review of *Marat/Sade*, *Peace News*, 4.9.1964.

— 'On Joan Littlewood and Peter Brook', *International Theatre Information*, Summer 1973.

— 'Acting and Being', *New Society*, 20.2.1975.

— 'The Trials of working with a Master Magician', *New Society*, 26.8.1982.

INNES, Christopher, *Holy Theatre*, Cambridge, Cambridge University Press, 1981.

JARRY, Alfred, *Ubu aux Bouffes*, Paris, C.I.C.T., 1977.

KALMAN, Jean, 'Par-delà Ubu, ou le globe el l'enfant', *Travail Théâtral*, no. 30, January/March 1978.

KANE, John, 'When my cue comes, call me and I will answer', *Sunday Times*, 13.6.1971.

— 'The Actor as Acrobat', *Plays and Players*, vol. 18, August 1971.

KAUFFMANN, Stanley and DRUTMAN, Irving, 'The Provocative *Marat/Sade*: was Peter Brook its brain?', *New York Times*, 9.1.1966.

KERR, Walter, 'The play is scanted in the scurry' (review of *A Midsummer Night's Dream*), *New York Times*, 31.1.1971.

KOTT, Jan, *Shakespeare our Contemporary*, London, Methuen, 1978.

KROLL, Jack, 'Placing the living Shakespeare before us' (review of *A Midsummer Night's Dream*), *New York Times*, 7.2.1971.

LABEILLE, Daniel, 'The Formless Hunch' (interview with Peter Brook), *Modern Drama*, vol. 23, no. 3, September 1980.

LAHR, John, 'Knowing what to celebrate' (interview with Peter Brook), *Plays and Players*, vol. 23, no. 6, March 1976: with a review of *The Ik* at the Round House in London.

LAWSON, Stephen R., interview with Peter Brook, *Yale/Theater*, vol. 7, no. 1, Fall 1975.

LEONARD, Hugh, 'Blue Murder' (review of *Marat/Sade*), *Plays and Players*, vol. 12, October 1964.

LEVIN, Bernard, review of *A Midsummer Night's Dream*, *The Times*, 30.9.1971.

— 'The Seeds of Genius: Watch them Grow', *The Times*, 3.4.1980.

— 'Two men on remarkable journeys', *The Times*, 26.6.1980.

LEWIS, Anthony, 'Peter Brook's Theatre is a Living Event', *New York Times*, 15.1.1971.

LIEHM, A. J., 'The Politics of Sclerosis: Stalin and Lear' (interview with Peter Brook), *Theatre Quarterly*, vol. 3, no. 10, April/June 1973.

MAROWITZ, Charles, 'Lear Log', *The Drama Review*, vol. 8, no. 2, Winter 1963.

— 'Notes on the Theatre of Cruelty' and review of *US*, *The Drama Review*, vol. 11, no. 2, Winter 1966.
— 'From prodigy to professional, as written, directed and acted by Peter Brook', *New York Times*, 24.10.1968.
— 'Brook: from *Marat/Sade* to *Midsummer Night's Dream*', *New York Times*. 13.9.1970.
— review of *A Midsummer Night's Dream*, *New York Times*, 13.10.1970.
— *Confessions of a Counterfeit Critic*, London, Eyre Methuen, 1973.
— *The Act of Being*, London, Secker and Warburg, 1978.
MILLON, Martine, 'Le Sens d'une Recherche: Entretien avec Peter Brook', *Travail Théâtrale*, nos. 18–19, January/June 1975.
MILNE, Tom, 'Cruelty Cruelty', *Encore*, vol. 11, no. 2, March/April 1964.
— 'Reflections on *The Screens*', *Encore*, vol. 11, no. 4, July/August 1964.
MOORE, James, interview with Peter Brook (*re Meetings with Remarkable Men*), *Guardian*, 20.7.1976.
MORLEY, Sheridan, 'Peter Brook: Quarrying theatre in Australia', *The Times*, 7.4.1980.
MOSSMAN, James, 'Throwing out the cobwebs' (interview with Peter Brook), BBC 2, 23.7.1971.
MUNK, Erika, 'Looking for a New Language' (interview with Peter Brook), *Performance*, vol. 1, no. 1, New York Shakespeare Public Theatre, 1971.
— 'The Way's the Thing', *Village Voice*, 12.5.1980.
NEIL, Boyd, 'Peter Brook: Larger than Life', *Scene Changes*, 13.6.1979.
OAKES, Philip, 'Something new out of Africa' (interview with Peter Brook), *Sunday Times*, 4.1.1976.
OIDA, Yoshi, 'Shinto Training of the Actor', *Dartington Theatre Papers*, Third Series, no. 3.
PARABOLA, 'Leaning on the Moment: a conversation with Peter Brook', *Parabola*, vol. 4, part 2, Spring 1979.
— 'Lie and Glorious Adjective' (interview with Peter Brook), *Parabola*, vol. 6, part 3, August 1981.
PITT-RIVERS, Julian, 'Peter Brook and the Ik', *Times Literary Supplement*, 31.1.1975.
PORTER, Andrew, 'In triumph through Persepolis' (reviews of *Orghast*), *Financial Times*, 11, 14, 16.9.1971: reprinted in *Theatre 72* (edited by Sheridan Morley), London, Hutchinson, 1972.
READ, Bill, 'Peter Brook: from Stratford-on-Avon to the Gare du Nord', *Boston University Journal* xxiv, no. 3, 1975.
REEVES, Geoffrey, 'The Persepolis Follies of 1971', *Performance*, vol. 1, no. 1, New York Shakespeare Public Theatre, 1971.
RICHIE, Donald, review of *A Midsummer Night's Dream*, *The Drama Review*, vol. 15, no. 3, Spring 1971.
RICH, Frank, 'Lust and Bloodlust' (review of *La Tragédie de Carmen* in New York), *New York Times*, 18.11.1983.
ROBERTS, Peter, review of *A Midsummer Night's Dream*, *Plays and Players*, vol. 18, October 1970.

RONCONI, Luca, interview with Peter Brook, *Cahiers Renaud-Barrault*, no. 79, 1972.

SCHECHNER, Richard (Ed.), '*Marat/Sade* Forum', *The Drama Review*, vol. 10, no. 4, Summer 1966.

— '*The Mahabharata*', *The Drama Review*, vol. 30, no. 1, October 1985.

SELBOURNE, David, 'Brook's *Dream*', *Culture and Agitation – Theatre Documents*, London, Action Books, 1972.

— *The Making of A Midsummer Night's Dream*, London, Methuen 1982.

SERBAN, Andrei, 'The Life in a Sound', *The Drama Review*, vol. 20, no. 4, December 1976.

SHAKESPEARE, William, *A Midsummer Night's Dream* (Brook's RSC Acting Edition), Chicago, The Dramatic Publishing Co., 1974.

— *Timon D'Athènes* (translation and adaptation by Jean-Claude Carrière), Paris, C.I.C.T., 1978.

— *Mesure pour Mesure* (translation and adaptation by Jean-Claude Carrière), Paris, C.I.C.T., 1978.

SHEVTSOVA, Maria, 'Peter Brook adapts *Carmen*', *Theatre International* 2, no. 10, 1983.

SHORTER, Eric, review of *Marat/Sade*, *Daily Telegraph*, 21.8.1964.

— 'Lost Man of British Theatre', *Daily Telegraph*, 17.10.1974.

— 'Timon of Paris', *Drama*, no. 115, Winter 1974.

— 'Gamlets, Gimmicks, Snooks and Puppets in Paris' (review of *Ubu*), *Drama*, no. 127, Winter 1977–8.

— 'Off the Cuff, with Peter Brook and Company', *Drama*, no. 129, Summer 1978.

— 'False Prophet?', *Daily Telegraph*, 12.2.1979.

— 'Brook and others in Avignon' (review of *Conference of the Birds*), *Drama*, no. 134, Autumn 1979.

— review of *The Cherry Orchard*, *Drama*, no. 141, Autumn 1981.

SMITH, A. C. H., *Orghast at Persepolis*, London, Eyre Methuen, 1972.

STOPPARD, Tom, review of *Orghast*, *Times Literary Supplement*, 1.10.1971.

STYAN, J. L., review of Theatre of Cruelty season, *Plays and Players*, vol. 11, March 1964.

SULIK, Boleslaw, 'Search for Commitment' (review of *Tell me Lies*), *Tribune*, 23.2.1968.

SUMMERS, Sue, interview with Peter Brook, *Screen International*, 27.8.1977.

TAYLOR, John Russell, 'Peter Brook, or the limitations of intelligence', *Sight and Sound*, vol. 36, no. 2, Spring 1967.

TAYLOR, Desmond Shawe, 'Brook's Triumph in the Bullring' (review of *La Tragédie de Carmen*), *Sunday Times*, 22.11.1981.

THEATRE EN EUROPE, 'Shakespeare and *The Mahabharata*' (interview with Peter Brook and Jean-Claude Carrière), *Théâtre en Europe*, no. 7, June 1985.

— *The Mahabharata* (many interviews and photographs), *Théâtre en Europe*, no. 8, October 1985.

TONKIN, Boyd, 'Maha Marathon' (review of *The Mahabharata*), *Drama*, no. 159, Winter 1986.

TREWIN, John C., *Peter Brook: A Biography*, London, Macdonald, 1971.

TRILLING, Ossia, 'Playing with Words in Persepolis' (account of *Orghast*), *Theatre Quarterly*, vol. 2, no. 5, January/March 1972.

TRUSSLER, Simon, 'Private Experiment – in Public' (interview with Peter Brook and Charles Marowitz *re* Theatre of Cruelty season), *Plays and Players*, vol. 11, February 1964.

TURNBULL, Colin, *The Mountain People*, London, Picador, 1974.

TYNAN, Kenneth, review of *King Lear*, *Observer*, 11.11.1962.

— 'Director as Misanthropist: On the moral neutrality of Peter Brook', *Theatre Quarterly*, vol. 7, no. 25, Spring 1977.

US, Playscript 9, London, Calder and Boyars 1968: includes two narratives (by Albert Hunt and Michael Kustow), full play text and a number of reviews.

VALDEZ, Luis, 'Pajaros y Serpientes' (conversation with Peter Brook), *Chicano Theatre*, Spring 1974.

WARDLE, Irving, 'Complex Simplicity' (review of *King Lear*), *Plays and Players*, January 1963.

— 'Second Thoughts on Brook' (review of *Oedipus*), *The Times*, 23.3.1968.

— 'Actors at their new exercise' (review of *The Tempest*), *The Times*, 19.7.1968.

— 'The Saint and the Sybarite (*re* Brook and Grotowski), *The Times*, 14.9.1968.

— 'To the heights on a trapeze' (review of *A Midsummer Night's Dream*), *The Times*, 28.8.1970.

— 'Conjuring buried music out of the earth' (reviews of *Orghast*), *The Times*, 10, 14.9.1971.

— 'Rituals in the Desert: the Shiraz Festival, 1970', *Gambit*, vol. 5, nos. 18–19, 1971.

— 'Paying the Price of Survival' (review of *The Ik*), *The Times*, 16.1.1976.

— 'The Indian Pilgrimage of Peter Brook', *The Times*, 5.5.1982.

— 'Images of tenderness, triumph and death' (review of *The Mahabharata*), *The Times*, 13.7.1985.

WEINRAUB, Bernard, review of *The Ik* (Round House, London), *New York Times*, 28.1.1976.

WEISS, Peter, *The Persecution and Assassination of Marat as performed by the Inmates of the Asylum of Charenton under the direction of Marquis de Sade* (English version, Geoffrey Skelton: verse adaptation, Adrian Mitchell: introduction by Peter Brook), London, John Calder, 1965.

— *The Investigation*, New York, Atheneum, 1966.

WILLBORN, Hugh, review of *The Mahabharata*, *Plays and Players*, October 1985.

WILLIAMS, David, *Theatre of Innocence and Experience: Peter Brook, 1964–1980*, Thesis, University of Kent, 1983.

— '"A Place Marked by Life": Peter Brook at the Bouffes du Nord', *New Theatre Quarterly*, vol. 1, no. 1, February 1985.

— In *Search of a Lost Theatre: The Story of Peter Brook's Centre*, Paris, C.I.C.T., 1986.

WILSON, David, review of *Tell me Lies*, *Sight and Sound*, vol. 37, no. 2, Spring 1968.

WILSON, Peter, *Sessions in U.S.A.: A Chronicle* (notes on the American journey, 1973: unpublished), Paris, C.I.R.T., 1973.